THE San Francisco POEMS

Victor di Suvero

Pennywhistle Press
Malibu & San Francisco
1987

ISBN 0-938631-00-4
Library of Congress Catalog Card Number 86-060724
Cover photos by Barbara Windom
Cover collage by The Groot Organization
Designed by John McBride
Composition at *turnaround* (Berkeley)
Printed in the USA

For Romana and Alexander
born in San Francisco
as these poems were.

The poems in this book span more than twenty five years. They are collected here as a celebration of the City of San Francisco and of its diversity.

By focusing on "place" perhaps "meaning" can be evoked.

By reflecting the specifics of the City perhaps the general sense of being in the City can be perceived.

The poetic process itself is made up of attempts to create different ways of looking at the world utilizing language. The attempt in these poems is to integrate an appreciation of the City from the varied points of view of immigrant, sailor, businessman, householder and citizen.

A thousand other locations and moments could and perhaps will be turned into other poems at another time. For this time these poems are here, to be shared with readers ready to appreciate yet another view of the City dedicated to that Saint Francis whose sense of himself with all aspects of Creation sometimes still enhances the way people are with each other and with the world.

VMdS

The
San Francisco
Poems

San Francisco

A marvel this microcosm!
This city state
With all its pain
This promontory, this place.

The kaleidoscope with all of us
Of every tribe
In shops and streets
Jostling our rainbow
Communality
With all the rest who came
Riding the whistling wind!

Souls first, then gold,
Then all the other stars
That shone for all of us
To draw us here.

The hills converge,
The fog comes in,
The air responds

The quail and otter,
The deer, the jays,
Miwok and Costanoans
Who were here before we came –
How do we honor them
For having made this place
So clear and sweet
For us?

In the Morning

In the morning, as the sun comes soaring
     over the East Bay hills almost seven
     hundred thousand people in San
     Francisco wake within a couple of
     hours of each other and bring
     their various energies out of the caves
     of their respective sleeps into the
     day.

They do this even
     when the fogs lie thickly upon the
     city darkening the sun.

I keep wondering whether one day
     after all these years of practice,
     with all that energy loosed at
     about the same time every
     morning, if we all happen
     to think about it at the same
     time, whether the entire city,
     with its hills and buildings
     and cable cars and boats
     and books and bakeries
     would suddenly

Cast off its moorings

Disengage itself from the net
     of its freeways

Rise into the sky
     up into the universe

To play with all those other
     vessels of energy we see

When we look up.

Russian Hill, Looking East

Dawn, clear, dawn,
After rain, clear

The East Bay sun jumps up
From the tip of Mt. Diablo –

The shadows
Run down the hill
And the morning
Is new again –

In the apartment
Seven year old Mozart plays away
On the resurrection machine
Reinventing
Bastian & Bastienne –

Music pours out
To meet the sun in the clear
Washed dawn
            as Chinatown
Sleep begins to unfold
And city birds chirp –

The cable car bells
Become counterpoint
In the music
            that grows
Up out of the city,
            early

When it can be heard
In the dawn, clear, dawn
After rain,
            sounding

New beginnings.

Cable Car

Mooring and tether,
Sling, stretched out wing –
Keeping it together
Making it fly!

Bottom of the hill –
Ring it!
Close to the bay –
Ring it!
Ring it!
Into sky!

Fisherman's Wharf
Russian Hill
North Beach
All tied together
Spliced, bound
With the cable
That moves the car –
That takes one up
That takes one down
Bringing one
From dawn of water
To rush of air.

Slap of cable,
Resting at midnight,
Paradigm, analog,
Up and down
Good for the show,

Mooring and tether
Where do we go?

Back and forth
It's how we do the ride
Up and down
It's how we are inside.

St. Francis

In Assisi they remember him.

In the city named after him

There is still only one generally
    visible statue of him.
They moved it off the steps of the
    church dedicated to him
Because the parish priest found it
      difficult to have the newlyweds
      pose for pictures in front of him.
Then the longshoremen offered a piece
    of their hardearned land down
    by Fisherman's Wharf and were
    pleased and honored to welcome him.

Sister Moon and Brother Sun shine
    out in the open on him
And all the tourists look and smile at him
As pleased as Benny Bufano was the
    day that Benny finished him
While the gulls and the pigeons perch on him
And the homeless sleep at his feet and
    wake and look up at him.

It seems that most of the things he had hoped
    to see in the world are not there for him.
Even though it's all done in his name
    and all the streets lead to him.
If we don't do any better perhaps we ought
    to think about taking the city's name
    and giving it back to him.

The Rincon Annex Post Office Murals

Like a collar, a necklace
An ornament of great worth
Around your throat
You wear the frescoes
That Refregier gave you
To remember what had made
Us, it, all happen.

In the dark corner closest to the water
The reed canoe, the Indians
Staring into the future
Where Drake and the Conquistadores,
Followed by the priests,
All began to add a little
As they took away
What they had come to take –

The scenes proceed
Until that glorious red shirted panel
With the miner's faces in ecstasy
Looking up to

Gold! Heaven on earth!

And all the rest that came after –
The forest of ships in the Bay!

The pale women landing
Where there was no law.

The newspapers, the Vigilantes
Where there was no law.
And then the Railroads
With Charlie Crocker and the Chinese
Working to carve mountains!

Then we come
To the day the earth shook
April's fire
With the dazed
Razed city that pulled itself
Into today's shape with a shrug
And Burnham's eye

Then comes Mooney
And the greenfaced Justice of the time,
Prepared once more
To do what served the powers

Clean the Unions came then
With Bridges
On the Waterfront
Overcoming
The rotten shape up,
The old ways.

And Strauss' Golden Gate next
And Pfleuger's Bridge on the Bay
Sewing it all together.

Next the shift into my time
The War came, I remember –
The Shipyards, I chipped steel there
Marinship, the ways.

All that which had to be done
Was done.

With the Four Freedoms flying
Bravely there on the wall
Backed by the world's Flags –

The Nations born here United!
Touching the Indians
In their reed canoe
In the corner
Closest to the water.

This land was swamp – mud,
Old tires, broken bottles
When the Post Office was built.

The government paid artists to paint
Their dreams instead of putting them on the dole.
The City was gifted.

Now the high rises crowd around,
The money boys say it's a waste
To have a post office with art
Take up so much space.

Like a collar, a necklace
An ornament of great worth
A mirror of memory
A way of looking
To see
Who we are and how we came
To be where we are.

It's like finding the necklace
Napoleon gave Marie Louise
In a pawnshop
My friend said –

But who would know it
To be what it is
If someone had not told us
That it started there
In the far corner
The one closest to the water.

Praise the one
who saves them!

The Cathedrals of Today are Banks

Working in the Bank of America is much
Like working in the Vatican used to be.

When the God lives, protocol is strict –
Bow three times and genuflect while approaching;
Bow again when leaving, many times –
Thank for favors received,
Pray for favors yet to come,
Voice muted, chasuble in order.

When Cortez got to Montezuma
The whole thing fell apart.

But it worked while it lasted.

So long as we continue to believe
In the sanctity of money
It will rule us

To break out of dogma
To do something for itself alone

Is the brave part.

The Bankers of Today

Oh, how the bankers of today
Hold their white hands
Like the priests of yesteryear
Folded over stomachs
Engorged with fear
And satisfaction!

Oh, how the bankers of today
With all good will
Say prayers for the fiscal health
Of their depositors
And borrowers!

Oh, how the priests of yesterday
Could cause the pyres
To be lit
So that the souls of those
Not shriven could go
Like comets
Into the undertow!

Marching through the centuries
They change their robes
But not their smiles.

The Program

Keep it simple,
The banker said.

No frills for the bottom line
No room for the seraphim.

More in, less out
Keep the balances up
No cherubim
No archangels
No room in the system
For them.

They don't compute.

But now –
Super Bowl tickets,
That's another matter!
They help the bottom line –
That stuff builds business
Just fine!

Story

At the Breakfast Club
There was a lot of talk
About the good servant
Who had made money grow
When his master
Had gone.

For the longest time
No one mentioned
The young Jesus
Driving
Those others
Out of the temple.

When one finally did
Another said
Yes,
And look what
It got
Him.

Sports

At the Banker's Club
At lunch
They talk about fishing
The Rogue River –
The steelhead,
The marlin at Cabo –
How it's going to look
Up there on the wall!

Down at Fisherman's Wharf
All day
The fishermen
Talk about money –
How little
How much
Where they're going to put it!

Montgomery Street/Dealing

It becomes an act of mutual faith
Intangible
            and, by becoming,
Creates things tangible
            as houses
Cars, warehouses, planes and TV sets.

The camel goes home with a new master.
There is wool in the house, a coat,
A painting, feathers, a ring;
Food on the table, hay in the barn.
Wood to be used – seashells.

The man dealing in the market place
Marshals hope
            trumps appetite with trust
Narrows the confines
            and sequentially
Limits the world to the one transaction only
Creating with all his skills
Something more than that which was.

Having brought grain from the field
Fish from the sea
            having caused coal
To roll into steel
Having invaded the atom
            and sent
Sensors soaring towards the stars
He stands generally unsatisfied
At the end of the deal
            because
He's been too busy and no one
Has bothered to teach him
That life is not divisible.

"The basis of credit
Is the abundance of nature."
Pound said that, not an economist.

Tell it to the Rotary, to the Chambers of Commerce
Tell it to the Medical Societies
Tell it to the professional ones, the believers,
Tell it to loan committtees and to appraisers.
That the spirit
            which is in all things
Is also in them.
And that the spirit is indeed
Against usury
That which takes without giving
It is against passive investments
Against safety forever
            in the name of Forest Lawn
And the heart of stone.

It condemns all churches
That maintain portfolios
That consider religion a Xmas Club
"Put away now and save," they say,
"And on that day for eternity
Rejoice!"

The spirit rejoices in sunlight
In that which can be done.

The spirit dances
St. Elmo's fire dances in the rigging,
Dances as the ship rolls,
Dying when caught
            and put in a jewelled box.

It is time to burn labels
And permit abundance.

Insta Cash

The ephemeral,
Blessed hopes,
A better life for the children –

One's trust that having worked
And saved and put away
Could add up to decency
Before death.

That's what it says
On the billboards
On the TV
On the radio.

And in the wings,
John Law and Richard Whitney
And J. David Dominelli
And the rest of that bunch
Itching to come out again

But no – it can't happen here
That was only greed –

Now that it's plastic
It's different –

Fastest balance on the block!

Jesse James was a primitive!

Statistics

More than ninety-six point nine per cent
Of our activities are spent
In various kinds of commerce.

One half of one per cent is spent on love
Including its janissaries and accoutrements.
Point two per cent is spent on running,
But often simply sweat.
One whole per cent is spent on dreaming
In all its forms.

Three and one half tenths of one per cent
Are spent doing good;
Feeding others, for example,
Others not related by blood, guilt or marriage;
Or burying those unable to bury themselves.

Two and one half tenths of one per cent
Of all our time is spent in praying –
Some call it reaching out.

The remaining eight tenths are dedicated
To that rare thing called "doing nothing"
Without which nothing does,
In fact, get done.

The Yellow Street Corner Box

Going by quickly in the morning
We only see the headlines.

The slaughter in the camps in September,
In San Salvador, in Soweto,
Arrives on paper – abstract,
Neat, with none of the smells,
Or the colors blood becomes in its trip
From red to black;
Or the ones flesh adopts, gray green,
Rotting to become dirt again.

All the acolytes of death are left out
In the morning paper –
The flies, the look of surprise,
The jaw dropped and held there for all time
The white of the bone sticking out of muscle.
The scream, echoing the knife's touch
Turning into
Silence after the truck with the killers
Has roared away
Taking with it
Even the sound of the wind.

Newspapers could be set in type
Made of twisted faces,
Made of holes where teeth
Or eyes once were.

Newspapers could be edited
In a manner consonant with the sound of murder,
And the arrogance of killers
Who never know why they're doing it.

Newspapers could be printed in ink
That smelled of wounds with maggots in them
And the unexpected sweetness of the unburied dead.

The comfort, not only of this city
But of all of the places
Where such papers would be printed and sold
Would be invaded

If they really knew
How to bring the news home.

Ding Dong Song

Kant's old "Ding an Sich"
The "Thing in Itself" is not
There any more
For most of us.

It's the money that buys
The plastic that buys
The credit that buys
What every one sells.

In order to move
It's at one remove
But teach
The children
To dig?

Telegraph Hill – 1985

After the Fire, build again –
Once the ant hill is kicked out and down
The leftover ones gather to build again
After the War, or the Fire,
To build again,

The Renaissance heritage teaches,
But once the figure is shattered
And the pieces scattered over the canvas
One builds again.

Once the mistake is made
One builds again.

Telegraph Hill, sandstone and serpentine
Signal point for the City,
Transmitter of the news of the world –
Formerly haven of homeless
When Ed Brady the signal master
Would trudge to the top to catch
The ships' flags as they cleared the Gate
To semaphore down to the merchants
At the Exchange that the Silver Cloud
Was coming in from Boston and
That old Watson was due in with his Girl
And that the Star of Alaska
Would be at the Cannery at noon.

Transmitter of news of the world
Patchen flat on his white bed
With his quarterback's body transmuted
Into a vibrant receiver translating
The pain of the world into angel talk

Telegraph Hill, concrete and asphalt
Incorporating American Dreams
In the Halls of the Tower
With frescoes of seraphim working
In gesso, on the docks, in the fields
In the street car and department store city
With furs on women,
And apples and bread lines
In the grey of the Thirties.

Western echoes of Gianiculum eagles,
Steps leading to an altar of glory
Perch like a torch
A power towering over the cars
And the buses
Creeping up to park and rest
While their cargo disgorges
To eat up the Bay and
Feed upon Alcatraz,

To view with surprise
The other hills, the sacred mountains,
Tamalpais and Diablo –
And the rest of the world of the West
Built by mistake on mistake –
With Columbus still looking West
Still looking for China
Placed by the North Beach
Merchants Association Committee
To look across the Bay
That Drake missed,
That the Spaniards found
Instead of Cibola.

When 1321 Montgomery burned in '62
Felix Rosenthal helped rebuild it –
Mel Fowler made a Phoenix for its front
More fitting for the Hill
Than the borrowed Imperial
Eagles of Rome,
Meeting above the steps.

Ride to the top of the tower
In the rockety cage –
Show your visitors the city
Poised like a flock of white birds
On its hills ready to fly –
Show them the cut of Columbus Avenue
Made by the track of the mules
Hauling the catch from Fisherman's Wharf
To the Produce Mart after the Fire,
Across Burnham's grid so set,
So square, show them Lombard
Snaking down Russian Hill
With its cover of flowers
Show it to them in the frame
Of the arches that make each view
A piece of an altar piece
Looking for the Virgin and Child
In this City that knows how
In spite of the murders,
Eight today –
In spite of the rapes,
Sixteen today –
In spite of the earthquakes,
One small one today –
In which we earn
Our daily bread.

Seacliff

This is the place the land stops.
Houses along the cliff are quiet,

•

Their few inhabitants at rest
Before their long trip into the stars.

•

It is so quiet
I hear snails calling,
Crawling, on the window glass.

•

Our wishes are like the stars
They help us set our course.

•

So many ways the sea comes
To touch the land
Riding and roaring on the rising beach below

•

Breaking on the rocks,
Gliding into lagoons,
Lapping up against man made docks,
Each time reminding us
Of the last time it took possession
When the Milky Way banded
The sky from South to North.

•

Our fears brilliant and visible
In the dark,
Shining like buoys, like lighthouses
Like bobbing salmon boats
Attracting us and warning us away.

The Left Hand Talks About The Sutro Tower

The thumb said "That big
"thing up the mountain looks like
"an up-ended piece of a giant
"metal mantis tossed out of
"some space kid's toybox landed
"there all red and white with
"red lights flashing on and off
"at night and in the fog."

The second finger said "No,
"that's a magic totem, it
"signifies the power of the place.
"It is a sign. It was built to honor
"the horizon and to supplicate the stars."

The third one said, "No –
"what it really stands there for
"is to remind us that in the highest
"place of all the Spirit always
"makes itself manifest – Macchu Picchu,
"the sacred places, Ararat, Sinai,
"Calvary, Tamalpais, and that mountain
"in Ceylon where Buddha took off."

The ring finger said "Well, what
"would you think about it if you
"were told that its purposes are myriad,
"that it disseminates information and
"is the translator of numbers, channels and
"challenges and brings news to mothers
"of the missing, sends salvos of
"satisfaction to the greedy, inspiration
"and dedication to the bedridden,
"fulfillment to the winners of elections,

"amplitude to the cornered, abundance
"to the needy, forgetfulness and laughter
"and delight to the many and hope against
"hope and evidence that we
"are all in fact angels and immortal
"and part of the light that was in the
"beginning and that will be without
"end and why do we treat each other
"as we do?"

"It is the trumpet the angel Gabriel
"had when he was a child",
The little one said.

Looking East to Potrero Hill

Houses sometimes smile,
All in a row,
Like dragon teeth
The pattern on the hill
That says "Oh, yes, that's the way it is".

Drawings
Done by children
Looking at clouds
Become smiles themselves,
Suddenly outside,
Outdoors.
Visible.

Night Watch – Pier 5

I sing you wavelet

Little wave lapping
This one piling
At pier head

Part of the surge
That came from
That wake
When that tug
Cut into that swell
Which itself came
Through the Gate
From the other side of Ocean
Moved by the Moon
Whose fixed orbit
Reflects the Sun
So as to send
Its ray down to us
To make you shine
Into my eye
For this one instant
Only

I sing you
Wavelet.

January Evening

Strong to be alive
At fifty six
Moon
Full
Crisp
Air
No wind
And the year beginning!

All the pockmarks
Ruts, holes and traps
Along the road count
For so little
When it's added up.

The moon itself is a little blurred
And I know it's my eye
Because it's sharp again
When I move my look.

How clear the air
How good to walk
Down Hyde Street
Where I can put one foot
In front of another
And have them both be mine.

Knowing as little now
As when I was last
So glad to be alive

Those forty years
Long past ago.

Upper Grant St. Bar Remembering

Spirit alone is not
Enough –

It takes body –
The temple of the spirit
The one that likes it
The one that makes it
Happen
To join with spirit
To make it conscious

It takes
It
To make it sing
Snap fingers
Dance like anything

It takes
It
To make it move
Just move
And
Dance like anything

It takes
It
To be moved,
To be,
And moving

Move
For
All time.

Body without spirit
Though, also,
Is not complete.

Without spirit
Body
Becomes corpse
And not much of anything.

Sure know
It
When
It is
Gone.

Aquatic Park, April

Because it's an early evening and the fog
    is full of horns and bells

Because all the butterflies have gone home
    not feeling very well,
Because the sea is hard and salt
    and full of shadows,
Because the empty people who are bored
    in the world are made of noise,

Because in this dark spring the tree
    in front is already late,

Because music brings the sun back into the heart,
Because the weather even when it's
    made of storms, is a surprise,
Because the grass in the park, when it's
    walked on, becomes a path

Because this time we'll go slowly so that
    we may arrive forever.

Vosnesensky

The Russian poet on Russian Hill
With his back to the bay
In the bay window
Held us all transfixed
With the sound
Of the bells of his mouth
So that we could tell
The big bells from the small,
The old ones muffled in snow
Under skies made of black leather,
Tolling, and the bright
Small child bells light
With their laughter.

He finished by asking
Us to send our sounds
To his country so that perhaps
His people would hear our bells
Instead of the rumbling
Coming out of the East.

Every one was still.

At that moment the bells
Of Saints Peter and Paul
On Washington Square
Struck ten.

In Order To Get Back To China

In order to get back to China
Where I had grown up
I had to go to 151 Potrero
Past the Gift Center
But before the Hospital
Where Chungliang Huang
Was doing his dancing.

In order to get back to China
Where I first saw the moon
And the sun
I asked
Chungliang to write
"Ming",
The word for "shining".

In order to get back to China
Where I had left so much behind
I had to go forward
And move my heart
Into the heart of the world.

And the sound of Chungliang's breath
Through the bamboo flute
Held in his magical hands
Became the promise itself
That leads me forward to China,

Once again.

Moonscape

Even the moon comes to Ghirardelli Square
To look at all the lights

Joining the rest of the tourists –
Holiday adventure!

Forgetting for a moment
The unsatisfied hungers
It has to look at
In most of the rest
Of the world.

The Moon
Sinks slowly

As if all the air
Had weakened
Finally
At the end of the year
And could not
Hold
That silver ball
Up there
Any longer.

On Parnassus

Without windows
The house is blind
The moon doesn't enter
The government can't
The air doesn't come
Plants die and
The street does not exist.

Without windows
One sees no faces
Prayers fall to the ground
The song remains a prisoner.

Seasons don't recognize themselves
And the future extinguishes itself.

I am enchanted
Now that I have become
All of the windows of the world
For you
In this wet
March
Looking out over the Panhandle

Looking out to the Pacific

To Betelgeuse
To Orion.

Cup of Coffee

At the counter
At Woolworth's
On Market
At Powell
The old man
Full of dreams
Splendid, scintillating dreams

Dreaming of tomorrow

Suddenly steps away
From the counter

Jumps into the future

And disappears.

Lines

The long lines on Golden Gate Avenue
Are grey, hungry, cold and patched.
Drugged, hung over, broke and broken
They wait with bundles, cold hands
And the runny noses and used eyes
Of survivors wearing other people's clothes –

Waiting for other people's hands
To spoon out the fish chowder and the rice
At St. Anthony's Dining Room
With not too much conversation
While patches of leftover fog
Drift around them in the late morning.

The long lines on outer Broadway are bright.
The guests polished and glittering in black
At night. They are hungry and cold and
Full of laughter waiting in lines
Under canopies with all the little lights
Bright as if it were Christmas again,
Waiting for the lobster and caviar and pates
Wearing other people's clothes, Armani and Blass.

Waiting for other people's hands
To help them and feed them in front
Of the house of the richest man in America
While the fog drifts around them in the evening.

Milton Komisar's Light & Sound Sculpture at the Art Institute

Light, light light light light
Green green green yellow pink
Pink Pink red pink green
Round red red red red Red
Yellow green pink Red round
Red yellow green
Arc pink yellow green
Blue red blue Red blue
Red red red red Red.

Circle Arc Circle Circle
Arm Arm Arm Arm bulb bulb
Bulb Bulb Arm Arm Circle
Circle Circle Circle Circle Circle
Green, yellow, yellow, Green, pink
Green, yellow, green, Bulb, Bulb
Arm, arc, arm, arm, Arm.
Circle round circle Bulb
Green yellow pink pink Red
Green yellow pink pink red
Green, green, Green, green, green,
Arc, Arm, bulb, circle
Circle, circle, circle, circle, Circle
Green, yellow, green, green, green.

All in black space –

This is the way
It is
When a star
Starts.

At Enrico's

You told him you had filled up too much of your space
With too many men, married men,
Men that belonged elsewhere
Men who were taking up
Too much room in your room under the eaves –
And how you feel crowded.

You asked him how he had been
After all the in between months.
He told you of his work and his plans.

You asked him again –

He tried to answer with news of his doctor,
Of pleasures postponed and imaginary,
Of his wife and his life and his children
And of distances and plans.

There was more coffee and then the check.

You told him proudly you had stopped smoking
(You were both pleased) and had renewed
Yourself with tennis lessons and really felt fit.

Walking out of the restaurant into the crowd,
Moving across Broadway you thought
Of your next day's destination.

You raised your beautiful head and the wind
Caught your hair.

Dinner at Kimball's

"But women have it here"
She said, lacing her fingers into a basket
    in front of her
Like a basket of reeds, a basket of rushes
"And it's always here, before and after
    children, even with no children at all!"

"It's always here," she said lifting
    her hands a little as if to show it off –
And the windows began to turn, slowly at first,
    and the tables began to turn
And the flowers and waiters and the
    people drinking and eating
All began to turn in a dance that
    became water and vortex
And rushed him into that secret place
    that changes its shape and its functions
Where his children had been made;
    and the shape of the future defined.

"Men always have to go poking around
    to get to the nest that is here"
She said, lifting the basket of
    her hands gently again into the air.

Portsmouth Square

At night the ghosts come back
Through the concrete that's been poured
Out and down to make five floors
Of garage happen, through the steel
Through the membranes
Through the planting and lawns.

In the summer fog
They murmur
The same things they were thinking
Just before they were killed
On the scaffolds – here.

Now,
To those who've just arrived
It looks like a Chinese kid's playground
Abandoned at night.

See,
The tot lot
With the swings –

No,
The vague shadow of those two men
Barely swinging in the air
Slowly moving across the grass
Is not
There!

That Somewhere Authority

That somewhere authority
Had the power to determine
For us
That which could be done
Was the fallacy –

That somehow we all
Have the power to determine
For ourselves
That which can be
Was forgotten.

The six million dead in the camps;
Martin Luther King, Jr.
On the motel balcony –
The students at Kent State
Dead on the lawn –
The 52,808 names
On the Vietnam Memorial –

The ache of one heart
Echoing loss –

And the moment in the night
When waking,
The fear comes
That there will be no morning
No matter what one has or has not done.

One breath very quickly then
Looking again for a way
To be somewhere else
Because somewhere authority
Had the power to determine.

Fragments of Martyrs

Fragments of martyrs
Are seldom heroic
A piece of St. Sebastian's ear,
The breasts of St. Agnes
Or the blood of San Gennaro
In the cathedral in Naples
Liquefying on order
Once a year –

History tells us
Such things are useful
But what can one do
With what's left –
Not only of one martyr
But of an entire group?

In the synagogues
In the temples
Only the names of the camps
Are remembered
Treblinka and Dachau
Not Isadore and Gretel
Not Volodya, not Primo
Not Rachele and Tess
Not Avram not Bruno
Not Solomon or Kitzel

Here they are, the minion,
Cast in bronze, white
With the color of lye
In accurate disarray
With one only
Still standing
By the barbed wire

As they all stood –
Before they went to be killed
In Auschwitz
In Belsen.

In Venice
Some of the greatest churches
Were built to celebrate
The kindness of God –
The deliverance of the people
From a plague
Which was not understood
At the time
As having sprung out of filth
And carried by rats –

In San Francisco,
On the promontory
Above the Golden Gate
Across from the Palace
Of the Legion of Honor
Overlooking the Pacific Ocean
And the still untouched hills of Marin
The Holocaust Memorial stands open
In the eye of the sky
In summer, in the fog
Insignificant, enormous
And as quiet as the waves out there
That wash over the 20,000 drums
Of atomic waste dumped
There before any one knew.

A few wilted flowers
At the feet of the standing figure –
On certain days candles,
A wreath even –
One day some incense
Was left burning –

The ashes of six million roasted hearts
Still fluttering in the wind

This time Segal
Not Goya
Tears the cry of the wind
Into silence
For all to hear

The silent Kaddish becomes
Shadow of sea gulls streaking
Across the parking lot

High to the north
Above the cliffs
A turkey buzzard soars

Perhaps one of these mornings
Early, with no live people around
Six or seven or twelve
Of those buzzards
Will come down
Across the parking lot
To see if it really is
A banquet spread
For them by those
Who go around
Killing their own kind

To discover that what appears
To be flesh will not tear,
Will blunt beaks and be inedible

For all time.

Note for the Voyage

Given:
>   One cannot take provisions

The baggage of the senses
Permitted for that galactic voyage
Is minimal.

We must learn to hold the essence
Of each sunset and each flower
Of each dancer and each song.

We must learn to carry
The taste of tears and apples
The smell of new mown hay
And the musky warmth of waking
Under covers, together, in caves
For our sustenance and growth.

To travel well we must be centered
And full of light and play.

We must learn to bring
Our lives with us
On that voyage to the stars
And must learn to pack
More neatly than Pharaoh.

All we have is the space
Within our skulls in which to place
Our consciousness of self,
Our loves, our artifacts
And the heritage of our humanity.

For My Mother

Venice and this city are the only two I know
Where the seagulls and the pigeons go
At dawn into a smudge of sky
To dance quadrilles together as they fly.

I walk down the street I used to run
When I was young and on my way to shipyard work.
Then my life lay before me like the sea.
Now all has changed except my eyes
That have seen wars come and go,
My own children grow and ships
I've sailed on sink and ventures drown;
Now my eyes look out to sea and see again
That world beyond horizon that you made for us.

The mountain's shoulder lunges through the clouds
As the gulls and pigeons dance
And wheel while sleep ridden tourists
Begin to stretch and grumbling rise
To lumber down to this piece of beach,
This launching place,
This bay of hopes you made possible for us.

All your dreams of right and freedom still sail on
Around the world, and come back home
To light and wheel as gulls and pigeons do,
At dawn in February, as I remember you.

Setting a Course

Gauging the wind
Feeling tide's rip
Learning the currents –
Befriending headlands
Markers, buoys, stars
The house near the point
And the whale's pastures –

Knowing which way to turn
When confronted by shoals
Skeletons of wrecks,
Monsoons, pirates, tankers
And other monsters –

Standing a watch alone
With the Pole star and
A large silent bird
Riding the wind beside you –

To learn this –
To become a sailor
Able to choose a landfall
The Tuamotos, Panama,
The Inland Passage or even
Back to the Gate –

To learn this
The heart soars
Over the hands cut by line,
Over the wet, the wind's bite
To come to port again.

The craft brings you there –
The art comes in the choice
Of harbor,
The destination.

Questions/Washington Square

How do we add it up?
Where does it belong?
Why is it?
What does it matter?

How do we know it?
Where did it come from?
Why is it lonely?
What does it do?

How do we trust it?
Where is it going?
Why is it pleasing?
What does it mean?

When will we know?
When will we sing?

All the answers
In all the books
Do not mean figs
Or dew drops
Unless the heart is clear,

Then
The sky is made of peacocks
And all the bells ring.

Coming Back To The House

Coming back to the house,
Across the Bridge from Marin
Looking through the spring black
With no moon at all
To the large yellow artificial diamonds laying at
The bay's eastern edge, knowing
The next twenty four
Hours,
Years
Are a lot less likely
To happen
Than the last –

Each day
Remembered
Is found again;
Each new month, treasured;
Each waking, thanked;
Each star, seen;
Each song, sung;
Each deal, done;

And still
The petals of the rose
Continue to unfold.

If It Had Happened

If it had happened Thirty years ago,
Instead of One Thousand
Nine Hundred and Eighty Four
Years back, in as unlikely
A place as Bethlehem was then –
Say, in the heart of Watts
Or on the outskirts of
Wellington, New Zealand
Not too far from an airport –
But nowhere near bucolic
Romantic shepherds
With their sheep and

He were to grow up

Just as the book says
He did

And today you were to hear
THAT voice
Unmistakable
Over the radio
Driving
Down Lombard
Telling you to let
The little children come to
Him – what would you do?

What would you do
At that intersection?

Postcards

In Golden Gate Park
The hummingbird in the greenhouse
Full of tropical flowers
Beats itself to death
Against the window panes
Fighting to get out.

•

On Columbus Avenue
The counterman at the café
Is busy saving poor Butterfly
While engineering the espresso.

•

The black policeman directs
St. Patrick's Day parade
With great power
Through Chinatown
And North Beach.

•

Seals look at tourists
Pointing at the seals
Barking at tourists
Who come to Seal Rocks.

•

Restaurants at the Wharf
Hire fishermen to furnish
Local color and action,
While the fish come from Alaska.

•

Kites on the Marina green
Fill the sky
And my heart.

•

Net Mender on the Wharf

Where do we begin?
With Abraham?
Or further back –
At the beginning?

Do I tell my children
That because of the Inquisition
An ancestor left Malaga
For Padua and Venice –
Some say by ship
Others say by foot up the coast –
And then across the mountains,
And across the sea.

The net mender wonders
If this be the beginning
Of the net he mends.

It always starts
With just a piece of string
A cord to tie us in
To let us go,
To be,
And

There are moments
When we are not the knots,
But the spaces in between
For which there is no name
But which is light

We know our end
But how do we begin?

North Beach – Easter

I

It is not simple.
The busy ness of it
When one discovers
Even the simplest thought
Has both inside and out
And all the permutations
Of the colors of the light
Up to and including
Joseph's coat –

Rexroth came early
Out of Indiana
Into the Promises –
Down from the Sierras,
The mountains of Muir
Reaching across the Bay –
Arriving here to find
Pasta and wine and bread
North of Broadway and
Sun Hung Yeung South
With wonton
And the sweet sour smells
Of tomorrow's chickens
And duck and fish
All waiting to be eaten –
The constant sacrifice.

Bakeries and restaurants
Bookstores and cafes
And the people in them
All quickly woven
Into the fabric
Of the days.

A chart evolves
To navigate
These waters.

II

Time's shadow
On the clocktower
Is fixed for one instant
Only
The rest of it runs down
Into the street, the park,
Becomes
The rose I hand you
Which
Can be found
In the Chinese movie
At the Palace
Where one can learn
That every thing
Is always both
Perfect and fallible
Sun and moon
Generative and receptive
Thrust and pull
And about as simple
As the music that we are

Made up of silences
And sounds.

Strong rope
Many strands
Each one
Weak
Being and non being
In the air –

Discovery of hexagrams!

The logic of artichokes!

III

Like begets like
And the dance continues.

Shiva's breath
Infuses Mulligan
And Maya
And they touch
And touch you
And touch me
Until dawn comes to wake us
With the sun smell
Of real bread
Made in brick ovens
By people you can touch
And talk to
In a place of clarity.

IV

Opinion or ecstasy
Religion or politics
The drug of choice
Always permits perfection.
It will not pay the rent
Or even stand scrutiny,
However
It becomes a sign
ONE WAY
STOP
WALK
DO NOT ENTER
And you choose
BROADWAY
where everything goes.

V

With
Clear
Eye
And
Determination
We say
This time it will be changed
This time
Our turn
All that
Which was
Is no more
Is over
Turned.

And Puccini's golden throated heroine
    of the moment sweeps out
    of the cafe into Columbus
    with cascades of love and pain
    once more

While we discover it again.

VI

And now
We are
In
City Lights
Between books and magazines
Between poetry and fiction
Between killers and saints
With each of those visions of the
    world ready to be chosen
    to help us in getting through
    the next day –
    out of the next labyrinth.

We pick up sustenance
To go and do it
One more time.

The tides lap continuously.

VII

Where we are
Is where it is –
The busy center
Is here.

From this place
We all move
Out to join
The procession
Of the stars.

VIII

The bells of St. Francis
Ring out over
The Little City Market
Where capretto sells for
Four dollars a pound
And the Paschal Lamb
Becomes the main course
Of the Feast of the Resurrection.

IX

Out of the tomb
The light

Out of the soldier's sleep
The waking

Out of the dark
The radiance!

BREEDING FODDER CROPS FOR MARGINAL CONDITIONS

Developments in Plant Breeding

VOLUME 2

The titles published in this series are listed at the end of this volume.

Breeding Fodder Crops
for Marginal Conditions

*Proceedings of the 18th Eucarpia Fodder Crops Section Meeting,
Loen, Norway, 25–28 August 1993*

Edited by

O.A. ROGNLI
*Department of Biotechnological Sciences, Agricultural University
of Norway, Ås, Norway*

E. SOLBERG
Løken Research Station, Heggenes, Norway

and

I. SCHJELDERUP
Holt Agricultural Research Station, Tromsø, Norway

Chapters indicated with an asterisk in the table of contents were first published in
Euphytica, Volume 77: 3, 1994

Kluwer Academic Publishers

Dordrecht / Boston / London

Library of Congress Cataloging-in-Publication Data

Eucarpia. Fodder Crops Section. Meeting (18th : 1993 : Loen, Norway)
    Breeding fodder crops for marginal conditions : proceedings of the
  18th Eucarpia Fodder Crops Section Meeting, Loen, Norway, 25-28
  August 1993 / edited by O.A. Rognli, E. Solberg, and I. Schjelderup.
        p.   cm. -- (Developments in plant breeding ; v. 2)
    Includes index.
    ISBN 0-7923-2948-1 (hb : acid free paper)
    1. Forage plants--Breeding--Congresses. 2. Forage plants-
  -Adaptation--Congresses. 3. Forage plants--Germplasm resources-
  -Congresses. 4. Agriculturally marginal lands--Congresses.
  I. Rognli, O. A. II. Solberg, E. III. Schjelderup, I. IV. Title.
  V. Series.
  SB193.5.E93   1993
  633.2'0823--dc20   94-21242

ISBN 0-7923-2948-1

Published by Kluwer Academic Publishers,

P.O. Box 17, 3300 AA Dordrecht, The Netherlands.

Kluwer Academic Publishers incorporates
the publishing programmes of
D. Reidel, Martinus Nijhoff, Dr W Junk and MTP Press.

Sold and distributed in the U.S.A. and Canada
by Kluwer Academic Publishers,
101 Philip Drive, Norwell, MA 02061, U.S.A.

In all other countries, sold and distributed
by Kluwer Academic Publishers Group,
P.O. Box 322, 3300 AH Dordrecht, The Netherlands.

Printed on acid-free paper

Printed in the Netherlands

Organized by the Fodder Crops Section of EUCARPIA – The European Association
for Research on Plant Breeding.

Organizing committée:

O.A. Rognli (chairman) – Dept. of Biotechnological Sciences, Agricultural University of
Norway, 1432 Ås, Norway
E. Torgersen Solberg   – Løken Research Station, Volbu, 2640 Heggenes, Norway
I. Schjelderup   – Holt Research Station, 9002, Tromsø, Norway

Financial support is gratefully acknowledged from:

The Norwegian State Agricultural Research Stations
The Norwegian Research Council
Hellerud Research Station and Seed Multiplication Farm

Table of contents

Preface

In 1990 Norwegian members of the Eucarpia Fodder Crops Section invited the section to hold its 18th meeting in Norway 1993. Arising from this invitation eighty members from 19 countries met at Loen, Norway from the 25th to the 28th August 1993 to consider the problem of 'Breeding for Marginal Conditions' a topic of major importance not only in the Nordic countries but throughout the range of environments represented by Eucarpia. The problems of adaptation and breeding for marginal conditions were last discussed by the Section at its meeting in Perugia in 1980. The Section President at the time, Professor Julén, in his paper highlighted the range of climatic and latitudinal effects that fodder crops are subjected to in the Nordic countries. It is difficult to realise that it is as far from Oslo to the North of Norway as it is from Oslo to the venue of our last meeting in Alghero, Sardinia. As far as wide scale adaptation of fodder crops is concerned the range of environmental conditions from Sardinia to Norway exemplifies the problems which we have to take into account when breeding for marginal conditions. During the course of the meeting we discussed various topics related to the theme of the problems of breeding for marginal conditions in five formal paper sessions. The subjects covered ranged from 'General Aspects of Adaptation to Marginal Conditions' in the opening symposium, through to 'Genetic and Genomic Aspects of Adaptation to Marginal Conditions'. For the opening symposium, Mr. M. Stubsjøen, of the Norwegian Royal Ministry of Agriculture, set the scene with a plenary paper on 'Norwegian plant production and its challenges'. This was followed by the President of Eucarpia, Professor Peter Tigerstedt who introduced the theme of the meeting with an overview of 'Variation, adaptation and selection in marginal areas'. In all a total of 26 scientific papers were presented over the three days of the meeting. In addition to the paper sessions three parallel workshops examined the problems of 'Why breed for marginal conditions', 'Specific versus general adaptation and strategies for breeding' and 'Quality in relation to breeding'. As well as this most comprehensive series of formal sessions an informal evening lecture on 'Seed production in Norway' was presented by Mr. R. Hillestad. The meeting finished with a visit to the Løken Agricultural Research Station, Valdres to see some aspects of the forage breeding programmes there and to a local highland farm. In addition some opportunities were made to visit some areas of outstanding natural beauty and to enjoy the local hospitality. We most gratefully acknowledge the support given to this meeting by the various official organisations, in particular the service of the Norwegian Agricultural Research Stations.

M.D. Hayward
President, Eucarpia Fodder Crops Section
Institute of Grassland and Environmental Research
Aberystwyth, Wales, UK

Introduction

O.A. Rognli et al. (eds.), Breeding Fodder Crops for Marginal Conditions, 3–10.
© 1994 *Kluwer Academic Publishers. Printed in the Netherlands.*

Norwegian plant production and its challenges

M. STUBSJØEN
Royal Ministry of Agriculture, P.O. Box 8007 Dep., 0030 Oslo, Norway

Norway is the most northern country in Europe. The topography and northern location give the country its most unique features. One is the extreme seasonal changes in daylight and temperature. Another is the nature.

About 60% of the land area consists of mountain peaks and plateaus above the timber line, and yet with a great variety of lichens, herbs and shrubs. Fjords and valleys have been carved into the terrain by ice and rivers, providing the basis for livelihood. About 22% of the land area is productive forests. Cultivated land is one million hectares, which is less than 3% of the total area, compared with 57% in the EC countries. About two thirds of the agricultural area and almost three quarter of the livestock production are situated north of 60 degrees of latitude. As a consequense, the climatic conditions for agriculture are quite different from, and much less favourable, than those of Continental Europe.

A considerable part of the country is north of the Arctic Circle. The Gulf Stream, which follows the whole costline, makes agriculture possible all over the country, even in the northernmost regions. Agriculture is carried out further north than in any other country worldwide. The arctic and subarctic climate limits the production potential and the yield. The growing season extends to just 190 days in the south and only 100 days in the northern part of the country and the mountainous regions. Over half the area of cultivated land is not suitable for cereal production. Cereal production is almost entirely concentrated in the flatish regions of south-eastern Norway and to some extent in Trøndelag. Compared to the most efficient EC countries, like Germany and Denmark, the Norwegian wheat yield is only two thirds. Livestock production is predominant, because most of the cultivated land is located in areas where the climate and terrain are most suitable for grass, which can also be grown in high land and in the far north. The short growing season combined with unstable weather during spring work and harvest, necessitates a high reliance on machinery and equipment at the farms. Animal husbandry requires well-insulated buildings and adequate storage for fodder and manure during the long winter periode spent indoors.

Mountains, lakes and forests divide the farm land into scattered, relatively small and often steeply sloping plots. These special topographical conditions limit the potential for structural rationalisation involving amalgamation of small farms into larger and more efficient units. They also lead to small and scattered units in the processing industry, as well as long distances for transportation of goods, resulting in high costs for production, sale and distribution.

The farm structure in Norway is also a result of strong historical and cultural traditions attached to owning a farm. By statute, the oldest child has the first priority to take over a family farm. Many farms have been within the same family for centuries. The few farms sold on the open marked, are subject to government concession.

The Norwegian agricultural policy has provided for the development of an extensive and differentiated support system to provide equal opportunities for income for all kinds of production in all areas of the country. It has also been a major objective of Norwegian agricultural policy to provide the same level of income and social conditions to farmers as industrial employees.

The supply situation during World Wars I and II drew attention to the concept of self-sufficiency. Important considerations in shaping Norwegian postwar agricultural policy, were increased production, self-sufficiency, and the availability of supplies for emergencies. There has been an increase in grain production particularly in the southern part of the country. There has also been made political decision, taking all factors into consideration, to exclude sugar, vegetable fat and protein feed from Norwegian agricultural production. In spite of developments after World War II towards larger farm units and reduced employment, small and scattered farms are still typical for Norwegian agriculture. The average farm size is 10 hectares of cultivated land. Only 13% of the farms have more than 20 hectares of farmland.

Nevertheless, on this small areas of farmland we have managed to meet the national demand by domestic production of milk and dairy products, meat, eggs, potatoes and store vegetables, and also to increase the production, where viable, of other vegetables, fruit, berries and wheat. Export of farm products are limited to occasional 2–3% over-production of milk, meat and eggs. The degree of self-sufficiency in cereals for human consumption has risen over the years, reaching 53% in 1991.

The diagram for distribution of gross income for agriculture by main products (Fig. 1) shows that livestock production, especially cow's milk, dominate the gross income for agriculture. The group of other activities includes sale of live animals and coars feed to private persons and industries outside agriculture, net result of export/import of live animals and incomes from rabbit meat and honey from bees.

The diagram for distribution of holdings by main line of production (Fig. 2) shows that 17.000 holdings or 17.4% have sheep as their main line of production. However, sheep production represent only 4.8% of gross income.

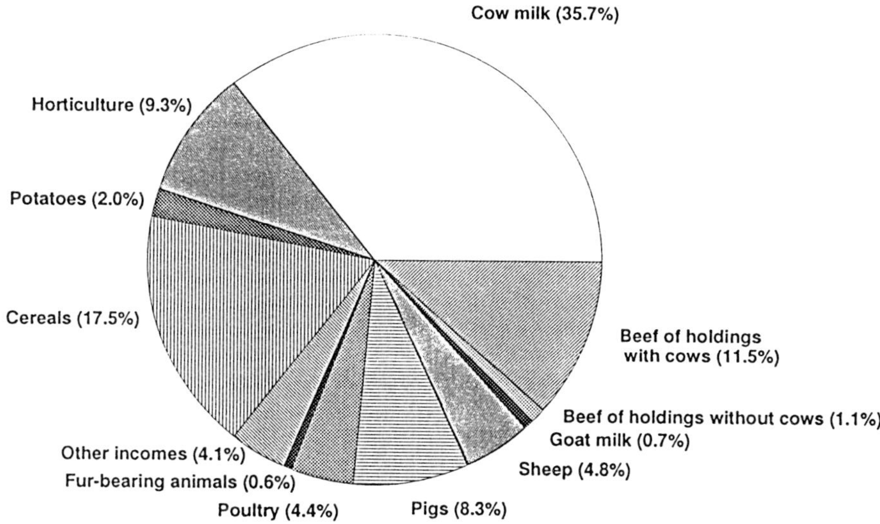

Fig. 1. Distribution of gross income for agriculture by main products, 1990.

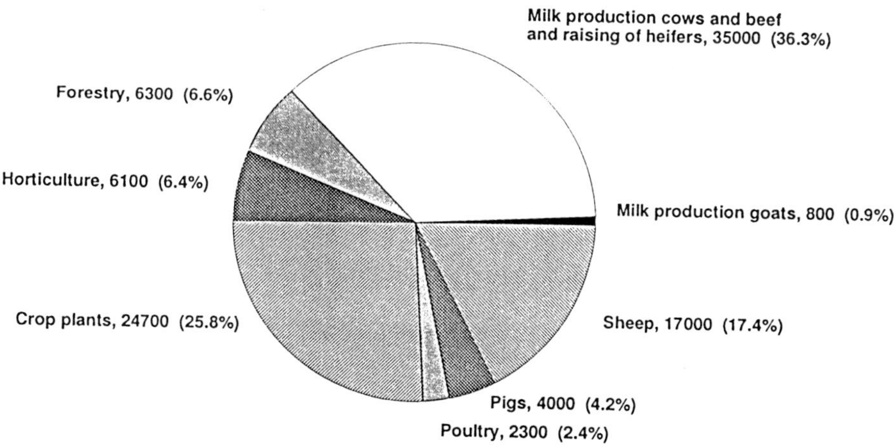

Fig. 2. Distribution of holdings by main line of production, 1990.

The sheep holders are to a great extend part-time farmers. So are the farmers producing cereals. As a matter of fact two out of three of the farmers in Norway have other employment in addition to farming. Our policy is to increase supplementary economic activities on the farms, first of all activities related to agriculture.

6

In the middle of the seventies a revised agricultural policy was presented in a White Paper. Production, income and efficiency were not any longer the only goals. The Government underlined the importance of regional policy, enviroment and natural resources.

Norway is the most sparsely populated country in Europe after Iceland. The population density for the country as a whole is 13 persons per square kilometre. The EC average is 11 times larger. Maintenance of settlements throughout the country is an important political aim.

In many areas, agriculture forms the basis for economic activity and hence for settlement. It is therefore an important element of general regional policy. Agricultural policy is particulary directed towards the stimulation of employment and economic activities in less favoured areas. This has been carried out by means of a number of different measures, and with the help of a support system that aims to promote equal income potential throughout the country, in spite of varying production conditions. Production based on grass and coarse feed, which covers more than half of the area used for agricultural purposes, is largely localised in less favoured areas. The most important agricultural products in these areas are milk, beef and mutton.

Environmental considerations and measures have acquired increasing importance in agricultural policy. A steadily growing proportion of the direct support to agriculture has wholly or partly been directed towards environmental considerations. The environment policy is designed both to remedy and to prevent environmental problems, and also to stimulate agriculture's production of public goods. At the same time, great importance is attached to production of public goods which are paid for through different forms of direct support. Measures favouring the cultural landscape, outdoor recreation and cultural heritage have been put into effect.

Norway attaches great importance to the development of a sustainable agriculture that does not reduce the production potential for future generations. There is a desire to reduce pollution of the natural environment, use of chemicals etc. in order to ensure a stable high quality of food products. Special emphasis is given to reduce soil erosion and loss of nutrients, to reduce pollution from sources such as silage, manure etc. and to encourage an ecological and environmentally sound production.

Our nature, as well as the cultural monuments of the past, form our common heritage which we want to hand on to future generations. The goal is to preserve the best of the past, linked to a present day moderate and considerate use of land. Many restrictions on the use of land have thus been introduced. Much effort is also made to take care of the cultural landscape, which has been shaped by the activities of man, whether these be farming, forestry, fishing, reindeer husbandry or industrial manufacturing.

Capacities for the assessment, study and systematic observation and evaluation of biodiversity need to be reinforced at national as well as international levels. Effective national action and international cooperation is required for *in situ* protection of ecosystems and for *ex situ* conservation of biological and genetic resources.

Laws and regulations, economic measures and information are used to achieve the objectives of environmental policy. General reduction of the intensiveness of agricultural production is a central element of the environmental programmes. Among the measures introduced to achieve these objectives, are some reduction of support linked to production and environmental taxes on commercial fertilizers and pesticides. The money from the taxes on fertilizers and pesticides has given an important economical basis for the rapid changes to more environmentally sound production methods in Norway. Systems are being developed to monitor effects on the environment and ensure the cost effectiveness of measures implemented.

The modern consumer as well as the Government is very conscious of the importance of proper nutrition and food quality. Quality and hygiene are key words for the entire food production chain from the field to the consumer's table. All food should be tasty, nutritious and safe. It should also be produced by farming and processing methods which are in harmony with ethical demands and environmental considerations. Other important elements in the Government launched food quality scheme, are more quality control, monitoring and introduction of a quality mark next year.

A low level of pollution of the environment forms an essential basis for the production of high quality food which satisfies all the various demands of the modern consumer. The optimal use of fertilizers and crop rotations are among the most cost effective ways of reducing water pollution. Our aim is that most of the farms shall have fertilizer and cropping plans. The plans should be based on correct prognoses of nitrogen fertilizer requirements. Soil sampling in spring and autumn is already being performed on a number of farms.

With regard to the plans for protecting the North Sea, it is estimated that the agricultural sector has decreased the loss of phosphorus to the waterways by 20–25% in the period 1985–92. This is mainly due to extended use of fertilizer plans, improved storage facilities for manure, spreading of manure only in the growing season, regulations on the number of animals per hectare and reduced tillage in the autumn. Furthermore, estimations indicate a reduction of nitrogen in the period from 1985–92 by 15–20%. This is achieved mainly by use of fertilizer plans, spreading of manure only in the growing season and split application of fertilizer in grain production. In addition the other measures mentioned for phosphorus also contribute to reduced nitrogen losses. For many of the measures, there is a time-lag from introduction until the loss of nitrogen to the North Sea is actually reduced, but the quality in many water cources are already improved.

There is a potential for further reductions by stricter implementation of most, if not all measures applied. We are also developing other means of preventing nutrient loss from areas. Vegetation zones between cultivated land and waterways and use of catch crops will help to stabilise soil and reduce the nutrient loss to the rivers. At the same time, these efforts will help to develop the cultural landscape.

Autumn tillage is a major contributory factor towards erosion and loss of nutrients. In areas with erosion problems we wish to motivate as many farmers as possible to grow cereals without autumn tillage. A compensation is paid in order to cover extra costs and possible yield losses. During a periode of three years the farmers in South-East Norway have changed to spring tillage of almost one third of the land for cereal production.

An important aim is to cut the use of pesticides to a minimum effective leval. Nature is on our side in this respect. The cold winter climate and moderate summer temperatures on the one hand, and small farms, often far apart, on the other, combine to create a situation in which plants are little exposed to parasites and diseases. It is then possible to produce grass, cereals, vegetables and fruits with a minimum use of pesticides.

Our phytosanitary regime is relatively strict. High production cost may be caused by imposition of quarantine or destruction of infected plants. It is also evident that phytosanitary measures have prevented introduction of harmful organisms in several cases. Regular reporting and control programmes are established for certain potato pests. Further, erradication programmes on fireblight, elm disease and cherry fruit fly are being run at present. The programme on fireblight seems to be especially succesful. The disease has attacked only a very limited area as it was found at an early stage of invasion. For a long time we have had programmes to ensure healthy, non-infectious planting material. The good health conditions of our animals and plants, enable society and farmers to reduce expences to medicines and chemicals, and also to ensure the consumers food of high quality. It is therefore extremely important for Norway to maintain the economical and social advantages of the existing health conditions for animals and plants.

Due to changes in international trade policy, Norway is facing a phytosanitary challenge. The Norwegian A-list contains at present 107 species, of which 27 are not mentioned in the annexes to Council Directive 77/93.

Nearly all sorts of plant consignments shall be accompanied by a phytosanitary certificate when imported. Plants and parts of plants intended for further growing, must have been under official phytosanitary supervision during the growing season previous to import. To prevent import of certain harmful organisms, there are several special conditions given for organisms, which have to be fulfilled. The phytosanitary challenge caused by changes in international trade calls upon increased international cooperation among the experts. In this connection we expect much of the work of EPPO (European and Mediterranean Plant Protection Organization).

In spite of our high phytosanitary standard, we cannot exclude the use of plant protection agents. The approval, sale and use are regulated by the Act of Plant Protection Agents. Only duly approved plant protection agents may be marketed in Norway. The requirements as to documentation accompanying applications are identical to those applied in the other Nordic countries. The process of approval includes biological testing carried out over at least two growing seasons. Approval of the agricultural authorities is required for both the sale and use of plant protection agents. The process of approval was recently reviewed and a new licensing scheme is introduced. According to the new scheme, the applicant is required to pass a government test. The Plant Inspection Service is currently carrying out projects of limited duration and geographic extent to ascertain farmers' handling of plant protection agents in practice.

Norwegian authorities run a long-term programme which is to reduce the use of chemical plant protection products to a minimum effective level. According to the programme we will use effective chemical protection agents when necessary in integrated management systems. A part of this, is the weather forecasts and warning systems which are being developed.

Technological innovations have played a significant role in transforming Norwegian agriculture. Like other industrialized countries the transition from horsepower to mechanical power increased the productive capacity of agriculture, even as farm labour requirements decreased dramatically. Agricultural productivity rose further as chemical fertilizers and pesticides increased yields and helped farmers control plant pests and diseases. Biotechnology and advanced computer systems are now introducing a new technological era in agriculture. They have the potential to increase resource productivity, preserve the environment and improve food safety and quality. Many of the new technologies will be commercially viable in the 1990s. However, they will not automatically be put into use. Today's public increasingly questions whether technological changes are always good or needed and is voicing new concerns about food safety, the environment and the changing structure of agriculture. These issues as, well as declining public confidence in institutions create an atmosphere in which agricultural biotechnology may not readily be approved for commercial use or adopted by industry. Lack of public acceptance could prevent some technologies from being used, even if they are approved by regulatory agencies.

Biotechnology is not so different from previous agricultural technologies as to raise novel scientefic issues conserning the safety of foods. What is substantially different, however, is the climate in which this new class of technologies is being introduced. Society in general is more sceptical of the need for new technologies. Lack of knowledge about agriculture and biology lead some people to misunderstand how and why these technologies are developed and regulated. Public confidence will sink further if the public feels that food safety standards are too lax, are fraught with scientific uncertainty or are not adequately enforced. To avoid this fate agricultural biotechnology must meet scientific standards of safety, and regulatory agencies responsible for determining the safety of new biotechnology products must have public confidence.

In Norway we have just got our Biotechnology Act, which is going to be administrated by the Ministry of Environment and the Ministry of Health. Regarding agricultural biotechnology the two ministries shall cooperate with the Ministry of Agriculture. In this way the politicians have underlined the environmental and food safety aspects.

Intellectual property protection is one of the most important incentives for commercial development of traditional and biotechnology-related processes and products. A few months ago Norway got its Plant Variety Protection Act so the plant breeders' right will now be regulated through the system of UPOV (International Union for the Protection of New Varieties of Plants).

Norwegian plant production is dependent on varieties suitable for our growing conditions. We are sure that the UPOV-membership will promote plant breeding. Traditional breeding programmes will continue, but we hope that the tools of biotechnology can be used selectively to engineer varieties fit for our climate. We also hope that our varieties can be used in other countries where the growing conditions are more or less similar to ours. On the grain sector we are organizing a marketing system, and we are going to carry out some marketing analyses in other sectors.

All these new challenges require that our well educated farmers need to be even more skilled. Especially the new technologies will demand greater attention to management issues than technologies in past. Advanced computer technologies can provide farmers with the ability to systematically make the best decision rather than arrive at decision in an ad hoc fashion. Weather and field condition for crop management can be monitored. Expert systems may help farmers to interpret these data and suggest appropriate management strategies such as irrigation, fertilization or pesticide treatment.

General aspects of adaptation to marginal conditions

O.A. Rognli et al. (eds.), Breeding Fodder Crops for Marginal Conditions, 13–19.
© 1994 Kluwer Academic Publishers. Printed in the Netherlands.

Adaptation, variation and selection in marginal areas

P.M.A. TIGERSTEDT
Department of Plant Biology, University of Helsinki, Box 27, SF-00014, Finland

Summary. The word adaptation and its derivatives are reviewed as well as the characteristics of environmental marginality. Plant traits are discussed in the light of their adaptive significance, specially pointing at their phenotypic expression under stress. Variation in marginal plant populations is discussed on the basis of accumulated knowledge on quantitative traits and isozymes. The common opinion that marginal populations are genetically depauperated is questioned on the basis of observations that show high degrees of environmental heterogeneity. This in turn would cause a disruptive mode of natural selection close to the species margin. Species' modes of adaptation and mating systems are briefly discussed and finally natural selection for stability is suggested to be of significance in marginal areas, a fact that should be duly recognized in modern plant breeding programmes aiming at maximum stability (sustainability) but not necessarily maximum yield.

Introduction

It can be taken as an axiom, that breeding under marginal conditions must be at the mercy of natural selection. Plant breeding away from the margin, in central areas of the species, may sacrifice adaptation to higher yields by manipulating important yield components of the plant, here crop physiology plays an important role for improving yields. Such tinkering with adaptation may only be done in marginal areas when dealing with annuals that only have to survive one growing season. Generally at the species margin, adaptation is of first order importance, yield comes second.

To find a proper starting point for this general presentation, the ambiguities that are inherent in the word 'adaptation' and its derivatives have been revisited, mainly on the basis of the work of Theodosius Dobzhansky, summarized in 'On Some Fundamental Concepts of Darwinian Biology' (1968).

Adaptation

Dobzhansky writes: 'When words are borrowed from everyday language to serve as technical terms, misunderstanding is liable to result. Adaptation is plagued with ambiguity, for it is used also in contexts which are biologically irrelevant. Pieces of furniture, or implements are said to be 'adapted' for certain purposes. Biological adaptation is concerned with survival and/or reproduction; it is found only in living bodies …'. Jepsen et al. (1949) have defined adaptation as 'Correlation in a way useful to the organism, between structure, function and environment'. I interpret this as a special trait useful to the organism. The same authors continue by adding 'Also the progressive

14

changes bringing about increase in such relationships in organisms'. Simpson (1953) adds to this 'An adaptation is a characteristic of an organism advantageous to it or to the conspecific group in which it lives', thus pointing at a population genetic interpretation. I interpret this as an evolutionary process dependent on conspecific groups and on the environment.

Adaptedness

Dobzhansky writes: 'Adaptedness first arose with the origin of life, since this life did not become extinct; the origin of life was, however, not an adaptation. … Man is not adapted to feed on pasturage, while horses and cows are so adapted; palms and bananas have no adaptedness to live in Canadian forests, while larches and spruces do have such an adaptedness; certain microorganisms grow in laboratory media and others do not. … In general, adaptedness can be achieved either by individual adaptability or by genetic adaptability'. My interpretation of the word adaptedness would be the degree or level of adaptation. How this should be measured is debatable. Dobzhansky has treated 'The problem of Quantification of Adaptedness' in the fundamental article mentioned earlier, he writes: 'For individual adaptedness, the probability of survival, of reaching the reproductive stage of the life cycle, and in the case of man, the degree of the sense of well being (which is also hard to measure), are thinkable criteria. For populations, a statistic has been proposed named variously the Malthusian parameter, intrinsic rate of natural increase, or innate capacity for increase'. This then becomes a population biological concept, related to the Lotka-Volterra equation of logistic growth and indeed developed further by population biologists.

Adaptability

The words of Dobzhansky: 'If a species could inhabit a single and perfectly constant environment, evolution could conceivably arrive at a genotype optimally adapted to that environment. Evolution would then come to a halt. In reality, not only every species but probably every individual has confrontations with many environments, because environments vary in space and in time. Adaptedness in a narrow range of environments is overspecialization; an overspecialized organism may be highly successful for a time, but it risks death or extinction if the environment changes. Hence the importance of adaptability.

Physiological and genetic adaptabilities must be distinguished. Every genotype has a 'norm of reaction', which is the array of phenotypes it can produce over the range of existing and possible environments'. I think adaptability can be defined as follows: To maintain itself in harmony with a changing environment, the organism must not only be adapted, but also adaptable.

Adaptive value

In conjunction with Darwinian fitness Dobzhansky writes: 'Natural selection is the process which tends to maintain or improve the genetic adaptedness in old environmnents, and contrive adaptedness to new environments'. Refering directly to the work of Darwin, I interpret adaptive value as fitness (w), given as 1-s, s being the selection coefficient. This, then can be taken further from the locus to the genotype and to the fitness of the population ($\overline{w}$).

Some related concepts

A whole range of important expressions originate from the above definitions, such as homeostasis, plasticity and flexibility. Also the confusing philosophy of acclimatization, including the interesting field of physiological preconditioning and general studies of acquired characters must be mentioned. The rest of this paper could be spent on the last mentioned alone. At this time I would like to emphasize just two, namely acclimatization and phenotypic plasticity. Acclimatization is the physiological adjustment to the environment, and is of outstanding importance in marginal plant cultivation. Phenotypic plasticity is the ability to change phenotype in different environments. Both have been of great importance in making use of G × E interactions in cultivated plants.

The marginal environment

Physiochemical factors, such as temperature, humidity, soil chemistry, wind, ice and snow may one at a time or by interaction set the limit for a plant natural distribution at the margins of species. Studies on cumulative mortality of perennial plants close to their margin have shown that, due to large variations in the environment in time plant stand mortality may accumulate in bursts, finally reaching over 90% and often causing complete eradication (Eiche & Gustafsson, 1970). This heterogeneity in time may be from day-to-day, week-to-week, month-to-month and between some seasons from year-to-year. Environments are weakly autocorrelated in time, to use the terminology of MacArthur & Levins (1967) or Levins (1968). Such conditions may frequently cause complete harvest failures and cultivated crops, perennials and trees must show highest possible tolerance to endure critical 'bottleneck' years.

Marginal environments appear to be very highly heterogeneous in space. Farmers or foresters, working in the Sahelian zone or in the subarctic, know the crucial importance of microsite selection when cultivating plants. Land inclination and profiles, water and nutrients may affect plant growth and survival in an almost threshold manner, the environment is highly mosaic in space, often much more so than under more central conditions.

The marginal environment may, due to 'bottlenecks', force plant populations towards a common durable modification. We can see that e.g. on the snow-pressure affected spruce trees or the wind stressed coastal tree populations. What we can not see directly, except after freezing mortality, is the influence of a critical temperature on hardiness or on the timing of flowering and seed set. This may restrict late flowering, late maturing individuals from reproduction, thus having fitness values of zero. It is particularly common in the north to have a complete failure of the generative cycle, due to distorted meiosis. Plants then turn to clonal growth and regeneration, an alternative mode of reproduction.

Observation of different quantitative traits under such conditions may cause us to classify them as having more or less adaptive significance. Traits of high adaptive value are forced to uniformity, while less adaptive ones may show much more variability within a population. This in fact may also be reflected in the genetic structure of populations, on the additive genetic variation of quantitative traits (Stern & Roche, 1974). As we shall see, this does not however eliminate genetic variation at the single locus level.

Plant genetic variation along the margin

A recent very large summary of allozyme diversity in plant species by Hamrick & Godt (1990), including 653 studies on 449 species representing 165 genera, indicates some interesting facts about genetic variation in plant species. I have extracted information on what is known about marginal plant species based on this large survey plus some special studies that are available on marginal populations (Tigerstedt, 1973, 1979; Alden & Loopstra, 1987; Tremblay & Simon, 1989).

- Plant species, on average, maintain higher levels of allozyme variation within populations than invertebrates or vertebrates. The reason for this must be the sedentary characteristic of plants; animal habitat selection is compensated for by higher genetic variation within the population and a much larger offspring number.
- Isozyme studies in marginal populations indicate, that just or nearly as much variation is retained in them as in more central populations.
- Perennial, outcrossing, windpollinated species of the later stages of succession have higher levels of allozyme variation within populations and less among populations than species with other modes of adaptation. Also they often conform on an allozyme level to a Hardy & Weinberg equilibrium. Thus an annual inbreeder would have more of its genet-

ic variation tied to populations in particular sites. In tree populations along the treeline, this generalization is not quite true, isolated pockets of trees may exhibit large differences in gene frequencies, although they are generally highly heterozygotic.

– Predominantly clonal plant species may maintain as much genetic diversity within populations as sexually reproducing species. This may indicate a heterozygous advantage of well adapted clones.

– Linkage disequilibrium is common in predominantly inbreeding species, specialized genotypes may be represented in certain marginal areas. In predominantly outbreeding species such chromosomal structures are very rare.

– Patterns of allozyme variation are not correlated with the variation of morphometric traits of a quantitative nature. Thus morphometric uniformity that may be caused by a marginal environment is not reflected at the allozyme level.

– In some cases environmental heterogeneity and genetic variation can be shown to be interdependent, in other cases the patchy genetic structure may be the result of limited pollen and seed dispersal.

Selection in marginal areas revisited

Natural selection is believed to have 3 fundamental modes; normalizing within populations centrally located, disruptive (diversifying) between populations in a heterogenous environment and directional in populations at species margins. This was the general model used by Carson (1955) for characterizing *Drosophila* populations and it was also generally accepted by e.g. Dobzhansky. Levins, in a series of papers (1962, 1963, 1964) and summarized in 1968 set the stage for a different model of natural selection, looking at mendelian species as adaptive systems. Here the species mode of adaptation was modelled on the basis of a fitness set and an adaptive function. Basically the important components in this model building was the tolerance of an individual in relation to environmental heterogeneity in space and time. This would cause species to adopt alternative modes of adaptation.

Since the early 1970s much new information about plant population genetic structures has accrued as allozyme analyses became available. At the moment, one has a fairly clear concept about population structure based on allozymes and also on morphometric traits. The first efforts to compare these two sources of variation show that they often do not match. At the moment one is turning once again to quantitative traits. By using molecular genetic markers one is now trying to explain the discrepancy between allozyme and morphometric variation. Results are not available as yet.

18

However, the high degree of genetic variation that populations exhibit at a species' margins questions the validity of simple directional selection that would cause genetic uniformity. Also, observations on environmental variation, often stochastic in nature at the margin, is much wider than earlier realized. This variation is both space and time dependent. Under such conditions natural selection on adaptively important traits may in fact have a strong diversifying component, perhaps masked by environmental pressures. In addition to this, plant populations at the margin are often sparse and isolated by distance. In the case of trees in Alaska and Finland, such population pockets may, due to drift, show high degrees of between population genetic diversity.

In large plant breeding efforts of today more emphasis than before is laid on breeding for wide adaptation, stability and tolerance. CIMMYT in Mexico, ICRISAT in the semi-arid tropics and IITA in the humid tropics have adopted a diversifying selection scheme in their breeding for wide adaptation, variously called divergent-convergent selection or shuttle breeding. This idea is also closely related to prebreeding and the efficient use of gene bank materials in breeding programmes. Breeding populations are thus 'shuttled' between several locations in the tropics/subtropics to retain high degrees of genetic variation, wide adaptation and disease resistance of a horizontal quality. The final step in such plant breeding programmes is usually done locally (nationally) by tapping breeding populations for their rich variation and higher than normal diversity.

I propose a similar approach in the effective use of gene bank materials specially adapted to the northern margins. Intercrossing populations of marginal species, that may show genetic diversity due to spatial isolation should create breeding populations with a maximum width of adaptation. Such populations should be the nuclei for breeding in marginal areas where adaptation and adaptability count first.

References

Alden, J. & C. Loopstra, 1987. Genetic diversity and population structure of *Picea glauca* on an altitudinal gradient in interior Alaska. Can. J. For. Res. 17: 1519–1526.

Carson, H.L., 1955. The genetic characteristics of marginal populations of *Drosophila*. Cold Spring Harbor Symp. Quant. Biol. 20: 276–287.

Dobzhansky, Th., 1968. In: Th. Dobzhansky, M.K. Hecht & W.R. Steere (Eds) On Some Fundamental Concepts of Darwinian Biology, Evolutionary Biology Vol. 2, North Holland, Amsterdam.

Eiche, V. & A. Gustafsson, 1970. In: M.K. Hecht & W.C. Steere (Eds) Population research in the Scandinavian Scots pine (*Pinus sylvestris* L.) Essays in Evolution and Genetics in Honor of Theodosius Dobzhansky, North Holland, Amsterdam.

Hamrick, J.L. & M.J.W. Godt, 1990. In: A.H.D. Brown, M.T. Clegg, A.L. Kahler & B.S. Weir (Eds) Allozyme diversity in plant species. Plant Population Genetics, Breeding and Genetic Resources, Sinauer Assoc. Inc.

Jepsen, G., G.G. Simpson & E. Mayr, 1949. Genetics, Paleontology and Evolution, Princeton Univ. Press.

Levins, R., 1962. Theory of fitness in a heterogeneous environment. I. The fitness set and adaptive function. Am. Nat. 96: 361–373.

Levins, R., 1963. Theory of fitness in a heterogeneous environment. II. Developmental flexibility and niche selection. Am. Nat. 97: 75–90.

Levins, R., 1964. Theory of fitness in a heterogeneous environment. IV. The adaptive significance of gene flow. Evolution 18: 635–638.

Levins, R., 1968. Evolution in Changing Environments. Princeton Univ. Press.

MacArthur, R.H. & R. Levins, 1967. The limiting similarity, convergence and divergence of coexisting species. Am. Nat. 101: 377–385.

Simpson, G.G., 1953. The Major Features of Evolution, Columbia Univ. Press.

Stern, K. & L. Roche, 1974. Genetics of Forest Ecosystems. Springer Verl.

Tigerstedt, P.M.A., 1973. Studies of isozyme variation in marginal and central populations of *Picea abies*. Hereditas 75: 47–60.

Tigerstedt, P.M.A., 1979. Genetic adaptation of plants in the subarctic environment. Holarctic Ecology 2: 264–268.

Tremblay, M. & J-P Simon, 1989. Genetic structure of marginal populations of white spruce (*Picea glauca*) at its northern limit of distribution in Nouveau-Quebec. Can. J. For. Res. 19: 1371–1379.

O.A. Rognli et al. (eds.), Breeding Fodder Crops for Marginal Conditions, 21–32.
© 1994 *Kluwer Academic Publishers. Printed in the Netherlands.*

Some consequences of adaptation to extreme environments

TOM MCNEILLY
*Plant Science Laboratories, Department of Environmental and Evolutionary Biology,
University of Liverpool, P.O. Box 147, Liverpool L69 3BX, U.K.*

Summary. The impacts of extreme environmental stress on plant populations in relation to the time scale of evolutionary change, and their consequences for the spatial scales of population differentiation are examined predominantly in members of the Poacea. Evidence from environmental situations in which genetically based population differentiation might reasonably be expected to have evolved but has not been recorded are examined. The impact of extreme selection pressures on genetic variability are briefly considered.

Introduction

Subjection of a group of individuals to stress implies a reduction in their performance, i.e. in their fitness. It follows from this that a group of individuals exhibiting genetically based variability in response to that stress, will, when subjected to it, undergo change due to selective survival of the better adapted, with a concurrent increase in group fitness. In other words natural selection will occur. The mathematical simulations of the outcome of selection on genetically variable populations by Fisher, Haldane, and Sewell-Wright in the 1930s and 1940s established that natural selection could indeed bring about evolutionary changes of the kind observed in nature. The selective advantages of their more fit individuals were extremely small compared with present day evidence about selection differentials in natural populations. As a consequence the time scales of change predicted were in terms of many generations.

The pioneering work of Turesson (1922), and of Clausen, Keck and Hiesey (1948) illustrated the degree to which intra-specific variation could be related to natural selection in response to heterogeneity in environmental stress, such as degree of exposure, woodland shade, shifting sand, low temperature. The differences they reported may have been the product of adaptive radiation, involving long-term gradual evolutionary change in response to relatively low selection pressures, as species gradually migrated to colonise new habitats in the post glacial.

More recent studies of selection in the wild suggest that selection pressures may be significantly greater than previously thought. These higher selection pressures have two major implications for our concept of natural selection. Firstly, if selection pressures are high, and the appropriate genetic variability is available, then change in population structure can be relatively rapid. Secondly, contrasting high selection pressures in adjacent habitats can lead

22

to the evolution of distinct populations separated by very small distances. Much, but certainly not all of the evidence for these possibilities comes from man-made environments such as those which are the products of the mining or smelting of the heavy metals – cadmium, copper, lead, zinc – and the toxic environments which they have produced in the past. They have the advantages from the viewpoint of the investigator that the metals constitute the over-riding stress factor in such environments, and their impacts are relatively easy and quick to quantify using simple measures of root or shoot growth (Bradshaw and McNeilly, 1981). Some of the consequences of this, and other environmental heterogeneity of diverse kinds will be examined in this paper.

Change in population structure – a time scale

In the United Kingdom high tension electricity cables are supported on steel towers, galvanised prior to erection. In high rainfall areas of the country considerable amounts of zinc have been removed from them in rain running down and dripping from the pylon structure. This zinc accumulates in the soil to such an extent that zinc tolerant populations of *Agrostis capillaris* have evolved beneath some of the pylons 16 years after they were erected, by which time the soils contained 1500–3300 μ g Zn g^{-1}, compared with 110–275 μ g Zn g^{-1} on adjacent control soils (Al-Hiyaly et al., 1988).

Whilst the dates of erection of these electricity pylons are precisely known, the point at which soil metal levels became sufficient to promote selection of tolerant individuals cannot be known. However, data from a site contaminated by copper from a smelter in south west Lancashire provides a clearer picture of the time scale of change under high selection pressures. Because of the extent of the emissions from the refinery, the lawns maintained for aesthetic purposes around the buildings were re-established at regular intervals on uncontaminated soil brought in to replace the soils which had become heavily contaminated with copper. By sampling *Agrostis stolonifera* from lawns of known age, it was shown (Wu and Bradshaw, 1972) that after only four years of input of aerially borne copper, copper tolerance had markedly increased in one of the populations. It was suggested that because of the occurrence of other known non-tolerant species in the lawn, and because of the absence of bare areas due to high copper toxicity, selection was just beginning to affect population genetic structure.

Recent studies in the Netherlands (Ernst, Verkleij and Vooijs, 1983) have provided evidence of a similar change over a shorter time scale in the vicinity of a zinc and cadmium smelter. *Agrostis canina* was sampled from the vicinity of the smelter in 1968 one year prior to its being commissioned, and over the following 5 years. A pronouonced increase in zinc tolerance was recorded after one year of emission from the smelter of zinc at a rate of 100 kg ha^{-1}.

These examples are from rather unusual environments with rather extreme characteristics and possibly unusually high selection pressures. What evidence for rapid change in population structure is there for more conventional situations? One of the earliest reports of rapid change in population structure and for this meeting a most appropriate one, was that described by Sylven in 1937. Amongst information relating to the problems associated with *ex situ* multiplication within Sweden of seed of forage grasses and legumes for extreme climatic conditions, Sylven described results from introducing white clover (*Trifolium repens*) from Denmark and Germany to Sweden. The Danish strains, Morsø and Strynø and an un-named German strain were established as leys at Svalöf. After 2 years growth a first generation seed sample was taken from each strain, and a further second generation seed sample was taken after some further years growth of the original leys. These seed samples were compared with samples of the original strains. After just two seasons growing at Svalöf, Morsø yielded 6.6% more green matter than the original Danish strain, and 15.5% more for the second generation sample. Corresponding figures for the German strain were + 29.1% after 2 seasons, and + 37.2% over control for the second generation sample. There was no change in green matter yield of Strynø, which appears to have lacked the genetic variation necessary to respond to selection due to its having been a more homogeneous and homozygous strain. More recent evidence of rapid change in response to pasture conditions comes from a selection experiment for increased yield in *Dactylis glomerata* using plants collected at Løken, Norway. Two groups of plants were raised (i) from seed originally obtained from intercrossing the 20 highest yielding clones from Løken, and (ii) from an unselected control seed sample from Løken. The two groups of plants were grown in separate plots, and dry matter yields assessed annually. Relative dry matter yield of the selected group decreased over a seven year period at an average rate of 1.8% per year, a significant decline occurring in the second year of the experiment (Aastveit, 1985). The change seems to have been due to natural selection for improved vegetative fitness, a feature lost during artificial selection for high yield. This is similar to findings in *Drosophila* where a marked reduction in fecundity was recorded in populations subjected to very high directional selection for abdominal chaeta number (Mather and Harrison, 1949). In this experiment selection was stopped after 24 generations, and fecundity recovered through natural selection, accompanied by a rapid reduction in chaeta number.

Evidence about the time scale of change due to selection in more normal situations comes from a study of the impact of three different management regimes, frequent grazing, infrequent grazing, or hay plus aftermath, on cultivar mixtures of *Lolium, Dactylis glomerata* and *Phleum pratense* (Charles,

24

1964). In the case of a mixture of *L. perenne* S23 and S24, and *L. multiflorum* S22, the proportion of the latter variety in the sward decreased from 80% of the total to 4% after 18 months. Over the same period of time S23 increased from 7% to 60%, and S24 from 13% to 36%. Population numbers declined during that period to about 12% of the original, implying very high selection pressures.

The occurrence of rapid changes in population structure of the kinds outlined above must require the operation of quite extreme selection pressures. Demographic studies of populations of plants and animals have been almost exclusively aimed at understanding population structure and dynamics. However, in that they record births and deaths over extended periods of time, they are recording the progress of natural selection although they lack information about the characteristics of survivors and non-survivors. A demographic study of the population dynamics of *Agrostis vinealis* on a small copper mine near Dolgellau, Gwynedd, North Wales (Farrow, 1983), gives an indication about just how extreme selection pressures may be. A census of births and deaths over a four year period was taken for adult plants, ramets derived from those adults, and for seedlings on areas of high and low adult plant densities. On the low density area, out of a total estimated seed input of 249,160 m^{-2} over the four years, 1925 seedlings m^{-2} resulted, of which only 47 survived until cessation of the study. On the high density area, total seed input over the four-year period was estimated at 99,385 m^{-2}, from which 87 seedlings m^{-2} resulted, of which 6 remained at the end of the study. In both sites survival was greater for the spring seedling recruits than for the autumn recruits – 9.4% vs 0.6% on the low density area, compared with 27.3% vs 0% on the high density area – despite autumn seedling numbers being 3 times greater than those of the spring seedlings. Clearly selection pressures at the seedling level are extremely high. If we look at the performance of adult individuals on the site, again based upon two weekly censuses, we can again see that there is a continual erosion of adult plant numbers over the period, although the rate of change is much lower than that of seedlings. Of 95 adult plants m^{-2} present on the low density area at the beginning of the study, 76 (80%) were alive after 4 years, and 321 (67%) out of 482 adults remained on the high density area. From these data the average half life of adult plants in the two areas were estimated at 20.7 years for the low density area, and 6.1 years for the high density area.

The highly copper contaminated Glasdir site supports a considerable *A. vinealis* population which can only have developed since the abandonment of the workings in 1914. Based upon the data obtained from this study, the numbers of individuals recruited annually could not account for the present population size. From visual estimates of population size at another similar site and for other species, the same picture is repeated – recruitment at the rates estimated from population dynamics studies cannot account for the numbers of individuals growing on them. It seems likely that in certain rather infrequent periods of two or more years, a number of environmental factors coincide favourably to allow significant recruitment of seedlings, significant numbers of which persist to produce adult plants. Clearly the critical stage for recruitment of individuals is germination, a process which almost certainly owes more to chance environmental influences than to the genotype of individual seeds. Differential survival of both seedlings and adults may on the other hand reflect differences in selective advantage due to genotype. It is also clear that selection in extreme environments is ruthless, but nonetheless, given the presence of appropriate genetic variation in potential colonisers such environments will be colonised.

Change in population structure – changes in space

At the beginning of this paper it was suggested that high selection pressures acting in adjacent extreme environments can bring about the occurrence of very sharp boundaries between populations. In such situations there is the possibility of gene flow between populations either by propagules and/or by pollen in outbreeding species. This can lead to blurring of the boundaries between the populations, the outcome being the result of interaction between the strength of the selection pressures operating and the extent of gene flow between the populations. Such a situation was described by Ennos (1985), where *Cynosurus cristatus* populations 100 m apart showed only weak genetic divergence because of the impact of gene (pollen) flow between them. Yet the populations of zinc tolerant *A. capillaris* from beneath electricity pylons described earlier exist on areas less than 100 m^2 surrounded by vast populations of non zinc tolerant individuals from which gene flow must be very considerable. Nonetheless these pylon populations retain their zinc tolerant identity. The contrasting outcomes in these two situations are almost certainly related to the differences in selection pressures operating in them, relatively weak selection in the *C. cristatus* populations contrasted with high selection for zinc tolerance in the *A. capillaris* populations. In the context of extreme environments there is a number of interesting cases where adaptive differentiation has been recorded for populations growing only a few metres apart, presumably in the face of considerable inter population gene flow.

A very elegant example of correlation between plant form and habitat type has been described for *Agrostis stolonifera* populations from a very exposed headland on the north west coast of Ynys Môn, Gwynedd, North Wales (Aston and Bradshaw, 1966). Stolon lengths were measured in a common garden experiment for populations from a very exposed cliff face and an

26

adjacent sheltered pasture. A second group of populations were sampled along a gradual sloping change from sea-level to the same pasture. Where the environment changed suddenly over a distance of 1.5 to 3 m, mean stolon length of the *A. stolonifera* plants changed from 17 cm to 47 cm over that same small distance. By contrast, where the environment changed gradually, stolon length also showed a gradual clinal change. The selective advantage of short stolons in exposed conditions is shown by the comparative loss of plant biomass of contrasting individuals subjected to gale force winds for 24 h. Pasture material lost 50% of its biomass, whereas cliff top material lost only 5% of its biomass.

Abandoned heavy metal mine wastes represent very extreme environments, and as we have seen tolerant populations maintain their integrity due to very high selection pressures favouring them. Many such wastes have very sharp boundaries where deposition of wastes has ceased. Several studies of the distribution of tolerance across such boundaries have been made, and show that tolerant and normal non-tolerant populations can be separated by as little as 1 m distance. Gene flow has also been shown to be high, but population integrity is maintained by the severity of selection against non-adapted types in both habitats (McNeilly, 1968). An even more remarkable example of population differentiation over a very small scale has been shown in the case of *Anthoxanthum odoratum* in the Park Grass plots set up at Rothamsted. Adjacent plots have, or have not received lime annually since 1903. Populations from these two types of plot differ completely in plant height even though they were separated by a distance of only 10 cm (Snaydon and Davies, 1976).

Alternative adaptive strategies

The evidence presented thus far suggests that in extreme environments natural selection will promote the evolution of genetically based adapted populations, and the death of the non-adapted, or in the absence of appropriate genetic variation, prevent the colonisation of such habitats. This latter situation appears to happen in the case of heavy metal tolerance in plants. An examination of the grass species present on normal soils along the periphery of the large heavily copper contaminated mine waste at Mynydd Parys, Ynys Môn, North Wales by Ingram (1988) and their occurrence on the toxic mine waste, showed that of the 15 grass species growing on normal soils, only five, *Agrostis capillaris, Holcus lanatus, Deschampsia flexuosa, Dactylis glomerata* and *Festuca rubra*, were found growing on the mine waste. Artificial selection for copper tolerance in the remaining 10 species produced no tolerant individuals, and Ingram concluded that colonisation was prevented because they lacked the appropriate variation – copper tolerance – necessary for the evolution of adapted individuals. We may however ask whether heterogeneity in environmental stress always leads to micro-evolutionary adaptations of the kind examined thus far.

Responses to shade/light and soil moisture were examined for populations of *Dactylis glomerata* and *Bromus erectus* from a *Quercus pubescens* wood and a grass sward, both of which were the result of natural colonisation of vineyards respectively abandoned 120 and 20 years prior to sampling (Roy, 1985). Despite the considerable differences in light and soil moisture between the wood and the sward habitats, no significant differences were found between the populations of either species for dry matter production in controlled experimental conditions. The *B. erectus* populations did not differ in the ratio spike biomass/leaf biomass in response to changing soil moisture. In addition, despite the onset of water stress conditions 6 weeks earlier in the sward than in the wood, differences in flowering time between populations, particularly in *B. erectus*, differed by less than four days. In this situation there was no evidence of adaptive evolution in either species. Given the time scales of change due to natural selection considered earlier it seems unlikely that time can have prevented adaptive change. It could be however that for these *Dactylis* and *Bromus* populations selection pressures were insufficient to cause such changes, since changes in phenotype in response to environment, phenotypic plasticity, may allow sufficient adaptive adjustments, rather than selection driven change in genotype. Indeed in *D. glomerata* where plants were grown in full incident light and 24% incident light, anthesis occurred up to twelve days later in the low light treatment than in full light conditions (Roy, 1985), a very convincing example of phenotypic plasticity.

A further situation in which phenotypic plasticity would appear to account for adaptation has been described in *Plantago major* spp *pleiosperma* by Blom and Lotz (1985). They sampled populations from situations in wich there were relatively extreme variations in environment, e.g. in grazing and flooding intensity, humidity, and soil chemical and physical conditions, all of which varied over very short distances. As a consequence individuals in a particular environment would likely be subjected to high levels of gene flow, a situation in which, unless selection pressures were extremely high, selection would favour phenotypically plastic responses to environmental heterogeneity. This is borne out by data from a transplant experiment, where variance in vegetative development was mainly affected by site variables, i.e. a phenotypically plastic response was induced. Other plant characters such as date of first flowering and reproductive effort showed at least some degree of genetic control, but they also had a phenotypic plasticity component. Remaining with the genus *Plantago*, a final example of the adaptive significance of phenotypic plasticity was shown by work of Gregor (1956). He examined a dwarf

28

population of *P. maritima* growing in an exposed area of Iceland consisting of a mosaic of hummocks and hollows. A corresponding mosaic of taller and dwarf plants was found in the wild, the taller plants growing in the hollows. When grown in an experimental garden however, these differences disappeared in five out of the six samples assessed. Again we see a phenotypically plastic response to environmental heterogeneity.

A consistent feature of the immediate environment of most plants is the presence of neighbours of the same or different species. Interactions between such neighbours occur as inter- or intra-species competition, from which, given time the evolution of co-adaptation between neighbours might be expected to occur. The possibility of co-adaptation between neighbouring individuals was assessed in a 10-year old pasture, and a permanent pasture known to be at least 40 years old, and probably much older (McNeilly and Roose, unpublished data). Genotype distribution within 0.25 m^2 quadrats on a 5-cm grid was determined using isozymes as markers (McNeilly and Roose, 1984), allowing precise identification of neighbouring genotypes. Interactions between 7 pairs of neighbours from the 10-year-old pasture and 2 pairs of neighbours from the permanent pasture were examined. Pairs were grown in mixed stands with each other, in mixed stands with the same group of alien genotypes from the same pasture, and in pure stands. Yields of dried green matter production were compared after 18 months' growth.

Neighbours yielded less when grown together than when they were grown either individually with aliens, or in pure stands. For 8 of the 9 pairs of neighbours, one individual significantly outyielded the other, and one of the other neighbours had been eliminated. No evidence of co-adaptation of known neighbours had occurred in either pasture. It would seem that the genotypic structure of these pastures is more likely the product of competitive exclusion of individual genotypes rather than of the evolution of co-adapted groups of individuals.

Populations in extreme environments – genetic aspects

Returning to a previous topic, heavy metal tolerance, it is a fact that whilst some contaminated sites cover many hectares, most are of modest size and a considerable number are measured in hundreds or tens of square metres. In all but a very small number, plant cover rarely exceeds 10% and therefore populations consist of small numbers of individuals. These populations are, as we have seen earlier, the product of very high selection pressures in their early evolution when it is likely that they would have gone through a bottleneck in which variation would have been drastically reduced. Bottlenecks would seem likely to be a common feature of populations of extreme environments both in the past and in the future. What then are the likely consequences of such a history for levels of genetic variability in metal tolerant populations and implications for other populations in extreme environments?

Variation in 10 morphological characters in adjacent mine and pasture populations of *Anthoxanthum odoratum* was examined by Antonovics and Bradshaw (1970) at a small lead/zinc mine. Four sites varying in distance from the mine/pasture boundary were sampled on the mine waste, and a further four were sampled into the pasture. For 8 of the 10 characters assessed, variation within the two populations was greater than that between them. The greatest amount of variability was found in the boundary sites where the tolerant mine and non-tolerant pasture populations were only 1–3 m apart, and gene flow would have been considerable. This gene flow would result in inter-population crossing leading to both heterogeneity and heterozygosity. More recent studies have revealed unexpectedly high amounts of both isozyme and morphological variability in tolerant populations of three species (*Arrhenatherum elatius, Silene vulgaris, Armeria maritima*) at different mine sites (summarised in Lefèbvre and Vernet, 1990). It does not seem plausible that the diversity of these populations is due to very precise selection for particular micro-niches, because of the extremely low frequency of successful seed establishment reported by Farrow (1983). Such variability appears be the product of genetic drift in the case of *Armeria maritima* on the Plombières lead/zinc mine has been suggested by Lefèbvre (1982). At Plombierès *A. maritima* occurs as a number of sub-populations which differ in heritable morphological characters. Different character combinations are not associated with any clear ecological differences on the mine. It seems that because gene flow in *A. maritima* is very restricted the sub-populations may have diverged through genetic drift during the early colonisation of the mine (Lefèbvre and Vernet, 1990). Such a situation may represent a more realistic model for populations in extreme environments than that of other mine colonisers.

What then are the likely fates of genetic variation in populations in extreme environments where gene flow from neighbouring populations is unlikely? What are the effects of genetic drift, mutation, immigration (gene flow), population sub-division, and various forms of selection likely to be on population heterozygosity? The impact of interacting effects of these factors were examined using simulations of populations of 20 to 500 individuals over 100 generations by Lacy (1987). The major factor affecting reduction in genetic variability was genetic drift, whereas mutation had no noticeable effect. Gene flow, even at very low levels from adjacent or exotic sources either halted or reversed the loss of genetic variation, a likely explanation of the high genetic diversity found in mine populations. With modest selection differentials (minimum relative fitness of 0.6) selection had no impact on genetic drift in populations of less than 100 individuals. Such selection differentials would seem to be rather low especially for extreme environments, suggesting that selection in such situations may well be sufficient to counteract genetic drift. Where simulated populations existed as groups of sub-populations, individual populations tended to lose variation, but in the group population as a whole, variation is maintained more successfully than in a single large population. These simulations were made for diploid dioecious species, whereas plants are predominantly polyploid and monoecious, and exhibit varying degrees of self fertilization, all features which would tend to reduce the impact of small population size in decreasing variability.

Finally let us consider the impact of bottlenecks on population variability, since almost by definition populations in extreme environments are likely to be subjected to varying numbers of bottlenecks in their histories and futures. Polans and Allard (1989) provide experimental evidence about the effects of bottleneck restriction where ryegrass (*Lolium multiflorum*) populations raised from wild collected seed were subjected to genetic stress by restricting the number of founder individuals to 2, 4, or 8 plants in each of three successive generations, followed by removal of breeding restrictions. The initial reduction in population size caused changes in allelic frequencies and levels of heterozygosity at 3 isozyme loci, a predicted consequence of genetic drift in such small populations. The smaller populations (2 or 4 founders) also suffered increasing loss of genetic diversity, as well as reduction in fitness. Despite removal of size restrictions from the populations, some of the deleterious effects of restriction in population size on fitness related characters were still evident after one generation of recovery. Random mating in mixtures of the inbred populations resulted in a rapid recovery of character expression to those of the original population, due to restoration of genetic diversity to a level equivalent to that in the original population. The practical implications of these data are that as a result of inbreeding, characters which are fitness related, and tend therefore to have predominantly non-additive genetic variation (Falconer, 1981) appear to be the most susceptible to inbreeding depression.

I have tried to present a brief account of experimental work illustrating what natural selection can achieve in response to extreme environmental factors, to illustrate what extreme can mean for seedling recruitment, to suggest that genetically based fixed responses to such selection can be substituted at least in some situations by phenotypically plastic responses, or lack of response, and finally to briefly introduce some of the genetic implications of small population size, a frequent characteristic of populations in extreme environments. In conclusion, what is perhaps most remarkable, is the extent to which plants are able to adapt to extreme environmental stress through natural selection, and survive apparently over long periods of time, in some cases as very small populations, in such stress environments.

References

Aastveit K 1985 Genetic aspects of climatic adaptation in plants. *In*: Plant Production in the North. pp. 23-42. Eds. Å Kaurin, O Juntilla and J Nilsen. Norwegian University Press, Oslo.

Al-Hiyaly SEK, McNeilly T and Bradshaw AD 1988 The effects of contamination from electricity pylons – evolution in a replicated situation. New Phytol. 110, 571–580.

Antonovics J and Bradshaw AD 1970 Evolution in closely adjacent plant populations VIII. Clinal patterns at a mine boundary. Heredity 25, 349–362.

Aston JL and Bradshaw AD 1966 Evolution in closely adjacent populations II. *Agrostis stolonifera* in maritime habitats. Heredity 21, 649–664.

Blom CWPM and Lotz LAP 1985 Phenotypic plasticity and genetic differentiation of demographic characteristics in some Plantago species. *In*: Structure and Functioning of Plant Populations 2. pp. 185–194. Eds. J Haeck and JW Woldendorp. North Holland Publishing Company, Amsterdam.

Bradshaw AD and McNeilly T 1981 Evolution and Pollution. Edward Arnold, London.

Charles AH 1964 Differential survival of plant types in swards. J. Brit. Grassl. Soc. 19, 198–204.

Clausen J, Keck DD and Hiesey WM 1948 Experimental studies on the nature of plant species. 3. Environmental responses of climatic races of *Achillea*. Carnegie Institute of Washington Publication 581. Carnegie Institute, Washington.

Ennos RA 1985 The mating system and genetic structure in a prennial grass, *Cynosurus cristatus* L. Heredity 55, 121–126.

Ernst WHO, Verkleij JAC and Vooijs R 1983 Bioindication of a surplus of heavy metals in terrestrial ecosystems. Env. Mon. Ass. 3, 297–305.

Falconer SJ 1981 An Introduction to Quantitative Genetics. Oliver and Boyd, Edinburgh.

Farrow SJ 1983 Population dynamics and selection in *Agrostis canina* on a small copper mine. Ph.D. thesis, University of Liverpool.

Gregor JW 1956 Adaptation and ecotypic components. Proc. Roy. Soc. B145, 333–337.

Ingram C 1988 The evolutionary basis of ecological amplitude of plant species. Ph.D. thesis, University of Liverpool.

Lacy RC 1987 Loss of genetic diversity from managed populations: interacting effects of drift, mutation, immigration, selection, and population subdivision. Conserv. Biol. 1, 143–158.

Lefèbvre C 1982 Variation et évolution chez une famille de plantes supérieures: Les *Plumbagnaceae*. Thèse d'Agrégation Enseignment Supérieur, Université Libre de Bruxelles, Bruxelles.

Lefèbvre C and Vernet P 1990 Micro-evolutionary processes on contaminated deposits. *In*: Heavy Metal Tolerance in Plants: Evolutionary Aspects. pp. 285–299. Ed. AJ Shaw. CRC Press, Boca Raton, U.S.A.

Mather K and Harrison B 1949 The manifest effects of selection. Heredity 3, 1–52.

McNeilly T 1968 Evolution in closely adjacent plant populations III. *Agrostis tenuis* on a small copper mine. Heredity 23, 99–108.

McNeilly T and Roose ML 1984 The distribution of perennial ryegrass in swards. New Phytol 98, 503–513.

Polans NO and Allard RW 1989 An experimental evaluation of the recovery potential of ryegrass populations from genetic stress resulting from restriction of population size. Evolution 43, 1320–1324.

Roy J 1985 Comparison of *Dactylis glomerata* and *Bromus erectus* populations from contrasted successional stages. *In*: Structure and Functioning of Plant Populations 2. pp. 51–64. Eds. J Haeck and JW Woldendorp. North Holland Publishing Company, Amsterdam.

Snaydon RW and Davies MS 1976 Rapid population differentiation in a mosaic environment IV. Populations of *Anthoxanthum odoratum* at sharp boundaries. Heredity 37, 9–25.

Sylven N 1937 The difference of climatic conditions on type composition. Bull. Bur. Pl. Genet. 21, 1–8.

Turesson G 1922 The genotypical response of the plant species to the habitat. Hereditas 3, 211–350.

Wu L, Bradshaw AD and Thurman DA 1975 The potential for evolution of heavy metal tolerance in plants 1. The rapid evolution of copper tolerance in *Agrostis stolonifera*. Heredity 34, 165–187.

Collection and evaluation of plant populations for forage production under marginal conditions

O.A. Rognli et al. (eds.), Breeding Fodder Crops for Marginal Conditions, 35–46.
© 1994 *Kluwer Academic Publishers. Printed in the Netherlands.*

Collecting and evaluating genetic resources of fodder plants from subalpine and alpine permanent grassland

U. SIMON
*Technical University Munich, Chair of Grassland and Forage Production, 85350
Freising-Weihenstephan, Germany*

Summary. The permanent grassland in the northern alpine and prealpine regions of Germany, Austria and Switzerland is characterized by a large genetic diversity of commercially important grass and clover species. This gene pool is endangered by the increasing practice of grassland renovation. The collection of genetic resources from that marginal habitat serves two purposes, therefore: Utilization of the gene pool in breeding programmes, and conserving the natural variation of endangered habitats. A considerable number of ecotypes of various species has been collected by several workers over a period of thirty years.
Special attention is given to the materials collected and evaluated by Scheller (several species), Tyler (several species), Spatz (perennial ryegrass), Krings & Simon (Italian ryegrass) and Simon (several species). The materials described contain genotypes which appear useful for the improvement of such agronomically important characters as date of heading, plant height, winter hardiness, persistency and rust resistance under marginal conditions. From Simon's collections six cultivars registered or applied for registration in the German List of Cultivars emerged.

Introduction

It is generally accepted that the availability of appropriate basic genetic materials is an indispensable prerequisite for any plant breeding programme aiming at the creation of improved cultivars (Simon, 1983; Tyler, 1987). Sources of such basic material may be existing cultivars, or the results of genetic manipulation such as crossing, inbreeding, induction of mutants and polyploids, genetic engineering and gene banks.

Many of the commercially important species which are useful for both fodder and non fodder purposes are integrated parts of the permanent grassland vegetation throughout Europe. It represents an excellent source of useful initial genetic breeding stock. It is quite logical, therefore, that this genetic potential is used extensively by plant breeders. The International Board for Plant Genetic Resources (IBPGR) established a Working Group on Forages, and the Report of this group (IBPGR, 1989) lists a considerable number of collecting activities for various species throughout Europe. Chorlton (1991) gives an account on the collection of genetic resources in the United Kingdom over the last thirty years.

In the northern alpine and prealpine regions of Germany, Austria and Switzerland permanent grassland covers from 50% up to 100% of the agricultural area. The botanical composition of this grassland is very variable

36

depending on the prevailing climatic and soil conditions, and on the type and intensity of management.

From the great diversity of external factors and due to natural selection a large genetic diversity within species has emerged. Grasslands ranging from elevations of about 400 m a.s.l. to approximately 1000 m a.s.l. include important grass species such as perennial and Italian ryegrass, fescue (meadow tall, red, sheeps), Kentucky bluegrass, orchardgrass, timothy, and bentgrass species. Among the legumes naturally occurring in this area are white clover, wild red clover, alsike clover, and birdsfoot trefoil. The habitats of some special purpose species like *Poa supina, Festuca violacea*, and *Festuca apennina* extend even above 1000 m a.s.l.

We feel that this wealth of genetic diversity presents a tremendous potential of resources for the genetic improvement of grass and clover species to be used under marginal conditions. Some of this valuable material is endangered by the increasing practice of grassland renovation, other is lost because grassland is destroyed for other reasons. The collection of genetic resources, therefore, serves two purposes: Making use of ecotypes in breeding programmes and conserving the natural variation of species in endangered habitats.

Collecting area

The collecting area extends approximately 150 km from east to west and 100 km from north to south. The southern border is the northern alpine limestone range with the Zugspitze (3000 m a.s.l.) as its highest elevation. Some climatic data of the area are presented in Table 1. From north to south, with increasing altitude, the mean annual temperature decreases from 7.5 to 6.0° C, the average temperature of the coldest month, January, decreases from - 2.2 to - 3.4° C, and the average temperature of the warmest month, July, drops from 17.0 to 15.1. Vice versa, the average annual precipitation increases from about 750 mm to about 1720 mm. For comparison, the respective data of Hamburg in northern Germany are presented. In addition to the described area, ecotypes were collected in the Bavarian Forest and in Switzerland.

Collecting and evaluating ecotypes

A considerable number of ecotypes of various species has been collected by various workers over a period of thirty years. Care was taken to collect only from habitats with a long history of grassland management without reseeding within fifteen to twenty years. Ecotypes were generally taken as plants, occasionally as seed. In one particular case seed of a perennial ryegrass dominant pasture was harvested by combine (Spatz et al., 1987).

Table 1. Climatic characteristics of collecting area from north to south, (Reichsamt für Wetterdienst, 1939)

Location	Elevation	Mean temperature ° C			Precipitation
	m	Jan.	July	year	mm yr^{-1}
Weihenstephan	450	- 2.3	17.0	7.4	748
München	530	- 2.2	16.9	7.5	904
Traunstein	597	- 2.4	16.5	7.1	1523
Kempten	705	- 2.7	15.4	6.4	1184
Garmisch-P.	715	- 2.9	15.4	6.7	1286
Oberstdorf	818	- 3.4	15.1	6.0	1721
Hamburg	29	0.3	17.1	8.5	740

Among the collections conducted within the last thirty years are those of Scheller, 1983; Tyler, 1986; Krings & Simon, 1990/91; Simon, 1963/93. Some results obtained by these workers will be reported here.

Collection Scheller

An extensive collecting programme was conducted by Scheller (1987) in 1983. All countries in the Bavarian subalpine region were sampled and supplemented by collections in the Bavarian Forest and a number of habitats in Switzerland. From each of 550 habitats 5 to 10 plants were taken adding up to a total of 8500 plants. The species included were primarily perennial ryegrass, and, to a lesser extent, Kentucky bluegrass, orchardgrass, and meadow fescue.

The collected ecotypes were planted in a spaced planted nursery for evaluation. In addition, part of the material was evaluated as clone propagules at an experimental site 730 m a.s.l. which is characterized by an exceptionally long snow cover.

The following characters were assessed: Spring vigour, vigour at cutting time, regrowth, rust resistance, winter hardiness, persistency.

The proportion of outstanding accessions according to their general appearance was in perennial rygrass 4%, Kentucky bluegrass and orchardgrass 15%, respectively, and in meadow fescue 10%. Outstanding ecotypes were concentrated in certain areas, e.g. Kentucky bluegrass in counties Miesbach, Rosenheim, Traunstein; orchardgrass in counties Freising and Allgäu; meadow fescue in counties Rosenheim and Freising. No such regional concentration of superior ecotypes was observed in perennial ryegrass. Selected ecotypes

Table 2. Classification of 'Spitalhof' ecotypes of perennial ryegrass according to date of heading; n = 359. Spatz, 1987

Days after April 1	42	49	52	56	63	70
Proportion of plants %	11	48	$\bar{x}$	33	4	4

were included in breeding programmes at the Bavarian State Institute for Soil Cultivation and Crop Production in Weihenstephan. Up to now, promising highly persistent and snow mold resistant strains have been developed from the collections of perennial ryegrass and orchardgrass (Scheller, 1993).

Collection Spatz

The pastures of the grassland and livestock experiment station Spitalhof near Kempten (730 m a.s.l.) are dominated by an unusually high proportion of perennial ryegrass. Since commercially available cultivars lack sufficient persistency at this location, the indigeneous perennial ryegrass seemed to be superior in this respect. Spatz collected 359 plants from the habitat and in addition, harvested by combine a perennial ryegrass dominant pasture at the stage of seed maturity in 1983. The plants exhibited a large variation with respect to the date of heading (Table 2). The range extends over a period of 28 days, which covers almost the range of the 69 forage cultivars of perennial ryegrass (30 days) described in the 'Beschreibende Sortenliste Gräser, Klee, Luzerne' (Bundessortenamt, 1991). The average date of heading of the population, 52 days after April 1, coincides with the Bundessortenamt classification 'very early to early' (Bundessortenamt, 1991).

The combine harvested seed was used for the establishment of variety tests at the site of collection, Spitalhof, and in Weihenstephan. The 'Spitalhof' population exceeded the three check varieties in dry matter production at both locations (Table 3 -, Spatz et al., 1987).

Collection Tyler

B.F. Tyler of the Welsh Plant Breeding Station Aberystwyth collected ecotypes within our area in 1986. The number of accessions was: Perennial ryegrass 65, tall fescue 35, and 5 each of meadow fescue and giant fescue. This material was included in the WPBS collection for regeneration and further evaluation at WPBS and Weihenstephan. No detailed information about the results is available up to now.

Table 3. Relative dry matter yield of the 'Spitalhof' perennial ryegrass population

Year	Average 3 check varieties	Relative dry matter yield 'Spitalhof' population at		$\bar{x}$
		Spitalhof	Weihenstephan	
1985	100	112	123	117
1986	100	114	110	112
$\bar{x}$	100	113	117	115

Collection Krings and Simon

Italian ryegrass is the most productive forage grass within a crop rotation in Germany. Most of the commercially available cultivars have been developed in sea-coast adjacent countries such as Belgium, the Netherlands, Denmark, and northern Germany. Consequently, they are adapted to a relatively mild climate. Disappointing results have often been obtained when this grass was grown in the relatively rough climate of southern Germany due to its limited winter hardiness and short life time. On the other hand it is known that ecotypes of Italian ryegrass are prevalent in some of the south German permanent grassland which has never been sown. We assumed that among these ecotypes individuals can be found which exceed the presently available cultivars in winter hardiness, persistency, and perhaps other agronomically important characters. For this reason the Association for the Promotion of the Private German Plant Breeding (GFP) supported a collection and evaluation programme which we conducted from 1990 to 1993.

Five individual plants were collected from each of 115 habitats, 19 of which are located in Switzerland around Zurich (Table 4). Only the 1990 accessions will be considered within the scope of this report.

Each collected plant was cloned into 25 parts. 20 clone plants were used to establish a polycross nursery to produce seed for progeny tests. Each polycross consisted of the 5 clones of one habitat. The remaining 5 plants were used to establish a maintenance nursery. Polycross seed was harvested in 1991. The average seed yield per plant among clones ranged from 1,5 g to 22,6 g, and the 1000 grain weight ranged from 1,5 g to 6,3 g. Judging from the 1000 grain weight and from the visual appearance of the clones, 35 accessions were classified as tetraploid. This is surprising, because indigeneous Italian ryegrass is never tetraploid. We concluded, therefore, that the tetraploids were not really ecotypes.

40

Table 4. Italian ryegrass ecotype collection

Region	Altitude range m	Number of habitats 1990	1991	total
Germany				
– Oberbayern	382–815	53	9	62
– Niederbayern	400–640	10	–	10
– Schwaben	600–860	16	8	24
Switzerland	400–820	19	–	19
Total	382–860	98	17	115

For the polycross progeny tests only ecotypes of above average seed setting capacity were selected. Progeny tests were conducted at five locations ranging in altitude from 45 to 1085 m a.s.l. The cultivars 'Lemtal' and 'Lipo' were used as check varieties.

The following characters were assessed for two consecutive years in the progeny tests and in some instances in the maintenance clones:
- date of heading
- plant height
- green and dry matter production (first cut, regrowth, total)
- rust resistance
- winter hardiness
- persistency

The material expressed a considerable variation of most of the characters tested, and many ecotypes compared favourably with the check varieties (Krings & Simon, 1993).

Plant height. The plant height was measured at the end of heading. Table 5 reveals a great variation in the height of the ecotypes. Interestingly, the plants grew much shorter at the higher altitude location. But at both experimental sites there were progenies that exceeded the check varieties in height. The tallest ecotypes were found in Switzerland.

Green matter production. Only the green matter production at two experimental sites in 1992 is reported here. Table 6 shows relevant figures for the first cut, the total of consecutive cuts, and the total green matter yield in 1992 at two experimental sites. Of the two check varieties, the tetraploid 'Lipo' is always superior to the diploid 'Lemtal' which confirms the general experi-

Table 5. Plant height (cm) of ecotype progenies at two locations 1992

Location	Check		Ecotypes		
	Lemtal (d)	Lipo (t)	min.	mean	max.
Hohenlieth (45 m)	102	110	84	102	114
Grünschwaige (435 m)	66	63	55	65	73

Table 6. Green matter yield (kg/plot) of ecotype progenies at two locations 1992

Location	Check		Ecotypes		
	Lemtal (d)	Lipo (t)	min.	mean	max.
First cut					
Thüle (100 m)	19.0	21.0	9.5	17.4	21.3
Grünschwaige (435 m)	19.3	21.2	9.1	18.2	25.0
Regrowth total					
Thüle	27.9	29.5	20.7	26.5	30.6
Grünschwaige	18.5	18.9	11.0	17.7	23.8
Year total					
Thüle	46.8	50.5	33.7	44.1	51.2
Grünschwaige	37.7	40.2	22.3	36.0	48.0

ence that tetraploids exceed diploid varieties in terms of green matter yield. Since ecotypes are diploid, they should be compared with the diploid check. In the first cut the mean green matter yield of the ecotype progenies was below that of 'Lemtal', but 27% of the progenies were superior to 'Lemtal', and 4% exceeded even the tetraploid check 'Lipo'. The early and tall types were the most productive ones in the first cut. Similar results were obtained for green matter yield in the regrowth and for total yield. We find particularly at Grünschwaige in southern Bavaria many promising ecotypes that exceed both check varieties in regrowth and total yield. The late ecotypes were more productive than the early ones in the regrowth which is in contrast to their behaviour in the first cut.

Table 7. Rust resistance of ecotype progenies at two locations 1992; 1 = very susceptible; 9 = very resistant

Location	Check		Ecotypes		
	Lemtal (d)	Lipo (t)	min.	mean	max.
Hohenlieth (45 m)	4.8	6.1	1.8	4.3	6.2
Grünschwaige 435 m)	5.3	6.5	1.6	3.7	6.4

Table 8. Winter hardiness of ecotype progenies at three locations 1992/93; 1 = very poor; 9 = very good

Location	Check		Ecotypes		
	Lemtal (d)	Lipo (t)	min.	mean	max.
Hohenlieth (45 m)	4.8	5.3	2.0	5.7	7.0
Grünschwaige (435 m)	1.6	1.4	1.0	2.0	5.0
Gereute (1085 m)	1.1	1.4	0.5	1.4	2.6

Rust resistance. The progenies are generally less resistant to rust – in most cases *Puccinia coronata* – than the check varieties (Table 7). Apparently, the ecotypes suffered more from rust attack at the higher elevated location Grünschwaige than at the lowland location. In fact, when comparing ecotypes from different altitudes, rust resistance decreases as altitude increases.

Winter hardiness. Data for winterhardiness are presented in Table 8. Obviously, the winter stress increases with increasing altitude of the testing sites. The duration of snow cover in the winter 1992/93, for instance, was 43 days in Hohenlieth (45 m), but 143 days in Gereute (1085 m). The important fact, however, is that the average winter hardiness of the ecotype progenies is superior to that of the check varieties. This is particularly true at the testing sites Grünschwaige (435 m) and Gereute (1085 m). We feel that the collected ecotypes include very valuable genetic resources for improving winter hardiness in Italian ryegrass.

Persistency. Italian ryegrass is less persistent than perennial ryegrass. To improve the persistency of Italian ryegrass is not only an important breeding aim in the highlands but in the lowlands as well. Persistency in this investiga-

Table 9. Persistency of ecotype progenies at two locations 1992; 1 = very poor; 9 = very good

Location	Check		Ecotypes		
	Lemtal (d)	Lipo (t)	min.	mean	max.
Hohenlieth (45 m)	2.8	2.7	1.2	2.2	7.0
Grünschwaige (435 m)	2.8	2.7	1.7	3.6	7.6

Table 10. Species and number of ecotypes collected by Simon 1963 to 1993

Species	Number	Species	Number
Agrostis stolonifera	13	*Lolium perenne*	87
Dactylis glomerata	20	+ seed ≈ 3000 plants	
Festuca apennina	5	*Phleum bertolonii*	23
Festuca pratensis	9	*Phleum pratense*	6
Festuca violacea	14	*Poa supina*	133
		Trifolium pratense	14

tion is expressed in terms of general appearance in the autumn 1992. The relevant data of one lowland (Hohenlieth 45 m) and one highland (Grünschwaige 435 m) testing site are presented in Table 9. It is very obvious that the progenies include ecotypes that are much more persistent than the check varieties. This is particularly true at Grünschwaige where persistency is greater than at Hohenlieth. Over 75% of the tested progenies exceed the best check variety in persistency here. In conclusion, the collected ecotypes include valuable genetic resources for improving both winter hardiness and persistency of Italian ryegrass particularly under highland conditions.

Collection Simon

Simons collection of ecotypes is summarized in Table 10. Comments are made on only a few of the mentioned species.

Agrostis stolonifera. This stoloniferous grass forms a very fine and dense turf when cut frequently very close to the ground. 'Schönbrunn' is one accession

44

Table 11 Performance of *Lolium perenne* synthetics of subalpine and alpine ecotypes at Grünschwaige (435 m a.s.l.). Recordings 1 = very poor; 9 = very good

Entry no. no.	Date of heading (days) % Gremie	1990/93 Vigour before 1st cut	1991/93 Winter kill	1990/91 Annual dry matter yield Gremie = 100 1990	1991	$\bar{x}$	1993 2 cuts
1	- 8	7.6	1.4	105	115	110	–
2	- 7	7.3	1.6	103	112	107	117
3	- 7	7.3	1.6	102	112	107	108
4	- 7	7.2	1.8	101	112	106	116
5	- 5	6.8	2.1	104	112	108	104
$\bar{x}$	- 6.8	7.2	1.7	103	113	107	111
Gremie[1]		5.7	3.2	100	100	100	100

[1] Bardonna in 1993.

which compares favourable with the Dutch cultivar 'Prominent'. The application for registration in the German List of Cultivars is pending.

Festuca violacea. Festuca violacea is an alpine grass growing between 1600 and 2500 m a.s.l. (Oberdorfer, 1990). This species has not been included in a breeding programme to the authors knowledge. It may have a potential for special purposes like seedings on ski tracks and avalanche prone sites in high altitudes. It is also useful as a forage grass. Our material has been collected in Switzerland at 2000 m a.s.l.

Lolium perenne. The collection of 87 ecotypes includes a seed population from the same habitat, Spitalhof, where Spatz took his material. We planted 3000 seedlings of the population in an observation nursery, and grew open pollinated progenies of the 600 superior plants which were also selected for seed set. We developed five synthetics from these and other ecotypes. The results of variety tests are presented in Table 11. With respect to the date of heading our ecotype-derived synthetics are exceptionally early. As compared with the check variety Gremie which is classified as 'very early' (Bundessortenamt, 1991) our synthetics are from 5 to 8 days earlier. There is no other cultivar in the German list within this heading time. Our material exceeds the check in vigour and winter hardiness, and in dry matter yield. The superiority of the synthetics is even greater in the second year than in the first year which indicates better winter hardiness and persistency. Two synthetics have up to now been applied for registration.

Poa supina. *Poa supina* is a short grass similar to *Poa annua*, but in contrast to *P. annua* perennial and with short above ground stolons. *Poa supina* is exceptionally wear-resistant; the turf recovers very rapidly after lesions. A fine example of a *Poa supina* dominant lawn is the soccer turf in the Olympic Stadion in Munich. *Poa supina* grows in highlands from about 500 to 2300 m a.s.l. (Oberdorfer, 1990) preferably at trampled habitats of ample nitrogen supply. We have up to now collected over 130 ecotypes which is probably the largest existing collection of *Poa supina*. The characteristics of this species are very variable and offer a good response to selection for wear and disease resistance, leaf length and width, colour, heading date, length of seed heads and seed set. A major constraint for the commercial utilization of the species was seed production. Now, after Berner (1993) devised specialized equipment for seed harvesting, ample commercial seed is available. We evaluate our accessions for both turf quality including wear-resistance and seed set. Our work resulted in one registered cultivar 'Posipa' and one cultivar applied for registration 'Horo'.

Trifolium pratense var. *spontaneum.* The wild red clover is a common species in single-cut and double-cut permanent meadows. The interest in this wild ancestor of the cultivated red clover is increasing because it is useful as a component of ornamental herbaceous seed mixtures, and landscaping mixtures. We select for low dry matter production, profuse flowering throughout the growing season, and persistency. One cultivar – 'Wiro' – has been applied for registration.

References

Berner, P., 1993. Personal communication.
Bundessortenamt, 1991. Beschreibende Sortenliste 1991. Gräser, Klee, Luzerne.
Chorlton, K., 1991. Genetic resources – conservation in the United Kingdom. IGER Report 1991: 33–34.
IBPGR, 1989. Report of a Working Group on Forage (Third Meeting). European Cooperative Programme for the Conservation and Exchange of Crop Genetic Resources. International Board for Plant Genetic Resources.
Krings, W. & U. Simon, 1993. Unpublished.
Oberdorfer, E., 1990. Pflanzensoziologische Exkursionsflora. Sixth ed. Eugen Ulmer, Stuttgart.
Reichsamt für Wetterdienst, 1939. Klimakunde des Deutschen Reiches. Berlin.

Scheller, H., 1987. Selektion in Ökotypensammlungen. DLG-Ausschuß für Gräser, Klee und Zwischenfrüchte. Bericht der 28. Fachtagung 1986: 54–62.
Scheller, H., 1993. Personal communication.
Simon, U., 1983. Utilization of genetic resources in breeding programmes. Eucarpia Fodder Crops Section. Report of Meeting 1982: 247–264.
Spatz, G., W. Schröpel & J. Bauer, 1987. Die autochthone Weidelgraspopulation 'Kempten', ihre Leistungsfähigkeit und Ausdauer im Vergleich zu Zuchtsorten. Das wirtschaftseigene Futter 33: 248–261.
Tyler, B.F., 1987. Description and distribution of natural variation in forage grasses. Eucarpia Fodder Crops Section. Report of Meeting 1987: 13–22.

O.A. Rognli et al. (eds.), Breeding Fodder Crops for Marginal Conditions, 47–60.
© 1994 *Kluwer Academic Publishers. Printed in the Netherlands.*

Potential for improving adaptation of *Lolium perenne* L. to continental climates in Norway

E.T. SOLBERG,[1] O.A. ROGNLI[2] & L. ØSTREM[3]
[1] *State Agricultural Research Station Løken, N-2940 Heggenes, Norway;* [2] *Agricultural University of Norway, Dept. of Biotechnological Sciences, P.O. Box 5040, N-1432 Ås, Norway;* [3] *State Agricultural Research Station Fureneset, N-6994 Fure, Norway*

Summary. Breeding of perennial ryegrass has been conducted in Norway for more than 30 years. The little progress achieved so far can, most probably, be explained by a restricted genetic variation within our indigeneous plant material. In order to increase the variation in the Norwegian ryegrass germplasm, we have tested populations of diverse origin and adaptations under contrasting climatic conditions in Norway. Data is presented for winter survival and dry matter yield obtained in two experiments, one in a dense stand with 20 populations of Norwegian and Russian origin, and one as a spaced plant experiment with 26 populations of Norwegian, Russian and Swiss origin. In both cases commercial foreign cultivars and breeding populations were included.
The results show that the commercial varieties were superior when grown in dense stand. The Norwegian material showed, however, a significant better adaptation at the continental location, measured as plant cover after three years. There was considerable variation between populations in all characters. In the spaced plant experiment, the Norwegian diploid breeding populations were the highest yielding. The commercial cultivars also performed well. Winter survival was generally good in this experiment, and only small differences between populations could be detected. Winterhardy and productive populations of different origin and contrasting adaptations have been selected, and breeding populations constructed. Surprisingly enough, Swiss Alp populations, presumably adapted to long lasting snow-cover, do not show any better adaptation to the continental climates in Norway than indigeneous ryegrass populations.

Introduction

Grass forage is the most important crop in Norway, with between 60 to 100% of the cultivated land being used for leys and pastures. Norwegian dairy farming is in general rather intensive, with high input of energy, fertilizers and feed concentrates which are produced off-farm. The roughage consist mainly of silage of perennial grasses.

The income of the farmers will greatly benefit from the use of long-lasting, high yielding and good quality species and cultivars for leys and pastures. Due to frequent winter-kill, Norwegian leys are short-lived (4–5 yrs). This is very costly, and winter-hardy and long-lasting cultivars, that also can tolerate intensive management, are therefore most welcome. In contrast to most of Europe, timothy (*Phleum pratense*) and meadow fescue (*Festuca pratensis*) are still the most important grass species for leys in Norway. This is due to their superior combination of winter-hardiness and quality. There is however an increasing interest in perennial ryegrass because of its high yield capacity, good response to fertilization, rapid establishment, tolerance

Table 1. Plant material used in Exp 1

Group designation/ ploidy level	Origin	Designation for cultivars/populations
FU/2x	Local populations from the South-West coast of Norway.	16-57-1 16-57-2 16-59-2 16-60-1 16-62-2 16-62-3
WIR	Populations from St. Petersburg and Pskov region (Vavilov Institute)	WIR 20258 (2x) WIR 35600 (2x) WIR 40697 (4x)
IBF/4x	Tetraploid populations from Dept. of Biotech. Sci., Agric. Univ. of Norway, Ås	Raigt1 Raigt2 Raigt3 Raigt4 Raigt5
IBF/2x	Diploid populations from Dept. of Biotech. Sci., Agric. Univ of Norway, Ås	Raigd1 Raigd2 Raigd3
CV/4x	Tetraploid Dutch and Danish commercial cultivars	Taptoe Tove Polly

to frequent cutting, and high quality. There is only one major problem: winter-survival is erratic and unpredictable in Norway. Rather winter-hardy varieties are on the market, and during the last years some of them have frequently been sown in mixtures with timothy, meadow fescue and clover for use in short rotation systems in the southern and western parts of the country. Their success however is mainly due to some exceptionally mild winters.

The natural distribution of perennial ryegrass is confined to the Western and South-Western coastal regions of Norway (below 62°N latitude). Some form of ryegrass breeding has been going on in Norway for more than 30 years. Much of this work has concentrated upon selection in the landrace 'Kleppe', originating from the South-Western coast of Norway. Simonsen (1976) demonstrated that the non-additive component makes up a large part of the genetic variation in total dry matter yield in this variety. Larsen (1979)

Table 2. Plant material used in Exp 2

Group designation/ ploidy level	Origin	Designation for cultivars/populations
CH/2x	Swiss alpine populations collected mainly in grazed hills and along roadsides.	Ba9436/Aurora/CH[a] Ba8692/Koma/PL[b] Ba9068/CH/300[c] Ba9105/CH/600 Ba9088/CH/707 Ba9091/CH/840 Ba9092/CH/860 Ba9089/CH/870 Ba9108/CH/980 Ba9100/CH/1276 Ba9097/CH/1600 Ba9101/CH/2030
IBF/4x	Tetraploid populations from Dept. of Biotech. Sci., Agric. Univ. of Norway, Ås.	Raigt1 Raigt2 Raigt3 Raigt4 Raigt5
IBF/2x	Diploid populations from Dept. of Biotech. Sci., Agric. Univ of Norway, Ås	Raigd1 Raigd2 Raigd3
WIR	Populations from St. Petersburg and Pskov region (Vavilov Institute)	WIR 20258 (2x) WIR 35600 (2x) WIR 40697 (4x)
CV/4x	Tetraploid Dutch and Danish commercial cultivars	Taptoe Tove Polly

[a] Registered cultivar 'Aurora';

[b] Polish cultivar 'Koma';

[c] the last number refers to altitude of collection site.

found considerable variation in frost tolerance, and good response to phenotypic selection in clonal experiments. In terms of registered cultivars, however, very little progress has been achieved. The scope for improving yield and winter-hardiness by selection within our indigeneous ryegrass material seems to be rather limited.

50

Systematic breeding efforts to broaden the genetic basis for developing Norwegian cultivars has been carried out only for the last 10 years. Some of the results of two breeding projects, in which different Norwegian breeding populations of ryegrass were compared to foreign ryegrass cultivars and populations under different climatic conditions in South-Norway, will be presented.

Materials and methods

Experiment 1

Plant material and experimental design
Field trials with populations sown in dense stands, were conducted at two locations (coastal climate) on the western coast of Norway (The State Agricultural Research Stations at Fureneset and Særheim), and at one location with a continental climate in South-Eastern Norway (Agricultural University at Ås). Description of the plant material used in Exp. 1 is presented in Table 1. In addition, 9 diploid commercial cultivars, and 31 diploid half-sib families (PC/2x) from a polycross, were also included.

The experimental design was a combination of an incomplete block and a split-plot design, with two levels of N- fertilization (high and low) as main-plots, and cultivar/populations at sub-plots, with two replicates.

Characters observed
Dry matter yield (t/ha), winter survival (percentage plant cover on plots in spring), and heading date (days from May 1) were recorded during three years of harvest. Forage quality parameters were estimated using NIRS-analysis, and artificial tests of resistance to low temperature fungi were conducted at the Plant Protection Institute at Ås. Only data on winter survival in the field, and dry matter yield, recorded in the trials at Fureneset and Ås, will be presented in this paper.

Experiment 2

Plant material and experimental design
The populations listed in Table 2 were tested in field trials with spaced plants at one continental lowland location (Ås), and one continental highland location (State Agricultural Research Station Løken) in South-East Norway. Fifty randomly selected plants from each population/cultivar were planted in rows spaced 60 cm apart, with plants 30 cm apart in the row, in two replicates.

Table 3. Average heading date, spring cover and dry matter yield (t/ha) of groups of ryegrass populations and cultivars estimated in a coastal (Fureneset) and a continental (Ås) climate in Norway (Exp 1)

Location	Group	No. of populations	Heading date (Days from 1 May)	Spring cover (%)		Dry matter yield (t/ha)			
				Mean	3. year	1. year	2. year	3. year	Mean
Coastal	FU/2x	6	41.2	78.9	61.3	15.32	8.40	11.18	11.63
	IBF/4x	5	40.4	78.3	55.5	15.31	8.14	10.50	11.32
	IBF/2x	3	41.8	82.6	67.9	15.14	8.71	11.06	11.64
	WIR/4x	3	40.4	82.8	64.6	15.92	8.94	11.35	12.07
	PC/2x	31	43.8	75.5	52.0	13.41	7.22	9.39	10.01
	CV/4x	3	39.9	92.2	88.8	17.64	9.74	12.90	13.43
	LSD 5%		0.4	6.2	6.7	0.96	0.66	0.57	0.55
Continental	FU/2x	6	45.2	77.7	90.9	13.58	6.71	8.33	9.54
	IBF/4x	5	44.0	93.3	96.0	15.65	8.30	8.65	10.87
	IBF/2x	3	46.1	83.3	93.3	12.58	7.31	8.49	9.46
	WIR/4x	3	43.8	85.4	95.4	15.19	7.38	9.96	10.85
	PC/2x	31	49.6	79.8	87.3	11.38	6.04	5.90	7.77
	CV/4x	3	42.6	77.8	90.4	16.73	7.20	10.38	11.44
	LSD 5%		1.3	5.4	2.9	0.73	0.42	0.53	0.44

Characters observed

Spring growth was recorded at Løken in 1990 as days from April 1 when 2 cm of the first new leaf was visible on three or more tillers on half of the plants in each row. Winter survival was scored in 1991 as damage from snow-mould fungii (*Microdochium nivale*) at Ås, and as a combined visual estimate of percentage plant cover and degree of growth vigour two weeks after observed start of growth (spring growth) at Løken. Heading date was recorded as days from May 1 when half of the plants showed two visible spikelets. Dry matter yield was recorded for 2 years as the sum of 3 cuts/season, except for the last year at Løken where only two cuts were taken.

Statistical analyses

Analyses of variance were performed using the SAS/STAT GLM procedure (SAS, 1987). Orthogonal linear contrasts were used to test differences between population/cultivar group means in Exp. 2.

52

Table 4. Analysis of variance of groups of ryegrass populations and cultivars estimated in a coastal (Fureneset) and a continental climate (Ås) (Exp 1)

Source	df	Spring cover in 3. year	Heading date	Dry matter yield (t/ha)			
				1. cut	2. cut	3. cut	Mean
Locations (L)	1	ns	***	ns	***	***	***
Years (Y)	2	***	***	***	***	***	***
Population groups	6	***	***	***	***	***	***
Between ploidy levels	1	***	***	***	***	***	***
Norwegian 4x vs. foreign 4x	1	ns	ns	***	***	***	***
CV/4x vs. WIR/4x	1	ns	*	***	***	***	***
PC/2x vs. other diploids	1	ns	ns	***	***	***	***
FU/2x vs. IBF/2x	1	***	*	ns	ns	ns	ns
Pop. groups × L	6	***	***	***	***	***	***
Pop. groups × Y	12	***	***	***	***	***	***
Pop. groups × L × Y	12	***		***	*	ns	***

Entries with *, **, and *** are significant at p ≤ 0.05, p ≤ 0.01, and p ≤ 0.001, respectively.

Results

Experiment 1

Mean values for different cultivar/population groups are presented in Table 3. The tetraploid commercial cultivars (CV/4x) were on average highest yielding irrespective of location and year. The local populations (FU/2x), and the diploid IBF/2x-populations were equal, while the polycross progenies had the lowest average yield. The tetraploid IBF/4x-populations performed well at the continental location Ås, but yielded less than the diploids at the coastal location Fureneset. The Russian populations (WIR) were equal to the IBF/4x-populations as Ås, and somewhat better than the diploid cultivars at Fureneset.

At the coastal location, the average plant cover in spring showed much of the same tendency as total yield. Although the differences between populations were small, they were significant, and the foreign commercial cultivars (CV/4x) were found to survive best in the coastal climate, while the IBF/4x-cultivars showed less survival at this location. However, at the continental location (Ås) the IBF-4x and the Russian WIR-populations showed a significant better plant cover after three years than the tetraploid commercial cultivars and the local populations.

The diploid populations (Fu/2x and IBF/2x) were both relatively late heading, while the commercial cultivars were rather early.

One landrace, 16-60-1, should be mentioned as promising. This is a rather early heading population with a very good winter-hardiness and reasonably high yield at the coastal location Fureneset. The Russian population WIR 40697 was also high yielding, especially at the continental location Ås, and relatively persistent at both locations. The IBF/2x-population Raigd2 was very persistent at Fureneset, but somewhat lower yielding than the two others. However, none of the populations reached the average yield of the foreign tetraploid cultivars 'Taptoe', 'Tove' and 'Polly' at the coastal location. At the continental location Ås, all the tetraploid IBF/4x-populations were much more persistent than the foreign tetraploid cultivars, and population Raigt5 was equal to 'Taptoe' in average dry matter yield.

The analyses of variance (Table 4) showed that there was significant variation between populations for all characters. There was no significant interaction between N-level and population/cultivar for dry matter yield or winter survival.

Experiment 2

Mean values for each population/cultivar group are presented in Table 5. Spring growth started on average a couple of days earlier in the IBF-populations compared with the other populations. Earliest spring growth was however observed in the Swiss population Ba9105, and one of the Russian populations. Another Swiss population, Ba9436/Aurora was also relatively early. However, heading was earlier in the Sw/2x-populations than in the Norwegian material. This is mainly caused by 4 very early heading Swiss populations, among them Ba9436/Aurora and Ba9105. The differences between these four populations and the rest of the material are more pronounced at the continental lowland location Ås, but statistically significant at both locations. Except the four populations mentioned, there were no significant differences between populations or groups of populations in heading date.

Winter survival was generally good, and there were only small differences in plant cover the second year. Resistance to snow-mould is however better in the Russian WIR-populations than in the Swiss material. The IBF-populations and the tetraploid commercial cultivars were moderately resistant.

The IBF/2x-populations were highest yielding both years at Ås and in the first year at Løken. In the second year at Løken the commercial cultivars were best. The Swiss material seems to have a relatively low yield capacity, Ba9097 being an exception at Ås. Other promising populations were the

54

Table 5. Average dry matter yield (kg/plot), spring growth, heading date and winter survival of groups of ryegrass populations and cultivars estimated at two continental locations, one lowland (Ås) and one highland (Løken) (Exp 2)

Location	Group	No. of populations	Total dry matter yield (kg/plot)		Spring growth (Days from 1 April)	Heading date	Winter survival
			1990	1991			
Highland	SW/2x	12	2.39	1.28	30.2	42.1	79.5[1]
	IBF/4x	5	3.29	1.41	27.2	44.6	79.0
	IBF/2x	3	3.39	1.61	28.8	46.7	79.7
	WIR/4x	3	2.72	1.63	30.3	44.7	77.7
	CV/4x	3	2.79	1.81	31.8	43.8	81.7
	LSD 5%		0.5	0.3	1.8	1.5	
Lowland	SW/2x	12	4.61	2.20		21.9	56.1[2]
	IBF/4x	5	4.83	2.56		28.0	65.0
	IBF/2x	3	5.80	2.94		29.8	61.7
	WIR/4x	3	5.72	2.62		29.1	70.8
	CV/4x	3	5.59	2.81		25.2	64.2
	LSD 5%	0.3	0.4		1.9		

[1] Recorded as plant cover in spring 1991 at Løken.

[2] Recorded as snow-mould injury in spring 1990 at Ås (0 = complete injury; 100 = no visible injury).

IBF/2x-populations Raigd3 and Raigd2. The Dutch cultivar 'Taptoe' also had a high average yield at both locations, while the Danish cultivar 'Tove' yielded well at Ås, and the Fu208 (WIR) at Løken.

The combined analysis of variance over locations and years showed significant differences between populations for all characters (Table 6). Two and three factor interactions between populations, locations and years were significant for first cut and total yield. Linear contrasts show that the Swiss material accounts for quite a large amount of the variation.

Discussion

Commercial cultivars

Danish and Dutch ryegrass cultivars are well adapted to the mild coastal climate of the West-Coast (Fureneset), while the continental climate at Ås seems to favour the Norwegian ryegrass populations. In continental regions the commercial foreign cultivars were in general outyielded by the diploid

Table 6. Combined analysis of variance over locations and years for the spaced plant trial (Exp 2)

Source	df	Dry matter yield cut no:				Spring growth	Heading date	Winter survival	
		1	2	3	Sum			Løken	Ås
Location (L)	1	*	ns	***	*				
Year (Y)	1	*	*	ns	**				
L × Y	1	*	ns	ns	ns				
Populations (P)	25	***	***	***	***	***	***	*	*
Between ploidy levels	1	**	ns	ns	*	ns	ns		
Swiss/2x vs. Norwegian 2x	1	***	***	ns	***	ns	***		
Norwegian 4x vs. foreign 4x	1	ns	***	**	*	**	ns		
CV/4x vs. WIR/4x	1	**	***	*	ns	ns	ns		
P × L	25	***	***	ns	***				
P × Y	25	***	ns	ns	***				
P × L × Y	25	***	*	ns	***				

Entries with *, **, and *** are significant at $P \leq 0.05$, $p \leq 0.01$, and $p \leq 0.001$, respectively.

IBF/2x-populations, except the last year at the continental highland location Løken the commercial cultivars were somewhat better. The winter survival of the commercial cultivars at Løken was surprisingly good, indicating that they must be winterhardy. However, it should be pointed out that the results were obtained in two years with a milder winter-climate than normal in the continental East-Norway, and with virtually no snow-cover. Winter-hardiness is a complex character determined by tolerance to low temperatures, long lasting snow-cover, ice and low-temperature fungi. Most emphasis has been devoted to increasing cold tolerance in North European ryegrasses (Fuller & Eagles, 1978, Humphreys & Eagles, 1988; Tcacenco et al., 1989). European cultivars will therefore perform well in winters with little or no snow, in which cold tolerance will be most important. Resistance against snow-mould is of course important only in regions with regular long lasting snow-cover (Gray & Copeman, 1975). This resistance was just about average among the commercial cultivars in our experiments, confirming that they are not particularily well adapted to snow-cover.

56

Norwegian breeding materials

It is well known from earlier breeding work that our indigenous ryegrass material, represented by the landrace 'Kleppe', has a relatively low yield capacity (Simonsen, 1971). According to Simonsen (1976) there should, however, be sufficient additive genetic variation within this population for improving yield by phenotypic selection. The original 'Kleppe' was not included in these trials, but the IBF-populations Raigd1 and Raigt1, and the polycross progenies, are of pure 'Kleppe' origin. Their performance shows that little progress has been achieved, at least when grown in the most favourable climates, from selections within 'Kleppe' based on clonal trials and subsequent polycross progeny testing. Although none of them performed well in dense stands, they gave quite good yields in the spaced plant trial at Løken. Most of the other diploid and tetraploid IBF-populations are based on more or less wide crosses, including Danish and Dutch cultivars. These populations performed significantly better than the pure 'Kleppe' selections, both in dense stands and as spaced plants. The difference may be due to increased heterogeneity, and/or to a hybrid effect. As production characters have been demonstrated to be controlled mainly by additive gene action (Cooper, 1961), it can also be due to additive genetic effects. If so, further improvement by selection within these 'wide cross' populations should be possible.

On average the yield of diploid IBF/2x-populations was no better than the local, unselected populations (Exp 1). As spaced plants, however, they performed very well, and much better than tetraploids. It is obvious from these results that the performance in dense stand cannot be predicted from spaced plant performance, as shown by Hayward & Vivero (1984). Both the polycross progeny group, and the IBF-populations have resulted from initial selections based on single plant performance.

The tetraploid IBF/4x-populations were less adapted to the coastal climate at Fureneset than diploid populations, while they were significantly better, and equal to the Russian populations, at the continental location Ås. This differential adaptation of tetraploid populations is probably due to increased resistance to snow-mould by polyploidization (van Bogaert, 1975).

Local Norwegian populations

The natural distribution of perennial ryegrass is confined to the South-Western coast of Norway, and the species are completely absent in continental regions. The lack of adaptation to snow-cover in our indigenous perennial ryegrass is therefore a major hurdle in adapting the species to continental regions. The local populations included in these trials originate from a rather limited geographical area with a relatively uniform climate. Despite this, there is variation between the populations both for winter survival and yield capacity, and some increase in adaptation to severe continental climates could probably be achieved by selection within such populations.

Swiss diploid populations from high altitude locations

Swiss alpine populations were included in order to find new, unrelated genetic variation for winter hardiness, especially tolerance to snow-cover. As pointed out by Lorenzetti et al. (1971), freezing tolerance increases with increasing latitude and altitude. The average dry matter yield of Swiss populations was low, but varied considerably (1.94–3.72 kg/plot). Population Ba 9097 was among the highest yielding populations at Ås, and was also the best Swiss population at Løken. Most of the Swiss populations have been collected at sites unmanaged or only grazed. Low yield potentials under our conditions can be an effect of both cross-latitudinal transfer, causing shifts in patterns of seasonal dry matter distribution due to interactions with daylengths and temperatures, and effects of adaptations to management at the collection sites. The highest yielding Swiss population, Ba 9097, was collected in a ley harvested for conservation. Average winter survival for the Swiss populations was good, at least at Løken. At Ås the populations exhibited great variability in resistance to snow-mould fungi, ranging from 30 to 87% undamaged leaves in spring. The correlation between percentage plant cover in spring and altitude of origin was weak and non-significant (r = 0.29). In this specific case, tolerance to ice cover has probably been more important than frost tolerance. However, the correlation between resistance to snow-mould and altitude was 0.51 and significant (P ≤ 0.05). Such a correlation has, as far as we know, not been reported before. However, Tronsmo (1984) has reported that hardening increases the resistance to snow-mould in addition to giving increased freezing tolerance. Thus our results are in agreement with those of Lorenzetti et al. (1971). Some Swiss populations are heading extremely early. Populations Ba 9436 (cv Aurora), Ba 9105, Ba 9097, and Ba 9092 started heading 10–14 days earlier than the other populations. Early ear emergence has been reported to be negatively correlated with winter-hardiness (Humphreys & Eagles, 1988; Tcacenco et al., 1989), except for ryegrass material collected in the Zürich region. These four populations mentioned showed very good winter survival and good snow-mould resistance. Ba 9436 and Ba 9105 originate from the Zürich region, and confirm their results, while the other two originate from other regions.

58

Russian populations

Little is known about the origin of the Russian (WIR) populations. In the dense stand trial the Russian populations gave significantly higher yields than the average of the Norwegian populations. Winter survival was excellent, and significantly better than the commercial cultivars, at the continental lowland location, Ås. The populations performed well in continental climates, but were less productive than the Danish and Dutch cultivars in the coastal climate. This result indicates that the Russian populations have been selected for agronomic performance. They are adapted to a continental climate, and as such supposed to have an adequate level of cold tolerance.

Differential response to N-level

Interactions between N-level and populations could not be detected, and confirms results reported by Wilkins (1987). Other investigations (Lee et al., 1977; Alcock & Harvey, 1985), have however indicated that interactions exist between populations and N-level when very low levels are compared to medium to high levels. However, as ryegrass is unlikely to be used under extremely low nutrient conditions in Norway, we conclude that populations selected at one nutrient level will perform well at all current levels in Norwegian agricultural rotation systems.

Concluding remarks

What is then the potential of improving adaptation of *Lolium perenne* to continental climates in Norway? The adaptation must include both survival and dry matter production under the actual climatic and management conditions. None of the populations tested in the present trials exhibited any improvements compared with the commercial cultivars at the continental lowland location Ås. The tetraploid IBF-population Raigt5 is probably one exception. However, according to results of official Norwegian variety trials, it does not seem very promising in any part of the country (Marum et al., 1992).

All evidence shows that the genetic variation within the Norwegian ryegrass material is rather narrow. Therefore, the best results have been obtained both in diploid and in tetraploid materials by hybridizing indigenous populations with winter-hardy foreign cultivars. It seems that the wider the crosses are, the better. The present material contains populations of very different origin, and with contrasting adaptation. The local populations (Fu/2x) are adapted to coastal climates, the commercial cultivars (CV/4x) to intensive management, the Russian populations (WIR) to continental climates, and the Swiss alpine populations (SW/2x) to high altitude and severe winter stress.

Irrespective of origin and adaptation, fairly high yielding populations can be identified in all groups. Construction of breeding populations with selected genotypes from two or more sources should make it possible to create sufficient genetic variation for increasing adaptation to continental climates in Norway. Two tetraploid breeding populations have already been established, one for the coastal climate based on the Danish cultivar Polly, and the most promising WIR-population (WIR 40697); and one for the inland climate based upon Polly, Tove, Taptoe, WIR 40697, and the two most promising tetraploid IBF/4x-populations Raigt2 and Raigt5. A diploid breeding population, aimed for Norwegian continental climates, has also been constructed, and includes Swiss alpine populations.

Acknowledgements

We are indebted to Mr. Einar Berg for his excellent technical assistance, and to The Norwegian Agricultural Research Council and The State Agricultural Research Stations for financial support.

References

Alcoc, M.B. & A. Harvey, 1985. The response of perennial ryegrass varieties to fertiliser nitrogen. Proceedings of the British Grassland Society's Winter Meeting 1985: 1–8.

Cooper, J.P., 1961. Selection for production characters in ryegrass. Proceedings of the 8th. International Grassland Congress 1960: 41–44.

Fuller, M.P. & C.F. Eagles, 1978. A seedling test for cold hardiness in *Lolium perenne* L. Journal of Agricultural Science, Cambridge, 95: 77–81.

Gray, E.G. & G.J.F. Copeman, 1975. The role of snow-mould in winter damage to grassland in northern Scotland. Annals of Applied Biology 81: 247–251.

Hayward, M.D. & J.L. Vivero, 1984. Selection for yield in *Lolium perenne*. II. Performance of spaced plant selections under competitive conditions. Euphytica 33: 787–800.

Humphreys, M.O. & C.F. Eagles, 1988. Assessment of perennial ryegrass (*Lolium perenne* L.) for breeding. Freezing tolerance. Euphytica 38: 75–84.

Larsen, A., 1979. Freezing tolerance in grasses. Variation within populations and response to selection. Meld. Norg. LandbrHogsk. 58 (42): 28 pp.

Lee, C.J., L.H. Davies, E.R. Armitage & A.E.M. Hood, 1977. The effects of rates of nitrogen application on seven perennial ryegrass varieties. Journal of the British Grassland Society 32: 83–87.

Lorenzetti, F., B.F. Tyler, J.P. Cooper & E.L. Breese, 1971. Cold tolerance and winter hardiness in *Lolium perenne* L. I. Development of screening techniques for cold tolerance and survey of geographical variation. Journal of Agricultural Science, Cambridge, 76: 199–209.

Marum, P., S. Rimmereid & T. Lunnan, 1992. Resultat av verdiprøving i fôrvekster 1992. Særtrykk fra Statens forskingsstasjoner i landbruk. 130 pp.

SAS, 1987. SAS/STAT Guide for personal computers, version 6 edition, Cary, NC, SAS Institute Inc., 1028 pp.

Simonsen, Ø., 1971. Forsøk med raigrassorter. Forskning og fors/ok i landbruket 22: 103–117.

Simonsen, Ø., 1976. Genetic variation in diploid and autotetraploid populations of *Lolium perenne* L. Hereditas 84: 133–156.

60

Tcacenco, F.A., C.F. Eagles & B.F. Tyler, 1989. Evaluation of winter hardiness in Romanian introductions of *Lolium perenne*. Journal of Agricultural Science, Cambridge, 112: 249–255.

Tronsmo, A.M., 1984. Induced resistance to biotic stress factors in grasses by frost hardening. Plant Production in the North. Proceedings from a Plant Adaptation Workshop in Tromsø, Norway, 4–10th September 1983.

Van Bogaert, G., 1975. A comparison between colchicine induced tetraploid and diploid cultivars of *Lolium* species. In: B. Nüesch (Ed.) Ploidy in Fodder Crops. Report of the Fodder Crops Section Meeting in Zürich, April 23–25, 1975: 61–78.

Van Dijk, G.E., 1980. Breeding *Lolium perenne* L. for yield and persistence under heavy nitrogen and infrequent cutting. Report of Eucarpia Fodder Crop Section Meeting in Perugia, Italy, 1979: 131–135.

Wilkins, P.W., 1987. Genotype/management interactions for plot dry matter yield in *Lolium perenne* L. Report of Eucarpia Fodder Crop Section Meeting in Lusignan, France, 1987: 153–159.

O.A. Rognli et al. (eds.), Breeding Fodder Crops for Marginal Conditions, 61–68.
© 1994 *Kluwer Academic Publishers. Printed in the Netherlands.*

Winter hardiness in marginal populations of timothy

I. SCHJELDERUP,[1] A.H. AASTVEIT[2] & K. AASTVEIT[3]
[1] *Holt, Research Station, P.O. Box 2502, 9002 Tromsø, Norway;* [2] *Dept. of Mathematical Sciences, Agricultural University of Norway, P.O. Box 5035, 1432 Ås, Norway;*
[3] *Måltrostveien 4, 1430 Ås, Norway*

Summary. A comprehensive collection of local fodder grass populations was carried out in the northern regions of Norway in 1972 and 1973. The main purpose was to find ecotypes with extreme winter hardiness. This paper gives results from experiments carried out with some of the timothy populations collected.

After testing in dense stand a few of the most promising populations were selected for investigation of genetic variation within populations by growing in duplicate blocs of 100 clones from randomly selected plants. Twenty-two clones were selected from each of six populations and planted in separate isolated polycross fields. During 1986 to 1990 the half-sib families from these polycrosses were grown in two series of experiments laid out at two locations, Tromsø and Alta.

Significant genetic variations were found for winter hardiness within all six populations tested, as well as interaction between families and locations, while the interaction effects between families and years were small and insignificant in all cases.

Winter hardiness was strongly genotypically correlated in the positive direction with visually estimated general performance, but not correlated with digestibility.

Introduction

Winter survival is no doubt an important fitness component of perennial plant populations growing in arctic and sub-arctic areas. In local populations from those regions one would therefore expect strong directional selection for winter hardiness, resulting in extreme winter hardiness and highly reduced genetic variation, or even fixation for genes governing this character.

In 1972 and 1973 a comprehensive collection of local fodder grass populations was conducted in the northernmost regions of Norway (Schjelderup, 1973, 1979). After seed multiplication the collected populations were tested in pure stand experiments with normal seed rates. Preliminary results from the first pure stand experiments with local populations of timothy (*Phleum pratense*) and the blue grass (*Poa pratensis*) showed only small and insignificant differences between populations for winter hardiness (Schjelderup, 1982).

A few of the most promising populations for dry matter yield and general performance were selected and investigated furtherly for genetic variation within populations. One hundred plants from each population were selected at random, cloned and planted in duplicate randomised block experiments at the research station in Tromsø. Based on the results from visual scoring of several characters with highest weight on general performance, 22 clones were selected from each of six populations and planted in separately isolated polycross fields, denoted 1/83, 2/83, 1/85, 2/85, 1/86, and 2/86 after the Pc-fields. During the years 1986 to 1990 the half-sib (HS) families from these polycross fields were grown in two series of experiments laid out at two locations. Tromsø and Alta. In this paper we present the results for winter hardiness variation in these series of experiments, and some genotypic correlations between winter hardiness and other agronomic characters.

The populations and the experiments

The local populations were collected from 12–15 years old leys (Table 1) following a procedure described by Schjelderup (1973). Their geographic origin is given in Fig. 1. All populations but one (011043) were collected as seeds taken from about 200 plants distributed over area of 0.2 to 0.4 ha at each location. Due to the scarcity of plants population 011043 was collected as vegetative plant parts. The populations 011035 and 011043 were used by Rognli (1987a, 1987b) in his studies of seed production of arctic timothy.

Engmo originates from a local population selected in Salangen (68°53′N) (cf. Fig. 1) after 1920. Pre basic (elite) seed production of Engmo has been continued for more than 60 years in Malangen at 69°25′N (Østgård, 1976). Because of the climatic constraints, high quality seed can only be obtained every third year on average in this area (Østgård, 1976). In years of crop failure the seed fields have been harvested for hay production. The commercial seed production of Engmo has been located in South-East Norway from around 1950.

The half-sib families from the 6 populations were laid out in two series of experiments, A and B. Series A comprised 4 individual experiments, two in Tromsø and two in Alta with 22 HS-families from Pc-fields 1/83 and 2/83 as well as Engmo, which is one of the two leading commercial varieties in North-Norway. Series B comprised 8 individual experiments, 4 in Tromsø and 4 in Alta with 22 HS-families from the Pc-fields 1/85, 2/85, 1/86, 2/86 and Engmo. Altogether 132 HS-families were tested in the two series of experiments.

All experiments had three complete randomised blocks, and the size of the drill sown plots was 4,5 m². The experiments were cut twice per year, the first one taken at heading time and the second one about 50 days later. The plot yields were not weighted. But before harvest all plots were visually evaluated for general performance using a scale ranging from 0 to 9 (best). In addition samples were taken from all plots after cutting and subjected to NIRS-analyses of quality characters.

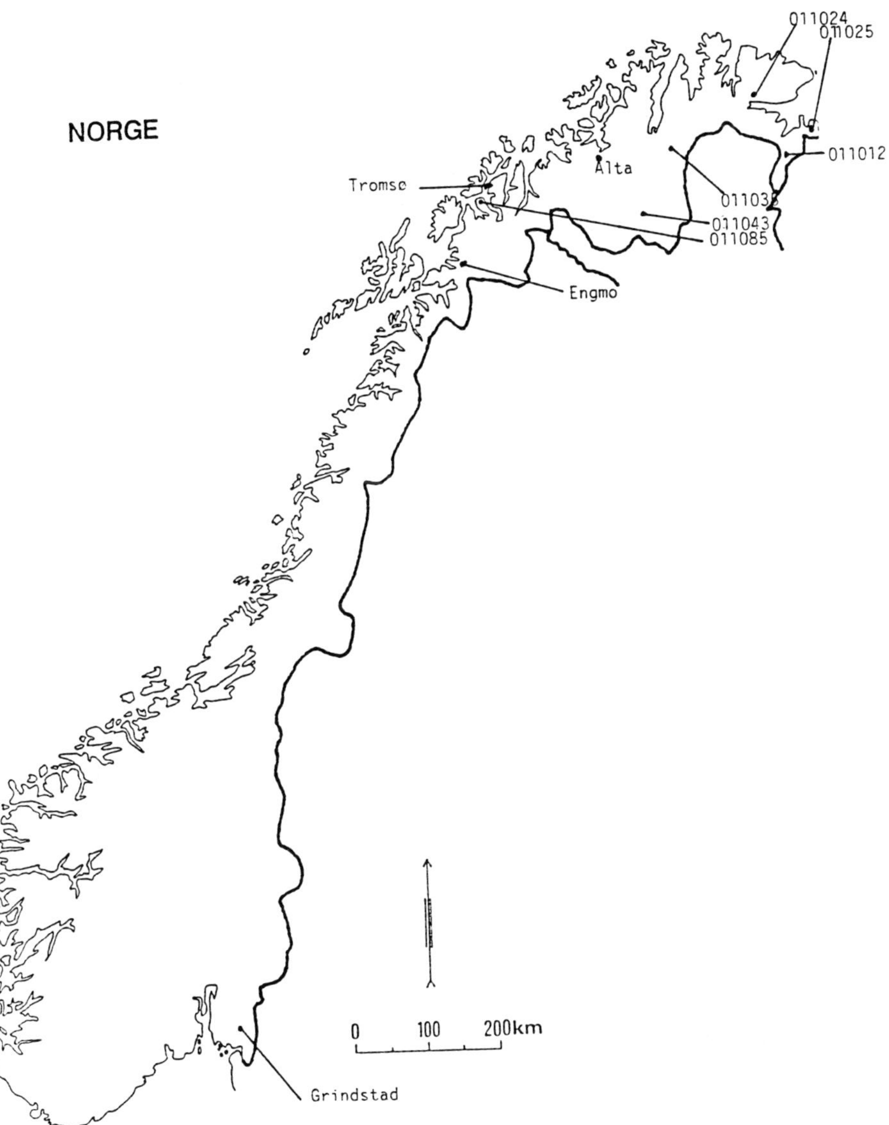

Fig. 1. The geographic origin of the collected timothy populations and the timothy varieties Grindstad and Engmo, and the experimental sites, Tromø and Alta.

Table 1. The populations investigated

Pc.No.	Population	Place of collection etc.
1/83	011035	Karasjok, Finnmark, 15 year old meadow. Origin unknown.
2/83	011085	Malangen, Troms. 100 m a.s.l. Old meadow. Origin unknown.
1/85	011043	Kautokeino, Finnmark, 355 m a.s.l. Old meadow. Origin: presumably Engmo.
2/85	011012	Svanhovd, Finnmark, 100 m a.s.l. 13 years old meadow. Origin: Engmo.
1/86	011024	South Varanger, Finnmark. Old meadow. Origin unknown.
2/86	011025	Grense Jakobselv, Finnmark, 20 m a.s.l. Old meadow, now harvested the last 3 years before collection. Origin unknown.
	Engmo	Local population from Salangen, Troms

Table 2. Distribution of HS-families and the cultivar Engmo for winter hardiness measured by ground cover in the spring and averaged over years

Population	Ground cover (%)										Average	Signific. level	SE
	10	20	30	40	50	60	70	80	90	100			
Tromsø													
011043				3	6	8	5				61.6	***	5.7
011012					2	4	8	8			75.0	***	4.1
011024					3	5	10	4			72.1	***	5.0
011025				1	3	4	9	5			71.7	***	5.5
Total				4	14	21	32	17			70.1	***	5.1
Engmo						1	2	1			74.8		
Alta													
011043	1		1		5	8	6	1			71.8	***	10.0
011012			1	1	11	8	1				77.8	***	4.4
011024					6	15	1				81.8	*	4.2
011025					6	16					82.2	*	4.2
Total	1		1	1	6	31	45	3			78.4	***	6.3
Engmo						2	2				79.4		

SE (Standard error) given are: For populations within, for Total between populations.

Table 3. Narrow sense heritabilities for winter hardiness for the timothy populations in series B

Population	Holt	Alta
011043	0.84 ± 0.09	0.81 ± 0.06
011012	0.88 ± 0.04	0.84 ± 0.06
011024	0.85 ± 0.07	0.56 ± 0.27
011025	0.88 ± 0.05	0.53 ± 0.23
Engmo[1]		0.46 ± 0.16

[1] From Schjelderup et al. (1992).

Results

Winter hardiness was measured by visual judgement of plot coverage in the autumn and spring in each of two years. In the A-series winter survival was in general good, and no significant differences were found between families. In the B-series, on the other hand, highly significant variations were found between families in all populations, in the first as well as in the second year of ley. Highly significant interactions between families and location were found in all populations, while the interaction effects between families and years were small and insignificant. The distributions shown in Table 2 are therefore based on average values over the two years at each location. Since each population had its own experiment with 22 HS-families and Engmo, the population means cannot be compared directly. All populations can, however, be compared with Engmo. On average over the two locations all populations were somewhat inferior to Engmo (not shown). The same was the case for the values over all populations at each location (Table 2). Significant genetic variation exists for winter hardiness within all the local populations tested, as can be seen from the distributions in Table 2 and the narrow sense heritabilities presented in Table 3. The most surprising results were obtained for the population 011043. This population was collected in the most marginal area for commercial timothy cultivation that probably can be encountered in the world (Rognli, 1987a). In spite of the fact that very few plants were left in the field at the time of collection, this population has a remarkably high genetic variation for the typical fitness character winter hardiness.

66

Table 4. Estimates of some important geno-typic correlations (r_g)

Character	r_g
Ground cover in the spring vs:	
– General performance	
Cut 1	0.85
Cut 2	0.86
- Digestibility (IVDDM-%)	
Cut 1	- 0.05
General performance at cut 1 vs:	
– Digestibility, Cut 1	- 0.77

Table 5. Comparison between the varieties Engmo and Grindstad for winter survival

Variety	Holt, Tromso 1931–35 Winter survival first year (%)	Alta, Finmark, 1984 Winter survival first year (%)
Engmo	75	80.2
Grindstad	24	21.0
Difference	51	59.2 ± 3.1

Genotypic correlations between winter hardiness and other characters

General performance, digestibility and protein content on average over locations and years were for the populations similar to that for Engmo. For general performance highly significant genetic variation was found in all populations. This character was genotypically highly correlated with winter survival. On average over all populations, years and locations this correlation was 0.85 in first cut and 0.86 in second cut respectively, as can be seen from Table 4. Based on data over two years highly significant genetic variation in digestibility (IVDDM-%) was found in only one population (011012) and only in Tromsø. At this location a genotypic correlation of - 0.77 was found between general performance and IVDDM-%. Winter survival was, however, not genotypically correlated with digestibility (V_g = - 0.05).

Discussion

The North-Norwegian timothy material has been introduced from regions further south. The variety Engmo has been developed from Mid-Norwegian (Trøndelag, 63°–64° N) timothy through natural selection early in this century (Østgård, 1976). Finnish timothy (Vasa) has also been sown in North-Norway. The present local populations can be traced back to these two gene sources.

There is a good reason to believe that the maintenance of Engmo from 1930 has had little influence on winter hardiness. This conclusion is based on the following facts: Flovik (1948) published results from experiments in Tromsø conducted during the years 1931–35 in which winter survival of Engmo had been compared to that for the variety Grindstad from South-East Norway. During the years 1983–86 we conducted an experiment in Alta with progenies from several polycross fields (Schjelderup et al., 1992). In this experiment Engmo and Grindstad were used as control varieties. The comparisons between Engmo and Grindstad for winter survival the first year of ley in 1931–35 and 50 years later are presented in Table 5.

Our experiments with HS-families have shown that Engmo is still quite genetically heterogeneous for genes governing winter survival. The best proof for this heterogeneity is, however, provided by Andersen (1971). In these experiments in Tromsø with generations of Engmo that had been seed propagated in South-East Norway for 0 to 6 generations he found an almost linear decrease for winter survival from about 78 to about 53 per cent. From a genetical point of view seed propagation in South-East Norway is therefore to be considered as reversed or backward selection.

Rognli (1987a) considers that timothy in the northernmost regions of Norway is at the margin of its distribution, since normal reproduction cannot be completed every year. In our preliminary studies of the collected local populations we did not find significant differences in winter survival between populations (Schjelderup, 1982). Rognli (1988) took this result as an indication of low genetic variation for winter survival within this material. He did not, however, find this result unexpected in view of the strong natural selection the materials have undergone.

In the present study we did also find low or absent genetic variation between local populations for winter hardiness, as in the preliminary results mentioned above. The present study has on the other hand revealed large genetic variation in winter hardiness within the populations. This result is in good agreement with the conclusions drawn by Tigerstedt (1983), namely that northern marginal populations often are very heterogeneous, with much more genetic variability than expected.

The high positive genotypic correlations found between winter survival and general performance was expected, since it was in accordance with earlier

68

experience. The genetic relationships between winter hardiness and quality are of great importance for the breeding strategy in northern regions. In this case winter survival and digestibility were uncorrelated. It should be remembered, however, that our data are rather limited at this point, and the problem of winter hardiness and quality needs to be studied further.

Conclusions

1. The present study has revealed that local populations from the northernmost regions of Norway possess high genetic variation for winter hardiness, which is a typical fitness character in these regions.
2. Winter hardiness was not correlated with digestibility, but was positively correlated with general performance.
3. Local populations of timothy from the northernmost regions of Norway should be considered as marginal, since normal reproduction cannot be completed every year.

References

Andersen, I.L., 1971. Overvintringsforsøk med ulike grasarter. Forskn. fors. Landbr. 22: 121–134.

Flovik, K., 1948. Kort utdrag av meldingene fra Statens forsøksgard Holt 1923–45. Publ. by Planteavlsutvalgene i Troms og Finnmark, Tromso 1948: 1–52.

Østgård, O., 1976. Timoteifrøavlen i Troms. Ny Jord (2) 1976: 55–62.

Rognli, O.A., 1978a. Genetic variation in arctic populations of timothy (*Phleum pratense*) I. Hereditas 107: 27–54.

Rognli, O.A., 1987b. Genetic variation in arctic populations of timothy (*Phleum pratense*) II. Hereditas 107: 75–94.

Rognli, O.A., 1988. Species aspects of breeding herbage varieties for northern marginal regions. J. Agric. Sci. in Finland 60: 181–189.

Schjelderup, I., 1973. Plan for innsamling av lokale plantepopulasjoner på Nordkalotten. Nord. Jordbruksforsk. (2) 1973: 223–241.

Schjelderup, I., 1979. Lokale populasjoner av grasarter. Norden 83 (6): 212–213.

Schjelderup, I., 1982. Test of local grass populations in North Norway. Eucarpia, fodder crop section, meeting, Wales, September 13–16th, 1982.

Schjelderup, I., K. Aastveit, P. Marum & A.H. Aastveit, 1992. Results of progeny testing and selection in timothy (*Phleum pratense* L.). Norw. J. Agric. Res.

Tigerstedt, P.M.A., 1983. Genetic mechanisms for adaptation. In: A. Kaurin, O. Junttila & J. Nilsen (Eds) Proc. from 'Plant Adaptation Workshop', Tromso, Norway, September 4–9, 1983: 205–218.

O.A. Rognli et al. (eds.), Breeding Fodder Crops for Marginal Conditions, 69–80.
© 1994 *Kluwer Academic Publishers. Printed in the Netherlands.*

Investigation of the adaptability of legumes in the Hungarian climate

ESZTER NEMESKÉRI
Agricultural University, Debrecen, P.O. Box 36, H-4015 Debrecen, Hungary

Summary. In this work we examine the adaptability of soybean and dry bean cultivars from the U.S. and Hungary on both field plots and in (plastic) greeenhouses, in order to select those genotypes most suitable for use in the Hungarian climate. Navy and Dark Red Kidney dry beans were sensitive to drought, particularly in sandy soil. Semideterminate or determinate bean varieties with well-developed roots can be effectively grown in slightly sandy soil. We pointed out that the percentage of shrivelled seed and yield per plant for both soybeans and dry beans are required to express the differences between cultivars and the relation between water circulation and pollination. This characterize the degree of adaptability for drought during the seed development period and should be taken into consideration when making breeding desicions.

Introduction

Climatic warming has increased the frequency of droughts in Hungary. This, in turn, has affected legume production, particularly the seed yield. In our country soybeans have primarily be grown for animal feed; use by the food industry is of lesser importance. Dry beans, on the other hand, are an important protein ingredient in food processing but are rarely used in animal feed because of their antinutritive qualities. Although they are utilized for different purposes, however, the problems encountered in production are quite similar. The biology of the soybean (*Glycine max* (L.) Merr.) is nearly the same as that of the dry bean (*Phaseolus vulgaris* L.) with the exception of the photoperiod. For soybean cultivars of diverse origin the duration of the initial photoperiod-insensitive phase is a strong determinant of the time to first flowering (Collinson et al., 1993). Although photoperiod-insensitive cultivars have been exploited in some species to broaden adaptation, insensitivity is frequently associated with extreme earliness (Lawn, 1989). The pre-flowering period should be at least 45 days long to allow sufficient vegetative growth for at least moderate seed yields (Hartwig, 1970). Hungary extends from 46 to 48 degrees latitude (equivalent to the northern U.S. and Canada), thus determining the choice of soybean cultivars from the U.S. for evaluation. One of the Hungarian joint-stock companies working in Bóly has determined that soybeans grown in Hungary require 1800–2500 HU during the growing season to guarantee maturity. Heat- and water stress affect soybean and dry bean productivity. The adaptability of a species under heat stress can be measured by the number of pods per plant (Bou et al., 1982). An insufficient water supply decreases both yield and quality (Flores and Fernando, 1982; Neyshabouri, 1982; Pechan and Webster, 1986). The root system influences

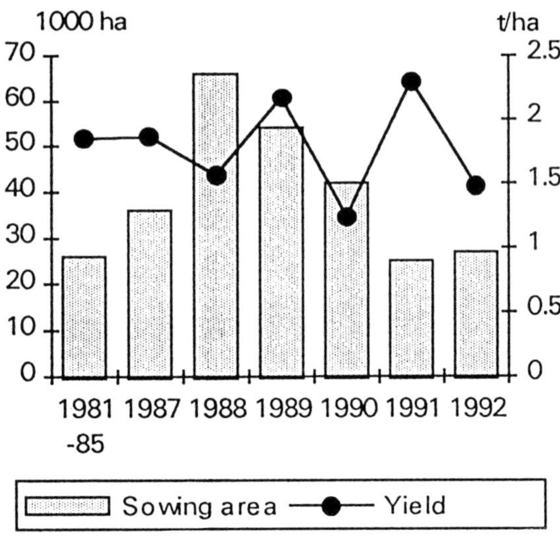

Fig. 1. Soybean production in Hungary.

the water circulation of the plant but there is no effect on the number of beans per pod (Nemeskéri, 1990). With field production, the high surface temperature of the soil results in numerous small ineffective nodules, which hamper growth (Piha and Munns, 1987). Lack of water in the upper soil accelerates the senescence of these nodules, more so for dry beans than soybeans (Smith et al., 1988). There was a significant correlation between the root weight and pod yield (R = 0.5) for beans grown in drought conditions. This allows for cultivar selection based on root weight. These cultivars realise, under drought conditions, 60% of the potential yield. (Nemeskéri, 1990)

Considering soybean production in Hungary during the last ten years, the area under cultivation increased until 1988 and decreased thereafter. The average yields were highly variable although a large number of cultivars were grown, most of them originating in the U.S. Dry bean production in Hungary has been less extensive, but the difficulties encountered are similar to those of soybeans (Figs 1 and 2). In Hungary the most productive region for both species is in the southwestern part of the country and in catchment basins. The Hajdú-Bihar and Szabolcs-Szatmár-Bereg counties are situated in northeastern Hungary, an area characterized by an unequal distribution of rain and frequent drought. This explains the low average yield in the region and thus the small number of hectares under bean production, as well as our decision to conduct experiments in these counties. We are interested in the adaptability of legumes to such marginal conditions as sandy soil, drought and water stress. In this work we examine the adaptability of soybean and dry

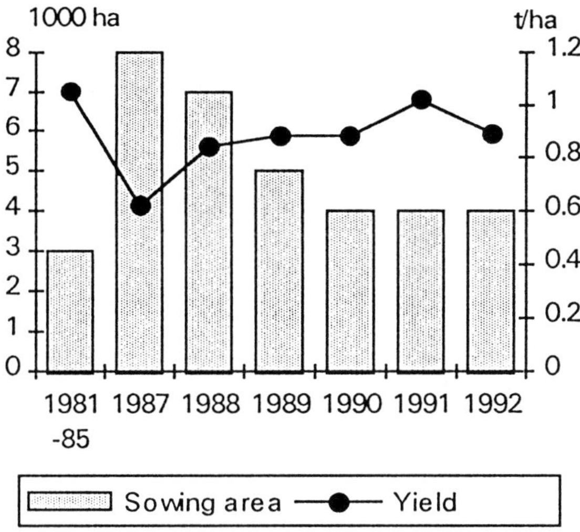

Fig. 2. Dry bean production in Hungary.

bean cultivars from the U.S. and Hungary on both field plots and in (plastic) greenhouses, in order to select those genotypes most suitable for use in the Hungarian climate.

Material and methods

At the Nyiregyháza and Debrecen Experimental Stations of Debrecen Agricultural University, we investigated the yield capacity of five Hungarian dry bean cultivars and two Hungarian lines (D-1076, D-830), an American dry bean cultivar and four American lines (see Table 1). The Nyíregyháza Research Station has clay washed brown forest soil with a low humus content (2.0%); experiments were conducted here from 1986 to 1988. At the Debrecen Experimental Station they were set up on chernozem soil with a 3.0% humus content. Both sets of experiments were performed in four repetitions under non-irrigated conditions. The trials were appropriately randomised and the yields were evaluated using ANOVA methods (Svab, 1981; Singh and Chaudhary, 1979). We used the American system of classification based on seed colour and shape for the purpose of typology. A Coco PV line originating in the Netherlands and most of the Hungarian cultivars were grouped with Cranberry beans. We made pair crosses among the Hungarian bean cultivar Start and the R86-139 Navy bean line originating in the U.S. In 1990 and 1991, the parents and their F_2 and F_3 generations were grown in both plastic greenhouses and the field on chernozem soil at the Debrecen Experimental

72

Table 1. Dry beans and their origin

Varieties	Seed colour	Seed type	Country of origin
White seed			
Start	white	NA	HUN
D79-054	white	NA	USA
D77-135B	white	GN	USA
Albamax	white	WK	HUN
R86-139	white	NA	USA
Coloured seed			
Express fürj	beige/red	CR	HUN
Tápiói círmos	beige/red	CR	HUN
Agate	brown/beige	PT	USA
Bólyi tarka	brown/beige	PT	HUN
D81-183	red	DRK	USA
D-1076	red	DRK	HUN
D-830	beige/red	CR	HUN
Coco PV select	beige/red	CR	NL

CR Cranberry; DRK Dark Red Kidney; GN Great Northern; NA Navy; PT Pinto; WK White kidney

Station. Applying SSD methodology, we selected for drought resistance based on analysis of yield. The plants were provided sufficient water using sprinkling irrigation until flowering and pod-setting. From 20 days after flowering we provided the greenhouse plants with 2 mm doses of water every other day to simulate drought during seed development. F_2 and F_3 lines from both crosses were examined; those lines for which both seeds per plant and pods per plant exceeded the population mean by more than one standard deviation were selected for (F_4 line) evaluation of adaptability and tested in the field. In 1991 and 1992, at the Debrecen Experimental Station five early and six medium-early soybean cultivars originating in foreign countries (provided by the Vetömag Seed Company) were analysed using the same experimental design as above. To test the difference between soybean cultivars with respect to adaptability, the experiments were set up in chernozem soil under non-irrigated conditions. The analysis of yield components was based on ten plants in two repetitions.

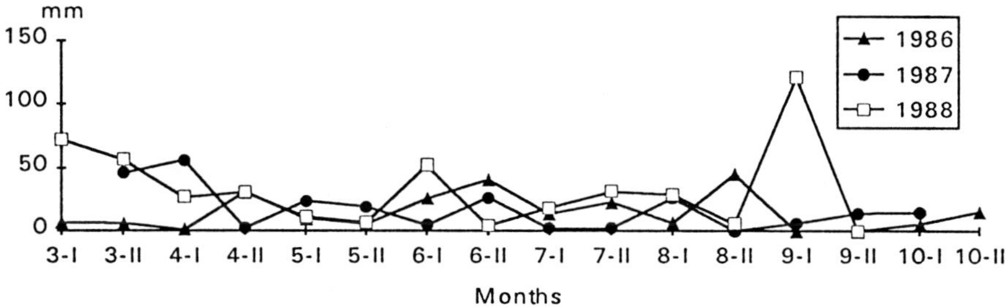

Fig. 3. Distribution of rainfall in Nyíregyháza.

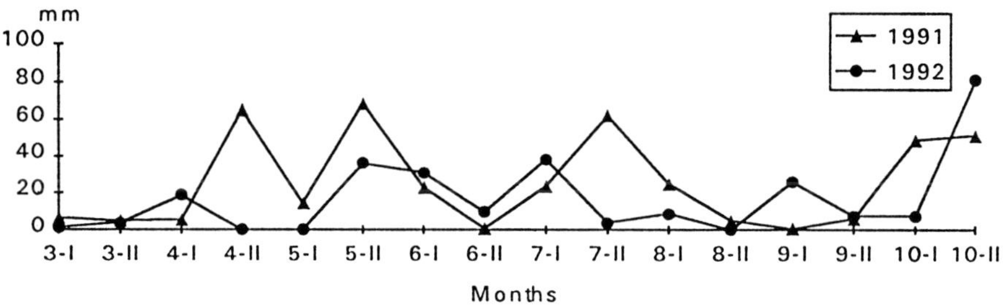

Fig. 4. Distribution of rainfall in Debrecen.

Result

1986, 1987 and 1992 were drought years (see Figs 3 and 4); this affected the flowering and fertility of beans.

Over the period examined, the mean yield for dry beans was higher on chernozem soil than on clay washed brown forest soil. The dry bush beans originating in the U.S. such as the D7-054 Navy and D81-183 Dark Red Kidney had low yields on both types of soil, particularly under drought conditions (Table 2). The semideterminate cultivars such as Bólyi tarka have a little longer duration of flowering than determinate ones and therefore better endured the short drought period. On clay washed brown forest soil, the cultivatrs selected from Hungarian regional beans yielded 70–80% as much as they yielded on chernozem soil. The Start cultivar, the R86-139 Navy and their crosses were tested with respect to drought tolerance (as in Bou et al., 1982). Comparing greenhouse yield of parents and F_2 progeny to that in the field, the number of pods per plant decreased only slightly in the greenhouse; the decrease in the number of seeds per plant was substantial (see Table 3).

Table 2. Yields of dry beans in different types of soils

Varieties	Country of origin	Seed type	Thousand grain weight (g)	Yield t/ha						
				years						
				1986	1987	1988	years' mean (a)	1991	1992	years' mean (b)
White seed										
Start	HUN	NA	183	2.18	1.55	1.88	1.87	2.75	1.58	2.17
D79-054	USA	NA	148	0.25	0.80	1.56	0.87	1.38	0.79	1.09
D77-135B	USA	GN	239	1.33	0.84	1.53	1.23	1.44	1.10	1.27
Albamax	HUN	WK	399	0.92	1.25	2.50	1.56	2.07	1.51	1.79
R86-139	USA	NA	150	–	–	–	–	1.08	0.95	1.02
Coloured seed										
Express fürj	HUN	CR	484	1.66	1.03	2.05	1.58	2.38	1.47	1.93
Tápiói círmos	HUN	CR	330	1.32	0.71	1.77	1.27	2.33	1.36	1.85
Agate	USA	PT	302	1.40	0.88	1.34	1.21	–	–	–
Bólyi tarka	HUN	PT	346	1.26	0.91	1.79	1.32	3.33	1.13	2.23
D81-183	USA	DRK	370	0.48	–	1.80	1.14	1.72	0.70	1.21
D-1076	HUN	DRK	540	–	–	–	–	2.18	1.00	1.59
D-830	HUN	CR	570	–	–	–	–	2.93	1.53	2.23
Coco PV select	NL	CR	490	–	–	–	–	1.47	0.94	1.21
LSD 5%				0.32	0.68	0.55		0.62		
Mean of varieties				1.14	0.97	1.82	1.34	2.09	1.17	1.63

Note: CR Cranberry; DRK Dark Red Kidney; GN Great Northern; NA Navy; PT Pinto; WK White Kidney;
(a) clay washed brown forest soil; (b) chernozem soil

Table 3. Changes in the yield components in Navy beans and F_2 progeny in greenhouses (a) and in the field (b)

Parent progeny	In greenhouse (a)			In field experiment (b)			Percentage of difference between (a) and (b)		
	Pod per plant	Seed per plant	Yield per plant (g)	Pod per plant	Seed per plant	Yield per plant (g)	Pod per plant	Seed per plant	Yield per plant
P_1 Start	32.4	98.89	22.94			21.56			+ 6.40
P_2 R86-139	30.0	94.00	14.66			6.55			+ 123.8
Mean of parents	31.2	96.45	18.80			14.06			+ 33.71
$P_1 \times P_2$ F_2 *population*									
D6-1	28.13	84.13	14.30	26.59	111.75	17.90	+ 5.79	- 24.72	- 20.11
D6-2	32.10	99.35	14.80	42.05	185.10	31.97	- 23.67	- 46.33	- 53.71
D6-8	36.70	95.10	17.60	42.83	164.67	27.84	- 14.31	- 42.25	- 36.78
D6-5	32.65	98.90	14.55	–	–	–	–	–	–

76

Table 4. Yield of selected F_4 bean lines from the F_3 greenhouse population

Progenies	Growing conditions					Difference of yield between (a) and (b) (%)
	(a)		(b)			
	Growth habit	Yield per plant (g)	Yield per plant (g)	Yield (t/ha)	Thousand grain weight (g)	
P_1 Start	D	22.56	9.09	1.58	171	40.29
P_2 R86-139	SD	10.65	5.62	0.95	158	52.77
Mean of parents		16.61	7.36	1.27	165	44.31
F_4 lines						
D6-202/7	D		7.75	1.55	147	
D6-202/8	D		8.75	1.75	147	
D6-202/13	SD		5.63	1.13	142	
D6-202/14	D-SD		3.61	0.72	155	
D6-202/18	D-SD		5.92	1.17	172	
D6-202/26	D-SD		7.92	1.58	161	
D6-202/27	D		8.13	1.63	160	
F_3 mean		17.70	6.82	1.36	156	38.50
D6-802/2	D		10.31	2.06	184	
D6-802/3	D		13.44	2.69	185	
D6-802/6	D		9.17	1.83	186	
D6-802/8	D		4.06	0.81	163	
D6-802/9	D		7.50	1.50	182	
D6-802/12	D		8.75	1.75	182	
D6-802/14	D		7.19	1.44	190	
D6-802/15	D		8.33	1.67	191	
D6-802/17	D		7.63	1.53	184	
F_3 mean		17.60	8.49	1.70	183	48.24
D6-502/6	D-SD		7.50	1.50	142	
D6-502/7	SD		8.10	1.62	148	
D6-502/8	D-SD		13.44	1.53	148	
D6-502/10	D		8.75	1.75	147	
D6-502/11	D		8.75	1.75	155	
D6-502/16	D		12.50	2.50	153	
D6-502/17	D		6.88	1.38	144	
D6-502/21	D		5.83	1.17	149	
D6-502/23	D		7.50	1.50	166	
D6-502/25	D		6.25	1.25	164	
D6-502/26	D		6.25	1.25	144	
D6-502/27	D		8.33	1.67	156	
F_3 mean		15.30	8.34	1.48	151	54.51

Note: D determinate; SD semideterminate; (a) dry condition; (b) field experiment

Table 5. Features of soybeans in Debrecen

Variety	Ripening time (days)	Plant height (cm)		Difference of height (%)	Number of branches	Yield t/ha (years)		
		1991	1992			1991	1992	years' mean
Early								
Mc Call	108–110	42	47	111.9	4	2.06	1.31	1.69
BS-38	108–110	50	58	116.0	2	1.13	0.92*	1.03
HM-262	111–114	67	71	106.0	2	1.75	0.17**	0.96
K-5551	113–115	63	54	85.7	1	2.14	0.33**	1.24
Polanka	109–110	58	44	75.9	3	2.25	0.36	1.31
Middle-early								
Evans	125–129	79	66	83.5	3	2.95	1.27	2.11
K-5709	124–129	89	62	69.7	2	3.11	1.47	2.29
Eszter	124–128	84	60	71.4	1	2.33	0.80	1.57
K-5846	124–129	90	43	47.8	3	2.56	1.43	2.00
K-4946	124–129	77	58	75.3	2	2.56	1.04	1.80
K-6660	111–115	83	61	73.5	1	2.17	0.29**	1.23
LSD 5%						0.80	0.93	

Note: shedding seed * moderate; ** strongly

From the F_3 breeding lines, where the yield per plant in the field was between 48 and 54% of that in the greenhouse, cultivars were selected for F_4 analysis for adaptability in the same fashion as described above. The resulting mean yield exceeded 1.5 tons per hectare under drought conditions (Table 4). We obtained similar results for the F_4 generation of cranberry dry beans. In a two-year experiment conducted by the Debrecen Institute of Agricultural Qalification, early soybeans matured within 110 days, and yielded between 2.8 and 3.5 tons/hectare, while the middle-early cultivars produced 3 to 4 tons/hectare. The average yield of cultivars investigated in our experiments were lower than above; however, there was insufficient rainfall and we did not irrigate. The height of middle-early soybeans decreased more than the earliest but their yield declined less (Table 5). There were differences in seed shedding in early soybean cultivars. The soybean cultivars with 3 or 4 branches could produce more pods than non-branching ones. For those cultivars with 2 or 3 branches, changes in the number of seeds per pod had only a slight effect on yield in comparison with changes in the number of pods per plant.

The relationship between fertilization and water circulation in the plant can be characterized by the percentage of shrivelled seeds (Table 6). When

Table 6. Yield components of soybeans in dry conditions

Variety	Pod per plant	CV (%)	Seed per plant	CV (%)	Thousand grain weight (g)	Percentage of seeds shrivelled	Potential yield (PY) (t/ha)	Realized yield (RY) (t/ha)	RY per PY (%)
Early									
Mc Call	48.8	53.17	111.1	53.00	125	17.50	4.94	1.31	26.50
BS-38	23.0	39.78	45.3	26.84	207	29.73	3.33	0.92*	27.60
HM-262	31.0	23.84	188.0	179.00	123	52.00	8.22	0.17**	2.07
K- 5551	13.1	55.42	15.3	69.15	139	25.00	0.85	0.33**	38.82
Polanka	20.0	74.00	45.2	74.85	85	15.66	0.43	0.36	83.70
Middle-early									
Evans	25.0	45.40	53.3	43.47	164	27.78	3.11	1.27	40.84
K-5709	29.1	30.79	76.8	28.95	103	13.48	2.81	1.47	52.31
Eszter	13.3	55.19	30.5	61.08	134	18.62	1.45	0.80	55.17
K-5846	16.0	55.81	43.4	60.58	104	5.62	1.61	1.43	88.82
K-4946	18.9	45.87	49.3	42.49	101	20.08	1.77	1.04	58.76
K-6660	31.7	59.78	35.1	126.13	136	68.15	1.70	0.29**	17.06
LSD 5%								0.93	

Note: shedding seed * moderate; ** strongly

the plants did not shed seeds, this figure was less than 20%, in which case early soybeans such as McCall grown on chernozem soil under drought conditions realized approximately 26% of their potential yield. Under the same conditions (drought, chernozem soil) fertilization had a markedly greater effect on most of the middle-early soybeans' potential yield than on earlier ones. Those cultivars had small leaves and a low percentage of shrivelled seeds realized between 52 and 88% of their potential yield.

Discussion

We analysed the adaptability of seven Hungarian and six American dry beans in field experiments on clay washed brown forest soil and chernozem soil without irrigation. Navy and Dark Red Kidney dry beans were sensitive to drought, particularly in sandy soil. These results are related to the water stress and high soil temperature, both of which decrease the number of root nodules and thus hamper growth and productivity (Piha and Munn, 1987; Smith et al., 1988). Semi-determinate or determinate bean varieties with well-developed roots can be effectively grown in slightly sandy soil. In comparison to the results published by Bou et al. (1982), we found that water stress and drought stress did not considerably affect the number of beans per pod, but did decrease the yield per plant. This can be explained by the water stress during the seed development period. We pointed out that the percentage of shrivelled seed and yield per plant for both soybeans and dry beans are required to express the differences between cultivars and the relation between water circulation and pollination. This characterize the degree of adaptability for drought during the seed development period and should be taken into consideration when making breeding decisions. Analyzing the yield of soybeans, we pointed out the number of seeds per pod (2 or 3) had a small influence on the yield while the number of pods per plant had a considerable influence. Genetic and climatic factors obviously influence pod development. The earliest, non-shedding soybeans with 2 or 3 branches had a shrivelled seed percentage of no more than 20%, and could produce 26% of their potential yield on chernozem soil under drought conditions. Medium-early soybeans with the same characteristics proved more adaptable; those cultivars with small leaves and a small percentage of shrivelled seeds produced between 52 and 88% of their potential yield. Although our experiments on the adaptability of soybeans considered only two years, the results for dry beans can be used to improve the genotypes of soybean grown in the Hungarian climate.

80

References

Bou JC, Kamp W and Summer VL 1982 Inheritance of resistance to temperature-drought stress in the snap bean. Journal of Heredity 73, 385–386.

Collinson ST, Summerfield RJ, Ellis RH and Roberts EH 1993 Durations of the photoperiod-sensitive and photoperiod-insensitive phases of development to flowering in four cultivars of soyabean (*Glycine max* (L.) Merrill). Annals of Botany 71, 389–394.

Flores L and Fernando L, 1982 Flowering, pod-set, yield and dry matter partitioning of beans (*Phaseolus vulgaris* L.). *In*: Response to Water Stress and Flower and Leaf Removal. Dissertation Abstract International Vol 44, No. 101.

Hartwig EE 1970 Growth and reproductive characteristics of soybeans (*Glycine max* (L.) Merr.) grown under short day conditions. Tropical Science 12, 47–53.

Lawn RJ 1989 Agronomic and physiological constraints to the productivity of tropical grain legumes and prospects for improvement. Experimental Agriculture 25, 509–528.

Nemeskéri E 1990 The water utilization by French beans crossed with regional varieties (Original title of the thesis 'Zöldbab fajták vizhasznosításának vizsgálata tájfajták bevonásával'). Gödöllö. 124 pp.

Neyshabouri MR 1982 Effects of water stress timing in the field on growth yield, and water use efficiency of soybeans (*Glycine max* (L.) Merr.) of varying growth habit. Ph.D. thesis, University of California, Davis 236.

Pechan PM, Webster BD 1986 Flower and pod-set of *Phaseolus vulgaris* under controlled environment conditions. Hort Science 21 (4), 989–991.

Piha MI and Munns DN 1987 Sensitivity of the common bean (*Phaseolus vulgaris* L.) symbiosis to high soil temperature. Plant and Soil 98, 183–194.

Smith DL, Dijak M and Hume DJ 1988 The effect of water deficit on $N_2(C_2H_2)$ fixation by white bean and soybean. Canadian Journal of Plant Science (Ottawa) 68. 4, 957–967.

Svab J 1981 Biometrical methods in research (Biometriai módszerek a kutatásban). Mezögazdasági kiadó. Budapest 1981.

Singh RK, Chaudhary BD 1979 Biometrical methods in quantitative genetic analysis. Kalyani Publishers. New Delhi, 1979.

O.A. Rognli et al. (eds.), Breeding Fodder Crops for Marginal Conditions, 81–87.
© 1994 *Kluwer Academic Publishers. Printed in the Netherlands.*

Variation within improved cultivars and landraces of lucerne in Central Italy

MARIO FALCINELLI[1], LUIGI RUSSI[1], VALERIA NEGRI[1] and
FABIO VERONESI[2]
[1] *Istituto di Miglioramento Genetico Vegetale, University of Perugia, Borgo XX Giugno 74,
06100 Perugia, Italy;* [2] *Dipartimento di Biotecnologie Agrarie ed Ambientali, University of
Ancona, Via Brecce Bianche, 60100 Ancona, Italy*

Summary. A variety must be distinguishable, uniform, stable and of sufficient productivity
to be officially registered. In Italy landraces of lucerne are still widely used because they are
characterized by a good persistence and productivity in their area of origin and adaptation.
The landrace from Casalina (20 km south of Perugia, Central Italy) has higher dry matter
production than many other commercial cultivars. The objective of this paper was to measure
the variation of the landrace Casalina and compare it with that of the commonest cultivars
available on the market and with some lines selected from the landrace Casalina.
The experiment consisted of 11 entries: Casalina, two selections from Casalina (one for high
seed yield and one for frequent cuttings), the registered landrace Italia Centrale and 7 registered
cultivars. Each entry was represented by 80 genotypes transplanted in the field 60 × 40 cm
apart in a randomized block design with 4 replications. In 1991 the following characters were
recorded on a single plant basis: time of first flowering, height, number of shoots and dry
matter yield at the first harvest, time of second flowering, leafiness, height, number of shoots
and dry matter yield at the second harvest, height, number of shoots and dry matter yield at
the third and fourth harvest. Height, number of shoots and dry matter yield at the first harvest,
dry matter at the second and third harvest were recorded during the 1992 season.
Casalina was as variable as the other entries in 77% of the comparisons; it was more variable
in 8% of the comparisons and less variable in 15% of the comparisons. In conclusion, the
variation of landrace Casalina is equal to or less than that of registered varieties so that it could
be directly registered at the National Registry of Varieties.

Introduction

Landraces are primitive cultivars and, according to the definition given by
Harlan (1975), are balanced populations in equilibrium with the environment
and pathogens; they are genetically dynamic with variations among sites
and populations (heterogeneity in space) and within sites and populations
(heterogeneity in time, i.e. variation between seasons and long term climatic,
biological and socio-economic conditions).

A landrace is continuously subjected to selective pressures within its area
of adaptation due to climatic, soil, biotic, and especially human factors.
Cross-fertilized species grown in mountain areas or in areas characterized
by natural obstacles have been subjected to restricted movement of their
pollen with the consequence of a limited gene flow. The restriction of gene
exchange, accompanied by even slightly different climatic, soil and biotic
factors could have led, with time, to populations specifically adapted to their

habitats and with well defined characteristics. The continuous selection by man, through the practice of sowing seed harvested from the best plants and with different crop management practices (soil cultivation, fertilization, time and methods of crop harvesting, etc.) could have further enhanced differences among landraces.

A wide range of environmental conditions are present in the Italian peninsula, which extends from 47° N to 37° N and is characterized by a continental climate in the north and a mediterranean climate in the south. In Central Italy the Appennine Mountains include several valleys (the Tiber Valley, the Nera Valley and others) and several plains at different altitudes. Many years ago differences for important agronomic characters were found in 4 landraces of maize (Bonciarelli, 1961) and in 5 landraces of lucerne (Lorenzetti et al., 1972) collected in these regions.

Although phenotypically similar, the individuals of a cross-fertilized landrace are highly heterozygous and genotypically different. Landraces are likely to be characterized by a much greater genetic variability than cultivars, whose fundamental requisites are uniformity, distincitiveness, and stability.

In 1992 there were 71 cultivars (35 from Italy, 10 from other parts of Europe, 21 from the USA and 5 from Australia) of lucerne (*Medicago sativa* $2n = 4x = 32$) registered in the Italian National Registry of Varieties, and 14 landraces. As a consequence of (i) their significant longer persistence, (ii) their good productivity, often higher than that of improved cultivars (P. Rotili, personal communication) and, (iii) the lower price of the seeds (50% less), landraces are used by farmers much more than varieties. In addition to the landraces registered *ex officio* by the Ministry of Agriculture in 1980, farmers also use on-farm seeds of landraces produced three or four years after establishment when the crop is no longer economically suitable for forage production (farmer-landraces). In Italy, recent estimates indicate that landraces represent over 80% of the lucerne seed market (Ligabue, 1993). However, registered cultivars are used more and more often by farmers because on-farm seed production is slowly being replaced by purchasing seed on the market.

European Community regulations aim to cancel landraces from the National Registry of cultivars and to abolish their marketing. In Italy landraces will be replaced by registered cultivars most probably by the year 2000. Without an effort to collect, evaluate and improve the existing landraces, precious and well adapted genetic materials will irreversibly be lost.

The objective of the present research was to evaluate the variation within the landrace Casalina, and compare it with that of two lines selected from Casalina, the registered landrace Italia Centrale and seven registered cultivars, including the National check, Equipe.

Materials and methods

The experiment was conducted at the experiment station of the Istituto di Miglioramento Genetico Vegetale, University of Perugia, located at San Martino in Campo, 10 km south of Perugia. The climate of Perugia is submediterranean (Le Houerou, 1977), with a long term average annual precipitation of 796 mm. Lucerne start growing in February-March and continues throughout the summer till October. In November many plants start to become dormant due to the cold temperatures and there is no growth during winter.

Eleven entries of *M. sativa* were used in the experiment: Casalina (the local landrace), two lines selected from Casalina: one for high seed production (Casalina SY) and one for a frequent cutting regime (Casalina FC), the registered landrace Italia Centrale, and seven commercial cultivars (Boreal, Delta, Equipe, Estival, Miral, Robot and Tornese).

Seedlings were grown in jiffy-pots in the greenhouse during the winter, and in March 1991 80 random plants per entry were transplanted in the field at distances of 60 cm between rows and 40 cm within the row. Plants were arranged in a randomized complete block design with four replicates, each plot consisting of 2 rows of 10 plants each.

During the 1991 growing season the following observations were recorded on a single plant basis: time of first flowering, plant height, number of shoots and dry matter yield at the first harvest; time of second flowering, leafiness, number of shoots, plant height and dry matter yield at the second harvest; plant height, number of shoots and dry matter yield at the third and fourth harvest. During the 1992 season the observations were: plant height at the first harvest and dry matter yield at the first, second and third harvest.

Data were subjected to hierarchical analysis of variance and variation within entries was computed on residuals. F-tests were performed to compare variability of Casalina and of Italia Centrale with that of the other entries.

Results and discussion

Significant ($P < 0.05$) differences of the variability between Casalina and all other entries are reported in Table 1. In 147 out of 190 F-tests (77%), the variation of Casalina was the same as in the other entries (F-ratios not shown). It was significantly more variable in 14 cases (8%), and less variable in 29 cases (15%).

Cultivars or populations of cross-pollinated species grown outside their area of adaptation are expected to show an explosion of variability mainly due to the interaction between the genotypes and the new environment (Mather, 1953). Several authors (Ludwig et al., 1953; Clausen & Hiesey, 1958; Cooper, 1959; Ceccarelli & Lorenzetti, 1977) have already reported this behaviour in

84

Table 1. Significant ($P < 0.05$) F-ratios between the variance of the lucerne landrace Casalina and that of each of the other lucerne entries for the agronomic characters evaluated. Numbers in bold means that the variance of Casalina was smaller than the variance of the entry used in the test, while numbers in italics means that the variance of Casalina was greater than the variance of the entry used in the test

Characters	Boreal	Cas.SY	Cas.FC	Delta	I.Centr	Equipe	Estival	Miral	Robot	Tornese
Season 1991										
1st flowering	2.61	2.20	2.66	2.65	2.19	3.22	5.35	2.90	–	2.91
DMY 1st harvest	*1.52*	–	–	–	1.68	–	–	–	–	–
Plant height	–	–	–	–	1.87	–	1.92	–	–	–
No. of shoots	–	–	–	–	–	–	–	*1.47*	–	–
2nd flowering	–	1.74	–	–	–	–	–	–	–	–
DMY 2nd harvest	–	–	–	–	–	–	–	–	–	–
Leafiness	*1.47*	–	–	1.67	–	–	1.93	–	1.98	–
No. of shoots	–	–	1.61	–	–	–	–	–	–	–
Plant height	–	–	–	–	2.37	–	1.49	–	–	–
DMY 3rd harvest	*1.87*	–	–	–	–	–	–	–	*1.54*	–
Plant height	–	1.97	1.81	2.29	2.24	–	1.57	–	–	–
No. of shoots	–	–	1.64	–	–	–	–	–	–	1.52
DMY 4th harvest	–	–	–	–	–	–	–	1.50	–	–
Plant height	–	–	–	–	–	1.57	–	–	–	–
No. shoots	–	–	–	–	–	–	1.52	–	–	–
Season 1992										
DMY 1st harvest	–	–	*1.47*	–	–	–	*1.68*	–	–	*2.01*
Plant height	–	–	–	–	–	*1.68*	–	*1.55*	–	*1.53*
DMY 2nd harvest	–	–	–	–	–	–	–	–	–	*1.72*
DMY 3rd harvest	–	–	–	–	–	–	–	–	*1.59*	*1.49*

a number of species; the entries of lucerne examined here showed the same behaviour. It is likely that some of the lucerne varieties tested in Perugia are characterized by a wide genetic base. For example, synthetics of lucerne released in the USA from both public and private companies are often developed by selecting parents from a large number of different sources, with the average number of parents being 92 (Short, 1986). If the varieties of lucerne were characterized by a narrow genetic base, then it is likely that they had been selected for an environment somewhat different from that of Perugia.

Casalina SY generally showed the same amount of variability as Casalina, but in 3 cases out of 19 (time of the first and second flowering and plant

Table 2. Significant ($P < 0.05$) F-ratios between the variance of the registered landrace of lucerne Italia Centrale and that of each of the other lucerne entries for the agronomic characters evaluated. Numbers in bold means that the variance of Casalina was smaller than the variance of the entry used in the test, while numbers in italics means that the variance of Casalina was greater than the variance of the entry used in the test

Characters	Boreal	Casalina	Cas.SY	Cas.FC	Delta	Equipe	Estival	Miral	Robot	Tornese
Season 1991										
1st flowering	–	*2.19*	–	–	–	**1.47**	**2.44**	–	*1.58*	–
DMY 1st harvest	**2.55**	*1.68*	*1.91*	*1.63*	*1.79*	**2.09**	–	*1.55*	*1.68*	*2.10*
Plant height	*1.75*	*1.87*	–	–	–	*1.91*	–	–	*1.61*	*1.68*
No. of shoots	–	–	–	–	–	–	–	–	–	–
2nd flowering	–	–	**2.10**	–	–	–	–	–	**1.73**	–
DMY 2nd harvest	–	–	*1.67*	–	–	–	–	–	–	*1.74*
Leafiness	*1.67*	–	–	–	**1.47**	–	**1.70**	–	**1.74**	–
No. of shoots	–	–	*1.92*	–	–	*1.48*	–	–	–	–
Plant height	**2.24**	**2.37**	*1.78*	**2.41**	*1.64*	**2.68**	*1.59*	**3.06**	*1.87*	*1.75*
DMY 3rd harvest	*2.04*	–	–	–	–	–	–	–	*1.68*	–
Plant height	*1.72*	*2.24*	–	–	–	*1.92*	–	*1.60*	*1.59*	*1.80*
No. of shoots	–	–	–	**1.66**	–	–	–	–	–	**1.53**
DMY 4th harvest	–	–	*1.67*	–	–	–	–	–	–	–
Plant height	–	–	–	–	–	–	–	–	*1.51*	–
No. shoots	–	–	–	–	–	–	**1.90**	–	–	**1.63**
Season 1992										
DMY 1st harvest	–	–	–	–	–	–	*1.57*	–	–	*1.89*
Plant height	–	–	**1.51**	–	–	–	–	–	–	–
DMY 2nd harvest	–	–	–	–	–	–	–	–	–	–
DMY 3rd harvest	–	–	–	–	–	–	**1.70**	–	–	–

height at the third harvest of 1991) it was more variable. Casalina FC was less variable than Casalina in only one case (plant height at the first harvest of 1992), and it was more variable in 6 cases out of 19. This suggests that the selection conducted in Casalina for high seed yield and the adaptation to a more frequent cutting regime did not restrict the variation for important agronomic characters.

The landrace Italia Centrale, registered *ex officio* by the Ministry of Agriculture for Central Italy, was one of the most variable entries for dry matter yield per plant at the first and second harvest of 1991 and plant height in 1991 (Table 2). Italia Centrale was less variable in only 7% of the 190 comparisons

86

with all other entries, but more variable in as many as 23% of them. This large variation could have been the consequence of a mechanical mixing of seeds produced by many farms licensed to multiply this landrace. A recent survey showed that Italia Centrale is multiplied by at least 53 farms scattered all over central Italy (F. Lorenzetti, personal communication), probably in areas with different environments.

Conclusions

The results indicate that Casalina is one of the most uniform of the entries tested in this trial. Its uniformity within its area of cultivation was somewhat expected while the large variation found in the cultivars recommended for Central Italy was totally unexpected. Their genetic base, although narrow compared with Casalina, was probably not narrow enough to restrict their phenotypic variation. This is a sufficient reason to state that Casalina is sufficiently uniform to be directly registered at the Italian National Registry of Varieties.

As Casalina is one of the less variable lucernes in the area of Perugia, other landraces of lucerne would probably show the same behaviour in their own area of adaptation. This has practical relevance both in breeding programmes and in seed legislation because in cross-pollinated species the uniformity and stability of landraces/varieties can be found only within their area of adaptation/selection. Therefore, public and private companies should be more careful in recommending improved varieties to farmers. In dense stand experiments conducted in our environment, Casalina has always shown a good yielding ability (Falcinelli et al., 1978) and was the best entry in another trial conducted for three years with the same materials included here (Russi et al., unpublished). Landraces are still so commonly used because it is difficult to outyield them in their environment. Farmers have always produced on-farm seeds only from the best fields of lucerne two to three years after establishment, thus conducting a sort of 'simple recurrent selection' where natural and human selection pressures have converged (Falcinelli et al., 1978).

One of the problems that farmers will be facing in the near future is that landraces will no longer be available on the market. It will be a disaster if good, adapted landraces (still common in Italy) are not collected soon and used in breeding programmes in order to develop varieties adapted to specific areas. A survey conducted in Central Italy by the Istituto di Miglioramento Genetico Vegetale indicated that some landraces, which were available from farmers in 1990 were no longer available in 1993. Therefore, the need of collecting and storing them is urgent because of their great value as a source of adapted and productive germplasm.

Acknowledgements

Research funded by the Italian Ministry of Agriculture and Forestry, project Foraggicoltura Prativa, subproject Miglioramento Genetico. Professor F. Lorenzetti, University of Perugia, critically reviewed the manuscript.

References

Bonciarelli, F., 1961. Studio agronomico comparato delle popolazioni umbre di mais. Maydica 6: 35–61.

Ceccarelli, S. & F. Lorenzetti, 1977. Within varieties variability in different adapted types of *Lolium perenne*. Proceedings of the XIII International Grassland Congress, pp. 329–332.

Clausen, J. & W.M. Hiesey, 1958. Experimental studies on the nature of species. IV. Genetic structure of ecological races. Carnegie Institute of Washington, Publication 615, 1.

Cooper, J.P., 1959. Selection and population structure in *Lolium*. II. Genetic control of date or ear emergence. Heredity 13: 445–449.

Falcinelli, M., F. Veronesi, S. Arcioni & A. Mariani, 1978. Studio preliminare per la costituzione di una varietà di erba medica utilizzabile per la disidratazione ed adatta all'Italia Centrale. Rivista di Agronomia 12: 191–201.

Harlan, J.R., 1975. Our vanishing genetic resources. Science 188: 618–621.

Le Houerou, H.N., 1977. Plant sociology and ecology applied to grazing lands research, survey and management in the Mediterranean Basin. In: W. Krause (Ed.) Application of Vegetation Science to Grassland Husbandry, pp. 213–274. Junk Publisher, The Hague.

Ligabue, M., 1993. Medica, oltre gli ecotipi. Terra & Vita 34, VI: 62–64.

Lorenzetti, F., S. Ceccarelli & Q. Catena, 1972. Caratterizzazione di ecotipi e selezione in erba medica. Sementi Elette 18, III: 17–28.

Ludwig, R.A., H.L. Barrales & H. Steppler, 1953. Studies on the effect of light on the growth and development of red clover. Canadian Journal of Agricultural Sciences 33: 274–287.

Mather, K., 1953. The genetical structure of populations. Symposium of the Society of Experimental Biology 7: 66–95.

Short, K.E., 1986. Breeding methodology for alfalfa: a survey summary. Proceedings of the XIII North American Alfalfa Improvement Conference, p. 57.

GENETIC VARIATION AND POPULATION STRUCTURE OF TRIFOLIUM FRAGIFERUM L. IN VARIOUS ENVIRONMENTAL CONDITIONS.

Z. BULINSKA-RADOMSKA
Plant Breeding and Acclimatization Institute
Seed Quality Department at Radzikow
05-870 Blonie
Poland

Twenty three populations of <u>Trifolium fragiferum</u> L. representing northcentral, southcentral and eastern Poland were electrophoretically analysed to elucidate the range and organization of allozyme variation in relation to their origin. Study was based on 9 polimorphic loci (8 enzyme systems). The enzyme loci assayed were as follows: alcohol dehydrogenase (Adh), aspartate aminotransferase (Aat1 and Aat2), esterase (Est), peroxidase (Prx), phosphoglucomutase (Pgm), shikimate dehydrogenase (Skd), malate dehydrogenase (Mdh) and leucine aminopeptidase (Lap). Data were analysed using Nei and Shannon–Weaver's statistics. Nei's statistics included the calculation of average unbiased gene diversity (He) for each population, the total gene diversity per locus (Ht) for all populations and partitioning it into intra (Hs) and interpopulational (Dst) components, and finally the calculation of relative interpopulational differentiation (Dst/Ht=Gst). Shannon–Weaver information index (H') was calculated for each locus and population, then these values were pooled and averaged for regions for each locus.

All the eastern populations were the most polimorphic. They had the highest number of alleles per locus and the highest proportion of polimorphic loci. Consequently the level of allozyme diversity (He) in eastern populations was much higher (0.330) than in northcentral (0.083) and south central (0.170) regions. Least variables were populations of northcentral Poland as evidenced by the lowest values of gene diversity (0.083) and Shannon–Weaver indices (mean 0.135). Mean values of the latter parameter for eastern and south central populations were 0.441 and 0.236 respectively. Various levels of polymorphism were observed across regions for most loci except for Adh. Eastern populations were monomorphic in Lap, whereas those of northcentral Poland were monomorphic in Mdh.

The pattern of diversity of Polish populations of <u>T. fragiferum</u> could be partly explained by climatic factors since other ecological variables were comparable for all regions. It seems that sharper climate was conducive to the accumulation of allozyme variation as populations from more severe conditions were more polimorphic than those from milder climate. In addition, the higher level of diversity displayed by eastern populations could be accounted for by the less advanced agricultural system in this region. Under such circumstances, species have greater chances than in areas of intensive agriculture to establish populations, persist and differentiate. For the majority of loci but one, Aat2 most of the allozyme variation resides within populations. Such pattern of distribution of variation is common for perennial, crosspollinated species.

O.A. Rognli et al. (Eds.) Breeding Fodder Crops for Marginal Conditions, 90–91.
© 1994 *Kluwer Academic Publishers. Printed in the Netherlands.*

FACTOR REGRESSION ANALYSIS OF NATURAL POPULATIONS OF RYEGRASS

Gilles Charmet & François Balfourier
INRA, Plant Breeding Station
63039 Clermont-Ferrand
France

Natural populations of grasses are widely used as genetic resources in breeding programmes. Therefore many plant breeders are collecting populations from the wild. Collection can either be systematic on a given area, or oriented by ecogeographic data. Particularly, in order to improve the adaptation to specific climatic conditions, plant breeders are looking for populations growing under similar conditions, which may have selected favourable genes. However the test of the efficiency of natural selection for the breeding objectives of Man is not obvious.

Generally the collection of populations is evaluated for agronomic traits. When carried out on a range of environments, such evaluations often exhibit a high level of genotype-environment interactions. One of the methods proposed to explain GxE interactions is factor regression analysis using covariates associated either to genotypes or to environments or to both (DENIS, 1988). In the case of the evaluation of natural populations in a multisite network, the same covariates can be used to characterize climatic conditions at either the site of origin or the site of evaluation.

Factor regression analysis has been carried out on a core collection of perennial ryegrass populations from France for the trait "summer growth score", using the two covariates: hydric balance HB (HB = rainfall - potential evapotranspiration for July-September) and Tmax, the average maximum temperature of July. The results are summarized in Table 1, which shows the F values of the different terms of the model (CHARMET et al 1993). The first line and column correspond to the regression of main effects on the covariates and, as expected, are highly significant. The lines and columns labelled by the covariates are the regression terms of the interaction on the 2-by-2 products of covariates, while the line and column "rest" are the regressions of the part of the interaction not accounted for by the products of covariates on a single covariate, and the rest x rest is the residue of unexplained interaction.

In this example, the method was succesful in explaining most of the interaction, as the term rest x rest is not significant. The most significant terms are the regression on the products HB x HB and Tmax x Tmax, which both have positive coefficients. This means that a population which originates from either a warm or dry site presents a positive interaction when evaluated in a warm or dry site respectively, as expected as a consequence of natural selection. Therefore the strategy of collecting from sites which present climatic characteristics similar to those where the variety is to be used must be encouraged. However a population component of regression on environmental covariates is also significant. Figure 1 illustrates this component of regression on hydric balance. The populations represented by empty symbols (negative coefficient of regression) therefore present a positive interaction in dry evaluation sites (negative hydric balance), in addition to the interaction which can be predicted by the regression on HB x HB. This population component can therefore be exploited through breeding to improve adaptation of perennial ryegrass to either drier or warmer regions, i.e. to marginal conditions for ryegrass growth.

REFERENCES.

CHARMET G., BALFOURIER F., RAVEL C., DENIS JB., 1993. Genotype x environment interactions in a core collection of French perennial ryegrass populations. Theor. Appl. Genet. (In press)

DENIS JB., 1988. Two-way analysis of variance using covariates. Statistics 19:123-132.

TABLE 1: F values of factor regression terms and their significance (* = S, ** = HS).

Location covariate	Population covariate			
	0	HB	Tmax	Rest
0	/	7.2**	10.8**	1.7*
HB	337**	6.2**	0.1	1.5*
Tmax	9.7*	1.0	11.4**	1.4*
Rest	55.7**	3.0*	1.7*	0.6

Figure 1

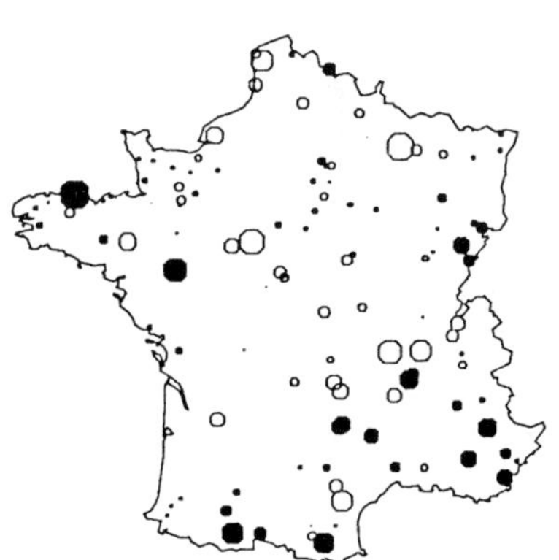

DESCHAMPSIA CAESPITOSA L. - PROPOSAL FOR LAWN IN SHADE CONDITIONS

S. PROŃCZUK
Plant Breeding and Acclimatization Institute,
Radzików, 05-870 Błonie
Poland

ABSTRACT. *Deschampsia caespitosa* is known to be a common weed grass on Polish pastures. The possibility for using this grass species for shade lawn has not been considered until now. While looking for shade-resistant breeding material, an ecotype of *D. caespitosa* was found growing on paths in the forest. Under pre-breeding tests in shade conditions, we compared this ecotype to other common lawn varieties in species - *Festuca rubra, Lolium perenne, Festuca arundinacea, Agrostis tenuis, Poa pratensis, Festuca ovina, Festuca heterophylla, Poa nemoralis.* The lawn utilization tests were made by the split plot method over three years in a park at Radzików (central Poland). The seed sowing density was $20g/m^2$. The grass was mowed 8 to 12 times per year. The following characters were tested: installation, general aspect, slow growth, sward density, colour, disease resistance and other. Data was collected from early spring to winter.
It was found that *D. caespitosa* could be a valuable species for shade lawns. The most valuable characteristics are: easy and fast installation, good lawn compactness, slow regrowth after cutting, fresh green colour especially in spring and summer. Some negative characteristics found are: slightly sharp leaves, rather rough turf, and a "whitening syndrome" after cutting.

O.A. Rognli et al. (Eds.) Breeding Fodder Crops for Marginal Conditions, 93–94.
© 1994 Kluwer Academic Publishers. Printed in the Netherlands.

THURINGIAN MALLOW (LAVATERA THURINGIACA L.) — AN ALTERNATIVE CROP FOR MARGINAL CONDITIONS AND WASTED LANDS

Z. STASZEWSKI, U. STASZEWSKA
Plant Breeding and Acclimatization Institute
Department of Genetics, Radzików,
05-870 Błonie
Poland

ABSTRACT. Thee field trials completed at Radzików in Central Poland showed that thuringian mallow would be a crop suitable for various utilization. It produces plants up to 1500 mm high, well branched and persistant. Each flower of mallow produces seeds giving 44 g seeds per plant. The yield of dry matter 27 t and seed yield 1 t per 1 ha were achieved.

1. Material and Metods.

Plant material consisted of:
RAH 1 - Thuringian mallow population bred at Radzików,
Malva verticilliata L. - population bred at Troubsko, Tschechs.
Radius - Lucerne variety registerd in Poland used as a standard,
Wielkopolski - Forage type sunflower cultivar.

The experiments were carried on in the field. Randomized block design was applied and 4 plants of mallow per sq. m density were used for seed harvest, while for forage yield 20 plants per sq. m were grown on. The plants excluding T. mallow were sown in a density generally recomended for a given crop.

2.. Results.

Thuringian mallow plants achieved remarkable size comparing to another crops. The plants had many stems which were well branched (table 1).

TABLE 1. A comparison of plant morphology characters.

Year of vegetation	Plant no. in a sample	Plant dry matter mass (g)	Stem lenght (mm)	Node no. per stem	Stem no. per plant	Number of 1-st (main) branches
2-1988	30	1193.0	1159	14.0	29.8	8.5
3-1988	49	539.3	1028	16.0	25.0	8.3
3-1989	30	661.6	1514	25.9	22.3	12.9
4-1989	49	239.6	1146	23.2	9.3	14.1

94

Mallow plants were producing very numerous flowers. Usually each flower set seeds due to extremal selfpollination, and gave 11-132 g seeds per plant. There were achieved seed yields 111-131 g per a m sq. on the plots, which contained 11.2-51.2% of hard seeds in various years. Hard seeds germinated well after scaryfication.

TABLE 2. Plant parts contents in T. mallow dry matter.

Dry matter content (%)	Stems (%)	Leves at flowering (%)	Flowers and buds (%)	Fiber in stems (%)	Leaves at early buds (%)
27.2	57.8	18.0	24.6	17.8	26.2

Thuringian mallow yielded better than lucerne and other crops which were compared and gave 22.7-27.1 t D.M. per 1 ha (table 3). The highest yields were obtained in second and third years of vegetation: frequent cutting diminished persistancy. Late harvested yield contained low deal of leaves, but more flowers and buds. The stems contained 17.8 per cent fiber (table 2).

TABLE 3. A comparison of biomass.

Species	Cut no. per year	Dry matter yield			
		Second year		Third year	
		(t/ha)	(%)	(t/ha)	(%)
Lavatera thuringiaca L.	2	27.1	18.1	22.7	19.4
Malva verticillata L.	1	14.1	16.1	12.5	16.7
Helianthus annuus L.	1	15.6	12.9	16.1	14.0
Medicago sativa L.	2	19.2	19.8	18.2	20.3

Lucerne was cut at flowering, other crops at early bud stage.

3. Conclusion.

Positive characteristic of thuringian mallow have rosed an expectation that it can be sown on lands taken out of production. This perennial species is well adapted to various regions in Europe and seems to be useful for marginal condition because of persistance, low demands for water and big production of seeds which fell down when were not harvested in a proper time.

Several ways of utilization shall be studied to state how this plant can be exploited in agriculture. The main purposes are following:

Growing for forage production in the field.

Growing on lands taken out of agriculture as an alternative crop to produce paper pulp. The same plantation can be used to produce honey and mallow seeds, or to pick up leaves and flowers for medicinal purposes.

Growing on wasted lands as an extensive field to prevent soil erosion. Autoseeding with seeds fallen down is expected. Plants can provide wild bees an animals with forage and nests.

Growing as medicinal plant to produce substances typical within Malvaceae.

O.A. Rognli et al. (Eds.) Breeding Fodder Crops for Marginal Conditions, 95–96.
© 1994 *Kluwer Academic Publishers. Printed in the Netherlands.*

EVALUATING GENETIC RESOURCES OF RED CLOVER IN MARGINAL GROWING CONDITIONS

M. UŽÍK
Research Institute of Plant Production
921 68 Piešťany
SLOVAKIA

In marginal, drier conditions, red clover has a low persistence, what is attributed to diseases, utilization regime, of variety growth rhythm of variety (Bird 1948, Choo 1984 etc.), and other factors. Since in our long-term program of research on genetic resources, persistence was studied, we will point out its dependence on some factors, or the possibilities of its improvement and refer to the resources of selection. We present the synthesis of results, which have been already published in part.

Materials and Methods
The results have been obtained according to the standard procedure of evaluation at individual plant growing in row-spacing, in the field or case trials. In total, more than 600 varieties have been evaluated.

Results
In the first stage of our research (1965-1975), we have evaluated more than 200 varieties of red clover (2n and 4n), when the native varieties appeared to be the most persistent and Swiss varieties of Mattenklee type, German, Swedish, Danish varieties, and varieties from USA were equal to them. Different persistence, or as the case may be also winterhardiness is usually connected with the growth rhythm (Bird 1948) . We have found out that relationship between the degree of generative development in sowing year and overwintering was different according to the studied set of varieties. Very strong relationship have been determined in the set of English varieties (r = -0.854++) and significantly poorer in the set of 150 varieties form 20 states (r = -0.422++). Similar results have been obtained also in the next stages of our research. From this it followed that persistence was conditioned by combination of other factors, including physiological necrosis of roots (Zeiders et all 1971).
We have found out that persistence of red clover varieties depends very much on precipitations in sowing year.

Year of establishment	·1977	·1978	·1985	·1989
Precipitation in mm	583,7	356,4	618,1	386,6
Persistence in 2 year	94,6a	54,36a	76b	39,41c

a - the same letters indicate the same set of varieties
From the point of breeding, variety x establishment year interaction is important (Užík 1983).

Group of varietes	n	% of persistance		Injury to root	
		77/78	78/79	on surface	on cross section
Above the average	13	95,4	65,6	4,1	2,19
Average	7	93,2	55,2	4,38	2,38
Below the average	9	93,9	37,3	3,77	2,12

In 1977/78, no differences as to persistence appeared between 29 varieties, while in the second trial in 1978/79, varieties could be divided to three different groups of persistence. The reason of a low persistence of the 3rd group can be attributed to a higher infection by root rot in spite of that this group had the lowest degree of injury. At a great difference in persistence (37.3% to 65.6%), degree of injury gives a distorted picture about the effect of root diseases on persistence, because it does not take in account plants died due to root rot. Therefore we use also another indicator, namely degree of resistance, which includes also plants died evidently because of root rot and it is more suitable also for estimation of selection progress .

Evaluation of genetic resources is evaluation of breeding progress, which can be documented on one of the last sets, in which a group of American varieties (W-115, Atlas, Persist, Starglo, Reddy, Redland, Arlington) have been included . These varieties were characterized by a low infection by virus diseases and powdery mildew, high persistence, as well as by survival in summer period, what indicates that this group of varieties is also tolerant to root diseases, but it had a low grain yield in the 2nd cut. Over the last 30 years of systematic study, foreign varieties of red clover were not more persistent than the native adapted varieties

Varietes	Number	Infection degree		Persistance %		Survival summe
		viroses	mildew	89/90	90/91	
European	7	2,38	3,06	33,88	79,91	61,92
USA strains	5	5,29	2,91	19,77	85,58	48,12
USA - varieties	7	1,71	2,04	59,32	95,13	82,53

It seems that drought stress creates also good selection conditions for improvement of persistence. Indirect selection in marginal conditions of clover (Piešťany) for suitable growing conditions (M.Šariš) was more efficient (127 %) than direct selection. High efficiency of selection in Piešťany can be attributed to the pressure of natural selection on nonadapted varieties, through a strong incidence of root and virus diseases (Užík 1991).

Selection locality	Numver of families	Progeny test			
		Piešťany		Malý Šariš	
		Weight of plant g	Persistance %	Weight of plant g	Persistance
Piešťany	15	182,33[P]	79,72[P]	456,33[N]	83,71[N]
Malý Šariš	15	145,85[N]	68,32[N]	386,50[P]	65,42[P]
(P = 100 %) N/P%		79,99	86,21	118,06	127,92

P - direct selection in Piešťany for Piešťany
N - indirect selection in Piešťany for Šariš and vice versa

References

Bird, J.N. (1948) 'Early and late type of red clover, Sci. Agr., 28, 444-453.

Choo, T.M. (1984) 'Association between growth habit and persistance in red clover', Euphytica, 33, 177-185.

Užík, M. (1983) 'Economic characteristics of selected clover cultivars', Ved. Práce Výsk. Úst. rast. Výr. Piešťany, 19, 33-47.

Užík, M. (1991) 'Influence of the environment on selection efficiency', Ved. Práce Výsk. Úst. rast. Výr. Piešťany,3,115-127.

Zeiders, K.E., Graham, H.J., Sprague, V.G. and Wilkinson, S.R. (1971) 'Internal breakdown of red clover (Trifollium ratense L.) in relation to environmental cultural and genetic factors', Agric. Res. Serv. 21, 34-126.

O.A. Rognli et al. (Eds.) Breeding Fodder Crops for Marginal Conditions, 97–98.
© 1994 *Kluwer Academic Publishers. Printed in the Netherlands.*

GENETIC RESOURCES OF OIL AND FODDER PLANTS IN THE GENEBANK STATION MALCHOW/POEL

E. WILLNER[1,3] and H. KNÜPFFER[2]
[1]*Institute of Plant Genetics and Crop Plant Research (IPK)*
Genebank, External Station Malchow
D-23999 Malchow/Poel, Germany
[2]*Institute of Plant Genetics and Crop Plant Research (IPK)*
Genebank
D-06466 Gatersleben, Germany

1. Introduction

The oil and fodder plant genebank station in Malchow/Poel comprises 16.742 accessions, mainly of the Gramineae, Leguminosae and Cruciferae. Since 1992 it belongs to the Institute of Plant Genetics and Crop Plant Research (IPK) Gatersleben. The establishment of the collection began in the early 1970s on the basis of breeding activities. The material includes wild species and landraces, as well as breeders lines and cultivars, both from Germany and abroad.

2. Genetic resources activities

2.1. REPRODUCTION

Viable seeds are needed for evaluation as well as for distribution to users. Therefore, the material has to be reproduced under conditions precluding genetic shift or contamination. The reproduction of cross-fertilizing Gramineae accessions is carried out in 10 m^2 plots isolated by rye plantings. Four accessions belonging to different species are grown on each plot. Cruciferae accessions are cultivated in double rows and isolated with crispac bags. Accessions of the Leguminosae are reproduced at Gatersleben in isolation boxes, using insects as pollinators.

2.2. LONG TERM STORAGE

Seeds are long-term stored in glass jars under vacuum. Although the sealing of the jars needs regular checking, this method of monitoring seed germinability and vitality is safe and cost-efficient since it does not require expensive cooling systems.

2.3. DOCUMENTATION

In 1992 the station obtained a 386 DX/40 MHz personal computer and the database management system dBASE IV for documentation (Willner, 1993). Documentation activities include, among others: inventorying the collection, validation of the data registered earlier, improvement of file struc-

---

[3]We thank the firms KWS Einbeck and DSV Lippstadt who supported the participation of E. W. in this meeting.

98

TABLE 1. Collecting expeditions

Year Collecting area

1984 Germany: nature reserves and landscape protection areas of the following districts of former GDR: Rostock, Magdeburg, Neubrandenburg, Dresden, Suhl

1985 Germany: biosphere reserve "Vessertal", nature reserve "Harzgrund"

1986 Germany: nature reserve "Oberharz"

1987 Germany: nature reserves and landscape protection areas in Spree-forest area

1988 Germany: Spree-forest

1989 Czechoslovakia: Beskids, Southern Moravia

1990 Germany: Poel island, nature reserves around Dresden and Erfurt; Southeast Poland

1991 Germany: GFP project, Mrs. Oetmann

tures, inclusion of further descriptors, integration of evaluation data, rationalization of seed management, identification of duplicates within the collection, and between Malchow and Gatersleben collections. The station will also participate in a centralized documentation system for genetic resources in Germany to be developed by the Zentralstelle für Agrardokumentation und -information (ZADI) in Bonn.

3. Results and conclusions

Genetic resources work aims at providing new gene sources to breeders. To widen the genetic diversity of the collection, especially of economically important grasses, material was collected and obtained from collectors in different climatical zones, partly from nature reserves (Table 1). The results of collecting are summarized in Table 2. Table 3 shows the composition of the whole genebank collection.

Bearing in mind the limited staff available, at present we have to concentrate on safeguarding the existing material by identical reproduction. Parts of the collection are grown for evaluation or comparison. We favour cooperation with plant breeders, scientific research institutions and other genebanks. The equipment (e.g. cold chambers, instruments) needs to be completed to ensure higher efficiency of the work.

4. References

Willner, E. (1993) 'Stand der Dokumentation genetischer Ressourcen in der Genbank-Außenstelle Malchow/Poel', in F. Schmidt (ed.), Pflanzengenetische Ressourcen — Situationsanalyse und Dokumentationssituation, Bonn, pp. 124—125.

Willner, E. and Müller, H. (1992) 'Bearbeitung genetischer Ressourcen in der Außenstelle Malchow', Vorträge für Pflanzenzüchtung 25, 29—30.

TABLE 2. Material from own collecting expeditions (1984—1991) maintained in the genebank (after Willner and Müller, 1992)

Species	Number of accessions
Gramineae	
Agrostis gigantea Roth.	26
Agrostis stolonifera L.	5
Agrostis tenuis Sibth.	23
Alopecurus pratensis L.	64
Arrhenaterum elatius Presl	45
Dactylis glomerata L.	210
Deschampsia caespitosa (L.) P.B.	11
Festuca arundinacea Schreb.	59
Festuca ovina L.	28
Festuca pratensis Huds.	150
Festuca rubra L.	86
Lolium multiflorum Lam.	13
Lolium perenne L.	403
Phalaris arundinacea L.	21
Phleum pratense L.	307
Poa nemoralis L.	6
Poa pratensis L.	247
Trisetum flavescens (L.) P.B.	25
Leguminosae	
Trifolium pratense L.	66
Trifolium repens L.	76
Other species	185
Total	**2056**

TABLE 3. Composition of the genebank collection (as of 1992)

Species	Number of accessions
Gramineae	*8.453*
Dactylis glomerata L.	983
Festuca pratensis Huds.	972
Lolium perenne L.	1.831
Phleum pratense L.	718
Poa pratensis L.	918
Leguminosae	*3.841*
Trifolium pratense L.	1.401
Medicago x varia Martyn	981
Cruciferae	*3.935*
Brassica napus f. annua	310
Brassica napus f. biennis	2.103
Other species	513
Total	**16.742**

Adaptation and breeding of forage crops for marginal conditions

O.A. Rognli et al. (eds.), Breeding Fodder Crops for Marginal Conditions, 101–127.
© 1994 *Kluwer Academic Publishers. Printed in the Netherlands.*

Specific adaptation and breeding for marginal conditions

SALVATORE CECCARELLI
*International Center for Agricultural Research in the Dry Areas (ICARDA), P.O. Box 5466,
Aleppo, Syria*

Summary. Breeding has been very successful in generating cultivars that in favorable environments, and together with large use of fertilizer and chemical control of weeds, pest and diseases, have increased agricultural production several fold. Today the environmental impact of high input agriculture in more favorable environments causes growing concern. By contrast, the impact of breeding in marginal environments has been elusive. The paper discusses evidence showing that the use of breeding principles developed for, and successfully applied, in favorable environments may be the main reason for the lack of breeding progress in marginal environments. Very little breeding work has actually been done in marginal environments, although the theory of correlated responses to selection indicates that selection conducted in good environments or in well-managed experiment stations is not expected to be very efficient when genotype by environment interactions of a cross-over type exist. The assumptions that heritability is higher under good conditions and that there is a carry-over effect of high yield potential are not supported by experimental evidence. If the target environment is below the cross-over point, selection has to be conducted for specific adaptation to that environment. The concept of wide adaptation has more a geographical than an environmental meaning, and it reduces genetic diversity and increases genetic vulnerability. Eventually the issue of genetic heterogeneity versus genetic uniformity is discussed in relation to specific adaptation to marginal environments.

Introduction

The objective of this paper is to discuss three issues related to breeding for marginal conditions, namely the effect of genotype by environment (G × E) interaction on the choice of the selection environment, specific versus wide adaptation, genetic uniformity versus genetic diversity. More in general, the paper addresses the question of whether breeding philosophies, methodologies and strategies developed for favorable environments are useful in marginal environments.

Most of the data are from one type of marginal environment and from one crop. The environment is a continental-mediterranean environment where winter cereals, and barley in particular, are grown without irrigation. The features of this environment are described in Fig. 1, which shows rainfall and temperature data in two contrasting cropping seasons at the driest of ICARDA's experiment sites (Bouider, 80 km southeast of Aleppo, in northern Syria with a long-term average rainfall of about 200 mm). In Bouider most of the barley breeding for marginal conditions has been conducted under rainfed conditions, without fertilizer applications and without chemical control of pests, diseases and weeds. The two cropping seasons had a very similar total rainfall, yet yields were very different (1.2 t/ha in 1986 and a crop failure

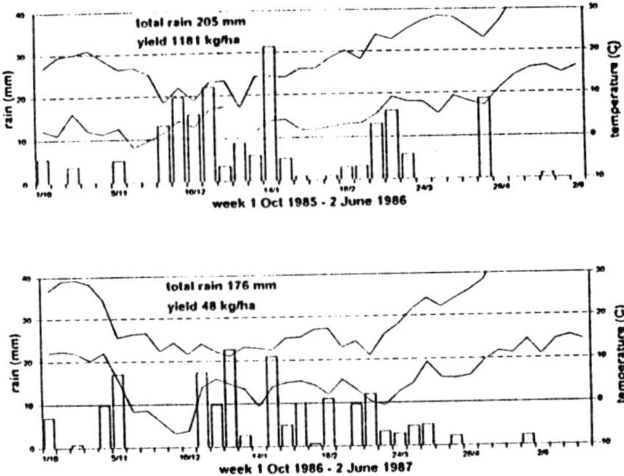

Fig. 1. Rainfall, minimum and maximum temperature in Bouider, northern Syria, in 1986 and 1987.

in 1987). The difference in total rainfall between the two cropping seasons (29 mm) was mostly due to the different amount of precipitation in April-May (42.6 mm in 1986 and 13.9 mm in 1987). The lower winter temperatures in 1987 prevented crop growth when moisture was not limiting, with the result that ground cover was still very poor by the end of March at the onset of increasing evaporative demand. Limited rainfall in April-May imposed drought stress on an already temperature-stressed crop. Therefore, the crop failure of 1987 was due to the concomitant effect of low temperatures and moisture stress.

In this type of environment not only low annual rainfall, but also rainfall distribution, low winter temperatures, high temperatures and hot winds during grain filling are important abiotic stresses. The frequency, timing, intensity and duration of each of these stresses, as well as their specific combinations, vary from year to year. However, low yields are common, crop failures occur once or twice in five years, and yields above 2.5 t/ha are very rare (Fig. 2). Low yields in these environments are highly predictable; the causes for low yields are not. Therefore, the environment has the typical characteristics (variable, unpredictable, low yielding) which are often indicated as 'impossible' for breeding work.

The crop I will refer to is barley. Barley is a useful crop for discussions of general issues related to breeding for marginal conditions because in many developing countries it is a typical crop of marginal, low-input, stressful environments (Ceccarelli, 1984). In these environments barley yields more than wheat in a range of environmental conditions, and is often the only possible rainfed crop. However, in developing countries barley yields have

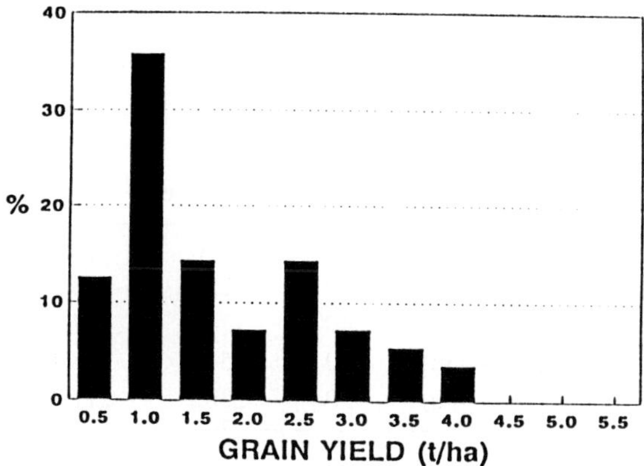

Fig. 2. Frequency distribution of barley yields in dry areas of Syria (less than 250–300 mm annual rainfall) between 1983 and 1993.

remained stagnant during the last twenty years despite the impressive yield increases in industrialized countries.

Barley is also a useful crop for discussions of breeding strategies in a farming system context, and particularly so in this meeting, because of its role as animal feed. In large areas of West Asia, North Africa, but also in the Andean and Himalayan countries and in China, barley straw, and in many cases both straw and grain are one of the major sources of animal feed, particularly for small ruminants. The strategies adopted by farmers who grow barley might be difficult to interpret if not considered in a perspective where the animals, and not necessarily the crop, are the actual agricultural product. Barley is used as animal feed, mostly for small ruminants, in a variety of ways which are largely dictated by the environmental conditions: a) straw, grain and stubble after a normal crop harvest; b) standing crop at maturity in dry years when the crop is too short to be combine-harvested, or alternatively hand pulled if the price of the straw is high enough to cover the labor cost; c) winter grazing (before stem elongation) in good years or by clipping the crop grown under full or supplementary irrigation. In extremely unfavorable years the crop is fully grazed before stem elongation: this is an example of sacrificing the crop to save the animals.

Yield stability, perceived by farmers as minimization of crop failures, is the most important socio-economic breeding objective in this type of marginal environment. If we can demonstrate that it is possible to improve the productivity of a crop such as barley in this type of marginal environment, the principles, or the strategy used, may be relevant to other crops in other types of marginal environments.

104

Table 1. Grain yield of barley (kg/ha) in five cropping seasons (rainfall in parenthesis) without and with fertilizer (60 kg/ha of P_2O_5 and 20 kg/ha of N)

Cropping season and rainfall	Without fertilizer	With fertilizer	Increase (%)
1981/82 (229 mm)	1720	2130	23.8
1982/83 (324 mm)	1320	2220	68.2
1983/84 (284 mm)	1040	1740	67.3
1984/85 (204 mm)	740	1540	108.1
1985/86 (278 mm)	750	2380	217.3

Table 2. Grain and total biological yield of barley (kg/ha) under rainfed conditions and with supplementary irrigation

Moisture regime	Moisture (mm)	Grain yield yield	Total biological yield
Rainfed (R)	185	400	2050
Irrigated (I)	417	3370	7570
Ratio (I/R)		8.4	3.7

Why breeding for marginal conditions?

Although I will only discuss different aspects of breeding for marginal conditions, one might argue whether breeding is in fact the best solution to increase agricultural production in marginal environments. Results obtained with fertilizer applications (Table 1) or with irrigation (Table 2) are spectacular, and yield increases far greater than the most optimistic breeding expectations. They are so spectacular and have been so well known for such a long time that one wonders why they have not been adopted on a much wider scale and why crop yields are still commonly reduced because of low use of fertilizer and/or by drought.

In the case of fertilizer, there are basically three reasons why this obviously beneficial agronomic practice has a low adoption rate in marginal environments: cost, availability and risk. Farmers are reluctant to use fertilizer in marginal environments because they cannot afford its cost, or because the fertilizer is allocated to better environments or more profitable crops, but mostly because they know that in very dry years there will be no crop, irrespective of fertilizer applications and that they will loose the additional investment made on fertilizer.

In the case of irrigation, which has a potential impact even greater than fertilizer, we must remember that the water used in many dry areas is often a non-renewable resource. The depth of the water table at ICARDA's main experiment station, located near Tel Hadya, 30 Km south of Aleppo, in northern Syria, has fallen more than 10 m during the last 10 years as a consequence of a dramatic increase in the use of supplementary irrigation by farmers around the station. In addition, irrigation brings problems of salinization. The accumulation of salts in agricultural soils is a problem that has plagued civilizations for thousands of years. It has been estimated that, considering competing needs and possible soil degradation, no more than 10% of the U.S. agricultural land will be irrigated. Therefore irrigation can only be a partial solution to the problem of drought even in developed countries (Boyer, 1982).

The conclusions are inescapable: water and nutrient resources are often limited, and economic and environmental problems are likely to restrain their use.

Breeding for marginal conditions

Breeding has been very successful in environments which are either naturally favorable or which can be made profitably favorable by adding irrigation and fertilizer and by chemical control of weeds, pests and diseases. Just a few examples give an idea of the yield gains obtained through breeding in various crops. The annual genetic gain in bread wheat in the U.S. from 1919 to 1987 has been 16 kg ha^{-1} yr^{-1} (Cox et al., 1988) and in U.K. between 1908 and 1985 38 kg ha^{-1} yr^{-1} (Austin et al., 1989). The genetic gain in maize hybrids released between 1930 and 1980 was 54.2% (Russel, 1984). Similar examples are available in many crops.

By contrast, yield improvements have been very elusive in marginal environments, to the point that the role of breeding for those environments is often questioned. What is not questioned is why it has not been possible to improve agricultural production by simply transferring into marginal environments cultivars and/or methodologies which have made breeding for favorable conditions so successful. The obvious hypothesis is that these cultivars, although often defined as 'widely adapted', are actually specifically adapted to conditions which are at or near the optimum for crop growth. Therefore, the superiority they have in these environments is not expressed in sub-optimal environments.

106

This brings up one of the major topics in discussing breeding strategies, namely G × E interaction, the importance of selection environment and of specific adaptation.

Genotype by environment interaction, selection environment and specific adaptation

Theory
The theory dealing with the relationship between selection environment and performance has been mainly developed by Falconer (1981) as a case of indirect selection. Selection is indirect when the breeder aims to improve a primary character by selecting for a secondary character. The justification for indirect selection is a higher heritability of the secondary character compared to the primary character. As pointed out by Falconer (1981), measures of the same character in two different environments should be regarded as two different characters.

If X is a marginal environment and A an hypothetical trait, we can select in the same environment aiming at a direct response to selection (R_X), or we can select for A in a more favorable environment (Y) aiming at a correlated response to selection in X (CR_X). The efficiency of indirect selection in Y versus direct selection in X is given by:

$$CR_X/R_X = r_G h_Y/h_X \qquad (1)$$

where r_G is the genetic correlation coefficient between A_X and A_Y, h_Y and h_X are the square roots of heritabilities of A in the two environments (Falconer, 1981).

When $h_Y = h_X$, the maximum value of CR_X/R_X is 1 when $r_G = 1$. Therefore, when heritabilities are the same, direct selection will always be more effective because the genetic correlation coefficient will always be less than one. The argument commonly used in favor of selecting in good environments is that heritabilities are higher in favorable environments than in poor environments (Blum, 1988). This issue will be covered later. With low genetic correlation coefficients (0.1–0.2), h_Y must be at least 5 to 10 times higher than h_X for CR_X to be greater than R_X. Therefore, heritability alone is not sufficient to determine the optimum selection environment. Moreover, when r_G is negative the magnitudes of h_Y and h_X are irrelevant.

With specific reference to selection in stress and non-stress environments, Rosielle & Hamblin (1981) showed that selection for tolerance to stress will reduce yields in non-stress environments and also reduce the average yield in stress and non-stress environments. Simmonds (1991), using numerical simulation, concluded that selection for low yielding environments must be conducted in low yielding environments; that using selection environments

Table 3. Grain yield (t/ha) in low and high yielding sites of the top 5% of the barley lines selected for grain yield either in low yielding (LYE) or high yielding (HYE) sites (modified from Ceccarelli et al., 1992)

Year	Testing site		Top lines in LYE		Top lines in HYE	
	LYE	HYE	G_{LY}	G_{HY}	G_{LY}	G_{HY}
1985	0.74	3.49	1.28	0.78	3.34	4.21
1986	1.14	4.01	1.94	1.34	4.14	4.97
1987	0.67	2.67	1.02	0.65	2.74	3.61
1988	2.91	4.42	4.20	3.38	4.67	6.10
1989	0.69	5.82	1.29	0.66	4.87	7.81
1990	0.47	3.35	0.79	0.43	3.07	4.12
1991	1.05	4.74	1.69	0.95	4.71	6.07
1992	0.90	4.63	1.31	1.03	4.80	5.79
Means	1.07	4.14	1.69	1.15	4.04	5.34

with intermediate yield levels is ineffective; and that alternating selection cycles in low and high yielding environments (shuttle breeding), is also ineffective, a conclusion reached earlier by Patel et al. (1987). Similarly, Smith et al. (1990) concluded that selection under low input conditions is essential if significant yield gains for such conditions are to be achieved.

Therefore, theory is very much straightforward: response to selection is maximized when selection is conducted in the environment where the future varieties will be grown. The theory also predicts that the environment of selection affects the pattern of response of genotypes to varying environments (Jinks & Connolly, 1973, 1975).

Experimental evidence: Selection environment and performance
Experimental evidence in barley comes from different sources. First, we compared the performance of barley genotypes in the lowest and in the highest yielding testing sites for eight cropping seasons (Table 3). The table gives for the lowest (LYE) and highest yielding (HYE) sites, the average yield of all lines, yield of the best 5% of the lines selected in low yielding sites (G_{LY}), and yield of the best 5% of the lines selected in high yielding (G_{HY}) sites. The average yield of the HYE sites (4.14 t/ha) was almost four times that of the LYE sites (1.07 t/ha).

In LYE sites the lines which had the highest yields in high yielding conditions had yields similar to the population mean and, on average, yielded 39% less than the lines which had been selected as high yielding in stress conditions. In HYE sites the situation was reversed. Lines which were high yielding under stress conditions had similar yields to the population mean and, on average, were 24% lower yielding than the lines selected as high yielding in non-stress environments. The trade-off between high yield potential in favorable conditions and high yield in marginal conditions is still present when genotypes with identical flowering dates and very similar early leaf area growth are compared (Hamblin, 1992). Therefore, indirect selection (in the absence of stress to improve yield in the presence of stress) will be less effective than direct selection (in the presence of stress).

The choice of the selection environment affects the choice of germplasm to be introduced in a breeding program. In marginal environments, local barley landraces outyield non-landrace material (Table 4). However, in high yielding environments the reverse is true. The data suggest that repeated cycles of selection in a given type of environment will reduce the frequency of lines specifically adapted to other environments.

Tables 3 and 4 indicate that correlated selection differentials in low yielding conditions for selections made in high yielding conditions are either negative or low. However, these differentials are only useful in predicting correlated responses to selection if the genetic correlation coefficient is known (Falconer, 1981). Estimates of genetic correlation coefficients between grain yield measured in low and high yielding sites were obtained from 58 pairs of yield trials in four cropping seasons (Ceccarelli et al., 1992). Among the 58 estimates of r_G, 27 were negative (Table 5). Of the 31 positive values, only 9 were greater than 0.4 and 6 of those were associated with low average yields in the highest yielding sites (ranging between 1812 and 3180 kg/ha). These yields are at or around the value where, in barley, a cross-over between genotypes with specific adaptation to different environments often occurs (Fig. 3). In only one case was a positive r_G associated with heritability estimates in the two environments, such that the CR_X/R_X ratio was greater than 1. In this case the pair of trials had the smallest difference between LYE (618 kg/ha) and HYE (1812 kg/ha) environments found among all 58 comparisons. Both these values are below the cross-over point in Fig. 3.

When the values of genetic correlation coefficients are considered in relation to the yield levels of the two environments used, it seems that high grain yield in high-yielding conditions and high grain yield in low-yielding conditions are under the control of different sets of alleles at most of the several loci that presumably control grain yield. The few estimates of genetic correlation

Table 4. Grain yield (kg/ha) under stress (YS) and grain yield under non-stress (YNS) of barley breeding lines classified according to the germplasm type

Type of germplasm	N^a	YS^b		YNS^c	
		Yield	Range	Yield	Range
Non-landraces	155	488	0– 893	3901	2310–4981
Landraces^d	77	788	486–1076	3413	2398–4610
Best check		717		4147	

^{a} Number of entries.

^{b} Average of two stress sites.

^{c} Average of three non-stress sites.

^{d} Pure lines obtained by pure line selection within landraces.

Table 5. Range of genetic correlation coefficients between yield measured in a low yielding and in a high yielding site and the ratio between correlated and direct response to selection (CR/R) in a total of 58 trials conducted in four cropping seasons (modified from Ceccarelli et al., 1992)

Year	Negative	0–0.2	0.2–0.4	0.4–0.6	0.6–0.8	0.8–1.0	CR/R >1
1986–87	6	1	4	1	2	3	1
1988–89	13	2					0
1989–90	5	7	2				0
1990–91	3	4	2	2		1	0
Total	27	14	8	3	2	4	1

coefficients available in the literature (Atlin & Frey, 1989, 1990; Ud-Din et al., 1992) agree with those reported here.

Experimental evidence: Selection environment and stability
Jinks & Connolly (1973, 1975) showed in *Schizophyllum commune* that environmental sensitivity was reduced if selection and environment effects were in opposite directions; sensitivity was increased if selection and environment effects were in the same direction. Recently Falconer (1990) reviewed published experiments to see if they agreed with the expectations based on the Jinks-Connolly model. He concluded that exceptions to expectation are

110

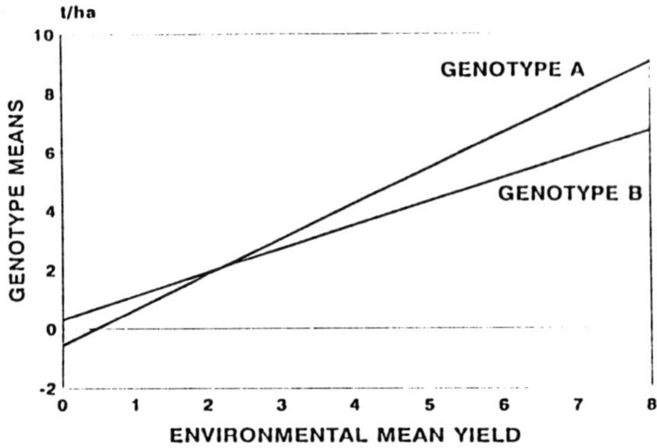

Fig. 3. Cross-over type of G × E interaction: A and B are typical genotypes selected in high and low yielding environments, respectively.

Table 6. Grain yield (kg/ha), linear regression coefficients (b) and coefficient of variation (C.V.) of barley lines selected for high grain yield in high (HY) and low (LY) yielding environments within two groups of 332 and 234 barley lines, respectively (modified from Ceccarelli & Grando, 1991a)

Selection environment	Testing environment		b	C.V.
	HY	LY		
Group 1 (n = 332)				
HY	5420	522	1.13	0.72
LY	4505	1186	0.82	0.54
Group 2 (n = 234)				
HY	6354	389	1.26	0.90
LY	4786	930	0.87	0.65

possible where large differences in additive genetic variances in the two environments (low and high) were coupled with a high genetic correlation.

Although the possibility of predicting or influencing environmental sensitivity is of great interest to plant breeding programs, surprisingly little data (Jinks & Pooni, 1982; Crossa et al., 1989) are available on crop plants which can be used to validate the Jinks and Connolly model. Ceccarelli & Grando (1991a) compared the stability across environments of the 10 genotypes with the highest grain yield under low yielding conditions and the 10 genotypes with the highest grain yield under high yielding conditions. The comparison was repeated twice, using two independent groups of 332 and 234 genotypes, respectively. The stability of the genotypes within each group was evaluated by linear regression analysis (Finlay & Wilkinson, 1963) and by the descriptive method of Francis & Kannenberg (1978) based on the relationship between mean and coefficient of variation.

The regression analysis produced a typical cross-over type of G × E interaction. In both groups the genotypes selected in poor conditions had a significantly lower slope and a lower coefficient of variation than the genotypes selected in good conditions (Table 6). There were no differences between the selection groups when the environmental means were near the cross-over point. This suggests that sites with intermediate levels of stress are unlikely to be useful for selection.

Therefore, experimental evidence is in full agreement with theory and indicates that the choice of selection environments affects both the performance of genotypes in specific environments and the response of genotypes to changing environments.

Genotype by environment interaction of cross-over type
In general, when different genotypes of a given crop are evaluated in a sufficiently wide range of environments, a cross-over type of G × E interaction is very common (Fig. 3).

Examples of cross-over type of G × E interaction can be found in the literature in a range of crops and environments, and for various stresses: Breese (1969) in cocksfoot, Arboleda-Rivera & Compton (1974), Hildebrand (1984) and Loffler et al. (1986) in maize, Simmonds (1984) in sugarcane, Lawn (1988) in chickpea, Ceccarelli (1989) in barley, Virk & Mangat (1991) in pearl millet, and Shannon & Francois (1978) in muskmelon in relation to salt tolerance. This indicates that, as a general phenomenon, genotypes selected under optimum growing conditions do not perform well under poor growing conditions, and vice-versa. In the presence of a cross-over type of G × E interaction, the plant breeder faces a dilemma in selecting the right genotypes for every environment. Because of its implications on breeding for marginal conditions, the phenomenon deserves an in-depth discussion.

There are four points to make about Fig. 3. Firstly, is that the definition of 'stress' environments plays a key role in determining breeding strategies. If we define 'stress environments' as those with an average yield above the cross-over point, then line A is 'widely adapted' to all environments. However, if we define 'stress environments' as having an average yield below the cross-over point, the 'wide adaptation' of line A has a lower limit at the cross-over point.

The second point relates to the type of comparisons made in the regression analysis illustrated in Fig. 3. The regression of a typical line (A) selected in

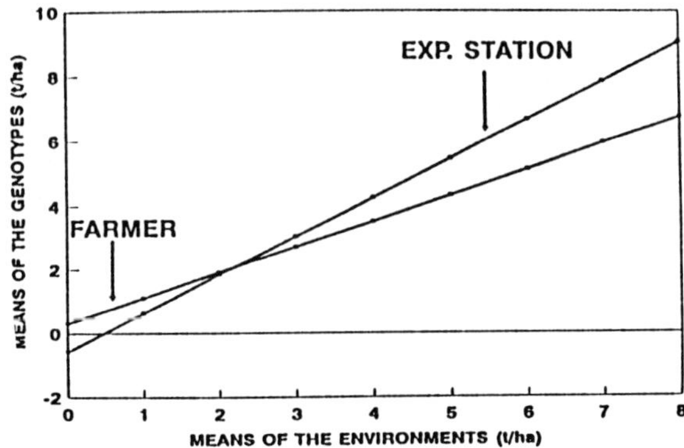

Fig. 4. Hypothetical G × E interaction of cross-over type between experiment stations and farmers fields.

optimum environments is often compared either with the average of all the lines in the experiment (it is unclear what this comparison means), or against a local check. Very seldom is line A compared with lines selected in stress environments below the cross-over point (such as line B). This is because it is assumed that high yielding environments allow the greatest expression of yield potential. One must ask why we need yield potential when we breed for environments such as those illustrated in Fig. 2, where the frequency of years with yield levels above 3 t/ha is less than 5% (or 1 in 20).

The third point is that the presence of a cross-over G × E interaction has often been neglected by either testing breeding material developed for favorable environments in foreign countries or by conducting selection and testing only above the cross-over point, and particularly in well managed experiment stations. Figure 4 shows that conditions in which selection is conducted in experiment stations could be above the hypothetical cross-over point in relation to the conditions in farmers' fields. When testing is conducted in many locations and selection is made for high average yield across locations, this is equivalent to selection for high regression coefficients (Simmonds, 1991). Even shuttle breeding can miss the presence of a cross-over G × E interaction if both environments are above the cross-over point. As the yields of many poor farmers are below the cross-over point, the chances of their being supplied with improved, stable germplasm is low.

The fourth point is that the existence of a cross-over G × E interaction has been allegedly disproved by the release of varieties for low yielding environments. This argument neglects the fact that many of these varieties have never been adopted by farmers or have been adopted in a different environment.

Hildebrand (1990) and Stroup et al. (1993) have presented similar concepts by discussing negative and positive interpretation of G × E interaction. The negative interpretation of G × E interaction implies that, in the presence of cultivars with the same overall mean yield and the same deviations from regression, the cultivar with b ≈ 1 is selected because it is more widely adapted according to Finlay & Wilkinson (1963). The cultivars with b > 1 are discarded because they perform poorly in poor environments, and cultivars with b < 1 are discarded because they are unable to exploit high-yielding environments. In practice, since most of the selection work is traditionally conducted either in favorable environments or under the well managed conditions of experiment stations (Simmonds & Talbot, 1992), cultivars with b ≥ 1 are frequently selected on the assumption that their high yield potential will have a carry-over effect in marginal environments. The positive interpretation recognizes the importance of specific adaptation and leads to the selection of cultivars with b > 1 for good environments and of cultivars with b < 1 for poor environments.

Heritability in low yielding environments

The most common justification for conducting selection in optimum environments, regardless of the nature of the target environment, is the lower heritability found in low yielding environments. The theory of correlated responses to selection shows that not only heritability, but also the genetic correlation coefficient has to be considered before deciding which is the optimum environment for selection. However, even if we want to consider heritability alone, the experimental evidence that heritability in low yielding conditions is lower than in high yielding conditions is far from unanimous (Table 7). Of particular interest are the data of Pederson & Rathjen (1981) (Table 8), which suggest a high degree of independence between yield levels and magnitude of heritability (r = - 0.034). Our experience with barley (Singh & Ceccarelli, in press) also suggests no relationship between yield level and magnitude of heritability. Therefore the conclusion that heritability in low yielding environments is lower than in high yielding environments is not supported by experimental evidence.

The magnitude of heritability is affected by the type of genetic material. We suspect that the genetic material used in those studies where heritability in low yielding environments was lower than in high yielding environments was selected in high yielding environments and then tested in low yielding environments. If G × E interaction of cross-over type exists, it implies a low average adaptation of this material to low yielding conditions, hence low heritability.

Table 7. Heritability estimates of grain yield at low- and high yield levels in different crops

Crop	High	Low	Reference
Cocksfoot	0.89	0.50	Breese, 1969
Maize	0.52	0.71	Selmani & Wassom, 1993
Wheat	0.78	0.32	Allen et al., 1978
Soybeans	0.56	0.31	Allen et al., 1978
Barley	0.47	0.54	Allen et al., 1978
Oats	0.56	0.63	Allen et al., 1978
Flax	0.44	0.56	Allen et al. 1978
Barley	0.65	0.66	Weltzien & Fischbeck, 1990
Oats	0.38	0.52	Johnson & Frey, 1967
Oats	0.67	0.32	Atlin & Frey, 1990
Wheat	0.89	0.74	Pfeiffer, 1988
Wheat	0.25	0.03	Roy & Murty, 1970
Wheat	0.33	0.68	Pederson & Rathjen, 1981
Barley	0.47	0.68	Singh & Ceccarelli, in press
Oats	0.45	0.32	Frey, 1964

Table 8. Heritability estimates in wheat. The data are the more extreme values from a set of 31 trials conducted in 9 locations over 5 years (modified from: Pederson & Rathjen, 1981)

Grain yield (t/ha)	Heritability
4.96	0.38
3.67	0.41
3.20	0.00
1.04	0.64
0.68	0.41
0.59	0.00
0.58	0.43

Wide adaptation

Many national and international breeding programs consider wide adaptation as a primary objective of a breeding program. Most of the evidence on wide adaptation comes from wheat and rice breeding where the use of dwarfing

Table 9. Grain yield of six wheat varieties under two irrigation regimes in Cd. Obregon, Sonora, 1982 (Rajaram et al., 1984)

Variety	Grain yield	
	5 irrigations (well-watered)	2 irrigation (stress)
Genaro 81	7461	4745
Lira 'S'	6920	4747
Veery 'S'	6819	4378
Neelkant 'S'	6758	4585
Junco 'S'	6346	4681
Tanager 'S'	5202	3637

and photoperiod-insensitivity genes allowed the spread of the same genotype over a wide geographical area. The hypothesis underlying wide adaptation is that high yield potential is an advantage even in marginal conditions when adaptation barriers such as photoperiod sensitivity are removed.

An example of wide adaptation is shown in Table 9 (Rajaram et al., 1984). The comparison of advanced bread wheat lines tested under well-watered (5 irrigations) and stress (2 irrigations) conditions shows that 'there are lines, such as Genaro 81 and Lira 'S' suitable for both regimes', and therefore widely adapted. The stress environment in this example is an environment with average yield of about 4.5 t/ha, and therefore these data agree with Fig. 3. The adaptation of these lines is wide only in an environmental range above 4.5 t/ha.

Another example of widely adapted genotypes illustrates one of the points made earlier (pg. 13). Based on the data of Fig. 5 (Osmanzai et al., 1987) Veery 'S' is classified as an input-efficient, input-responsive cultivar, with high yield potential and superior yield performance over the entire range of environments, including moisture stress conditions. What the data 'actually' show is only that the performance of Veery 'S' is better than the mean of all genotypes. The critical comparisons with the top yielding cultivars in moisture stress environments and with the top yielding cultivars in high yielding environments are in fact missing. The importance of these comparisons is shown in Table 10. Within two groups of breeding lines we selected with the same selection pressure lines specifically adapted to low- or high-yielding conditions (top lines in LYE or HYE) as well as those performing well in both (widely adapted). The widely adapted lines yielded more than the best check in very contrasting environments. However, they have a yield disadvantage

116

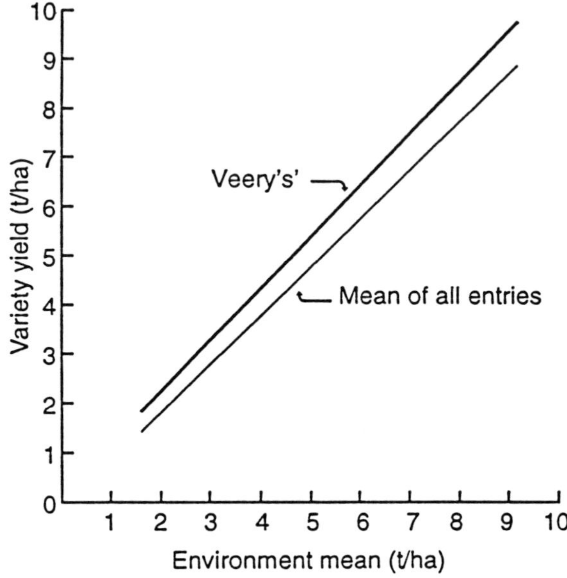

Fig. 5. Grain yield of Veery S regressed over the mean yields of 72 locations (from Osmanzai et al., 1987).

of 10–30% when compared with lines selected for specific adaptation. This yield disadvantage is the cost of wide adaptation.

These examples, as well as those presented earlier, suggest that most of the controversy on wide versus specific adaptation and related breeding strategies is due to definitions of stress environments which are often very different.

The widespread adoption of high yielding wheat and rice varieties in many different countries has been taken as a demonstration of wide adaptation. An analysis of the environments where 'widely adapted' cultivars have been successfully adopted shows that all the environments are either similar, or are made similar by the use of irrigation and/or fertilizer. Therefore, the term 'wide adaptation' has been used in a geographical, rather than in an environmental sense. In fact the adoption of 'widely' adapted cultivars in marginal environments has been negligible (Byerlee & Husain, 1993). While the advantages of wide adaptation over time are obvious, it is less clear why breeders have been fascinated by the possibility of finding cultivars widely adapted over space, i.e. cultivars which are superior in very different environments.

Farmers are basically interested in a constantly superior performance of a cultivar on their own farm and it is not sure that a farmer will understand why a cultivar which performs very well in the environment in which he

Table 10. Grain yield (kg/ha) of barley lines selected from two different groups of breeding lines for performance across environments (widely adapted) and for performance in specific environments (top lines in LYE or HYE)

Material	No.	YS	YH
First group			
Widely adapted	5	908 (- 28.2%)	5811 (- 9.6%)
Top lines in LYE	5	1265	4410
Top lines in HYE	5	574	6430
Best check		678	5544
Second group			
Widely adapted	4	945 (- 12.4%)	6025 (- 11.2%)
Top lines in LYE	4	1079	4013
Top lines in HYE	4	449	6783
Best check		887	5587

LYE = low yielding environments;
YS = Yield in low yielding environments;
HYE = high yielding environments;
YH = Yield in high yielding environments.

is farming is not made available because it does not perform well under conditions which never or seldom occur on his farm. Therefore, farmers are indifferent to spatially widely adapted cultivars but rather are interested in cultivars specifically adapted to their conditions, needs and uses, and which have a high degree of stability over time. Even assuming that breeding for truly wide adaptation is possible, it will result in few cultivars being grown throughout very large areas. It is now recognized that this is potentially a very dangerous philosophy in relation to resistance to pests and diseases. Man is already depending for his food supplies on too few species. Reducing the number of genes within a species can only increase the vulnerability of our crops and jeopardize food supplies. It has been documented that the release of a few successful new cultivars over large areas has led to the displacement of many old cultivars, many of which may possess useful genes for future needs. Wide adaptation therefore is not a healthy, or sustainable, solution to the long-term problem of maintaining genetic diversity.

118

Specific adaptation: A lesson from landraces

A feature of plant breeding in developed countries and for favorable environments has been the narrowing of the genetic base accompanied by a trend towards homogeneity: one clone, one pure line, one hybrid (Simmonds, 1983). Although genetic uniformity is now being questioned in developed countries (Wolfe, 1991), it is still very popular in breeding programs and seed production systems of developing countries at both the national and international level. This is in contrast with one of the characteristics of agriculture in marginal environments: the genetic diversity either in the form of mixed cropping or in the form of genetically heterogenous cultivars, or both. Genetically heterogeneous landraces (also called farmers' varieties, old cultivars or 'primitive cultivars') are still the backbone of agricultural systems in many developing countries, mainly in marginal environments. In these environments the replacement of landraces by modern, genetically uniform varieties bred for favorable environments has proved to be a difficult task at the levels of inputs farmers can afford. Not only will germplasm such as landraces play an important role in the success of a breeding program for marginal environments, but its study may teach the breeder an important lesson about adaptation strategies to marginal environments.

Landraces are typically mixtures of different genotypes. In self-pollinated crops they are mixtures of (probably) a high number of homozygote genotypes (Brown, 1978, 1979; Grando & McGee, 1990). Therefore landraces contain a large amount of genetic variation within an adapted genetic background. In the case of self-pollinated crops, this genetic variation is readily usable. Selection within landraces is one of the easiest, oldest and cheapest methods of plant breeding, but often scientists in developing countries are discouraged from using their locally adapted germplasm on the basis of its low yield potential and susceptibility to diseases.

Landraces played two important roles in barley breeding for marginal environments at ICARDA. First, they have shown a breeding avenue based on the combination of the appropriate selection environment with the exploitation of the specific adaptation of landraces and their genetic variability. Second, they have contributed to a better understanding of adaptation to marginal conditions.

Selection environment and use of landraces

A large collection of barley landraces was made in 1981 in Syria and Jordan (Weltzien, 1988) by visiting 70 farmers' fields and collecting 100 individual heads in each field. A preliminary evaluation of the progenies of individual heads (pure lines) revealed variation both between and within collection

Table 11. Number and frequency of lines outyielding the best check in marginal conditions obtained with two contrasting breeding strategies, namely selection in marginal conditions with adapted germplasm and selection in favorable conditions with improved (= non-landraces) germplasm (Ceccarelli & Grando, 1991b)

Breeding strategy	Total number of lines tested	Number (N) and frequency (%) of entries outyielding the best check	
		N	%
Selection in marginal conditions and use of adapted germplasm	1742	33	1.89
Selection in favorable conditions and use of improved germplasm	4510	3	0.07

sites for many plant characters of agronomic importance (Ceccarelli et al., 1987) and for disease reaction (van Leur et al., 1989). Because of the large number of pure lines, only 600 to 700 new lines are evaluated each year in the routine yield testing together with lines derived from the crossing program and unrelated to landraces. The sites used for yield testing range from marginal (average yields of about 0.5–1.0 t/ha) to favorable (average yields of about 4.5–6.0 t/ha). In 1991 we analyzed the data of three yield testing cycles (1986–1988, 1987–1989 and 1989–1990) in which a total of 6252 lines (1742 landraces and 4510 non-landraces) were yield tested. We found only 36 lines (0.6%) outyielding consistently the local landrace in marginal environments. Of those, 33 were pure lines extracted from landraces which were identified in our driest experiment site (Bouider) and 3 were non-landraces identified at our highest yielding site. A breeding strategy for marginal environments which combines direct selection under farmers' conditions (specific adaptation) and use of locally adapted germplasm is therefore 28 times more efficient than a strategy based on selection in high yielding conditions and using non-landraces material (Table 11).

Selection of pure lines from landraces conducted in marginal conditions and at low levels of inputs is a promising avenue. Figure 6 shows the performance of three pure lines (Arta, Tadmor and Zambaka) selected from Syrian

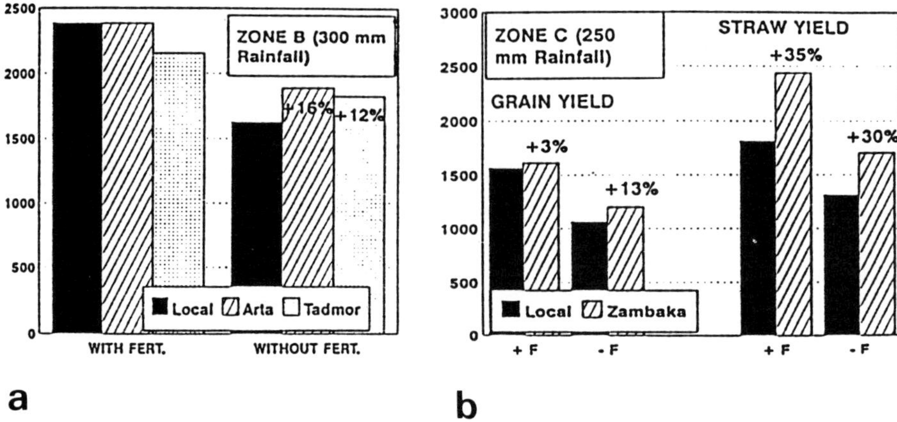

Fig. 6. Yield advantage of three pure lines selected from barley landraces, Arta, Tadmor (6a) and Zambaka (6b), in environments with 300 and 250 mm average annual rainfall, respectively. Values are means of 12 (6a) and 8 (6b) locations, plot size is 1 ha.

landraces and tested in farmers' fields (plot size of 1 ha) in two rainfall zones of Syria: zone B and zone C with long term average rainfall of 300 and 250 mm, respectively. Through this strategy yield increases of 12–16% are possible in these difficult conditions even without fertilizer. Although successful, we wonder whether this is a sound strategy in the long-term. Pure line selection within landraces is only a short-term strategy used to prove that this type of germplasm has an important role to play in breeding for marginal conditions. In the longer term, the best pure lines are used in crosses either with other pure lines from landraces or with non-landrace material, or as mixtures of pure lines, which are a sort of 'improved landraces'. The latter is likely to be the best long-term avenue to cope with the unpredictable variability of abiotic stresses. Only limited data are available on performance and stability of mixtures (Grando & McGee, 1990) and it is premature to draw conclusions.

Pure lines or mixtures?

Landraces are very well adapted to marginal conditions (both climatically and agronomically). The understanding of the basis of the adaptation of landraces was therefore important in a breeding program aiming to increase barley yield and stability in marginal conditions. We evaluated a number of morphological and developmental traits in landrace and non-landrace material hoping to find a relatively simple explanation to the superiority of the landraces under farmers' conditions in marginal environments. The choice of the traits was

Table 12. Means of morphological, developmental and agronomic traits in 1041 modern (unrelated to Syrian landraces) barley genotypes compared with 322 pure lines extracted from Syrian landraces[a]

Traits	Non-landraces n = 1041	Landraces (n = 322)
Early growth vigor (1 = good; 5 = poor)	2.5 b	3.2 a
Growth habit (1 = erect; 5 = prostrate)	2.8 b	4.0 a
Cold tolerance (1 = toler.; 5 = susc.)	3.0 a	1.3 b
Days to heading (from emergence)	117.9 b	121.2 a
Grain filling duration (days)	39.3 a	35.5 b
Yield potential (kg/ha)	4398.0 a	3293.0 b
Yield under stress (kg/ha)	483.1 b	984.0 a

[a] Means followed by the same letter are not significantly ($P < 0.05$) different based on t-test for samples of unequal size.

limited to those that are easy, cheap and quick to measure, as these are essential requisites for use in a breeding program. The results were discouraging (Table 12). Landraces differ from non-landraces in a number of traits which together appear to form an adaptive complex. Moreover, these traits are not present in just one combination within landraces, but they are present in different combinations in different individuals. When we classified 322 lines derived from Syrian landraces in 9 classes according to all possible combinations of three scores for early growth vigor (< 2.5 = good, 2.5–3.5 = intermediate, and > 3.5 = poor) and three scores for growth habit (< 2.5 = erect, 2.5–3.5 = intermediate, and > 3.5 = prostrate) we found the combinations shown in Table 13. Genotypes with different combinations of traits are likely to have a specific advantage in specific combinations of the abiotic stresses occurring in a continental-mediterranean environment.

If the genetic structure of landraces is considered as an evolutionary approach to survival and performance under arid and semi-arid conditions (Schulze, 1988), then it appears that during millennia of cultivation under

Table 13. Frequency of different combinations of early growth vigor (GV), and growth habit (GH), and mean values of cold tolerance (CT), days to heading (DH), and length of the grain filling period (GF) in a sample of 322 lines of barley landraces collected in the dry areas of Syria

Groups		%	GV	CH	CT	DH	GF
Good vigor	Erect	0.0	–	–	–	–	–
"	Semiprostrate	1.2	2.2	3.3	1.6	118.8	37.4
"	Prostrate	5.3	2.4	3.9	1.4	119.8	36.6
Interm. vigor	Erect	0.0	–	–	–	–	–
"	Semiprostrate	6.2	2.9	3.4	1.5	119.7	35.8
"	Prostrate	65.1	3.1	4.0	1.4	121.2	35.4
Poor vigor	Erect	0.0	–	–	–	–	–
"	Semiprostrate	0.0	–	–	–	–	–
"	Prostrate	22.1	3.9	4.2	1.3	121.9	35.4
L.S.D.$_{0.05}$			0.2	0.1	0.1	0.6	0.7

adverse conditions, natural and artificial selection have not been able to identify either an individual genotype possessing 'a trait' associated with its superior performance, or an individual genotype with a specific architecture of different traits. On the contrary, the combined effects of natural and artificial selection has led to an architecture of genotypes representing different combinations of traits. In marginal environments a population with such an architecture of genotypes is probably the best solution to long-term stability (Ceccarelli et al., 1991).

Conclusions

Breeding for marginal environments has traditionally consisted of either testing germplasm developed for other environments, or selecting under favorable conditions. This is based on the assumption that it is not possible to detect and use genetic differences at low yield levels and there is a carry-over effect of high yield potential in favorable environments. Very little breeding work for marginal environments includes selection of parents and segregating populations in environments climatically and agronomically similar to farmers' conditions.

Training scientists from developing countries, where improving agricultural production in marginal conditions is more urgent, has been based on breeding methods and philosophies used in favorable conditions. As a consequence of this training, in most developing countries experiment stations are concentrated in the most favorable environments. Those which are in marginal environments are managed according to 'recommended' agronomic practices and yields levels are much higher than in farmers' fields. Therefore, the success of the concept of wide adaptation has been based on this combination of breeding and training: varieties developed under favorable conditions in one country were tested and released by collaborators trained to test and select under equally favorable conditions in many other countries.

Both theory and experimental data show that this type of breeding has a low probability of success in marginal conditions because of G × E interactions. But, instead of recognizing that it is possible to make use of G × E interaction by breeding for specific adaptation, it has often been concluded that breeding for conditions below the cross-over point is not possible. Two solutions are usually recommended for these conditions. Firstly, when the same crop is grown both in favorable and marginal conditions, breeding efforts should concentrate on favorable conditions. At the country level, larger increases of national production can be obtained by increasing production in good environments through the joint effect of improved varieties and improved agronomic practices. However, such a strategy will neglect many poor farmers who could represent the majority of the farmers in the country. We believe it is possible to increase agricultural production at the country level and at the same time to serve small, resource-poor farmers by recognizing that the two types of environments need separate breeding programs, with different objectives, methodologies and type of germplasm.

Second, it is recommended that the introduction of inputs, such as fertilizer and irrigation, is an essential prerequisite for successful breeding work (Austin, 1989). However, breeding for an agronomically improved environment dictates the type of germplasm which will best exploit it and is based on genetic uniformity − the reverse of the biological diversity requisite for minimizing risk in most natural systems (Wilkes, 1989).

This paper shows that for a typical crop of marginal and unpredictable environments such as barley, it is possible to exploit genetic differences for specific adaptation to marginal environments under farmers' conditions and improve yield without additional inputs. Breeding for specific adaptation not only offers a solution on how to improve agricultural production in marginal environments, but can do so in a sustainable way both in relation to environmental impact and genetic diversity.

Breeding for sustainability has been defined as a process of fitting cultivars to an environment instead of altering the environment (by adding fertilizer, water, pesticides, etc.) to fit cultivars (Coffman & Smith, 1991). Also, it has been recognized that the key to increased production with fewer external

124

inputs, a condition which is more self-sustaining, less harmful to the environment, and yet productive enough to meet the increasing demand for food, will be through a reevaluation of the identification and use of selection and testing environments (Bramel-Cox et al., 1991). Most of our results have been obtained on farmers' fields, under rainfed conditions and without fertilizer or pesticides. Yet it has been possible to detect genetic differences which can be of immediate benefit to farmers at no additional cost.

Exploiting specific adaptation implies that the number of varieties (not necessarily homogeneous) of a given crop grown at any time will be large. The benefits of maintaining genetic diversity within a crop over large areas has been discussed extensively in the literature in relation to resistance to pests and diseases and does not need further justification. The major disadvantage of disseminating many varieties among farmers is seed production. However, the dissemination of specifically adapted varieties among resource-poor farmers does not have to follow the conventional release-seed production-seed certification schemes used in developed countries. Indeed, there are examples of successful dissemination of varieties through non-market methods (Grisley, 1993).

Eventually, if we extend the concept of G $\times$ E interaction to cover different levels of management within the same environment, the question is whether the yield levels attainable with environmentally friendly levels of inputs are above or below the cross-over point. It is obvious from our previous discussion of the cross-over type of G $\times$ E interaction that if these levels are below the cross-over point, the optimum compromise between productivity and sustainable use of inputs cannot be achieved by the use of cultivars specifically bred for high-input agriculture.

Acknowledgements

Part of this work has been supported by the Government of Italy and OPEC Fund for International Development. The author thanks Dr. S. Grando for critically reviewing the paper and Mr. B. Wedeman for editing the manuscript.

References

Allen, F.L., R.E. Comstock & D.C. Rasmusson, 1978. Optimal Environments for Yield Testing. Crop Science 18: 747–751.

Arboleda-Rivera, F. & W.A. Compton, 1974. Differential response of Maize (*Zea mays* L.) to Mass Selection in Diverse Selection Environments. Theoretical and Applied Genetics 44: 77–81.

Atlin, G.N. & K.J. Frey, 1989. Predicting the relative effectiveness of direct versus indirect selection for oat yield in three types of stress environments. Euphytica 44: 137–142.

Atlin, G.N. & K.J. Frey, 1990. Selecting oat lines for yield in low-productivity environments. Crop Science 30: 556–561.

Austin, R.B., 1989. Maximizing crop production in water limited environments. In: F.W.G. Baker (Ed.) Drought resistance in cereals, pp. 13–25. ICSU Press by CAB International.

Austin, R.B., M.A. Ford & C.L. Morgan, 1989. Genetic improvement in the yield of winter wheat, a further evaluation. J. Agric. Sci., Camb. 112: 295–301.

Blum, A., 1988. Plant breeding for stress environments. CRC Press, Boca Raton, Florida.

Boyer, J.S., 1982. Plant Productivity and Environment. Science 218: 443–448.

Bramel-Cox, P.J., T. Barker, F. Zavala-Garcia & J.D. Eastin, 1991. Selection and testing environments for improved performance under reduced-input conditions. In: D.A. Sleeper, T.C. Barker & P.J. Bramel-Cox (Eds) Plant breeding and sustainable agriculture, Considerations for Objectives and Methods, pp. 29–56. CSSA Special Publication no. 18.

Breese, E.L., 1969. The measurement and significance of genotype-environment interactions in grasses. Heredity 24: 27–44.

Brown, A.D.H., 1978. Isozymes, plant population genetic structure, and genetic conservation. Theor. Appl. Gen. 52: 145–157.

Brown, A.D.H., 1979. Enzyme polymorphism in plant populations. Theor. Pop. Biol. 15: 1–42.

Byerlee, D. & T. Husain, 1993. Agricultural Research Strategies for Favoured and Marginal Areas, The Experience of Farming System Research in Pakistan. Experimental Agriculture 29: 155–171.

Ceccarelli, S., 1984. Utilization of landraces and *H. spontaneum* in barley breeding for dry areas. Rachis 3 (2): 8–11.

Ceccarelli, S., 1989. Wide adaptation. How wide? Euphytica 40: 197–205.

Ceccarelli, S., S. Grando & J.A.G. van Leur, 1987. Genetic diversity in barley landraces from Syria and Jordan. Euphytica 36: 389–405.

Ceccarelli, S., E. Acevedo & S. Grando, 1991. Breeding for yield stability in unpredictable environments, single traits, interaction between traits, and architecture of genotypes. Euphytica 56: 169–185.

Ceccarelli, S. & S. Grando, 1991a. Selection environment and environmental sensitivity in barley. Euphytica 57: 157–167.

Ceccarelli, S. & S. Grando, 1991b. Environment of selection and type of germplasm in barley breeding for stress conditions. Euphytica 57: 207–219.

Ceccarelli, S., S. Grando & J. Hamblin, 1992. Relationships between barley grain yield measured in low and high yielding environments. Euphytica 64: 49–58.

Coffman, W.R. & M.E. Smith, 1991. Role of Public, Industry, and International Research Center Breeding Programs in Developing Germplasm for Sustainable Agriculture. In: D.A. Sleeper, T.C. Barker & P.J. Bramel-Cox (Eds) Plant breeding and sustainable agriculture, Considerations for Objectives and Methods, pp. 1–9. CSSA Special Publication no. 18.

Cox, T.S., J.P. Shroyer, B.H. Liu, R.G. Sears & T.J. Martin, 1988. Genetic improvement in agronomic traits of hard red winter wheat cultivars from 1919 to 1987. Crop Science 28: 756–760.

Crossa, J., B. Westcott & C. Gonzales, 1989. The yield stability of CIMMYT's maize germplasm. Euphytica 40: 245–251.

Falconer, D.S., 1981. Introduction to quantitative genetics. 2nd Ed. Longmann Group Ltd., London.

Falconer, D.S., 1990. Selection in different environments, effects on environmental sensitivity (reaction norm) and on mean performance. Genetic Research Cambridge 56: 57–70.

Finlay, K.W. & G.N. Wilkinson, 1963. The analysis of adaptation in a plant breeding programme. Aust. J. Agric. Res. 14: 742–754.

Francis, T.R. & L.W. Kannenberg, 1978. Yield stability studies in short-season maize. I. A descriptive method for grouping genotypes. Can. J. Plant Sci. 58: 1029–1034.

Frey, K.J., 1964. Adaptation Reaction of Oat Strains Selected Under Stress and Non-Stress Environmental Conditions. Crop Science 4: 55–58.

Grando, S. & R.J. McGee, 1990. Utilization of barley landraces in a breeding program. In: Biotic Stresses of Barley in Arid and Semi-Arid Environments. Montana State University Press.

126

Grisley, W., 1993. Seed for Bean Production in Sub-Saharan Africa, Issues, Problems, and Possible Solutions. Agricultural Systems 43: 19–33.

Hamblin, J., 1992. Can resource capture principles assist plant breeders or are they too theoretical? 52nd Nottingham Easter School (in press).

Hildebrand, P.E., 1984. Modified stability analysis of farmer managed, on-farm trials. Agron. J. 76: 271–274.

Hildebrand, P.E., 1990. Modified stability analysis and on-farm research to breed specific adaptability for ecological diversity. In: M.S. Kang (Ed.) Genotype-by-Environment Interaction and Plant Breeding, pp. 169–180. Dept. of Agron., Louisiana Agric. Expt. Stn., Baton Rouge, U.S.A.

Jinks, J.L. & V. Connolly, 1973. Selection for specific and general response to environmental differences. Heredity 30: 33–40.

Jinks, J.L. & V. Connolly, 1975. Determination of the environmental sensitivity of selection lines by the selection environment. Heredity 34: 401–406.

Jinks, J.L. & H.S. Pooni, 1982. Determination of the environmental sensitivity of selection lines of *Nicotiana rustica* by the selection environment. Heredity 49: 291–294.

Johnson, G.R. & K.J. Frey, 1967. Heritabilities of Quantitative Attributes of Oats (*Avena* sp.) at Varying Levels of Environmental Stress. Crop Science 7: 43–46.

Lawn, R.J., 1988. Breeding for improved plant performance in drought-prone environments. In: F.R. Bidinger & C. Johansen (Eds) Drought research priorities for the dryland tropics, pp. 213–219. ICRISAT, Patancheru, AP 502324, India.

Loffler, C.M., M.T. Salaberry & J.C. Maggio, 1986. Stability and Genetic Improvement of Maize Yield in Argentina. Euphytica 35: 449–458.

Osmanzai, M., S. Rajaram & E.B. Knapp, 1987. Breeding for moisture-stress areas. In: J.P. Srivastava, E. Porceddu, E. Acevedo & S. Varma (Eds) Drought Tolerance in Winter Cereals, pp. 151–161. John Wiley & Sons, New York.

Patel, J.D., E. Reinbergs, D.E. Mather, T.M. Choo & J.D. Sterling, 1987. Natural Selection in a Double-Haploid Mixture and a Composite Cross of Barley. Crop Science 27: 474–479.

Pederson, D.G. & A.J. Rathjen, 1981. Choosing trial sites to maximize selection response for grain yield in spring wheat. Aust. J. Agric. Res. 32: 411–424.

Pfeiffer, W.H., 1988. Drought Tolerance in Bread Wheat – Analysis of Yield Improvement over the Years in CIMMYT Germplasm. In: A.R. Klatt (Ed.) Wheat production constraints in tropical environments, pp. 274–284. CIMMYT, Mexico DF, Mexico.

Rajaram, S., B. Skovmand & B.C. Curtis, 1984. Philosophy and methodology of an international wheat breeding program. In: J.P. Gustafson (Ed.) Gene manipulation in plant improvement, pp. 33–60.

Rosielle, A.A. & J. Hamblin, 1981. Theoretical aspects of Selection for Yield in Stress and Non-Stress Environments. Crop Science 21: 943–946.

Roy, N.M. & B.R. Murty, 1970. A selection procedure in wheat for stress environments. Euphytica 19: 509–521.

Russel, W.A., 1984. Agronomic performance of maize cultivars representing different eras of breeding. Maydica 29: 375–390.

Schulze, E.D., 1988. Adaptation mechanisms of non cultivated arid-zone plants, useful lesson for agriculture? In: F.R. Bidinger & C. Johansen (Eds) Drought research priorities for the dryland tropics, pp. 159–177. ICRISAT, Patencheru, AP 502324, India.

Selmani, A. & C.E. Wassom, 1993. Daytime chlorophyll fluorescence measurement in field grown maize and its genetic variability under well-watered and water-stressed conditions. Field Crops Research 31: 173–184.

Shannon, M.C. & L.E. Francois, 1978. Salt Tolerance of Three Muskmelon Cultivars. J. Amer. Soc. Hort Sci. 103: 127–130.

Simmonds, N.W., 1981. Genotype (G), environment (E) and GE components of crop yields. Expl. Agric. 17: 355–362.

Simmonds, N.W., 1983. Plant Breeding, The state of the art. In: T. Kosuge, C.P. Meredith & A. Hollaender (Eds) Genetic engineering of plants. An Agricultural Perspective, pp. 5–25. Plenum Press, New York.

Simmonds, N.W., 1984. Decentralized selection. Sugar Cane 6: 8–10.

Simmonds, N.W., 1991. Selection for local adaptation in a plant breeding programme. Theor. Appl. Genet. 82: 363–367.

Simmonds, N.W. & M. Talbot, 1992. Analysis of on-farm rice yield data from India. Expl. Agric. 28: 325–329.

Singh, M. & S. Ceccarelli, 1994. Estimation of heritability using varietal trials data from incomplete blocks. Theoretical and Applied Genetics (in press).

Smith, M.E., W.R. Coffman & T.C. Barker, 1990. Environmental effects on selection under high and low input conditions. In: M.S. Kang (Ed.) Genotype-by-Environment interaction and plant Breeding, pp. 261–272. Dept. of Agron., Louisiana Agric. Expt. Stn., Baton Rouge, U.S.A.

Stroup, W.W., P.E. Hildebrand & C.A. Francis, 1993. Farmer participation for more effective research in sustainable agriculture. In: Technologies for sustainable agriculture in the tropics, Am. Soc. Agron. Spec. Publ. (in press).

Ud-Din, N., B.F. Carrer & A.C. Clutter, 1992. Genetic analysis and selection for wheat yield in drought-stressed and irrigated environments. Euphytica 62: 89–96.

Van Leur, J.A.G., S. Ceccarelli & S. Grando, 1989. Diversity for disease resistance in barley landraces from Syria and Jordan. Plant Breeding 103 (4): 324–335.

Virk, D.S. & B.K. Mangat, 1991. Detection of cross over genotype by environment interactions in pearl millet. Euphytica 52: 193–199.

Weltzien, E., 1988. Evaluation of barley (*Hordeum vulgare* L.) landraces populations originating from different growing regions in the Near East. Plant Breeding 101: 95–106.

Weltzien, E. & G. Fischbeck, 1990. Performance and Variability of Local Barley Landraces in Near-Eastern Environments. Plant Breeding 104: 58–67.

Wilkes, G., 1989. Germplasm preservation, objectives and needs. In: L. Knutson & A.K. Stoner (Eds) Biotic diversity and germplasm preservation, global imperatives, pp. 13–41. Kluwer Academic Publishers, the Netherlands.

Wolfe, M.S., 1991. Barley diseases: maintaining the value of our varieties. Barley Genetics VI: 1055–1067.

O.A. Rognli et al. (eds.), Breeding Fodder Crops for Marginal Conditions, 129–141.
© 1994 *Kluwer Academic Publishers. Printed in the Netherlands.*

Cooperative breeding for the northern marginal areas

ÁSLAUG HELGADÓTTIR & HÓLMGEIR BJÖRNSSON
The Agricultural Research Institute, Keldnaholt, 112 Reykjavík, Iceland

Summary. A joint breeding project for the northern areas of Scandinavia and Iceland was initiated in 1981 under the auspices of the Nordic Council of Ministers. Initially, efforts concentrated on cooperative trials in which both early and more advanced breeding material was tested at a number of experimental stations in the northern regions. This was followed by a joint breeding programme for timothy with the primary aim of developing varieties that possess broad adaptation to a range of Nordic climates and managements and can be grown throughout the northernmost part of Scandinavia. Each of the five national breeding stations originally provided 12 timothy genotypes for the project giving a total of 60 genotypes. The parental genotypes were compared as spaced plants at all five stations and their polycross progeny were grown under sward conditions at the same sites. On the basis of results obtained from these field trials parent clones have been selected and intercrossed to form synthetic populations.

Introduction

In northern marginal areas agriculture is mostly based on herbage production. However, the climate at northern latitudes places heavy demands on the fodder plants grown in this region and well adapted plants are crucial for a reliable herbage production. Winters are long and severe conditions for overwintering plants, such as hard frost, ice encasement and prolonged snow cover, often occur. Long photoperiods and relatively low temperatures characterize a rather short growing season (SNP, 1992). As both photoperiod and temperature are known to influence various growth processes, commercial grass varieties bred outside these areas are of limited value. Locally bred grass varieties are of primary importance and several valuable cultivars have resulted from national breeding activities over the years. However, the seed market is limited in these areas making breeding efforts at a national level relatively expensive. In the Scandinavian countries conditions for plant growth vary more within a country than between regions at comparable latitudes in the different countries. In order to stimulate cooperation of plant breeders across the borders the Nordic Council of Ministers established Internordic Plant Breeding (now merged with the Nordic Gene Bank). The purpose was to make the breeding process more efficient and economic in the region.

A joint breeding project for the northern areas, NORDGRASS, was initiated in 1981 with the aim of developing herbage varieties adapted to Northern Scandinavia (Manner, 1983). The geographic area for the breeding work was defined as Iceland and Greenland and the northern parts of Norway, Sweden and Finland. The following national institutions cooperate in the breeding

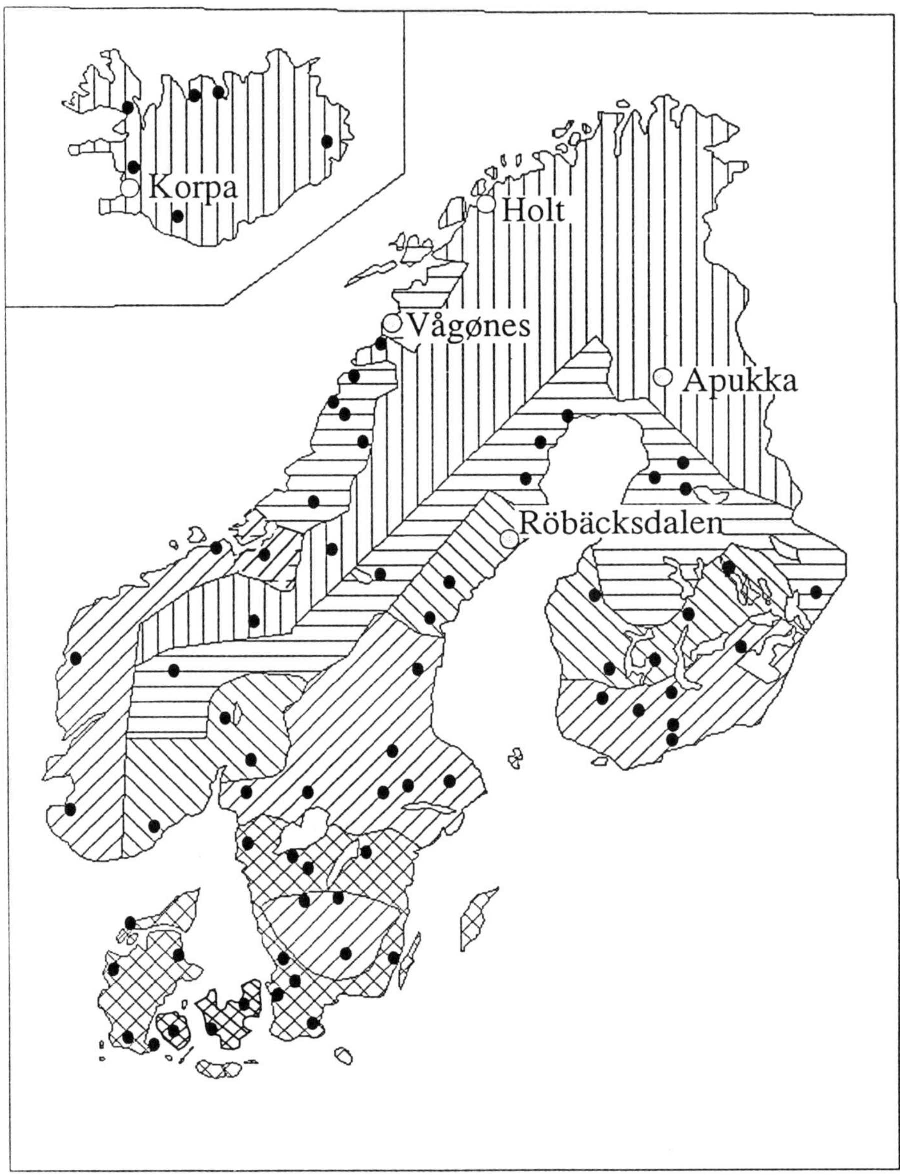

Fig. 1. Geographic location of experimental stations in the Norgrass project, and schematic agroclimatic zones developed for test sites of timothy in the Nordic countries (from Björnsson, 1993, with correction).

Table 1 Analysis of variance for total dry matter yields in variety trials with timothy (*Phleum pratense*), meadow grass (*Poa pratensis*), meadow fescue (*Festuca pratensis*) and red fescue (*Festuca rubra*), grown at various locations in northern Scandinavia and Iceland

	P. pratense		P. pratensis		F. pratensis		F. rubra		
	df	MS	df	MS	df	MS	df		MS
Location	5	394952***	6	265020***	6	149738***	9		854396***
Variety	8	896*	13	9381***	9	3259***	13		22176***
L × V	40	356	70	2072***	47	1052***	109		2930***
Error a	114	400	224	448	150	229	321		887
L × Y_1^1	6	66557***	7	234827***	7	32374***	10		96135***
V × Y_1	8	668	13	810	9	1451***	13		4958***
L × V × Y_1	40	415	70	1032***	47	427	109		1416*
Error b_1	129	383	243	429	169	264	347	1033	
L × Y_2^2	4	126808***	6	130976***	4	91360***	6		92778***
V × Y_2	8	278	13	2237**	9	816*	13		604
L × V × Y_2	24	359*	58	1082***	23	344	57		1112
Error b_2	93	207	204	393	98	224	207		601
Total	479		950		578		1214		

[1] Y_1 = linear contrast over years (Yr_1-Yr_3), with error b_1.

[2] Y_2 = quadratic contrast (Yr_1-2*(Yr_2)+Yr_3), with error b_2.

project: The Agricultural Research Centre, The Experimental Station for Lappland, Apukka, Finland (66°35′N); Svalöf Weibull AB, The Northern Branch, Röbäcksdalen, Sweden (63°49′N); The State Agricultural Research Stations, Vågønes (67°17′N) and Holt (69°39′N), Norway; The Agricultural Research Institute, Keldnaholt, Iceland (64°09′N); The Royal Veterinary & Agricultural University, The Experimental Station Høbakkegård, Denmark (55°44′N). Originally Denmark represented Greenland but later took on an active role of plant and seed multiplication. All the northern stations are located within the same or close-by agroclimatic zones developed for timothy, based on results of variety trials carried out at a national level in the Nordic countries (Fig. 1) (Björnsson, 1993). Climatic conditions at the test sites have been presented elsewhere (Dennis & Helgadóttir, 1988).

The Nordgrass project has comprised three main phases. Initially, efforts concentrated on cooperative trials in which both early and more advanced breeding material was tested at a number of experimental stations in the northern regions. In this way it was possible to study the response of different species to the environmental conditions at the various locations. This was followed by a joint breeding programme for timothy with the primary aim of developing varieties that possess broad adaptation to a range of Nordic climates and managements and can be grown throughout the northernmost part of Scandinavia. A genecological study, a by-product of the timothy breeding project, is currently being undertaken which aims at investigating the effects of different climates, managements and seed production conditions on the genetic structure, adaptability and stability of northern timothy genotypes. Finally, a new project for breeding forage legumes was initiated 1992. The aim is to increase the use of forage legumes in the northern areas by developing adapted varieties as the present commercial varieties lack sufficient winter hardiness. The present paper will primarily deal with the second phase of the Nordgrass project.

Variety testing in different environments

Joint variety trials including varieties, local populations and advanced breeding materials began in 1982. The aim was to coordinate variety testing and identify varieties with wide adaptation. A total of 71 populations of timothy (*Phleum pratense*), smooth meadow grass (*Poa pratensis*), meadow fescue (*Festuca pratensis*), red fescue (*Festuca rubra*) and red clover (*Trifolium pratense*) have been compared at various test sites in the northern areas. These trials were the first to simultaneously compare locally adapted varieties at comparable latitudes in Finland, Iceland, Norway and Sweden. They gave valuable results for dry matter production, yield stability, persistence and quality, and formed the basis for further selection (Helgadóttir, 1989a, 1989b). A new set of variety trials within the project has now been started.

The results for timothy show that there were differences in yield between northern varieties and no interactions between varieties and test environment were detected (Table 1). However, when the results were reanalysed, assuming that the experimental sites belonged to three different agroclimatic zones (Fig. 1), interactions were found between varieties and zones (Björnsson, 1993). This implies that, as the varieties were all adapted, they may have to show wider adaptability than the original analysis would suggest when grown over the whole region. For smooth meadow grass, meadow fescue and red fescue various G × E interactions were detected (Table 1) indicating that different varieties have to be grown in different areas.

The timothy breeding project

Timothy is the most valuable fodder species in the northern areas (Simonsen, 1985). The stability and high degree of adaptation of the timothy varieties

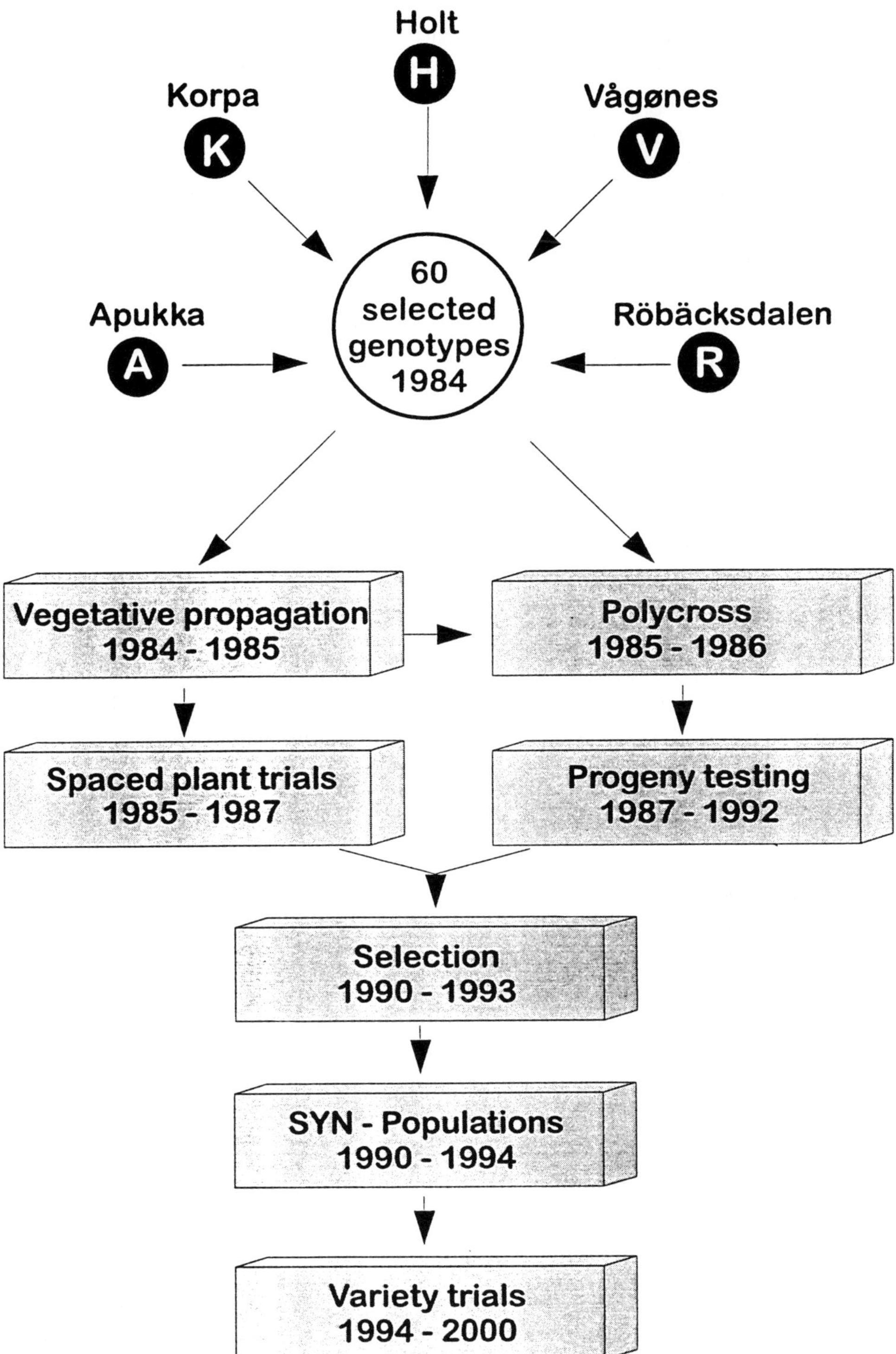

Fig. 2. Schematic presentation of the joint breeding programme for timothy.

found in the variety trials encouraged the initiation of a joint breeding programme designed to develop varieties that can be grown throughout northern Scandinavia using pooled germ plasm from these areas. Breeding methods have followed traditional lines and are outlined in Fig. 2. Each of the five national breeding stations originally provided 12 timothy genotypes for the project giving a total of 60 genotypes. The parental genotypes were compared as spaced plants at all five stations (Helgadóttir & Kristjánsdóttir, 1991) and their polycross progeny were grown under sward conditions at the same sites (Helgadóttir et al., 1993). On the basis of results obtained from these field trials parent clones have been selected and intercrossed to form synthetic populations. After comparable testing of the synthetic populations new varieties will hopefully emerge.

Experimental approach

For the spaced plant trials the 60 parental genotypes were arranged in a randomized block experiment with three replicates at each of the five sites. Five ramets of each genotype were arranged in a row, making up each plot. Three genotypes were in short supply bringing the total number of genotypes included in the analysis down to 57. The polycross of the 60 parental genotypes followed the layout of Olesen & Olesen (1973). The progeny testing trials consisted of 60 half-sib families and four reference varieties, Bottnia II and Saga from Sweden, Bodin from Norway and Adda from Iceland, making a total of 64 entries. The experimental design was an 8×8 lattice with four replicates at each site.

A number of characters were measured on the genotypes in the spaced plant trials in each of two years but only two will be presented here; impression score (0–9; 9 = max.) and total yield (sum of dry matter yield per plot harvested at the end of June and end of August). In the polycross progeny trials the plots were harvested twice a year for three years, at the time of heading of timothy in early July and at the end of August. Various other measurements were taken but in the present paper analyses of total dry matter yields (sum of first and second cut) will be presented. Winter kill did not affect any of the experiments and timothy was the dominant component in the harvest.

The spaced plant trials

Results from the spaced plant trials revealed that there were large differences between genotypes for most characters irrespective of origin, and the performance of the individual genotypes was highly dependent on the test site (Table 2). As the main purpose of the breeding project was to identify genotypes that are adapted and stable over the whole region, a general superiority

Table 2. Analysis of variance (MS) for total yield and impression 1986 of timothy genotypes grown as spaced plants at Apukka, Korpa, Holt, Vågønes and Röbäcksdalen

Source	df	Total yield	Impression
Location (L)	4	2095423***	98.5***
Origin (O)	4	94913	12.5
L × O	16	28762*	4.1*
O/Genotypes	53	85331***	11.1***
L × O/G	212	15164***	2.3***
Residual	561	4823	0.9

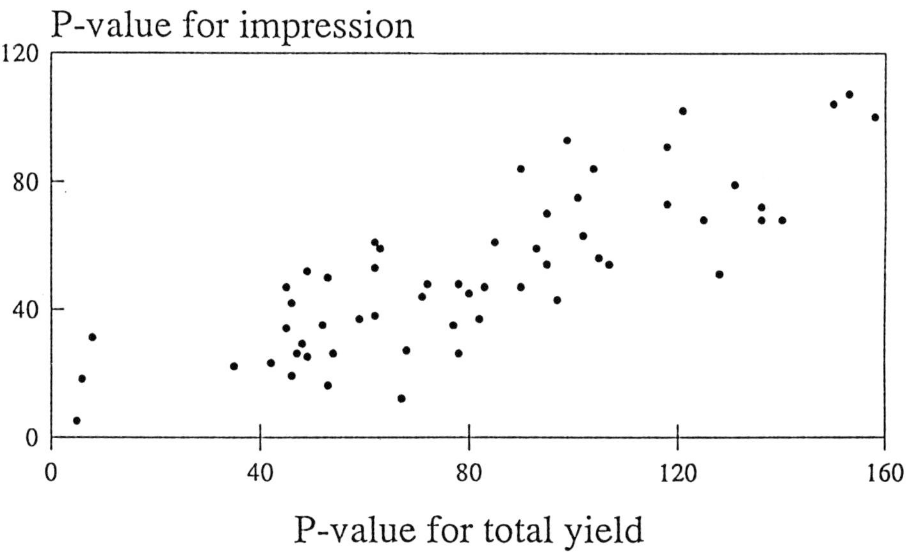

Fig. 3. P_i-values for total yield and impression of spaced plants in the joint timothy breeding project.

136

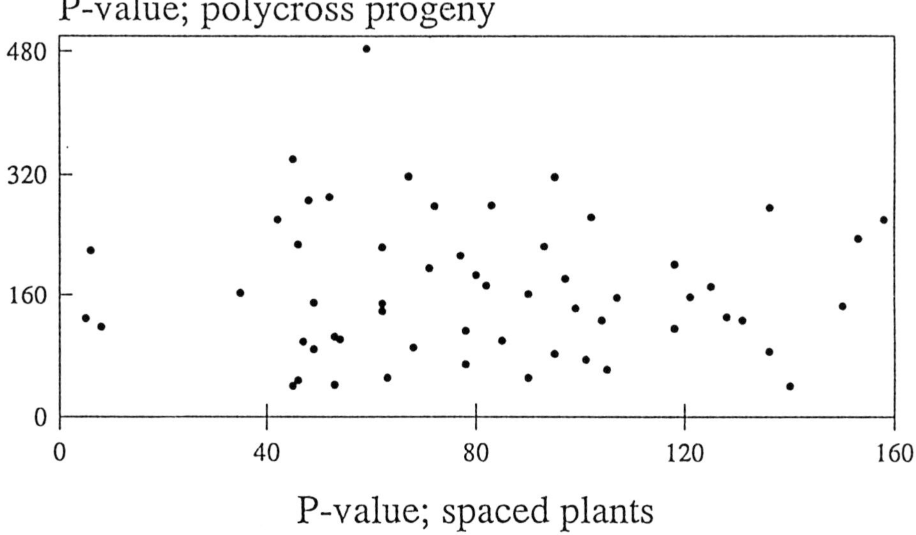

Fig. 4. Relationship between P_i-values for total yield of spaced plants and of their polycross progeny grown under sward conditions.

measure (P_i-value) proposed by Lin & Binns (1988) was used. The P_i-value is defined as the distance MS between the highest yielding genotype in each environment (year and site) and the test genotype. Hence, for genotype i the P_i-value was calculated as

$$P_i = \Sigma(Y_{ijk} - M_{jk})^2/2n, \tag{1}$$

where M_{jk} is the environmental maximum for site j and year k and Y_{ijk} is the genotype yield. A genotype that is high ranking in yield over all environments therefore has a low P_i-value. Eliminating the mean deviation of a genotype from the maximum a general measure of the G × E interaction due to the ith genotype was obtained as

$$GE_i = \Sigma((Y_{ijk} - Y_{i..}) - (M_{jk} - M_{...}))^2/2(n - 1). \tag{2}$$

A plot of P_i-values for total yield and impression (Fig. 3) shows that in ranking the genotypes impression did not entirely reflect differences in yield. With respect to the latter three genotypes were clearly superior having the lowest P_i-values, whereas P_i-values for impression identified a greater number of superior genotypes. The GE_i was generally low and non-significant for genotypes with low P_i-values.

The polycross progeny testing

In the series of experiments comparing the polycross progeny, the same families are expected to be top yielding at a test site in all years, provided that they are also stable for variable seasonal differences. However, differences between half-sib families were generally small and the top ranking families varied between the test environments, partly as a result of experimental error (Helgadóttir et al., 1994). In order to get a more stable evaluation of the families the superiority measure was modified such that the environmental maximum of Lin & Binns (1988), used for the results from the spaced plant trials, was replaced by a site index. This was obtained by selecting the 16 highest yielding families on average over years at each site. For each year the M in equations (1) and (2) was replaced by the mean of these 16 families.

The yield of the polycross progeny under sward conditions was regressed on the yield of the parental genotypes as spaced plants and no correlation was found. This is clearly demonstrated in Fig. 4 which shows the P_i-values for the two test conditions. Consequently, selection of genotypes is entirely based on results from the polycross progeny testing. A number of half-sib families gave yields superior to the reference varieties but the ranking of the families varied between test environments (Helgadóttir et al., 1994). Variance components derived from the three-way analysis of variance revealed that the three factor interaction entries $\times$ sites $\times$ years was dominant and the interaction of entries $\times$ sites was also important. This means that it is essential to base the selection of families on both mean performance and the variation attributable to the response of families to sites on one hand and years within sites on the other.

By ordinary analysis of variance methods the GE_i of equation (2) was thus further divided into a mean square for sites, S_i, with four degrees of freedom and a mean square for years within sites, SY_i, with 10 degrees of freedom. From the difference between the two a component for interaction with sites was calculated for each entry as

$$V_i = (S_i - SY_i)/3. \tag{3}$$

This component is a function of the differences in response of the entries to the environmental conditions prevailing at the various experimental sites and can be regarded as a measure of adaptability. Half-sib families with a low value for this component show general adaptability whereas high values may indicate special adaptability. The two factor interaction of entries $\times$ years was found to be zero in the analysis of variance (Helgadóttir et al., 1994). Hence, SY_i is composed of an experimental error plus the three factor interaction entries × years × sites. It estimates the variance of response of the families to unpredictable environmental variation and is regarded as a measure of stability.

In order to choose parental genotypes for the production of synthetic populations, a number of half-sib families were first selected which had low P_i-values and were thus consistently high yielding over all test environments (Fig. 5a). The GE_i value varied somewhat for the selected families and by studying the measure of adaptability and stability derived from the interaction in conjunction with the P_i-value the final nine half-sib families were identified that are both stable with respect to unpredictable environmental variation and that show general adaptability (Fig. 5b).

Discussion

In the spaced plant trials variation in yield between individual genotypes was large and their response was highly dependent on the test site. The performance of the half-sib families did, however, not correlate with the performance of the parental genotypes and only one genotype ranked among the top eight genotypes in the two sets of experiments. This result was not surprising as it has generally been difficult to predict the sward yield from the yield of spaced plants (e.g. Lazenby & Rogers, 1960; Opsahl, 1964). A more promising approach would be to define ideotypes possessing specific morphological characteristics associated with high yield (Jönsson et al., 1992).

In the present work the main aim was to obtain timothy varieties that are high yielding over the whole of northern Scandinavia and Iceland. Results from the polycross progeny testing revealed significant yield differences between half-sib families. The variation in yield was, however, rather restricted, the highest yielding family giving only 14% higher yield that the lowest yielding family. This may reflect the fact that timothy is not indigenous in northern areas. It has been introduced from more southerly regions and mostly originates from a few closely related varieties (Rognli, 1988).

The results from the polycross progeny trials also revealed the presence of interactions between half-sib families and both years and test sites, contrary to the results obtained in the variety trials with timothy (Table 1). As a large part of the variation was attributable to the three factor interaction between entries, sites and years it was of primary importance to elucidate these G × E interactions in order to meet the breeding objectives, i.e. to identify consistently high yielding genotypes stable across all test environments. The method adopted from Lin & Binns (1988a) and modified for the present work has proved successful to meet these aims. The calculations are relatively

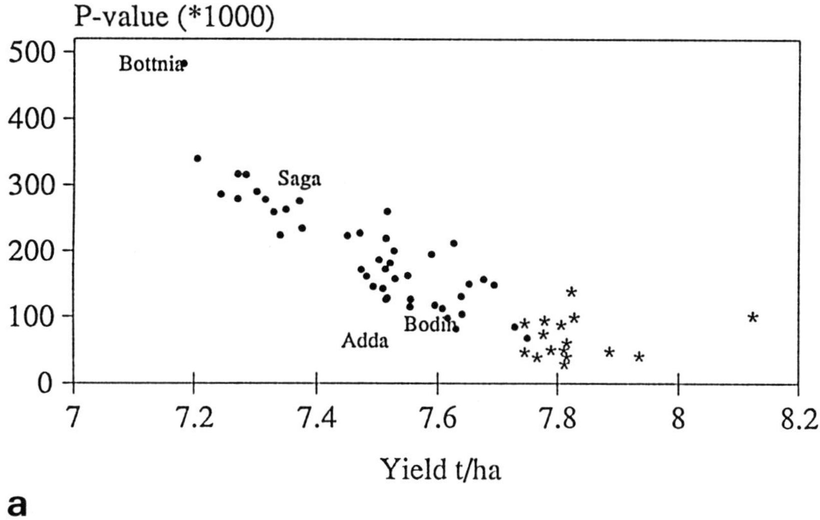

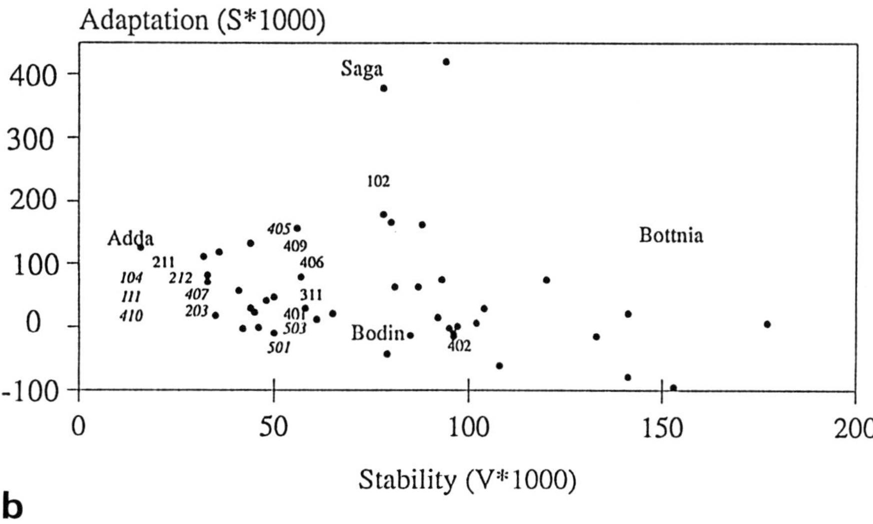

Fig. 5. Relationship between P_i-values and mean yield over years and test sites (a) and measures of adaptability (V_i) and stability (SY_i) (b), for 60 timothy half-sib families originating from Apukka (101–112), Korpa (201–212), Holt (301–312), Vågønes (401–412) and Röbäcksdalen (501–512) and four reference varieties in the polycross progeny testing. Preliminary selections are designated by asteriks (a) and numbers (b) and the final selections are shown in italics (b).

simple and can be displayed graphically. Firstly, one parameter, the P_i-value, is used to rank the families by comparing their performance at each test site and year with a site index. Secondly, high yielding families showing high values for interaction with the site index (G × E part of the P_i-value) are discarded. Thirdly, analysis of variance of the G × E value for each family was used to obtain a measure of adaptability, derived from the response of the families to predictable environmental conditions as represented by different sites, and a measure of stability, derived from the response to unpredictable irregularities in the environment as represented by random variation between years within sites. By this approach nine superior genotypes have been selected and are currently being used to produce synthetic populations.

Conclusions

Often the limiting factor in plant breeding is testing of breeding material under a wide range of environmental conditions. The experimental stations participating in the Nordgrass cooperative project cover a range of environments varying from continental to maritime and from 63° N to 69° N giving the opportunity to extensively test both advanced and early breeding material. This has been successfully carried out for variety trials in a number of important fodder species in these areas. More importantly, a joint breeding programme for timothy has been successful in identifying high yielding genotypes across the area and that are stable to random variations in the environment. The fruitful cooperation in the Nordgrass project has stimulated the initiation of new projects such as an investigation on the effects of different climates, managements and seed production conditions on the genetic structure, adaptability and stability of northern timothy genotypes, and breeding of herbage legumes for the northern areas.

Acknowledgements

The NORDGRASS project is a cooperative project funded by The Nordic Gene Bank. Members of the project group, B. Dennis (Denmark), P. Pärssinen & O. Nissinen (Finland), :Á. Helgadóttir & T. Tómasson (Iceland), A. Larsen & I. Schjelderup (Norway), E. Lindvall & A. Wiberg (Sweden), have been responsible for carrying out experiments at their local sites. T.A. Kristjánsdóttir assisted in the statistical analysis of the data.

References

Björnsson, H., 1993. Zones for performance testing of timothy (*Phleum pratense* L.) in the Nordic countries. Acta Agric. Scand. Sect. B, Soil and Plant Sci. 43: 97–113.

Dennis, B. & Á. Helgadóttir, 1988. Breeding herbage species for northern Scandinavia. In: Natural Variation and Breeding for Adaptation, pp. 169–177. Proceedings of the Eucarpia Fodder Crops Section Meeting, Lusignan, France.

Helgadóttir, Á., 1989a. Breeding herbage species for northern areas. 1. Variety trials with timothy (*Phleum pratense* L.). Acta Agric. Scand. 39: 243–254.

Helgadóttir, Á., 1989a. Breeding herbage species for northern areas. 2. Variety trials with smooth meadow grass (*Poa pratensis* L.). Acta Agric. Scand. 39: 255–268.

Helgadóttir, Á. & T.A. Kristjánsdóttir, 1991. Simple approach to the analysis of G × E interactions in a multilocational spaced plant trial with timothy. Euphytica 54: 65–73.

Helgadóttir, Á., H. Björnsson & T.A. Kristjánsdóttir, 1994. Analysis of a site × year experiment with timothy polycross progeny. Unpublished.

Jönsson, H.A., U. Kristiansson, C. Nilsson & J. Sjödin, 1992. Morphological characters in spaced plants associated with forage yield under sward conditions in timothy (*Phleum pratense* L.). Acta Agric. Scand. Sect. B, Soil and Plant Sci. 42: 18–25.

Lazenby, A. & H.H. Rogers, 1960. The evaluation of selection indices for yield in grass breeding. Proceedings of the 8th International Grassland Congress, Reading.

Lin, C.S. & M.R. Binns, 1988. A superiority measure of cultivar performance for cultivar × location data. Can. J. Plant Sci. 68: 193–198.

Manner, R., 1983. The co-operative Nordic project on grass breeding for northern areas. Symposium on Nordic Co-operation in the Field of Plant Breeding. Acta Agric. Scand. suppl. 23: 116–121.

Olesen, K. & O.J. Olesen, 1973. A polycross pattern formula. Euphytica 22: 500–502.

Opsahl, B., 1964. Contributions to the breeding methods of timothy. Meld. Norg. Landbr. Högsk. 43 (12): 1–86.

Rognli, O.A., 1988. Species aspects of breeding herbage varieties for northern marginal regions. J. Agric. Sci. Finl. 60: 181–189.

Simonsen, Ö., 1985. Herbage breeding in northern areas. In: A. Kaurin, O. Junttila & J. Nilsen (Eds) Plant Production in the North, pp. 277–295. Norwegian University Press, Oslo.

SNP, 1992. Agroklimatisk kartlegging av Norden. Grunnlang og framlegg til gjennomforing av soneinndeling. Samnordisk Planteforedling. Skrifter og rapporter nr. 5, 97 pp.

O.A. Rognli et al. (eds.), Breeding Fodder Crops for Marginal Conditions, 143–147.
© 1994 *Kluwer Academic Publishers. Printed in the Netherlands.*

Breeding of amenity grasses adapted to marginal conditions

ERNST LÜTKE ENTRUP
Deutsche Saatveredelung, Thüler Strasse 30, 33154 Salzkotten-Thüle, Germany

Introduction

In Germany and other European countries, breeding of amenity grasses with special characters is started in beginning of the 50s. With the increasing demands on amenity grasses, for ornamental lawns, grassland and green areas in parks as well as for sports turf and other pastures like roadside-turf and slopes under marginal conditions, became more and more important. Due to the knowledge and practice with grasses, the success is up to the forage plant breeders who adapted to this new breeding perspective during the past 40 years. For example in the Netherlands the breeding of lawn grasses have begun very early, using forage plant breeding as the basis. Seeds of unproved vaneties have been up to now an important export item. In Great Britain, lawngrass is an important factor for sports and leisure purposes. In Germany, the annual use of forage- and lawngrasses is of about 53,000 t. About 50% are for agricultural forage use with stagnating tendency, and the other 50% are for lawgrass use which depend on increasing or stagnating economic trend. In nearly all fields where lawngrasses are used, the latter are subjected to extreme conditions. Therefore, it is important and necessary, that selection is carried out under marginal conditions. Breeders of lawngrasses have to consider conditions, selection of the original material and trials required for the development of specific types of lawngrasses.

Choice of lawngrass species in a moderate European climate area

There are only a few species regarded as lawngrasses as shown below.

Selection of ecotypes on marginal sites

When selecting ecotypes for breeding lawngrasses it is important to choose sites where nature or the environment already has selected a permanent inter-vention with marginal conditions. These sites are described as follows:
  a) Old sports fields which have not been renewed and where plants could live, even after an extensive use by sportsmen. These fields must be sound and the plants must have anti-stress characters;

Table 1. Lawngrass species in the moderate climate area

Lolium perenne	*Festuca* ssp.	*Poa* ssp.	*Agrostis* ssp.
early	rubra rubra	pratensis	capillaris
medium	rubra commutata	supina	stolonifera
late	rubra trichophylla	alpina	canina
	ovina	annua	

b) Strongly frequented roadsides in recreation areas where the daily stress factor and man destroy a lot of plants;

c) In the highlands, long winters and long snow-periods are not only a recreation and winter-sleep period for species growing in an altitude of 500–600 m, but also a prepration period for resistance against a lot of diseases and weather conditions. This field is the ideal site for *Poa pratensis* and *Poa supina*, while *Poa alpina* is more often found in higher altitudes;

d) In coastal areas salt-tolerant festuca forms can be selected. On humid hills and highlands *Agrostis* species can be found. Other examples with eoctypes which are already pre-selected by nature though a 'selection-margin' can also be found.

Breeding is important for closely mown very fine ornamental lawns and on golf-greens

Closely mown lawngrasses have to cope with special problems. Due to a very low space of assimilation only those species which have a creeping or prostrate form of sprouts and leaves can be used. Low based leaves are preferable for a close mowing from 0,3 to 1,0 cm. On golf-greens, which consist of approx. 100% *Agrostis* sp., the lawn adapts itself to the daily cutting regimen. Ornamental lawn with longer cutting intervals may have height of approx. 1.0 cm with an *Agrostis/Festuca*-lawn. Close mowing of *Poa pratensis* is not always possible, but experiences at Bingley indicate, that the variety Limousine very well adapted to close mowing of 0,5 cm thus making this variety suitable as roll-lawn on golf-greens. Close mowing poses the disadvantage of a high susceptibility to fungus and immigration of *Poa annua*.

Table 2. Valuation of grass species by lawn conditions

Species	Cutting tolerance	Wear tolerance	Dryness tolerance	Shadow tolerance
Agrostis canina	9	3	1	1
Agrostis stolonifera	8	5	3	2
Agrostis capillara	8	4	4	3
Festuca ovina	4	3	6	3
Festuca rubra rubra	6	4	4	4
Festuca rubra commutata	7	5	5	4
Festuca rubra trichophylla	7	5	6	4
Lolium perenne	6	8	6	3
Lolium perenne	8	9	6	4
Poa pratensis	8	8	6	7
Poa supina	9	9	6	9
Poa annua	8	9	5	7

1 = no tolerance

9 = high tolerance

Breeding of high wear resistance mainly concerns the sports turf

On football fields, tennis grounds and golf-greens the grass species have to cope with high stress. Of the aforementioned species, varieties of *Lolium perenne* and *Poa pratensis* have shown the best results under these conditions. The first selection progress starts with the selection of the ecotypes. In an early stage of testing we try to get the best results by using wear machines in order to check the conditions. It appears that the wear as well as the cut resistance are of importance. In the area of the goal on the football field, on the kick-off of a golf-green, or on a tennis ground, barren areas due to insufficient tolerant varieties can be easily found. Hard tests of the test stations of the BSA or at Bingley show clearly the extreme points of the varieties. The best varieties are listed with a special mark in the variety list.

Dry and wet sites demand adapted species and varieties

The lawngrasses have to cope with extreme conditions: on poor and dry sites as well as on clay soils with wet conditions. The undemanding species *Festuca rubra* and *Festuca ovina* grow quite well and only extensively. If intensive grass maintenance is desired, these species are urf to prefere. Therefore, in dry periods you can find they bestone to look at lawn of *Poa pratensis* and *Lolium*

146

perenne. For the breeder it is important to look in dry areas for these species and to collect these preselected plants directly on the site. A very extreme site for lawngrasses are humid sites connected with shadow influence. In various trials *Poa supina* showed good results. *Poa supina* due to its shadow influence is a not-to-be-missed mixture partner.

Breeding of salt-tolerant species is required for varieties for roadsides, salt contaminated soils and erosion protection in coast areas

Salt tolerance on lawngrasses and the outside influence of dry salt on roadsides are of great importance. In coastal areas the lawngrasses are the most important building material to dyke strengthening and erosion protection. The roadsides along the motorways and the green middle stripes are exposed to the dry salt in the winter. For these purposes grasses, which have a salt tolerance, are therefore needed. Tests showed that species red fescue (*Festuca rubra trichophylla* – litoralis –) has a good salt tolerance. Perennial ryegrass (*Lolium perenne*) consists of forms which obtain a degree of salt tolerance. The breeder collects ecotypes in coastal areas, where the salty seawater has already carried out a preselection. These grasses have to pass a special salt test.

In permanent greenkeeping of ski-runs in wintersport areas soil and environmental protection should be considered

The increasing winter sports with expanded ski-areas and high stress on ski-runs become a big problem in alpin-regions due to the destruction of covering vegetation with terrible consequences. People are busy to regenerate the green areas in the snowfree summer months by resowing. The use of autochthon species is a goal to ensure the success of maintenance of the green cover. For this purpose we collect forms of *Poa alpina* and red fescue as ecotypes, selected in a way that we can produce a material which is also suitable for the seed production. Trials with the material selected and multiplied in other climatic areas show that these forms are very well suitable for the maintenance of ski-runs. The method of use of autochthon grasses with the reproduction in other areas and the repatriation to its original site have meanwhile become the standard practice,

Conclusions

This contribution should show, that especially the lawngrasses are used under various marginal conditions. For the breeder it is important to collect the ecotypes, i.e. the basis material, under the desired conditions which would then allow for the natural adaptability of these ecotypes.

References

Ellenberg, H., 1982. Vegetation Mitteleuropas und den Alpen 5. Auflage, Stuttgart.

Fischer, W. and Lütke Entrup, E., 1978. Die wichtigsten Gräser – Ihre Bedeutung für Landwirtschaft – Rasen – Landschaftsgestaltung. Druck Mensing, Hamburg, 2. Auflage (vergriffen).

Hape, F., 1983. Rasen (bearbeitet von H. Schulz). Verlag Eugen Ulmer, Stuttgart.

Klapp, E., 1937. Taschenbuch der Gräser. Verlag Paul Parey, Berlin, Hamburg.

Kley, G., 1984. Züchterische Entwicklung salzverträglicher Sorten für Saatgutmischungen zur Begrünung salzbelasteter Standorte (Deichvorland – Straßenbegleitgrün) Rasen/Turf/Gazon 4.

Köck, L., 1975. Pflanzenbestände von Skipisten in Beziehung zur Einsaat und Kontaktvegetation. Rasen/Turf/Gazon 6, 103–108.

Köster, P., 1984. Fertigrasen – die Problemlösung salzbelasteter Oberböden? Rasen/Turf/Gazon 4.

Lütke Entrup, E., 1986. Begrünung extremer Standorte aus Sicht der Saatgutmischungen. Rasen/Turf/Gazon 4.

O.A. Rognli et al. (eds.), Breeding Fodder Crops for Marginal Conditions, 149–158.
© 1994 Kluwer Academic Publishers. Printed in the Netherlands.

Breeding winter hardy grasses

ARILD LARSEN
*Norwegian State Agriculture Research Stations, Vagones Research Station, N-8010 BODO,
Norway*

Summary. Perennial grasses are vital for Norwegian agricultural production. The nature
and extent of winter damage on grasslands is highly dependent on climatic conditions, and
determines both persistency and yield. Physical stresses such as frost and ice encasement
predominate in coastal regions with an unstable winter climate, while biotic stresses such as
low temperature fungi are more common in the inland regions. Development of hardening
depends on plant adaptation and climatic conditions during autumn and winter. New winter-
hardy cultivars should be bred for wide adaptation to winter stresses. The genetic background
for the most important character, freezing tolerance, seems to be of polygenic nature with
mainly additive gene action. Selection for increased freezing tolerance has been effective over
generations in grasses, and in most grass species ample variation still exists to be exploited by
breeding. However, in some species like perennial ryegrass, modern biotechnological methods
should be used to improve freezing tolerance and winter hardiness.

Introduction

Perennial grasses are the basis for dairy and meat production in Norway. Good
winter survival and yield stability are therefore vital for animal production
and for agriculture economics. The goal for both breeding and cultivation
is an intact stand of plants in spring, ready for production as soon as the
growth conditions are favourable. Winter hardiness of plants is not a simple
character, rather a supercharacter composed of several components whose
impact will vary with the climatic conditions. This paper gives an overview
of factors to be considered when breeding winter hardy cultivars in Norway,
such as stresses causing winter damage, development of hardening in the field,
available laboratory tests, genetic aspects of winter hardiness, and breeding
strategies.

Winter conditions in Norway

Several surveys of Norwegian grasslands have given good information on the
nature of winter damage to meadow plants (Sterten, 1954; Andersen, 1960,
1963, 1966; Årsvoll, 1973, 1975). According to these, the main stresses caus-
ing winter damage can be classified as follows: Physical: Frost, ice encase-
ment, water-logging, desiccation, soil heaving. Physiological: Insufficient
climatic adaptation, poor plant condition in autumn, carbohydrate starvation.
Biotic: Low temperature fungi; *Microdochium nivale, Typhula incarnata, T.
ishikariensis, Myriosclerotinia borealis, Sclerotinia trifoliorum.*

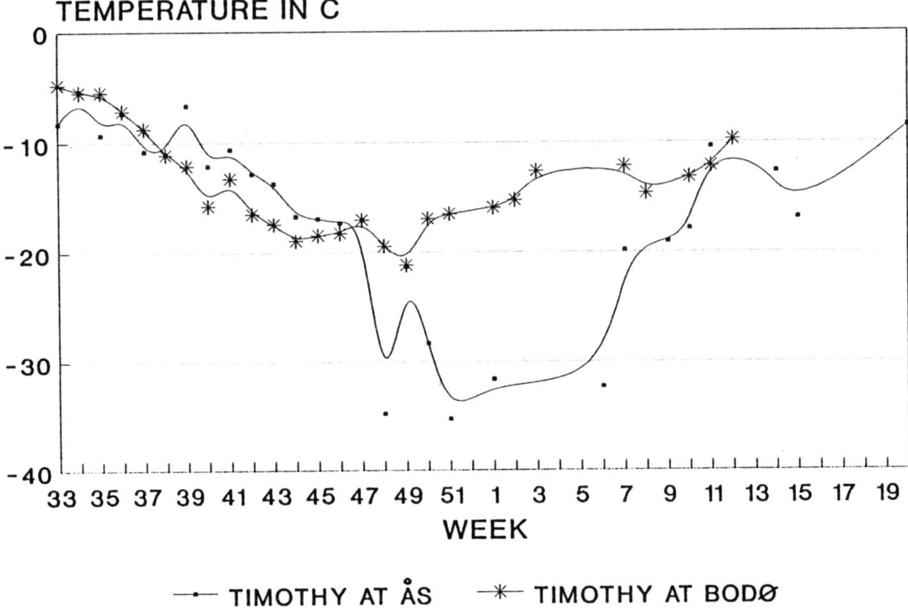

Fig. 1. Development of hardening during autumn and winter, measured as freezing tolerance (LT$_{50}$), in timothy (*Phleum pratense*) grown in the field at Ås, S.E. Norway, and Bodø, N. Norway. Mean values for the three cultivars 'Engmo', 'Grindstad' and 'S352'.

The most important physical stress is ice encasement. This dominates on level fields in the coastal regions of Norway where the winter climate is unstable. Frost damage is also important in these regions. In field studies frost damage may be underestimated since frost can cause yield reduction without completely killing the stand, whereas injuries due to fungi and ice are more easily recognized. The biotic damage caused by the low temperature fungi *T. ishikariensis* and *M. borealis* occur mainly in the inland regions after a long duration of snow cover. The fungus *M. nivale* may attack susceptible grasses in the coastal regions after just a short spell of snow, and *S. trifoliorum* is able to damage red clover (*Trifolium pratense*) in humid autumns. The nature of winter damage is therefore highly related to winter climate and will vary between years and locations.

Hardening under natural conditions

Hardening or acclimatization means altering the phenotype according to changing environmental conditions. Cold hardening occurs during autumn as temperature, photoperiod and light intensity decrease. Grasses possess low tolerance to winter stresses during active growth. Genetic differences in tol-

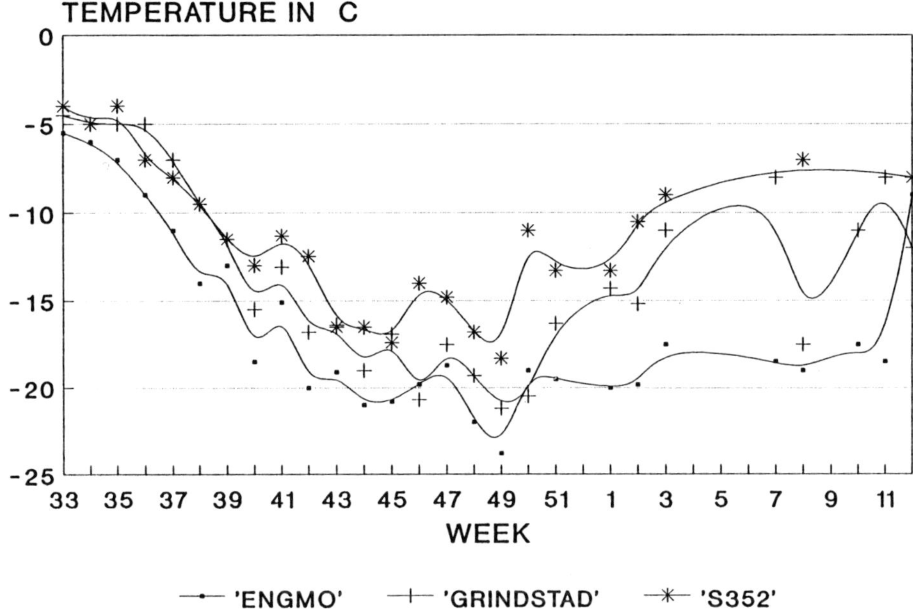

Fig. 2. Development of hardening during autumn and winter, measured as freezing tolerance (LT$_{50}$), in three cultivars of timothy (*Phleum pratense*) grown in the field at Bodø, N. Norway.

erance develop during the hardening period. It is therefore of interest to study the conditions and level of hardening in the field at different locations and in different plant materials.

Development of freezing tolerance in grasses, assessed as LT$_{50}$-values, was studied at Ås in S.E. Norway and at Bodo in N. Norway. At both locations a steady increase in tolerance was observed from mid August to early November, as shown for timothy (*Phleum pratense*) in Fig. 1. In the coastal climate at Bodø the tolerance of timothy was reduced from January, while at Ås, with a more continental climate, a pronounced increase in tolerance occurred from December to mid February, associated with a period of hard frost. The level of hardening was, in spite of the northern location, generally lower in the coastal climate at Bodø (Larsen & Tronsmo, 1991).

At Bodø the most winter-hardy timothy cultivar 'Engmo' started hardening earlier and possessed a higher tolerance throughout the winter then the south Norwegian cultivar 'Grindstad', and the British cultivar 'S352' (Fig. 2). The greatest differences between cultivars did not occur at the stage of maximum tolerance, but at the stage of dehardening in late winter. At this stage 'Engmo' maintained a higher tolerance than the more southern cultivars. The longer maintenance of tolerance at dehardening in the most hardy cultivar

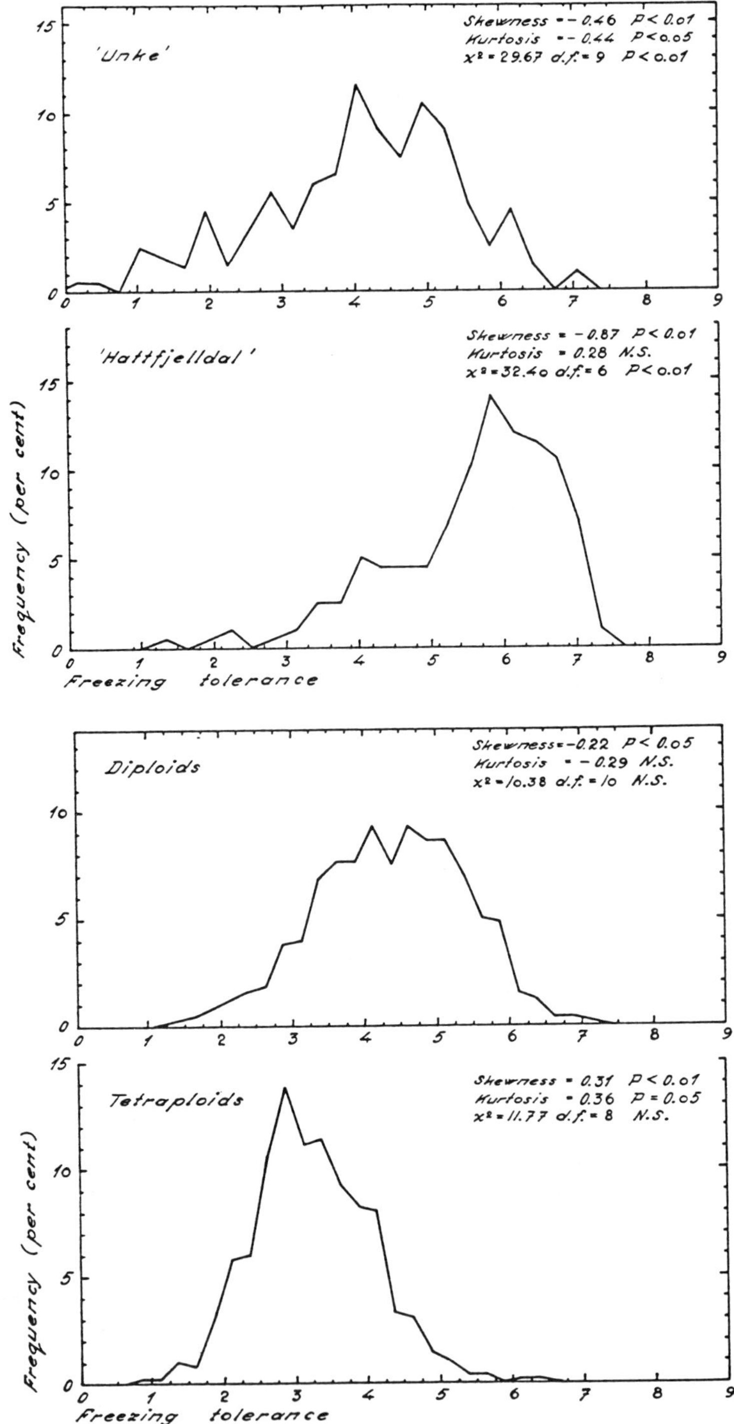

Fig. 3. Frequency distributions of clonal mean values for freezing tolerance (0 to 9) of 200 genotypes from the cultivars 'Unke' and 'Hattfjelldal' of *Dactylis glomerata* (upper), and of 498 genotypes of the diploid cultivar 'Loken' of *Festuca pratensis* and 483 genotypes of the

is in agreement with results from *Lolium perenne* (Eagles, 1984; Eagles & Williams, 1992).

When performing laboratory tests for winter hardiness in a breeding program, it is of interest to recognize that the level of hardening is lower in a maritime then in a more continental climate, and that the best differentiation between cultivars can be obtained at the stage of dehardening. However, laboratory tests which include dehardening can be more time consuming and expensive.

Laboratory tests for components of winter hardiness

Good differentiation in breeding materials and reproducible results may be difficult to obtain in the field because of the complex winter conditions and the variation of stresses between locations and years. Therefore, several tests in controlled environment have been developed to measure tolerance to winter stresses. The most widely used test is for freezing tolerance, which has been performed in a number of ways. These tests are simple and can be finished in relatively short time. Useful tests for resistance to ice encasement and for different species of low temperature fungi are also used. These tests are, however, more complex and time consuming.

The value of studies under artificial conditions to predict winter hardiness in the field and the usefulness of these in a breeding program have been debated. To evaluate the different tests used in the Nordic countries a joint project under the auspices of the Nordic Gene Bank was started in 1989. Reliable field results are often the greatest problem for evaluation of laboratory tests. Field tests with a collection of cultivars of winter cereals and perennial forage plants were therefore conducted at many locations in the Nordic countries over three years.

The results for winter wheat showed that freezing tests gave the best agreement with overall field winter survival, with correlation coefficients of 0.8 to 0.9 for the best performed tests. The results were similar for winter barley, while for winter rye the freezing tests correlated better with survival in field without snow than with the overall survival. Tests for tolerance to ice encasement and low temperature fungi showed lower correlation with field survival. Ice encasement tests gave highest correlations with field survival without snow cover, while tests for resistance to fungi showed better correlations under snow conditions (Hjortsholm, 1993). The field tests with grasses and red clover are still running, and the results have not been analyzed.

Earlier studies with grasses in Norway have demonstrated correlations between field survival and freezing tolerance of about 0.7 to 0.8 for red fescue (*Festuca rubra*), timothy and reed canary grass (*Phalaris arundinacea*), and correlations for low temperature fungi of about 0.4 to 0.6 in red fescue and

154

Table 1. Broad sense heritability, responses to selection and realized heritability after one generation of selection for high and low freezing tolerance in grasses, where 5 to 7 percent of the populations were selected for high and low freezing tolerance. Score 0 - killed and 9 - no damage (From Larsen, 1979)

Species/ cultivar	Herita- bility b.s.	Direction of selection	Freezing tolerance 0–9	Response to selection	Realized herita- bility
Cocksfoot					
'Unke'	0.73	High 5%	4.26	1.20	0.50
		Low 5%	1.97	- 1.09	0.35
		Not select.	3.06		
'Hattfjell- dal'	0.55	High 5%	5.01	0.52	0.35
		Low 5%	4.11	- 0.38	0.13
		Not select.	4.49		
Meadow fescue					
'Loken 2x'	0.65	High 5%	6.44	0.75	0.39
		Low 5%	4.97	- 0.72	0.33
		Not select.	5.55		
'Loken 4x'	0.63	High 5%	5.20	0.56	0.30
		Low 5%	3.99	- 0.65	0.42
		Not select.	4.64		
Per. ryegrass					
'Kleppe'	0.74	High 7%	6.15	0.63	0.39
		Low 7%	4.77	- 0.75	0.42
		Not Select.	5.38		

timothy (Larsen, 1989). It can be concluded that freezing tests have shown the most consistent results and should be used in breeding programs for increased winter hardiness in grasses.

Genetic control of tolerance to winter stresses

Detailed genetic studies of freezing tolerance in grasses have not been reported. The most detailed studies of the genetics for tolerance to winter stresses have been done in winter cereals, e.g. freezing tolerance in winter wheat (*Triticum aestivum*) has been studied extensively. Analyses of diallel crosses have been reported by Gullord (1974), Parodi et al. (1983), Sutka (1981) and Sutka et al. (1986), and the results can be summarized as follows:
  – No significant average cytoplasmatic or maternal effects existed.
  – Both significant additive and non-additive gene action were present.

– The non-additive genetic variation was due purely to dominance.

– The dominance effects were incomplete and considerably lower than the additive genetic variation.

– Genes with additive and dominance effects were independently distributed among parents.

– Both average general (GCA) and specific (SCA) combining ability were significant.

Gullord (1974) showed dominance to be predominantly in direction of high freezing tolerance, while Sutka (1981) reported dominance to be mainly in direction of low tolerance. Broad sense and narrow sense heritability varied in these studies from 0.7 to 0.9 and from 0.7 to 0.8, respectively. Brule-Babel & Fowler (1988, 1989) showed for both wheat and rye (*Secale cereale*) that heritability was lower for crosses between cultivars with high freezing tolerance, compared to crosses between cultivars with greater differences in tolerance.

Studies of genetic variation of freezing tolerance within populations of grasses have showed significant variation between genotypes. Examples of variation among clones are presented in Fig. 3 for two cultivars of cocksfoot (*Dactylis glomerata*), and for a diploid and a corresponding tetraploid population of meadow fescue (*Festuca pratensis*) (Larsen, 1979). Calculation of heritability in broad sense, responses to selection and realized heritability in these materials, and for a local Norwegian population of perennial ryegrass (*Lolium perenne*) are shown in Table 1. Because of significant differences between clones within all populations rather high values were calculated for broad sense heritability. Selection for freezing tolerance for one generation in the three grass species, resulted in significant responses both for high and low tolerance. In cocksfoot both broad sense and realized heritabilities were higher in the Danish cultivar 'Unke' than in the N. Norwegian cultivar 'Hattfjelldal'.

Continued selection for high tolerance for three generations in cocksfoot resulted in increased freezing tolerance, while selection for low tolerance gave no significant response (Larsen, 1985). The rather high realized heritabilities obtained in these selection experiments, indicate that in grasses, like winter wheat, freezing tolerance is a quantitatively inherited character, mainly with additive genetic variance. This gives the possibility for selecting plants with greater freezing tolerance.

For resistance to low temperature fungi higher genetic variation and higher estimates for broad sense heritability were observed in diploid than in tetraploid perennial ryegrass. This could be expected from the tetrasomic inheritance in the tetraploids (Larsen & Tronsmo, 1991) (Table 2).

156

Table 2. Genetic variation and broad sense heritability for resistance (0 to 9) to low temeprature fungi in 200 clones of diploid (2x) and tetraploid (4x) perennial ryegrass from the local population 'Kleppe' (From Larsen & Tronsmo, 1991)

Fungus	Genetic variation		Broad sense heritability	
	2x	4x	2x	4x
M. nivale	80	42	0.79	0.66
T. ishikariensis	89	26	0.74	0.58
S. borealis	11	20	0.48	0.66

Selection for resistance to low temperature fungi in perennial ryegrass has not given consistent results. This may be due to low genetic variation in the initial material and because of insufficient stress conditions during testing. Heritability estimates for resistance to freezing and low temperature fungi in half-sib families, from polycross groups in cocksfoot, showed generally lower heritability for resistance to fungi than for freezing tolerance (Tronsmo, 1993).

It is important to know if correlations exist between tolerance to the different winter stresses. Positive phenotypic correlations between tolerance to freezing and ice encasement have been shown, while correlation between these physical factors and resistance to low temperature fungi been more varying (Larsen, 1989). Tronsmo (1993) reported very high genetic correlation between resistance to the different species of low temperature fungi, indicating a common genetic background for resistance.

Breeding for better winter hardiness

Breeding for winter hardiness is breeding for adaptation, and as the winter conditions for grasslands vary considerably even within Norway, and between years, new cultivars should possess tolerance to several winter stresses. The cultivars should, however, also be adapted to the climate in the growing season, and have the ability to produce high yield of good nutritive value.

We could consider breeding cultivars for more specific environments instead of adaptation to a range of winter stresses. Since the correlations between tolerance to winter stresses seems to be variable and not always positive, it would be easier to breed cultivars for either continental or coastal conditions. Such cultivars would, however, have a limited cultivation area and also be unstable because of the year to year variation.

Tests for freezing tolerance seems to give the best indication of the overall wintering ability for gramineous plants. These tests have also proved to be the most reliable under controlled climate conditions, and have shown to be more efficient than tests for tolerance to ice encasement and resistance to low temperature fungi. Freezing tolerance can be handled as other quantitative characters in a breeding program, and selection could be conducted either as a truncation or in index selection.

In most grasses there is still ample natural variation for tolerance to be utilized in breeding. However, in some species, such as perennial ryegrass, more modern breeding methods may be needed to increase variation for winter hardiness. Crossing and transfer of genetic material from *Festuca* species is a potential way of increasing variation for freezing tolerance (Humphreys, 1993). In winter wheat somaclonal variation for freezing tolerance have been reported by Lazar et al. (1988) and by Galiba & Sutka (1989). Offspring from a few regenerated plants showed increased freezing tolerance, however, use of these materials in breeding and development of cultivars has not been reported. This technique may also be used in grasses. Reports indicate that molecular markers may be available in selection for freezing tolerance in gramineous species (Houde et al., 1992).

New cultivars of grasses bred for broad adaptation to winter conditions, should be selected for tolerance to freezing and ice encasement, and for resistance to low temperature fungi. If the resources are limited and only one test for winter hardiness can be conducted, freezing tolerance should be chosen. This character has shown the most consistent results, given the best response to selection and shown the best correlation with winter survival in field. In our present forage breeding program we are trying to include laboratory tests of the initial breeding material, and of half-sib families during progeny tests. Tolerance under field conditions is a very important selection criterium, and should be considered whenever winter damage occurs in breeding materials.

References

Andersen, I.L., 1960. Overvintringsundersokelser i eng i Nord-Norge. I. Forsk. Fors. Landbr. 11: 635–660.

Andersen, I.L., 1963. Overvintringsundersokelser i eng i Nord-Norge. II. Forsk. Fors. Landbr. 14: 639–669.

Andersen, I.L., 1966. Overvintringsundersokelser i eng i Nord-Norge. III. Forsk. Fors. Landbr. 17: 1–20.

Årsvoll, K., 1973. Winter damage in Norwegian grasslands, 1968–1971. Meld. Norg. LandbrHogsk. 52 (3), 21 pp.

Årsvoll, K., 1975. Fungi causing winter damage on cultivated grasses in Norway. Meld. Norg. LandbrHogsk. 54 (9), 49 pp.

Brule-Babel, A.L., & D.B. Fowler, 1988. Genetic control of cold hardiness and vernalization requirement in winter wheat. Crop Sci. 28: 879–884.

158

Brule-Babel, A.L. & D.B. Fowler, 1989. Genetic control of cold hardiness and vernalization requirement in rye. Genome 32: 19–23.

Eagles, C.F., 1984. Effect of temperature on hardening and dehardening responses in *Lolium*. In: H. Riley & A.O. Skjelvåg (Eds) The Impact of Climate on Grass Production and Quality, Proc. of the 10th General Meeting of the EGF. The Norwegian State Agricultural Research Stations: 287–291.

Eagles, C.F. & J. Williams, 1992. Hardening and Dehardening of *Lolium perenne* in Response to Fluctuating Temperatures. Annals of Botany 70: 333–338.

Galiba, G. & J. Sutka, 1989. Frost resistance of somadones derived from *Triticum aestivum* L. winter wheat calli. Plant Breeding 102: 101–104.

Gullord, M. 1974. Genetics of freezing hardiness in winter wheat (*Triticum aestivum* L.) Ph. D. Dissertation. Michigan State University: 70 pp.

Hjortsholm, K., 1993. Comparisons of different laboratory methods testing winter hardiness in cereals, Röbäcksdalen meddeler. Rapport 11: 1993, 127–128.

Houde, M., S.D. Rajinder & F. Sarhan, 1992. A molecular marker to select for freezing tolerance in Gramineae. Mol. Gen. Genet. 234: 43–48.

Humphreys, M.O., 1993. Genetic resources for improved climatic adaptation within the ryegrass/fescue complex. In: D. Wilson, H. Thomas & K. Pithan (Eds) COST, Crop Adaptation to Cool, Wet, Climates, Aberystwyth, Great Britain, pp. 281–287.

Larsen, A., 1979. Freezing tolerance in grasses. Variation within populations and response to selection. Meld. Norg. LandbrHogsk. 58 (42): 28 pp.

Lazàr, M.D., T.H.H. Chen, L.V. Gusta & K.K. Kartha, 1988. Somadonal variation for freezing tolerance in a population derived from Norstar winter wheat. Theor. Appl. Genet. 75: 480–484.

Parodi, P.C., W.E. Nyguist, F.L. Patterson & H.F. Hodges, 1983. Traditional combining-ability and Gardner-Eberhart analysis of a diallel for cold resistance in winter wheat. Crop. Sci. 23: 314–318.

Larsen, A., 1985. Response to selection for freezing tolerance and associated effects on vegetative growth in *Dactylis glomerata*. In: Å. Kaurin, O. Junttila & J. Nilsen (Eds) Plant Production in the North. Norwegian Univ. Press: 116–126.

Larsen, A., 1989. Foredling for overvintringsevne hos engvekster, Norsk landbruksforskning. Supplement No. 5 1989: 75–80.

Larsen, A. & A.M. Tronsmo, 1991. Seleksjon for resistens mot overvintringssopp i engelsk raigras (*Lolium perenne* L.). Nordisk Jordbruksforskning 73: 516.

Larsen, A. & A.M. Tronsmo, 1991. Natural hardening in grasses, Sveriges Lantbruksuniversitet Raporter Nr. 53. The 4th Plant Cold Hardiness Seminar, 26.

Sterten, A.K., 1952. Melding om undersøkelser over engvekstenes overvintring. I. Undersøkelser i tiden fra 1949 til våren 1951. Forskn. Fors. Landbr. 3: 31–47.

Sutka, J., 1981. Genetic studies of frost resistance in wheat. Theor. Appl. Genet. 59: 145–152.

Sutka, J., O. Veisz & G. Kovacs, 1986. Genetic analysis of the frost resistance and winter hardiness of wheat under natural and artificial conditions. Acta. Agron. Scient. Hungarica 35: 227–234.

Tronsmo, A.M., 1993. Resistance to winter stress factors in half-sib families of *Dactylis glomerata*, tested in a controlled environment. Acta Agric. Scand., Sect. B, Soil and Plant Sci. 43: 89–96.

O.A. Rognli et al. (eds.), Breeding Fodder Crops for Marginal Conditions, 159–165.
© 1994 Kluwer Academic Publishers. Printed in the Netherlands.

Breeding white clover for tolerance to low temperature and grazing stress

I. RHODES, R.P. COLLINS & D.R. EVANS
Institute of Grassland and Environmental Research, Welsh Plant Breeding Station, Plas Gogerddan, Aberystwyth, Dyfed, SY23 3EB, UK

Summary. Low temperature and grazing are the two major stresses limiting white clover yield in mixed swards grown in the marginal areas of the UK. White clover has traditionally been used to improve productivity in such areas but is increasingly being used to reduce input costs in more productive areas. Considerable genetic variation exists in characters associated with cold tolerance, low temperature growth and grazing tolerance. This paper describes recent progress in developing varieties tolerant to three major stresses and which give greater and more reliable production.

Introduction

Traditionally white clover has been used to improve the productivity of marginal land in the United Kingdom. This land is usually situated at altitudes above 200 metres and is characterised by soils of low nutrient status and pH, subjected to severe winter conditions and utilised through continuous sheep grazing, sometimes combined with beef production. However, more recently there has been a resurgence of interest in the use of white clover in intrinsically more productive areas, to reduce the financial and economic costs of livestock agriculture.

White clover is almost universally grown with grasses and must be present in sufficiently large quantities to fully exploit its high nutritional and nitrogen fertiliser saving benefits. Available evidence suggests that the optimum clover content is approximately 30 per cent of the annual dry matter yield, although it may vary from as little as five per cent in early spring up to 60 per cent in July/August. Significantly greater annual contents of clover, with concomitant reductions in the grass, have often been associated with collapses in clover content arising from loss of the protection from cold stress and grazing provided by the grass tillers (Rhodes, 1991). Thus a compatible grass/clover mixture is one which has sufficient clover to optimise its nutritional and nitrogen saving benefits within a high yielding grass background.

The amount of clover in a pasture is determined not only by its direct responses to environmental and edaphic factors, but also by its interactions with companion grass, grazing animal, *Rhizobium* bacterium and pollinating insects. These factors control the invasiveness of the clover which can be quantified by the length of stolon per unit ground area and leaf production per unit of stolon length. The latter character is of course dependent upon such factors as leaf number and rate of leaf appearance and constitutes the bulk of agronomic yield.

Over a range of stolon densities from approximately 20 to 100 metres per square metre, there is a strong positive linear relationship between stolon length in spring and annual clover yield. Beyond approximately 100 metres of stolon, the response in yield declines rapidly (Rhodes, 1991).

Under realistic agricultural conditions, two factors in particular viz winter kill of stolon and grazing (particularly by sheep) result in stolon density values in the linear phase of this relationship, with stolon length being the major component limiting yield and causing yield differences between varieties. Where grass/clover swards are cut (which is unusual in the UK) or following mild winters, stolon amounts are very large and inter varietal differences in yield between varieties are often related to other characters such as leaf size (Rhodes, 1991). Grazing and low temperature are of course two of the major limiting factors in the marginal areas of the UK and this paper will review progress in the breeding in the UK of white clover tolerant to these stresses.

Winter survival and low temperature growth

A general perception of white clover has been that it grows slowly in spring when grass growth is rapid, with resultant competitive suppression of the clover, which has the knock on effect of reducing annual clover yield.

Comprehensive studies throughout the 1970s and 1980s (Harris et al., 1983; Collins et al., 1991) highlighted the overriding importance of stolon survival over winter in determining the subsequent yield of clover. What the farmer may have seen as poor spring growth is in fact low yield due to winter kill and resulting patchiness of the clover.

New varieties of white clover are required with good cold hardiness, coupled with active leaf expansion at low temperature, a combination of characters that has hitherto been unobtainable.

Considerable genetic variation exists in cold hardiness as measured by the damage to stolons over winter. At Aberystwyth, the new cold hardy varieties AberCrest and AberHerald suffered smaller proportional losses in stolon length than the most commonly used variety, Grasslands Huia (Table 1). Similar rankings for the cold hardiness of these varieties were obtained using an artificial freezing test (Collins & Rhodes, 1991). Extensive and rapid death of stolon during winter in this location occurs during periods of sub zero temperature associated with a strong dehydrating wind.

In further experiments pot grown plants which had been subjected to natural winter conditions were placed in a temperature gradient tunnel at temperatures ranging from 3 to 15° C to simulate spring temperatures. Differential death of stolon had occurred during the winter period with the varieties show-

Table 1. Winter damage and low temperature growth

	Field Stolon length per unit ground area m/m^2		Controlled environment Leaf yield per unit stolon length at 6° C mg/mm
	November	March	
AberCrest	144	103	3.51
Huia	158	57	2.00
Menna	159	81	2.51

ing the same ranking for cold hardiness (measured by stolon death) as in Table 1.

Rates of leaf expansion and leaf dimensions were measured during this simulated spring growth, revealing leaf expansion rates per unit of stolon length in AberCrest and AberHerald at least as great and often greater than those in less cold hardy material (Table 1). Final leaf size was also greater than in control varieties Huia and Menna, although at other times of the year in the field AberCrest produces smaller leaves than Huia and Menna.

In the majority of winters throughout the 1980s, when AberHerald, Aber-Crest and their progenitors were being evaluated, substantial winter kill of stolon occurred. The cold resistance of these two varieties coupled with good low temperature growth resulted in substantial improvements in both spring yield and total annual yield (Table 2). The improvements in annual yield were substantial, often being in excess of 25 per cent over the widely used control varieties.

Subsequent field studies involving these two varieties have coincided since 1989/90 with a series of mild winters at Aberystwyth with little winter kill of stolon being recorded, even in susceptible varieties. In these conditions, striking differences emerged between AberCrest and AberHerald in their leaf development and dry matter yield. AberHerald on the one hand responded to the mild winter conditions by expanding leaf area rapidly, producing very large leaves and high spring yields (Table 3). In contrast, AberCrest did not respond to these mild winter temperatures.

Preliminary studies indicate that AberCrest requires a combination of higher spring temperatures and spring daylengths for rapid leaf expansion.

162

Table 2. Annual yield of clover following cold winter t/ha

	t/ha
AberCrest	4.3
AberHerald	4.1
Huia	2.7
Menna	3.4

Table 3. Spring yield and percentage clover after mild winter, March 1992

	Clover yield kg/ha	Clover as percentage of sward yield
AberHerald (Medium leaf)	545	40
Menna (Medium leaf)	198	16
Alice (Large leaf)	428	25

AberHerald by contrast can expand leaves rapidly in short winter photoperiods in mild conditions. In addition, whilst AberCrest has little or no vernalisation requirement for flowering, AberHerald requires longer periods of chilling.

The daylength and temperature requirements of AberCrest may be a survival mechanism preventing winter kill in an environment subjected to alternate cold and milder periods in winter. By contrast the material from which AberHerald was developed originated from an environment with more prolonged and consistent cold conditions not requiring such survival mechanisms.

Grazing tolerance

General relationships have been established between leaf size, stolon density, yield and persistency (Rhodes & Harris, 1979). Thus across the whole spectrum of leaf size there exists a positive relationship between leaf size and yield under cutting and a negative relationship between leaf size, yield

Table 4. Clover and total dry matter yields t/ha

	Clover	Clover + grass
Cattle grazing		
AC39	4.1	9.9
Olwen	3.2	9.2
Continuous sheep grazing		
AC39	3.1	8.1
Olwen	1.9	7.2

and persistency under intensive sheep grazing. Traditionally, white clover varieties have been classified into arbitrary leaf size categories. Small leaved varieties have a dense network of thin stolon and are primarily used for intensive sheep grazing. By contrast large leaved varieties used for cattle grazing and conservation have less but thicker stolon. General purpose varieties for sheep and cattle systems are usually of a medium leaved type, whilst very large leaved varieties, used rarely in the UK but more frequently in southern Europe, are primarily for cutting or lax cattle grazing.

This overall relationship, however, hides much more complex relationships within leaf size categories. Moreover, a major aim of current breeding programmes is to produce varieties which have greater flexibility in grazing tolerance thus blurring the arbitrary divisions between leaf size categories. It has already proved possible to breed more grazing tolerant large leaved varieties by increasing the amount of stolon without sacrifice in leaf size. Further grazing tolerance has been obtained by selecting for short internode length and profuse rooting at nodes, the result being that stolons adhere more effectively to the soil and are less susceptible to removal. This is exemplified in the variety AC39 (Table 4) which, as expected, outyields Olwen under hard sheep grazing but is also more productive under cattle grazing.

Conversely, more productive small leaved types have been produced without loss of persistency. One of the first attempts to achieve this was in the cultivar Gwenda. In Northern Ireland, where Recommended List testing of varieties involves grazing evaluation, Gwenda shows one of the highest persistencies under grazing combined with a yield potential exceeded by only one large leaved variety. At Aberystwyth, Gwenda outyielded the very persistent variety S184 and was equally persistent under hard grazing (Table 5).

164

Table 5. Clover yield under cutting and grazing t/ha
(Aberystwyth)

	Cutting			Continuous sheep grazing		
	Year 1	Year 2	Year 3	Year 1	Year 2	Year 3
Gwenda	3.4	4.4	2.2	1.5	4.7	3.3
S184	4.2	3.9	1.9	1.9	4.3	2.5

A further exciting development is the possibility of utilising the wide range of variation in intra plant morphological plasticity to give greater flexibility in response to management. White clover in general changes its morphology in response to contrasting environments and managements, but genotypes show considerable variation in the extent of this response. A new variety, Ac3715, showing extreme plasticity, has been produced and early research shows a good performance over a wider range of defoliation managements (Rhodes et al., 1993).

The successful development of the type of varieties described in this section will present increasing problems for statutory National List and Recommended List testing where decisions on the value of varieties for agricultural use are usually made by extrapolation from simplistic cutting evaluation.

Conclusions

The extensive and largely untapped genetic resources of white clover have provided the raw material for major improvements in the tolerance of white clover to the major stresses of temperature and hard grazing which characterise marginal areas of the UK. Attention to these problems has already resulted in the development of clover varieties, using conventional breeding techniques, which are consistently higher yielding. Clearly other stresses are features of marginal areas in the UK, foremost amongst these are competitive, edaphic, nutritional and moisture stress. Extensive genetic variation exists for response to all these factors giving rise to optimism that further progress can be made by incorporating desirable traits into an already reliably productive genetic background.

References

Collins, R.P., M.J. Glendining & I. Rhodes, 1991. The relationship between stolon characteristics, winter survival and annual yields in white clover (*Trifolium repens* L.). Grass and Forage Science 46: 51–61.

Collins, R.P. & I. Rhodes, 1991. Genetic variation in cold tolerance and spring growth in white clover. In: White Clover Development in Europe. REUR Technical Series 19, FAO Rome, pp. 11–14.

Harris, W., I. Rhodes & S.S. Mee, 1983. Observations on environmental and genotypic influences on the overwintering of white clover. Journal of Applied Ecology 20: 609–624.

Rhodes, I., 1991. Progress in white clover breeding. In: White clover development in Europe. REUR Technical Series 19, FAO Rome, pp. 1–9.

Rhodes, I. & W. Harris, 1979. The nature and basis of differences in sward composition of grass-clover mixtures. In: A.H. Charles & R.J. Haggar (Eds) Changes in sward composition and productivity. Occasional Symposium No. 10, British Grassland Society, pp. 55–60.

Rhodes, I., K.J. Webb, D.R. Evans & R.P. Collins, 1993. Problems, potentialities and progress in white clover breeding. In: Proceedings of XVII International Grassland Congress, New Zealand (in press).

O.A. Rognli et al. (eds.), Breeding Fodder Crops for Marginal Conditions, 167–178.
© 1994 *Kluwer Academic Publishers. Printed in the Netherlands.*

Selection for improved adaptation of white clover to low phosphorus and acid soils

J.R. CARADUS
AgResearch Grasslands, Private Bag 11008, Palmerston North, New Zealand

Summary. A total of 490 white clover genotypes were grown in competition with *Agrostis tenuis* and repeatedly defoliated, in a glasshouse trial. The percentage change in shoot yield from the first to the last harvest (harvest 6) was negatively correlated with the soil-P level from which ecotypes were collected. High- and low-yielding genotypes were selected from this study and compared in a field trial on a low-P soil (12 mg Olsen P/kg soil), in a grazed mixed species sward. Over the first year there was no significant difference in spread into the sward, and over three years no significant difference in persistence. Selection in glasshouses for yield is unlikely to improve edaphic stress tolerance in the field.
In a field study in New Zealand, comparison of six ecotype populations showed that after one year the highest-spreading population had been collected from a low-P soil while the lowest spreading population came from a high-P soil, although the correlation between spread and soil-P from which ecotypes were collected was not significant (r = - 0.67 p > 0.05). However, in another field trial in England it was shown that populations collected from low-P soils not only outyielded those collected from high-P soils but that they also responded less to added P. It was concluded that populations collected from low-P soils will be a useful source of germplasm to identify genotypes adapted to low-P soils. Successful identification of such genotypes is most likely to be made in the field rather than in controlled more artificial environments.

Introduction

Nutrient imbalances in agricultural soils have been ameliorated traditionally by the application of fertilisers. However, in some areas this practice has or will become economically untenable and environmentally unacceptable. In response to this situation attempts have been made to change plants to suit existing conditions by either the introduction of alternative species or selection within existing species. Selection of cultivars or genotypes with improved nutrient characteristics that allow growth, and additional persistence for perennial species, at low levels of nutrients have been termed selection for either increased nutrient efficiency or tolerance to low levels of a particular nutrient.

This approach is particularly relevant in a country like New Zealand where the cost of phosphorus (P) fertiliser import, manufacture, and application can prove excessive and when prices for exported agricultural products, on the world market, have not increased as rapidly as the cost of imports. In Europe, environmental concerns and legislated demands to reduce nitrogen fertiliser inputs may increase interest in identifying grasses with more efficient uptake and utilisation of nitrogen (den Nijs, 1989; Poisson, 1989). In New Zealand

Table 1. Description of collected white clover population

No	Locality	Grid reference	Dominant species	No of genotypes collected	Aspect	Grazing intensity	Soil[a] pH	Soil[b] Olsen P (ppm)	%P First two leaves	%P Second two leaves	%N first four leaves
1	Rangiwahia	N139/432967	*Agrostis*	23	southeast	lax	5.5	2	0.17	0.13	2.40
2	Rangiwahia	N139/432967	*Agrostis, Cynosurus, Anthoxanthum*	26	northwest	hard	5.3	2	0.20	0.15	2.76
3	Rangiwahia	N139/432983	*Lotus, Agrostis, Anthoxanthum*	33	west	–	5.4	3	0.20	0.14	2.99
4	Waituna West	N144/190752	*Agrostis, Anthoxanthum*	21	northwest	–	5.5	3	0.22	0.12	2.72
5	Sandon Block	N139/184896	*Agrostis, Cynosurus*	21	north	hard	5.5	3	0.23	0.18	2.68
6	Sandon Block	N139/232888	*Agrostis*	23	east	–	5.3	4	0.19	0.12	2.40
7	Pohangina	N144/237565	*Agrostis, Cynosurus*	30	east	lax	5.5	4	0.26	0.17	2.70
8	Rewa	N144/078765	*Agrostis*	35	north	lax	5.6	5	0.28	0.20	3.04
9	Pohangina	N144/262604	*Agrostis*	30	east	lax	5.1	7	0.25	0.16	2.53
10	Sandon Block	N139/207867	*Cynosurus, Agrostis,* moss	20	southwest	hard	5.2	7	0.29	0.17	3.00
11	Kimbolton	N144/293644	*Agrostis, Cynosurus*	32	north	hard	5.3	12	0.28	0.16	2.54
12	Rangiwahia	N139/413942	*Agrostis, Anthoxanthum, Trifolium pratense*	29	roadside	lax	5.7	13	0.25	0.17	2.56
13	Kimbolton	N144/308678	*Agrostis, Cynosurus*	34	north, roadside	hard	5.3	16	0.23	0.15	2.37
14	Kimbolton	N144/293644	*Agrostis, Holcus*	14	north	un-grazed	5.2	17	0.21	0.17	2.74
15	Massey dairy farm	N149/105309	*T. repens, Lolium*	25	flat	lax	6.2	22	0.45	0.26	3.95
16	Massey sheep farm	N149/095303	*T. repens, Lolium*	32	flat	lax	6.4	22	0.48	0.30	4.40

[a] 1 : 1 soil : water mixture.

[b] Extracted in 0.5 M sodium bicarbonate; ppm is equivalent to mg/kg soil.

Table 2. Leaf size and spread of white clover populations grown on a low phosphorus soil, in a grazed mixed species sward. Means and standard errors are given. The description of population is given in Table 1

Population	No of genotypes	Leaflet width (mm)	Spread (cm)		Persistence score (36 months)
			6 months	12 months	
1 Rangiwahia A	19	9.8 ± 0.4	6.6 ± 0.3	15.4 ± 1.3	0.89 ± 0.12
6 Sandon Black B	21	9.0 ± 0.4	6.5 ± 0.2	17.5 ± 1.0	0.84 ± 0.09
11 Kimbolton A	16	10.5 ± 0.6	5.9 ± 0.3	13.6 ± 1.0	0.74 ± 0.07
12 Rangiwahia D	17	13.1 ± 0.5	6.3 ± 0.3	14.5 ± 1.3	0.80 ± 0.11
15 Massey dairy	20	13.3 ± 0.6	5.4 ± 0.3	10.9 ± 0.9	0.97 ± 0.11
16 Massey sheep	28	12.8 ± 0.5	5.9 ± 0.2	15.4 ± 0.8	0.66 ± 0.09
Hill country	20	11.3 ± 0.9	7.1 ± 0.2	17.4 ± 0.9	1.22 ± 0.14
Huia	20	15.2 ± 0.5	7.3 ± 0.2	13.2 ± 0.7	0.93 ± 0.07

phosphatic fertiliser is applied predominantly to stimulate and improve the growth of the legume component of the sward.

Approaches taken to identify white clover genotypes more tolerant of low-P soils include: (a) empirical field screening in a low-P environment, (b) screening for growth in a low-P soil in a more controlled environment, and (c) selection for adaptive plant characters. Only the first two will be examined here; the last has been recently reviewed (Caradus, 1990).

The aim of this study was to examine the significance of screening a range of white clover ecotypes and cultivars for adaptation to low P soils in a controlled environment and in the field.

Methods and materials

Growth of white clover genotypes in a low phosphorus soil in a glasshouse

To circumvent problems associated with soil heterogeneity in hill country pastures a glasshouse trial was conducted to compare the growth of white clover genotypes in a well mixed low phosphorus soil (5 mg Olsen P/kg soil). The soil was an Egmont sandy loam subsoil (NZ Soil Bureau, 1968) to which 100 mg P/kg soil was added as superphosphate to give an Olsen P level of 10 mg P/kg soil and pH of 5.6. Into trays (42 × 30 × 6 cm depth) of the soil, seed of *Agrostis tenuis* was sown at 3.5 cm centres. After 3 months, rooted stolon tips of white clover genotypes were planted between the *Agrostis* seedlings. There were 487 white clover genotypes representing

16 white clover populations (Table 1) and three cultivars, Huia, Kent Wild White and a Hill Country selection. Each genotype was represented by three stolon tips in each of three replicates.

Every three weeks, from late September to early January, white clover shoots were cut back to rooted nodes, genotypes bulked within replicates and weighed dry. There were six harvests. At each harvest the *Agrostis* was cut to 2 cm height. Selections were made of genotypes for yield based on dry weight at the sixth harvest. Low-yielding genotypes had less than 10 mg shoot dry weight and high-yielding genotypes had more than 100 mg shoot dry weight at the sixth harvest. Both groups of genotypes were grown in the field study described below.

Spread of white clover genotypes in a low phosphorus soil under grazing in the field

A total of 182 white clover genotypes comprising six ecotypes, two cultivars (Table 2) and the two selections described above were grown in a low P soil, in a mixed species sward under set-stocked grazing by sheep. Soil-P levels were measured before planting by taking 2.5 cm diameter cores to 7.5 cm depth at 3 m centres across the trial area.

The study was located on a hill country research farm, 'Ballantrae', southern Hawkes Bay. All resident clover was removed using dicamba prior to planting. Seedlings were grown initially for 10 weeks in a glasshouse before transplanting into rows in the field. Five plants per genotype were planted per 0.5 m row, with 1 m between rows. The trial consisted of eight randomised complete blocks. The site was set stocked with sheep at 12 stock units per ha.

Measurements were made of leaflet width, while still growing at Palmerston North; and at Ballantrae, spread after 6 and 12 months, density score (1, open to 3, dense) and leaflet width after 6 months, and persistence score (0, absent to 5, a large amount of clover present) after 3 years. In this instance good persistence was defined as a situation where populations are at a density that achieves the expectations of the specific ecosystem (Marten, 1989).

Evaluation of white clover populations collected from soils of different pH and phosphorus level

Four populations (each of 20 genotypes) were collected from the Park Grass experiment, Rothamsted, England; two (A and B) from unfertilised plots which were either unlimed or limed and two (C and D) from fertilised plots which were either unlimed or limed (Table 3).

The trial was in the New Forest, England on a plateau gravel soil (Geological Survey of England and Wales, Sheet 330), which had a pH of 4.8 and soil-P

Table 3. Description of the soil from which the four populations from the Park Grass experiment, Rothamstead were collected

Population	Soil[a] pH	Extractable				
		P[b]	K[c]	Ca[d]	Fe[d]	Al[d]
		(ppm)[e]	(ppm)	(%)	(ppm)	(ppm)
A	5.2	0	134	0.21	4.6	28.0
B	7.1	2	55	0.42	2.9	8.5
C	4.8	144	374	0.13	2.6	37.0
D	6.7	117	423	0.58	2.3	15.0

[a] 1 : 1 soil : water mixture.
[b] Extracted in 0.5 M sodium bicarbonate.
[c] Extracted in 1 M ammonium acetate.
[d] Extracted in 0.1 N acetic acid.
[e] ppm is equivalent to mg/kg soil.

content of 3 mg Olsen P/kg soil. Two P levels (0 and 500 kg P/ha/yr added as superphosphate) and two liming treatments (0 and 1 t/ha/yr) were applied as main plots in a split plot design. Populations constituted the sub-plots, randomly arranged within each main plot; there were three replicates. The experimental area was set stocked by cattle and ponies. Growth was recorded after 6 and 18 months by harvesting material above 1.5 cm and separated into grass and white clover before weighing dry. Leaflet width was also measured at 18 months.

Results

Growth of white clover genotypes in a low phosphorus soil in a glasshouse

Twelve of the 16 collected populations had significantly ($p < 0.05$) higher mean harvested shoot dry weights than Huia (Table 4). Collected populations with highest mean shoot dry weight yields were Waituna West (population 4) and Rangiwahia D (12); and lowest yields were Massey dairy (15) and sheep (16) farms. The two small-leaved cultivars Kent Wild White and Hill Country selection had mean shoot yields significantly ($p < 0.05$) lower than all collected populations and Huia. At harvest 6, 15 of the collected populations had significantly ($p < 0.05$) higher yields than Huia (Table 4). The lowest yielding collected population was Massey sheep farm (16). Mean harvested shoot yields were negatively correlated with soil pH from which populations were collected and with %P and %N of leaf material at time of collection (Table

Table 4. Shoot dry weight and reduction in yield of white clover populations grown in low phosphorus soil in a glasshouse under six 3-weekly defoliations. The description of populations is given in Table 1

Population	Harvested shoot dry weight (mg)		Harvest 6 yield as % of harvest 1
	Mean	Harvest 6	
1 Rangiwahia A	80.6	51.8	46
2 Rangiwahia B	74.0	48.0	49
3 Rangiwahia C	64.5	44.9	54
4 Waituna West	90.2	53.6	44
5 Sandon Block A	68.3	50.3	53
6 Sandon Block B	71.4	59.6	68
7 Pohangina A	70.9	47.1	48
8 Rewa	65.9	50.9	59
9 Pohangina B	78.0	41.3	35
10 Sandon Block C	75.9	51.1	49
11 Kimbolton A	71.7	47.7	38
12 Rangiwahia D	89.0	48.7	38
13 Kimbolton B	73.2	56.3	52
14 Kimbolton C	69.7	29.0	26
15 Massey dairy	55.2	33.1	38
16 Massey sheep	55.9	22.9	25
Kent Wild White	39.5	18.5	31
Huia	58.4	16.5	18
Hill Country	34.5	18.9	29
p	***	***	***
$LSD_{0.05}$	9.2	11.2	11

5). With harvest there was a trend of decreasing magnitude of correlation coefficient with soil pH and increasing magnitude with soil-P level (Table 5).

Huia had the lowest yield at harvest 6 as a percentage of yield at harvest 1; significantly ($p < 0.05$) lower than all but two collected populations (14 and 16) and Hill Country selection (Table 4). Highest yields at harvest 6 relative to that of harvest 1 were Sandon Block B (6) and Rewa (8). There was a significant trend for collected populations with the highest yields at harvest 6 as a percentage of harvest 1 to come from low-P soils and those with lowest yields at harvest 6 as a percentage of harvest 1 to come from higher-P soils (Table 5).

Table 5. Correlation of collection site characteristics with dry weight yield at each harvest, mean yield and percentage change in yield from harvest 1 to harvest 6 of white clover genotypes grown in a low P soil in a glasshouse. Significant (p < 0.05) coefficients highlighted, df = 14

	pH	Soil-P	%P leaves 1 + 2	%P leaves 3 + 4	%N leaves 1 - 4	N/P ratio	Harvest 1
Harvest 1	- 0.34	0.02	- 0.28	- 0.36	- 0.47	- 0.11	–
Harvest 2	- 0.36	- 0.13	- 0.36	- 0.43	- 0.47	0.08	*0.95*
Harvest 3	- 0.28	- 0.35	- 0.43	*- 0.49*	- 0.41	0.36	*0.81*
Harvest 4	- 0.23	- 0.40	- 0.45	*- 0.50*	- 0.44	0.37	*0.72*
Harvest 5	- 0.17	*- 0.56*	*- 0.49*	*- 0.51*	- 0.41	*0.51*	0.24
Harvest 6	- 0.10	- 0.44	- 0.26	- 0.35	- 0.31	0.17	0.01
Mean	*- 0.51*	- 0.46	*- 0.63*	*- 0.71*	*- 0.71*	0.31	*0.83*
Percentage change	- 0.34	*- 0.67*	*- 0.49*	*- 0.51*	- 0.43	0.38	- 0.39

Table 6. Comparison of white clover genotypes selected for high and low yield in the glasshouse and when grown in the field in a low P soil at Ballantrae

Selection group	n	Yield in low-P soil in glasshouse (mg)		Leaflet width (mm)	Spread in field (cm)		Density score 6 months	Leaflet width (mm) 6 months	Persistence score 36 months
		Harvest 1	Harvest 6		6 months	12 months			
Low yield	17	81	7	10.3	6.0	15.0	1.57	5.4	0.9
High yield	19	128	121	11.5	6.4	15.9	1.84	5.0	1.0
p		***	***	ns	ns	ns	**	**	ns
LSD$_{0.05}$		22	8	–	–	–	0.18	0.28	–

Comparison of genotype groups selected for high or low yield based on harvest 6 showed that they also differed (p < 0.001) at harvest 1 (Table 6). However, there was no significant difference between selections for spread or persistence in a grazed mixed species sward on a low-P soil (Table 6). However, the high yield selection was denser and smaller leaved after 6 months growth in the field. Leaf size did not differ when plants were grown in the glasshouse in pots (Table 6).

Table 7. Mean clover yield (mg/m^2) of populations, grouped on the basis of soil-P content and soil-pH of site of origin, after 6 months growth in a low P soil in the New Forest

P application (kg P/ha/yr)	Soil type of population group				P	$LSR_{0.05}$
	Low-P		High-P			
	Acid	Alkaline	Acid	Alkaline		
0	820	1247	307	33		
500	1040	1247	647	540	*	× 1.88
Mean	920	1247	440	133	**	× 1.40
0		1007		100		
500		1140		587	**	× 1.40
Mean		1073		247	***	× 1.13

Table 8. Mean yield, response to P fertiliser (yield low-P/yield at high-P) of populations grouped on the basis of soil-P content and soil-pH of site of origin, after 18 months in a low P soil in the New Forest

Population group	Clover yield (mg/m^2)	L/H ratio	Leaflet width (mm)
Low soil P	53	2.58	4.4
High soil P	9	0.35	4.3
P	**	(0.10)	ns
$LSD_{0.05}$	× 2.08	–	–
Acid soil	29	0.64	3.9
Alkaline soil	17	1.40	4.9
P	ns	ns	***
$LSD_{0.05}$	–	–	0.3

Spread of white clover genotypes in a low phosphorus soil under grazing in the field

The mean soil-P level of the site was 12 mg Olsen P/kg soil, with the coefficient of variation being 23% and range of 6.4 to 20.4 mg Olsen P/kg soil.

All the collected populations had smaller ($p < 0.05$) leaf size than Huia (Table 2). However, only population 6 had leaf size significantly smaller than that of Hill Country selection. Spread at 6 months was greater ($p < 0.05$) for Huia than all other populations (Table 2). The collected populations with the greatest spread at 6 months were from Rangiwahia A (population 1) and Sandon Block B (6), both collected from low-P soils. At 12 months, Huia had a much lower spread than most of the other populations. There was no clear and consistent relationship between spread at this time and P level of soil at collection site of populations. However, the greatest spread was for Sandon Block B (6) from a low-P soil and the lowest spread for Massey dairy farm (15) from a high-P soil.

The Hill country selection had the best persistence over three years; the Massey sheep population (16) the poorest (Table 2). There was no clear linear relationship between P level of soil at collection site and population persistence.

Evaluation of white clover populations collected from soils of different pH and phosphorus level

After 6 months, populations (A and B) from low-P soils had greater dry weight yields ($p < 0.001$) than populations (C and D) from high-P soils, particularly when comparing ($p < 0.01$) low-P and high-P populations from the more alkaline plots (i.e., populations B and C) (Table 7). Populations collected from low-P soils were also less responsive to added P ($p < 0.01$) than populations collected from high-P soils (Table 7). This again was most apparent ($p < 0.05$) when comparing populations from low-P and high-P alkaline plots (Table 7).

After 18 months, populations collected from low-P soils were still more ($p < 0.01$) productive than those from high-P soils, but differences in response to added P were less ($p < 0.10$) (Table 8). Populations collected from high-P and low-P soils did not differ in their mean leaflet width. However, populations from acid soils had significantly ($p < 0.001$) smaller leaf sizes than those from alkaline soils (Table 8).

Discussion

Identification of tolerance to low-phosphorus soils

In both glasshouse and field trials it was possible to identify differences in tolerance to low-P soils among populations and cultivars of white clover. In some, but certainly not all, cases the most low-P-tolerant populations based on yield at low P were those collected from low-P soils; alternatively those populations least tolerant of low-P soils were often collected from high-P soils. This relationship between low P tolerance and P status of sites from which populations were collected was most evident in the glasshouse trial (Table 5) and the New Forest field trial (Table 8). Snaydon & Bradshaw

176

(1962) found that two white clover populations collected from acid, low-P soils had greater survival rates than the cultivar Kent Wild White and a population collected from a calcareous soil when planted into an acid, low-P upland soil. In other studies Snaydon (1962, 1971) found that white clover populations collected from high- and low-pH soils performed relatively better on its native soil type.

A major problem with empirical studies in which there is only a single low P level is that differences between lines could simply be due to differences in tolerance to other environmental stresses such as defoliation management. The best lines, therefore, could equally have been those most tolerant or adapted to the management system used as those tolerant of the low soil-P status.

For this reason differences in tolerance to low P have been determined on the basis of variation in P response, as occurred in the New Forest trial. P response is broadly defined as the change in dry matter yield with increase in P supply and can be measured in a number of ways, such as a ratio of yield at low P divided by yield at an adequate level of P supply (e.g. Table 8) or by using fitted curves (Caradus et al., 1992). Identification of edaphic ecotypes based on differences in P response in pot studies have been few. Caradus & Snaydon (1986) summarised 19 studies, ranging from solution culture to field trials, investigating the P response of collected populations of white clover. Statistically significant correlations between P response and P content of the soil from which these populations were collected occurred only when P supply was close to optimum. This may indicate a fairly slight difference in the optimum P concentration, rather than a difference in tolerance to low P supply.

The New Forest trial has shown that low-P populations can not only grow better than high-P populations on low-P soils, but that they also respond differently to added P. Bradshaw (1969) surmised that a plant growing at 90% of its maximum yield is in some ways more fit than another plant growing at only 50% of its maximum yield, because the latter is under physiological stress and may have lowered resistance to other adverse factors of its environment. The low-P-adapted populations were not only higher yielding but also responded less to added P than populations collected from high-P soils, i.e., they were under less physiological stress when no P was added than the high-P populations (Table 7).

Relationship between glasshouse and field results

Selection for yield at low P in the glasshouse trial had little or no effect on performance in the field on a low P soil. Previous studies have shown that variation for response to P in glasshouse trials is often poorly correlated with response to P in the field (Caradus & Snaydon, 1986). Additionally, selection under artificially controlled conditions may result in a loss of fitness for field adaptation (Devine, 1982).

Major problems with screening under controlled conditions are the presumptions (a) that there is a single limiting factor and that it can be identified as being important in the field, (b) that this factor does not interact with other factors, and (c) if using solution culture, nutrient uptake characteristics are more important than root morphology characteristics in identifying adaptive mechanisms.

Conclusion

Populations of white clover do differ in their tolerance of low P and these differences can be related, in some instances, to the edaphic origin of the populations. Selection for yield at low levels of P supply in controlled or artificial environments is unlikely to provide germplasm with improved growth on low P soil in the field.

References

Bradshaw, A.D., 1969. An ecologist's viewpoint. In: I.H. Rorison (Ed.) Ecological Aspects of the Mineral Nutrition of Plants. British Ecological Symposium 9: 415–427.

Caradus, J.R., 1990. Mechanisms improving nutrient use by crop and herbage legumes. In: V.C. Baligar & R.R. Duncan (Eds) Crops as Enhancers of Nutrient Use. Academic Press, Inc., San Diego, pp. 253–311.

Caradus, J.R., A.D. Mackay, S. Wewala, J. Dunlop, A. Hart, J. van den Bosch, M.G. Lambert & M.J.M. Hay, 1992. Inheritance of phosphorus response in white clover. Plant and Soil 146: 199–208.

Caradus, J.R. & R.W. Snaydon, 1986. Response to phosphorus of populations of white clover. 3. Comparison of experimental techniques. New Zealand Journal of Agricultural Research 29: 169–178.

Den Nijs, A.P.M., 1989. Plant breeding research for quality. Prophyta 6: 46–47, 50.

Devine, T.E., 1982. Genetic fitting of crops to problem soils. In: M.N. Christensen & C.F. Lewis (Eds) Breeding Plants for Less Favourable Environments. John Wiley and Sons, New York, pp. 143–173.

Marten, G.C., 1989. Summary of the trilateral workshop on persistence of forage legumes. In: G.C. Marten, A.G. Matches, R.F. Barnes, R.W. Brougham, R.J. Clements & G.W. Sheath (Eds) Persistence of Forage Legumes: proceedings of a trilateral workshop. Honolulu, Hawaii, 18–22 July 1988. ASA, CSSA, SSSA, Madison, Wisconsin, USA, pp. 569–572.

New Zealand Soil Bureau, 1968. Soils of New Zealand, Part 3 DSIR Soil Bureau Bulletin 26: 84–85.

Poisson, C., 1989. Diversification des prairies semées d'aujourd'hui et de demain. Perspectives en selection. Fourrages 119: 253–267.

Snaydon, R.W., 1962. The growth and competitive ability of contrasting natural populations of *Trifolium repens* when grown on acid and calcareous soils. Journal of Ecology 50: 439–447.

Snaydon, R.W., 1971. An analysis of competition between plants of *Trifolium repens* L. populations collected from contrasting soils. Journal of Applied Ecology 8: 687–697.

Snaydon, R.W. & A.D. Bradshaw, 1962. The performance and survival of contrasting natural populations of white clover when planted into an upland *Festuca/Agrostis* sward. Journal of British Grassland Society 17: 113–118.

O.A. Rognli et al. (Eds.) Breeding Fodder Crops for Marginal Conditions, 179–180.

EARLY TEST TO DETERMINE THE EFFECTIVENESS OF SELECTION MADE FOR RESISTANCE FOR FREQUENT CUTTING AND PERSISTENCE ABILITY OF ALFALFA (Medicago sativa L.)

I. BÓCSA
GATE Agricultural Research Institute,
H-3356 Kompolt, Fleischmann u. 4, Hungary

Introduction

The problem of resistance to frequent cutting has been studied by numerous authors since 1970 (Demarly and Guy 1970 cit. Mansat 1972; Arcioni et al. 1980, Veronesi et al. 1981, 1982, 1986; Bócsa et al. 1980, 1983). Until now the results of selection have resulted in improvement of persistence (Veronesi 1982) but in general the authors have reported the results after only one or two selection cycles. Usually the early cut was made during the complectly vegetative stage (30-40 cm in height) and the control plots were cut at 10 % blooming, always using at the beginning of the second year adult field grown plants. The duration of the testing was generally two years wich is less than one selection cycle.

Material and methods

Our basic supposition is that resistance to frequent cutting is manifested at the juvenile stage. In preliminary studies we have determined that the optimum stage for cutting of the juvenile plants is at 2 months and 6 leaf stage. The frequency of cutting is every 20-25 days. The plants were grown in 60 x 40 x 25 cm trays and there were approximatly 100 plants pro tray. In each tray two rows of selected CF and two rows of control were grown in the greenhouse, if the climate allowed in the spring the trays were moved cut side. After the cutting trials the surviving plants were crossed to make the syn-1 generation. In the field they open pollinated. In each cycle we used seed from the syn-1 generation. During the course of this work we selected 3 cycles and our work continues.

The trials and selection were combined in the same generation, since after 3-4 cuttings most of the plants had died. The few surviving plants were selected for the next generation.

Results and discussion

The number and percentage of the surviving plants after each cycle (average of 4 replicates) of the selected (CF) and control variety (Sz-4) was the following:

Breeding cycle (generation)	Number of surviving plants		Percentage of surviving plants	
	CF	Sz-4	CF %	Sz-4
1	15	19	4,2	5,6
2	49	17	12,1	4,9
3	98	21	24,6	5,4
$SD_{5\%}$	21,3			

After three breeding cycles the difference in yield between the selected (CF) and control (Sz-4) population were as follows:

Cutting stage	CF g/container greenmass	%	Sz-4 g/container greenmass	%
6 leaves stage (average of three cuts)	150[xx]	161	93	100
10 % blooming (average of two cuts)	641	86	743[x]	100

When the cutting happens in 6 leaves stage then plants tolerate only 3-5 cuttings and after this the population thins quickly so the experiment will no longer be valuable. At the 10 % flowering stage the control (Sz-4) exceeded the selected variety (CF) by about 15 %; whereas at the 6 leaf stage the yield of the selected CF variety exceeded the control by 38 %. These data illustrate a relationship in yield between cutting stage and variety.

We found a correlation to 0.65 (significant) between the yields of test plants of 6 leaves in containers and on the fields at adult stage.

We can establish that the resistance to frequent cutting as such is manifested at a very young stage. So we can use test plants in containers rather than field plants for selection of CF variety.

The total of the 3 breeding cycles (testing selecting and synthesizing) was 38 month. The traditional method of breeding takes 100-102 month in the best of condition. An intermediate method would be to harvest field grown plants at the 6 leaf stage, but this method will take longer than the container method. This work is currently in progress because the container method is artificial and therefore we suppose that it does not account for interactions with the climate (winter effect) or diseases.

Literature

Arcioni, S.-Ceccarelli, S.-Falcinelli, M.-Mariani, A.-Veronesi, F.: 1980. Preliminary study for obtaining a Medicago sativa L. variety to be used for dehydratation and adapted to Central Italy. Genetica Agraria, 34. 355-357.

Bócsa,I.-Buglos,J.-Sziráki, I.-Manninger, K.: 1980. Breeding lucerne under stress conditions for frequent cutting and his biochemical aspects. Eucarpia Meeting of Fodder Crops Section, Perugia, 105-110.

Bócsa, I.-Buglos, J.-Sziráki, I.: 1983. Breeding lucerne for tolerance to frequent cutting and physiological aspects of tolerance. Z. f.Pflanzenz. 90: 222-228.

Mansat, P.: 1972. Improving the quality of forage crops; modification of plant type and selection for a biochemical character. Proc. 6th Eucarpia Congr. Cambridge, 197-206.

Veronesi, F.-Mariani, A.-Falcinelli, M.-Arcioni, S.: 1981. Adaptation of two lucerne population to different cutting regimes. Agronomie, 1: 733-738.

Veronesi, F.-Arcioni, S.-Mariani, A.-Falcinelli, M.: 1982. Risposta alla selezione per la produzione foraggera in erba medica. Rivista di Agronomia, XIV: 366-372.

Veronesi, F.-Mariani, A.-Falcinelli, M.-Arcioni, S.: 1986. Selection for tolerance to frequent cutting regimes in lucerne (Medicago sativa L.). Crop Sci. 26: 58-61.

O.A. Rognli et al. (Eds.) Breeding Fodder Crops for Marginal Conditions, 181–182.
© 1994 *Kluwer Academic Publishers. Printed in the Netherlands.*

THE SEED YIELDING ABILITY OF SYNTHETIC POPULATIONS (SYN-1, SYN-2) OF ALFALFA *(Medicago media Pers)* IN CLIMATIC CONDITIONS OF POLAND

S. M. DYBA, S. M. ROGALSKA
Agricultural University Poznan
Department of Genetics and Plant Breeding,
60-625 Poznan, Wojska Polskiego 71 c
Poland

ABSTRACT. In Polish climatic conditions alfalfa tends to set insufficient amounts of seeds contributing to the reduction of its cultivation. This is why one of the most important objectives of breeding of synthetic cultivars of this plant is high seed yield as well as high yield of fresh matter. In years 1987, 1988 and 1989 an experiment was established with 9 synthetic populations of alfalfa in generations Syn-1 and Syn-2 using the system of complet random blocks in four replications with the aim to evaluate the yields of fresh matter and seeds. The seeds were sown in rows 40 cm apart on 10 m² plots. Polish cultivars of alfalfa "Radius" and "Boja" served as models. Variance analysis was performed and coefficients determining the repeatabilities for fresh matter and seed yields as well as for traits connected with them were calculated.
The inbred lines were selected from 56 inbred lines on the basis of general combining ability (g.c.a.) and specific combining ability (s.c.a.). The seed yield of the discussed populations was a mutable trait as evidenced from the results of the conducted variance analysis. The analysis of variance revealed significant differences in seed yields between individual populations.Tables 1 and 2 show seed yields of synthetic populations.

TABLE 1. Seed yield of alfalfa Syn-1 populations

N_o of Syn population	Seed yield in dt/ha 1988	1989	x	V %	Weight 1000 seeds (g)	Offals %
1	3.89	4.27	4.08	14.5	2.14	7.8
2	5.65	6.25	5.95	19.1	2.48	11.2
3	3.19	3.78	3.48	23.6	1.96	8.8
4	6.71	7.11	6.91	9.2	2.54	9.4
5	7.47	6.92	7.19	18.7	2.37	6.5
6	4.17	4.29	4.23	27.2	2.22	14.3
7	4.44	3.76	4.10	21.8	2.24	11.4
8	7.23	6.84	7.03	16.0	2.61	8.2
9	4.32	6.32	5.32	16.3	2.43	9.8
Radius	5.18	5.48	5.33	17.9	2.36	8.1
Boja	3.37	3.69	3.53	24.4	2.25	11.0

TABLE 2. Seed yield of alfalfa Syn-2 populations

N_o of Syn population	Seed yield in dt/ha 1988	1989	x	V%	Weight 1000 seeds (g)	Offals %
1	3.19	3.52	3.36	18.1	2.25	9.2
2	4.39	4.85	4.62	23.6	2.51	14.0
3	3.27	3.91	3.59	14.4	1.86	10.4
4	4.52	5.89	5.20	21.2	2.62	10.1
5	6.55	6.15	6.35	19.7	2.43	9.6
6	3.52	4.60	4.06	24.3	2.37	16.2
7	3.16	2.77	2.96	20.8	2.25	11.7
8	5.78	6.18	5.98	31.4	2.67	10.3
9	5.26	5.47	5.36	30.0	2.29	14.8
Radius	4.99	5.33	5.16	16.5	2.40	10.4
Boja	3.53	3.15	3.34	23.5	2.38	10.9

Average seed yields from Syn-1 and Syn-2 were compared with average seed yields of model cultivars in both yiers of the experiment. Majority of the synthetic populations responded to site conditions similarly with the exception of Syn5,4 and 8 populations gave in Syn-1 and Syn-2 seed yields significantly higher than other synthetic populations and than model cultivars.
Syn5 proved to be the best of all the examined populations as its yields were the highest and most stable. This population exemplifies specific genotype response of the inbred lines which formed it, giving both high seed and fresh matter yields of 893.3 dt/ha in Syn-1 and 881.2 dt/ha in Syn-2.

O.A. Rognli et al. (Eds.) Breeding Fodder Crops for Marginal Conditions, 183–184.
© 1994 *Kluwer Academic Publishers. Printed in the Netherlands.*

PREDICTION OF SEED YIELD VALUE OF SYN-2 ON THE BASIS OF SEED YIELDING OF SYN-1 OF SYNTHETIC POPULATIONS OF ALFALFA *(Medicago media Pers).*

S.M.ROGALSKA, S.M.DYBA
Agricultural University Poznan,
Department of Plant Genetics and Breeding
60-635 Poznan, Wojska Polskiego 71c
Poland

ABSTRACT. The objective of the research work was to study repeatability and possibility of prediction of seed and fresh matter yields as well as the value of 12 other traits in plants of Syn-2 on the basis of the value of these traits in Syn-1 of nine synthetic populations of alfalfa. With this in mind,the third order curvilinear regression analysis was performed which allowed to determine the first order linear and parabolic regression equations for the examined traits. Data were processed according to programs ABS-42, ABS-45 and ABS-91 and programs elaborated by prof.Z.Kaczmarek from the Plant Genetics Institute of PAN.
Despite the fact that all the examined populations differed among themselves with regard to the analyzed traits the calculated trait repeatability coefficients were almost identical for all populations. For this reason all the nine populations were treated as one, and the data in Tab.1 are mean values of coefficients from nine synthetic populations of lucern.

TABLE 1. Values of trait repeatability coefficients in generations of lucern synthetic populations

Trait	Coefficient of repeatability
1. Fresh matter yield	0.814
2. Dry matter yield	0.834
3. Seed yield	0.837
4. Number of seeds/pod	0.880
5. Number of flowers/ inflorescens	0.915
6. Number of pods/infructescences	0.856
7. Number of inflorescences/shoot	0.894
8. Number of infructescences/shoot	0.908
9. Pod setting	0.924
10. Plant height	0.791
11. Number of shoots	0.837
12. Protein content g/DM	0.737
13. Protein yield	0.825
14. Digestibility	0.716
All coefficients were highly significant at $\alpha = 0.01$	

The calculations are in keeping with the true observations. The perfomed analysis of the third

184

order curvilinear regression allowed to determine the first order linear regression equations for the majority of the analyzed traits. The only exceptions was the number of flowers in the inflorescens for which parabolic curvilinear equation was applied. The clculated determination coefficients were highly significant for the following traits:pod setting, number of seeds/pod, number of pods/shoot, number of flowers/inflores-cence, DM yield, fresh matter yield and plant height. The determination coefficient for the seed yield was significant at the level of $\alpha=0,05$. It is evident from these calculations that the prediction of trait values in Syn-2 and consecutive generations for synthetic populations of lucern is highly probable. The determined linear regression equations with positive values of determination coefficients give a linear description of the dependence of the value of a given trait in Syn-2 and succesive generations on the value of this trait in the Syn-1 generation. In Syn-2 a varied drop in seed and fresh matter yield was observed in populations with the exception of the population Syn5. In both generations it showed the same increase in seed and fresh matter yields in comparision with models. Assuming that the seed yield is a function of heterozygosity (J.Dudley 1964), then its value will depend on the distribution of allele in parental inbred lines, irrespective of inbred generation.

TABLE 2. Trait values in Syn-2 populations predictet on the basis of their values in Syn-1 population

Trait	Regression equation	Determination coefficient
1. Seed yield	$Y(Syn\text{-}2) = 0.75 + 0.71X(Syn\text{-}1)$	76.72
2. Seeds/pod	$Y(Syn\text{-}2) = -5.36 + 1.23X(Syn\text{-}1)$	93.24
3. Pod setting	$Y(Syn\text{-}2) = -7.72 + 0.95X(Syn\text{-}1)$	95.89
4. Pods/shoot	$Y(Syn\text{-}2) = 0.68 + 0.92X(Syn\text{-}1)$	93.46
5. Pods/infructescence	$Y(Syn\text{-}2) = -1.93 + 0.97X(Syn\text{-}1)$	83.80
6. Inflorescences/shoot	$Y(Syn\text{-}2) = 3.24 + 0.73X(Syn\text{-}1)$	77.36
7. Flowers/inflorescence	$Y(Syn\text{-}2) = 23.00 + 3.25X(Syn\text{-}1) - 0.054X^2(Syn\text{-}1)$	92.10
8. Fresh matter yield	$Y(Syn\text{-}2) = 4.84 + 0.94X(Syn\text{-}1)$	91.36
9. Dry matter yield	$Y(Syn\text{-}2) = 2.45 + 1.24X(Syn\text{-}1)$	89.78
10. Protein content	$Y(Syn\text{-}2) = 2.24 + 0.91X(Syn\text{-}1)$	73.24
11. Protein yield	$Y(Syn\text{-}2) = 1.56 + 0.60X(Syn\text{-}1)$	85.34
12. Plant height	$Y(Syn\text{-}2) = 7.71 + 1.00X(Syn\text{-}1)$	95.87
13. Number of shoots	$Y(Syn\text{-}2) = 12.56 + 0.76X(Syn\text{-}1)$	81.39
14. Digestibility	$Y(Syn\text{-}2) = 3.45 + 0.63X(Syn\text{-}1)$	82.50

References:
Dudley, J.(1964) 'A genetic evaluation evaluation of methods of utilizing heterozygosity and dominance in autotetraploids', Crop Science, 4, 410-413.

DIFFERENCES BETWEEN FORAGE GRASS AND LAWN GRASS BREEDING

U. FEUERSTEIN
Deutsche Saatveredelung (DSV)
Weissenburger Str. 5
59557 Lippstadt
Germany

ABSTRACT. In the lower latitudes the same species of grasses are important as forage grasses and main lawn grasses. Only the red fescues as a very fine grass do an exception. Its importance in forage production is rather low. But forage and lawn grasses are not the same. The special necessities of each type of utilisation require different selection strategies.

1.   Importance of forage grasses and lawn grasses.

In all west European countries the consumption of seeds for the use in forages and the use in lawns is more or less about 50 %. The consumption of forage grasses is decreasing whereas the consumption of lawn grasses increases in relationship to the activities in the civil construction sector.

In spite of the great importance of the lawn grasses the scientists take more interest in the breeding of forage crops. But also many breeders give more emphasis to the breeding of forage crops than they do to breeding of lawn grasses.

The different interest in these both breeding directions is caused by the different determination of the variety value.

For forage grasses the value can be determined easily in form of yields. Progress in breeding can be well documented. For the lawn grasses the determination of the value depends of the estethic point of view. Here, an objective determination of the value is much more difficult.

These different evaluations of the breeding directions also become clear in the variety inscriptions. All grasses have to be tested in the DUS-test, but only for the forage grasses we have the agricultural value. France is an exception, here also a VCU-test is realised for the protection of the consumer. In the other countries only a description of the variety is necessary.

2.   Strategies of selection

The planned utilisation for a grass decides about is main breeding objektives (table 1). There are, of course, a lot of general characters being of importace for both types pf utilisation. Here we must point out the winterhardiness and the sward-density. But there are also some characters which are only important just for one utilisation system. Typical characters for the forage grasses are the yield of dry matter and the digestibility as well as the resistance to Xanthomonas. Typical characters for the lawn grasses are the fineness if the leaves, the colour of leaves and the resistance to Corthicium. The character "mass growth" is that one in which both utilisation types are mostly different. For the forage grasses there is desired a very fast growing where as for the lawn grasses reduced growth is to be wished.

186

TABLE 1. Main points in the breeding of lawn grasses and forage grasses.

characters	forage grasses	lawn grasses
general characters		
sward density	+++	+++
resistance	+++	+++
winterhardiness	+++	+++
early development	++	++
resistance to rust	+++	+++
resistance to Fusarium	+++	+++
resistance to leaf spots	++	++
seed yield	+++	+++
characters for lawn grasses		
adaptibility to low cutting	+	+++
leaf size	0	+++
coloration of cutted areas	0	+++
leaf colour	0	++
resistance to Corticium	0 .	++
characters for forage grasses		
dry matter yield	+++	0
distribution of yields	++	+
mass growth	+++	0
digestibility	++	0
resistance to Xanthomonas	++	+

+++	great importance	++	medium importance
+	low importance	0	without importance

3. Differences of varieties

Observing forage grasses and lawn grasses there is to be seen that
lawn grasses have more fine leaves. Our own investigations show that
the mean dry matter productivity of the lawn grasses is about 70 % in
relation to the forage grasses. We also have to realize that though
systematic breeding on very low cutting heights the basal leaf at the
stem of the lawn grasses will be deeper than at forage grasses. It
should be expected that these differences also could be shown in the
allelfrequences of the grasses. Nevertheless, analysis of the tables
of LALLEMAND et al. 1991 does not show systematic differences for the
mostly checked isozym phosphoglucose isomerase (PGI). Considering the
acid phosphatase (ACP) the "a" allel is more frequently being found in
forage grasses than in lawn grasses. Outstanding differences are to be
seen at the isocitrat dehydrogenase (IDH). Here the "b" allel in lawn
grasses is much more frequent and the "c" allel much more seldom than
in forage grasses. But generally there are in every case floating
differences.

4. References

Lallemand, J., Michaud, O. and Greneche, M. (1991) "Electrophoretical
description of ryegrass varieties: a catalogue", Plant Varieties and
Seeds 4, 11 - 16.

O.A. Rognli et al. (Eds.) Breeding Fodder Crops for Marginal Conditions, 187–188.

PHENOTYPIC RECURRENT SELECTION FOR FREQUENT CUTTING REGIMES IN LUCERNE: RESULTS ON FORAGE YIELD AND QUALITY

A. MARIANI (1), S. TAVOLETTI (2), M. TUZI (2) and F. VERONESI (2)

(1) *Italian Research Council, Forage Plant Breeding Institute, 06128 Perugia, Italy*
(2) *University of Ancona, Department of Agricultural and Environmental Biotechnologies, 60100 Ancona, Italy*

Introduction

Lucerne (*Medicago sativa* L., 2n=4x=32) is gaining new attention in EC Countries as a result of public concern about sustainable agriculture. The use of lucerne in modern rotations is based on the improvement of forage quality through intensive management. As a consequence, it is important to develop varieties which give good results when the cutting interval is shortened.

Materials and Methods

Sixty seven clones from phenotypic recurrent selection for resistance to frequent cutting (Selected, S) [2,3] and 33 clones from the initial material (Control, C) were transplanted in Spring 1989 as spaced plants in a field nursery and evaluated in the 1990-92 period under 2 harvest treatments: frequent , F (cut 5 times per year when plants were 40 to 50 cm tall) and infrequent, I (cut 4 times per year at 1/10 bloom stage). A split plot design with 3 replications was used under dryland conditions. Data reported regard total dry matter yield (DMY, kg m^{-2}, sum of 1990-92 cuts), Autumn survival percentage in the 1990-92 period and, for the 1992 growing season, Meat FU and Milk FU (per kg of DM) determined according to the INRA methodology [1]

Results and Discussion

Since Autumn 1991 (Table 1) survival percentages of C materials under the I and F harvest treatments (76% and 55%) were significantly lower than that of S materials under F harvest treatment (96%) which, on the contrary, showed a high survival percentage (74%) even in Autumn 1992. DMY of S materials was 54% and 32% higher than DMY of C materials under F and I harvest treatments (Table 1). S and C materials showed yield reductions of 23% and 44% from I to F harvest treatment, while DMY of S materials under the F harvest treatment was 8% higher than that of C

188

materials under the I harvest treatment. S and C materials did not differ either for Meat or Milk FU within harvest treatment (Table 1) while data relative to the F harvest treatment were significantly higher than those of the I harvest treatment.

TABLE 1. 1990-92 Autumn survival (%) and total DMY (kg m^{-2}); 1992 average Meat and Milk FU (per kg of DM) of selected (S) and control (C) materials in relation to frequent (F) and infrequent (I) harvest treatments.

| | | Autumn survival | | | DMY (kg m^{-2}) | FU (per kg of DM) | |
		1990	1991	1992		Meat	Milk
S	F	98a	96A	74A	2.50B	0.76A	0.83A
	I	99a	96A	84A	3.08A	0.66B	0.74B
C	F	88b	55C	36B	1.62C	0.76A	0.81A
	I	93ab	76B	43B	2,33B	0.66B	0.74B

Means within column followed by different capital or small letters are significantly different at 1% and 5% level.

Conclusions

Selected materials are characterized by an increased persistence, a higher DMY and a forage quality not different from control materials; the reduction in DMY related to the increase in cutting frequency is, in agreement with our previous findings [3], far less pronounced in S than in C materials while S materials under F harvest treatment produced 8% more than C materials under I harvest treatment. As a consequence, the selected materials seem to be well suited for modern systems of lucerne exploitation.

References

[1] Jarrige, R. (1988) 'Alimentation des Bovins, Ovins et Caprins', INRA, Paris.
[2] Veronesi, F., Mariani, A., Falcinelli, M. and Arcioni, S. (1986) 'Selection for tolerance to frequent cutting regimes in alfalfa', Crop Sci. 26, 56-63.
[3] Veronesi, F., Mariani, A. and Tavoletti, S. (199-) 'Breeding for lucerne tolerant to frequent cutting: results and perspectives'. In press on the Proceedings of the X Eucarpia Medicago spp. Group Conference, Lodi, Italy, 15-19 June 1992.

GENOTYPE-ENVIRONMENT INTERACTIONS OF SOME EARLY MATURING BARLEY LINES GROWN AT EXTREME HIGH-LATITUDE LOCATIONS

M. NURMINIEMI, AND O.A. ROGNLI
Agricultural University of Norway
Dept of Biotechnological Sciences/Genetics
N-1432 Ås, Norway

1. Introduction

Barley is the most important cereal crop in Scandinavia. Scandinavian barley breeding has rather similar objectives. As a means of encouraging collaboration and exploitation of genetic variation, covariation, responsiveness and stability of important traits, a joint Nordic research program on barley breeding was set up and founded by the Nordic Councils of Ministers. We present results obtained in this research program from 1987 to 1989 (SNP p 87:1).

2. Material and methods

The barley lines originated from Nordic plant breeding companies and research stations. Plant material used is presented in Table 1., and includes early maturing feedtype barleys.

Four locations represent two marginal and two favourable growing conditions: Korpa (63°50N 20°24W) in Southern Iceland and Röbäcksdalen (63°51N 20°16E) in Northern Sweden are marginal, and Ås (59°40N 10°48E) in Southern Norway and Viikki (Helsinki, 60°15N 25°3E) in Southern Finland are favourable.

Among many traits days from sowing to heading (SOWHD), yield (YIHA), lodging (MLODG) and accumulated effective temperature sum at heading (ETSHD) were observed.

Analysis of variance and covariance were applied to the data according to the following mixed model:
$$Y_{ijkl} = \mu + G_i + E_j + Y_k + B_{jl} + (GE)_{ij} + (GY)_{ik} + (EY)_{jk} + (GEY)_{ijk} + error,$$ where μ stands for grand mean, G_i for genotypes, E_j for locations, Y_k for years, B_{jl} for blocks within location and $(GE)_{ij}$, $(GY)_{ik}$, $(EY)_{jk}$ and $(GEY)_{ijk}$ designate interactions. Location and interaction involving location are handled as fixed effects. Other main effects and their interactions are all considered as random effects.

GE- and GY-interactions were investigated by regression analysis, and Shukla's S^2_i statistics were used to determine the significance of deviation from regression for each genotype. Genotypes showing significant deviations were considered as unstable according to the stability concept of Shukla.

3. Results

<u>GE-interactions</u> were highly significant ($p \leq 0.001$) for yield, very significant ($p \leq 0.01$) for lodging, but non-significant for SOWHD and ETSHD. <u>GY-interactions</u> varied from non-significant for yield, significant ($p \leq 0.05$) for lodging to highly significant for SOWHD and ETSHD. <u>GEY-interactions</u> were significant ($p \leq 0.05$) for yield, highly significant for SOWHD and ETSHD and non-significant for lodging.

Table 1. Significance of the deviation from regression for each genotype for the traits days to heading (SOWHD), effective temperature sum at heading (ETSHD) and lodging (MLODG). Probabilities: *=0.05, **=0.01, ***=0.001.

	SOWHD		ETSHD		MLODG	
INTERACTION	GE	GY	GE	GY	GE	GY
GENOTYPE						
1. Hja 673/Pomo	*			*		
2. Eero-mutation	*	***		***		
3. Sigur F						
4. Tampar	***		***			**
5. Mari/Tampar// Akka/Sigur F (2-rowed)	**	***	***	***		
6. Otra/Vigdis//Agneta			*	*		
7. Bodø			*	*		
8. Fræg					*	
9. Fræg-mutation	**	***	*	***	*	
10. Fræg-mut./Domen-mut.			**			
11. Varde						
12. Yrjar		*	**	**		
13. Eero/Pomo//Potra						
14. Agneta	*					
15. Bamse	**	*	*	***		
16. Silja						
17. Arla (2-rowed)			**			
18. Akka (2-rowed)			*			
19. Lise/Paavo//Agneta	*		***			

Results for yield are not presented in Table 1., because Sigur F (old landrace cultivar from Faroe islands) was the only variety that showed significant deviation from regression for GY-interactions of yield. None of the genotypes tested had a significant instability for GE-interactions of yield. Tampar (also from Faroe islands) was the only one showing instability for GY-interactions of lodging. Line no. 5, originating from a cross (Mari* Tampar) * (Akka*Sigur F), had a greater instability for SOWHD and ETSHD than its 6-rowed parents. Stability for lodging was improved due to 2-rowed parents Mari and Akka.

Norwegian Fræg-mutant line showed a greater instability for SOWHD and ETSHD than its parent. Both lines no.8 and 9. were unstable for GY-interactions for lodging. Crossing of a Fræg-mutant line with another mutant line of 2-rowed Domen improved stability, but still left GE-interactions for ETSHD significant. Yrjar showed a greater growth instability than one of its parents, Varde, which was released in 1941.

The Swedish sister varieties Agneta and Bamse had different patterns for stability, and Agneta had smaller deviations from regressions for SOWHD and ETSHD than Bamse. Arla showed a greater instability for GY-interactions of ETSHD than its backcrossing, Akka.

The Finnish lines no. 1 and 2 had both significant deviations from regression for GE-interactions of SOWHD and GY-interactions for ETSHD. Line no. 1 originates from a cross of Hja 673*Pomo. Pomo is a late maturing barley, and that could have caused instability for SOWHD. Line no. 13 was very stable, and it has Pomo as one of its grandparents, so Pomo's influence is not unambiguous.

There is no indication that elder material is consistently more stable (better adapted) than newer breeding lines for any trait tested. The daylenght insensitive variety, Mari, is one of the parents of Eero. It is difficult to judge whether Mari, which is in the background of line no. 2 and 5, has turned daylenght sensitiveness (linear effect of locations) to insensitiveness (deviation from regression). It is certainly not the case for line no. 13.

O.A. Rognli et al. (Eds.) Breeding Fodder Crops for Marginal Conditions, 191–192.
© 1994 *Kluwer Academic Publishers. Printed in the Netherlands.*

STABILITY OF QUALITY TRAITS IN FODDER CEREALS

P. Peltonen-Sainio, and J. Peltonen
Department of Plant Production
Section of Crop Husbandry
Box 27, Viikki
FIN-00014 University of Helsinki, Finland

1 INTRODUCTION

High quality cereal grains are annually required for processing in feed industry. However, the variation in both grain yield and quality is considerable owing to several risk factors endangering fodder cereal production in the marginal growing conditions of Finland [1, 2]. Therefore, stability in the expression of traits contributing to high grain quality is needed and should be included as a goal in breeding programs [3]. The objective of the present study was to evaluate the existence of genotype x environment (GxE) interaction and the phenotypic stability of quality traits over varying environments in barley (*Hordeum vulgare* L.) and oats (*Avena sativa* L.) by using the Finlay-Wilkinson [4] regression method and Eberhart-Russell [5] stability analysis, both previously used in the evaluation of stability of yield performance with environment.

2 MATERIALS AND METHODS

The phenotypic stability of quality characteristics of 11 barley and 8 oat cultivars were analyzed on a basis of 41 and 38 experiments, respectively. Field experiments during seven successive growing seasons (1982-1988) were conducted in greatly varying environments at the Anttila Experimental Farm (60°25′ N) and at the Nikkilä Experimental Farm (61°33′ N) of the Hankkija Plant Breeding Institute. For example, soil types varied from finesand to clay and mould, soil pH values from 4.3 to 6.7, fertilizer levels from 0 to 151 kg N ha^{-1}, and crops were irrigated/non-irrigated. The following results were collected from the annually published Trial Results of the Hankkija Plant Breeding Institute [6]: 1) hectolitre weight (kg), 2) 1 000 grain weight (g), 3) grain protein concentration (%) analyzed from whole grain meal, 4) protein yield (g/m^2), and 5) husk content (%) of oats measured twice from 100 grains.

Significant differences between cultivars in the examined quality traits and GxE interaction were evaluated by ANOVA. The phenotypic stability of quality traits indicating significant GxE interaction ($P \leq 0.05$) was computed using the Finlay-Wilkinson and Eberhart-Russell stability analyses.

3 RESULTS AND DISCUSSION

There were significant differences ($P \leq 0.001$) between cultivars in all of the quality traits studied. For protein concentration in barley, and grain weight, hectolitre weight, protein yield, and hull content in oats, the cultivars included in this study responded in a similar fashion to varying growing conditions showing insignificant GxE interaction. In contrast, grain weight ($P \leq 0.05$), hectolitre weight ($P \leq 0.001$), and protein yield ($P \leq 0.05$) in barley, and protein concentration ($P \leq 0.05$) in oats indicated a significant GxE interaction. The results were supported by Eberhart-Russell analysis.

The Finlay-Wilkinson analysis did not show any clear trend that high hectolitre weight or grain weight in barley was associated with instability (Fig 1). For example, the barley cultivar *Ida* combined high hectolitre weight and grain weight with relatively stable performance. However, low protein yield in barley was associated with stable performance and a high protein yield with instability.

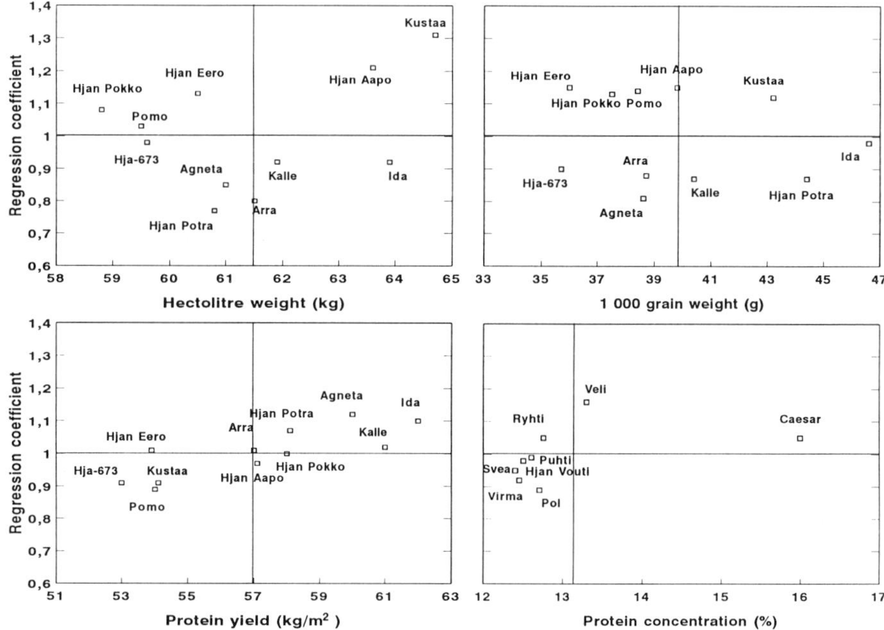

Figure 1.   Finlay-Wilkinson plot for hectolitre weight, 1000 grain weight, and protein yield in barley and for protein concentration in oats.

In oats, there was a clear trend showing high protein concentration to be associated with weaker stability (Fig. 1). The naked oat cultivar *Caesar* had the highest protein concentration (16%), the expression of which was somewhat unstable. Based on the findings of this study, the use of easily measured stability indices (e.g. b_i and s^2_d), in addition to mean values of quality traits, is recommended as it would give further information about the sensitivity of different cultivars in responding to varying environments.

4 REFERENCES

[1] Mukula, J. & Rantanen, O. 1989a. Ann. Agric. Fenn. 28, 29-36.
[2] Mukula, J. & Rantanen, O. 1989b. Ann. Agric. Fenn. 28, 37-43.
[3] Peltonen-Sainio, P. & Peltonen, J. 1993. Acta Agric. Scand., Sect. B, 43, 45-52.
[4] Finlay, K.W. & Wilkinson, G.N. 1963. J. Agric. Res. 14, 742-754.
[5] Eberhart, S.A. & Russell, W.A. 1966. Crop Sci. 6, 36-40.
[6] Anon. 1982-1988. Trial Results. Hankkija Plant Breeding Institute. Helsinki.

O.A. Rognli et al. (Eds.) Breeding Fodder Crops for Marginal Conditions, 193–194.
© 1994 *Kluwer Academic Publishers. Printed in the Netherlands.*

SELECTION FOR FODDER YIELD AND QUALITY AMONG POPULATIONS OF WHITE CLOWER

KÅRE RAPP
Holt Research Station
P.o. Box 2502,
9002 Tromsø.
Norway

ABSTRACT. In order to see if it is possible to select for better fodder quality together with the selection for fodder yield in white clover, the chemical content in the populations was analysed, and correlation coefficients to the dry matter yield in the same material were calculated. Based on the variability observed and the correlation coefficients calculated, it is drawn a conclusion that it is possible to select for fodder yield and quality at the same time. One method is to use the analyses of the ash content, the analyses of the Kjeldahl-N, and the values for dry matter yield in one and the same index. Another method is to use a sort of tandem method for fodder quality, in combination with an index selection for dry matter yield, winter hardiness and other agronomic characters.

1. Introduction, material and methods

The breeding program on white clover in Norway is based on some 90 populations collected from all over the country, between 58°- and 71°N, and ca. 10 - 500 m a.s.l.

The populations are tested in open field plots at the Agricultural Research Stations Holt (70°N, 50 m a.s.l.) and Apelsvoll (62°7 N, 250 m a.s.l.) for two years.

Based on the wide variability between populations, a selection was done for a fodder type using a simple phenotypic index where the following characters and economic values were used: winter hardiness 0.20, plant hight 0.10, fodder yield 0.50, and over all score 0.20 (Rapp 1992).

The best 10 populations selected have been seedraised, and are now put into the official variety testing system, before a final selection will be done.

In addition, it is also of interest to see if it is possible to select for a better fodder quality in the material. Therefore, the total content of minerals (ash), crude fiber, and Nitrogen using the Kjeldahl method, were analysed in all populations. The correlation coefficients between these characters and the data observed for dry matter yield among populations were calculated.

2. Results

The variability of the content of ash, crude fiber and Nitrogen from the Kjeldahl method, as percent of the dry matter, are given in figures 1, 2, and 3, respectively.

The correlation between ash content and the Kjeldahl-N is r = 0.4, whereas there is a negative correlation between the Kjeldahl-N and crude fiber content (- 0.61) (Figure 4).

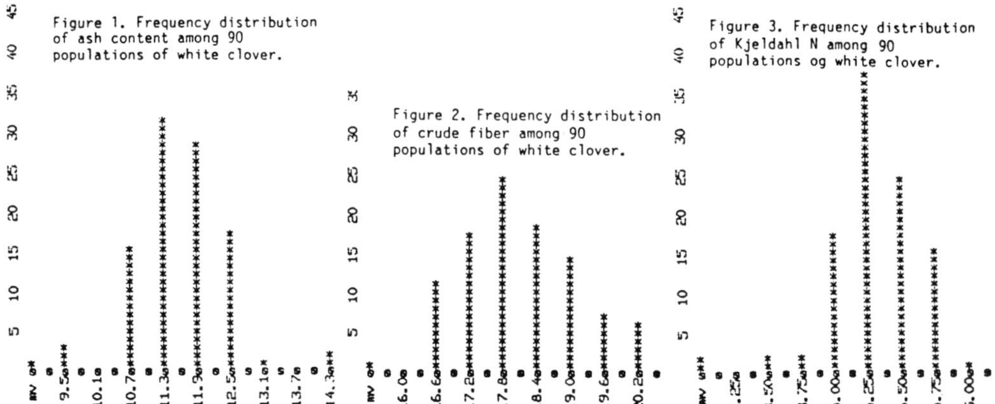

Figure 1. Frequency distribution of ash content among 90 populations of white clover.

Figure 2. Frequency distribution of crude fiber among 90 populations of white clover.

Figure 3. Frequency distribution of Kjeldahl N among 90 populations og white clover.

Finally, there is a positive correlation between the Kjeldahl-N and the dry matter yield in this white clover material (r = 0.43) (Figure 5).

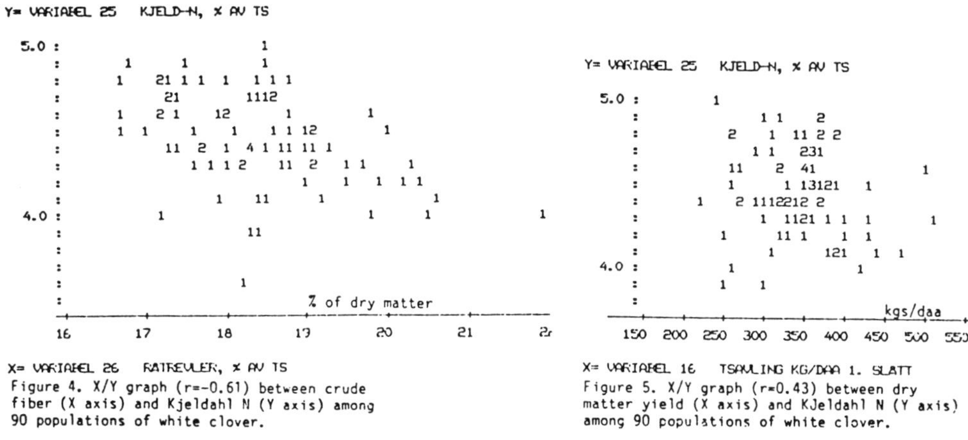

Figure 4. X/Y graph (r=-0.61) between crude fiber (X axis) and Kjeldahl N (Y axis) among 90 populations of white clover.

Figure 5. X/Y graph (r=0.43) between dry matter yield (X axis) and Kjeldahl N (Y axis) among 90 populations of white clover.

3. Conclusion

The wide variability, and the positive correlation between contents of ash and Kjeldahl-N, and between Kjeldahl-N on one hand and dry matter yield on the other, indicate that it is possible to select for crude protein and mineral content together with dry matter yield in white clover. One method is to use the analyses from Kjeldahl-N and the ash content in one and the same index as the values of dry matter yield. Another method is to use a sort of tandem method for fodder quality, in combination with an index selection for dry matter yield, winter hardiness and other agronomic characters.

It is not possible to select for higher values of crude fiber using the index method, because there is a negative correlation between the content of crude fiber on one hand and the content of ash and Kjeldahl-N on the other hand.

4. Literature

Rapp, K. (1992) 'Selection on white clover (Trifolium repens) for fodder production and turfs in Norway', Proceedings of the 14th General Meeting of EGF, Lahti, Finland, June 1992, pp. 465-466.

O.A. Rognli et al. (Eds.) Breeding Fodder Crops for Marginal Conditions, 195–196.
© 1994 *Kluwer Academic Publishers. Printed in the Netherlands.*

THE ROLE OF THE EARLY CUTTING REGIME IN THE LUCERNE NUTRITIVE VALUE IMPROVEMENT: FIBRE AND CRUDE PROTEIN CONTENT.*

P. Rotili, N. Berardo, G. Gnocchi, and C. Scotti.
Istituto Sperimentale per le Colture Foraggere,
Viale Piacenza 29, 20075, Lodi Italy.

Introduction

This work is the introductive part of a research programme in progress at our Institute. The final aim of this programme is to build up new cultivars for drying (meal and hay) adapted to intensive forage systems such as those used in the irrigated plains of Northern and Central Italy. The traits we have studied are saponin content, crude protein and fibre content, dry matter yield and persistence.

Materials and methods

Three experiments were conducted. In the first experiment four populations were utilised: Equipe (Italy), Sewa (Egypt), Victoria (Spain), Julus (Sweden). Boxes/plots: diameter 40 cm, height 82 cm; 30 plants/plot corresponding to a density of 254 plants/m^2. Two cutting regimes: early cut at 50% of plants with green bud and normal cut at 50% of flowered plants. In the second experiment Equipe and Sewa were used. Boxes/plots: 60x70x100 cm; density: 400 plants/m^2. Aerial biomass was studied at three cutting regimes: 30 cm; 60 cm; flowering. In the third experiment 10 varieties were utilised (from Italy, France, Spain, Greece). The cultivars, six time replicated, were arranged as a split-plot design with cutting treatments in main plot and cultivars in subplot. Cuts were made at two different phenological stages: 50% of blue bud (Early cut) or 50 % flowering (Normal cut). The analysis of the protein content in the first experiment was performed with a Technicon AutoAnalyzer Apparatus II generation. Concerning the second and third experiment, crude protein (CP), neutral detergent fibre (NDF), acid detergent fibre (ADF) and acid detergent lignin (ADL) were determined in leaves and stems *via* near infrared reflectance spectroscopy (NIRS).

Results

Crude protein content Table 1: in general the cultivar effect is negligible in comparison with the cutting time effect. This is evident for leaves and stems both in spring (first cut and successive regrowth) and in summer (third cut and successive regrowth). The CP content of the stems and leaves changes according to their age (Rotili et al., 1989). Within each phenological stage there is no significant difference among cultivars neither for stems nor for leaves.
Fibre content Table 1 : no significant differences among cultivars are detected when the analysis is made on stems and leaves at the same stage. A remarkable difference is observed between the biological stages of the plant for NDF, ADF and ADL (Rotili et al., 1992). The crude protein content decreases through the biological stages; the opposite is true for the fibre content.

*Work supported by the Italian Ministry of Agriculture, Project "Foraggicoltura Prativa"

TABLE 1. Crude Protein (CP) and fibre fractions (NDF, ADF) at different stages, II cycle.

	LEAVES						STEMS					
	EQUIPE			SEWA			EQUIPE			SEWA		
	CP	NDF	ADF	CP	NDF	ADF	CP	NDF	ADF	CP	NDF	ADF
Cut at 28 cm												
0 - 28 cm	41.7	27.5	15.1	40.9	26.7	15.9	21.4	44.9	36.9	21.5	42.6	34.9
Cut at 60 cm												
0 - 28 cm	34.5	28.6	15.6	33.6	28.7	17.9	16.5	54.6	48.3	14.2	57.6	50.1
28 - 60 cm	40.3	24.0	14.1	39.8	23.9	15.4	22.1	43.6	37.0	21.8	46.1	35.8
Cut at 50% bloom												
0 - 28 cm	29.9	23.0	17.5	28.4	26.7	18.2	11.6	63.8	55.1	10.9	65.9	55.3
28 - 60 cm	33.0	22.5	15.4	30.6	25.4	17.1	12.7	59.7	52.0	12.3	63.1	52.6
60 cm TOP	36.1	17.5	12.5	33.5	22.4	15.1	20.1	42.4	37.0	16.3	49.1	41.4

Discussion and conclusions

Within all analysed cultivars we have not found utilizable variability for CP, NDF, ADF and therefore we have concluded that it is almost impossible to obtain positive results in breeding work and variety constitution. At the same time we can say that it is possible to improve these traits by selection for physiological traits such as leaf persistence, onset of senescence and resistance to early cutting regime. But the consequence of early cutting is a decrease in biomass and increase in mortality. Mortality is the consequence of the fact that, at cutting time, not all the plants have reached the maximal recovery of the root reserves. The plants having reached it are advantaged in comparison with the others; these last undergo a delay in regrowth and development which increases from one cycle to the next. As a consequence of the interference effects, these plants become step by step weaker and finally die. Such a process is particularly drastic in the early cut regime. Our data concerning protein content of the roots show that this trait is severely affected by the cutting regime (Rotili et al., 1989). In the normal cut (50% flowering) the root crude protein content (% on total root DM) reaches a maximum at the flowering stage and the minimal level at the green bud stage. This trend of variation is similar to the root biomass trend. So it seems that the mortality of the plants is the consequence of the progressive decrease of the crude protein root reserves. It is to be underlined that while in the roots the maximal level of crude protein content is at flowering, in the aerial part at the same stage CP is at the minimal level: the trend of the crude protein content in the aerial part is the opposite of the root part of the plant. In conclusion we can state that breeding for crude protein and fibre content in lucerne is not feasible, because of the poor variability of these traits. Nevertheless, it is possible to improve both characteristics by indirect ways, like breeding for resistance to the early cut. In practice the best moment for cutting lucerne should be at the 50% blue bud stage rather than at 50% green bud stage: this stage seems indeed to be more suitable for an advantageous equilibrium among nutritive value and biomass production per hectare.

References

Rotili, P., Zannone, L., Gnocchi, G., Proietti, S. and Scotti, C. 1989. Analysis of aerial part and roots of the lucerne crop to improve the breeding method. Proceedings of the XVI International Grassland Congress. pp.485-486.
Rotili, P., Valentini, P., Berardo, N. and Zannone, L. 1992. Stratigraphical analysis of experimental lucerne meadow. Proceedings of the X International Conference Eucarpia Medicago Spp Group, I.S.C.F., Lodi, pp. 120 - 126.

Morphological and physiological aspects of breeding for marginal conditions

Improvement of snow mould resistance by conventional and in vitro techniques

ULRICH K. POSSELT & FREDY ALTPETER
Landessaatzuchtanstalt, Universität Hohenheim, D–70593 Stuttgart, Germany

Summary. Under our climatical conditions *Microdochium nivale* is the main pathogen which causes snow mould in grasses. Like many *Fusarium* species, *M. nivale* is able to produce toxins like Deoxynivalenol (DON). In vitro selection with callus cultures from two populations of perennial ryegrass and DON as selective agent was carried out in a one step (subculture) or two step procedure (induction plus subculture). The regenerants from in vitro selection and a seed derived control from the two populations were artificially inoculated with *M. nivale*. Significant improvement of snow mould tolerance in the high DON variant could be found. Additionally, a toxin test was established which allows to screen large numbers of mature embryos without laborious callus culture. The sexual progenies (R1) of the regenerants were subjected to both the snow mould and the toxin test. Toxin and pathogen resistance were not always in good accordance. The application of both tests in practical plant breeding is discussed.

Introduction

Snow mould, caused by *Microdochium nivale* (Fr.) Samuels & Hallet (syn. *Gerlachia nivalis*, syn. *Fusarium nivale*) is one of the most important diseases causing winter damage on grasses in temperate and cooler regions. In parts of Scandinavia snow mould may be due to attack by other pathogenic fungi like *Typhula* sp. and *Sclerotinia borealis* (Jönsson & Nilsson, 1985).

Besides snow mould, *M. nivale* also causes seedling blight. This is due to the fact, that the pathogen is both seed transmitted and soil borne. In the soil the fungus exists saprophyticly on dead plant parts. Infection mainly comes from the soil by growth of mycelia which penetrates the lower stem parts. Under snow cover (preferably on non-frozen soil) the fungus develops especially well. After winter, snow mould patches can be seen. However, *M. nivale* can also be found in later growth stages under favorable wet and cool environmental conditions and at temperatures from near freezing to around 16 °C. The pathogen becomes inactive as the canopy dries and warms up (Smiley, 1983).

M. nivale damages cereals too, especially rye and wheat. Besides snow mould, root and stem rot, head blight may occur. Other *Fusarium* species are also involved in these diseases. *Fusarium* species like *F. culmorum*, *F. avenaceum* or *F. graminearum* are known to be toxin producers. In a previous study a toxigenic isolate of *M. nivale* could be identified. Toxins like Deoxynivalenol (DON) are harmful to animals and humans (Marasas et al., 1984).

Because snow mould selection in the field is very much depending on the environmental conditions, several attempts have been made to establish artificial selection schemes (Arsvoll, 1977; Nilsson & Weibull, 1981; Jönsson & Nilsson, 1985; Posselt, 1987) including in vitro selection (Posselt, 1991).

The aim of our work was to investigate whether improvement in toxin resistance is associated with an improvement in pathogen resistance, and if the resistance is transmitted to its sexual progeny.

Material and methods

Plant material and in vitro selection

From two populations of *L. perenne* (cv. Loretta = WD02 and an experimental Synthetic = WD 51) callus cultures were established from mature embryos according to a method previously described (Schmidt & Posselt, 1991) and only slightly modified. DON was produced according to a method described elsewhere (Altpeter & Posselt, 1994). Callus was induced from 1000 explants in each variant: a control without DON (D0) and a selection variant with 200 μg DON (D200). Since on the latter many calli did not survive, the number of calli were reduced to 200 before subculture in each of the 3 variants:

1. control with no DON during subculture (D0/D0)
2. no DON followed by DON in subculture (D0/D400) and
3. DON during induction and during subculture (D200/D400).

The duration was 5 weeks for induction and 4 weeks for subculture. After transfer to DON-free medium plants (Ro) could be regenerated from all variants. The Ro-plants were transferred to soil and vegetatively multiplied to obtain enough plants for the snow mould test and sexual propagation. Additional control plants were raised from seeds of the two populations.

One plant from each Ro-genotype and selection variant was placed in a separate glasshouse for isolated interpollination in six crossing blocks. Seeds were harvested from each plant separately. The raised R1-plants from each parental plant are halfsib-families. They were vegetatively multiplied and subjected to a snow mould test. Spare seeds from the R1 were used in a toxin test.

Inoculum production

M. nivale isolates were maintained under cool conditions (+ 4 °C, dark) as permanent cultures in test tubes containing sterilized soil.

Inoculum for a first progagation was produced by placing aliquots of the soil colonies on plates (60-mm diameter) containing malt extract (ME) medium (2%) solidified with agar (0.8%). The plates were incubated at 25

°C in the dark for 4 days. The growing mycelium was used to start a mass propagation in liquid culture (modified after Miedaner et al., 1993).

M. nivale was cultured in SN medium (Nirenberg, 1981) supplemented with 1% extract of yeast (Y) powder. This SNY solution was placed in 1000 ml Erlenmeyer flasks with barriers (400 ml/flask), autoclaved, and inoculated with actively growing mycelium plugs from the MEA plates (ten plugs per flask). The flasks were incubated on a shaker (100 rpm) at 25 °C in the dark for 3 days. Mycelium cultures were broken to a suspension by a Waring blender.

Vermiculite (Klein, Zellertal, Germany; sieved to a size of 2–6 mm) was saturated with SNY solution, autoclaved and mixed with the liquid mycelium culture (300 ml with 1800 ml vermiculite). The vermiculite-mycelium mixture was incubated in dark in plastic trays with 100% relative humidity in a growth chamber at 13 °C immediately after preparation. During the two day incubation the vermiculite was uniformly colonized by *M. nivale*. Snow mould mycelium grew rapidly only in fresh preparation and every storage procedure (drying, freezing, etc.) reduced vitality.

Toxin test

Mature embryos from the various HS-families were plated on an artificial medium (MS, 30 g/l maltose, 0.2 mg/l kinetin) containing D 1400. After 14 days, germination percentage was counted and seedling growth scored.

Snow mould test

Plant material had 3–5 tillers and were trimmed to a height of 5 cm before placing in a cold room. Temperature was initially 10 °C and then gradually reduced to 2 °C. A 8/16 hrs (day/night) light regime (3000 lx) was applied. After this hardening period plants were inoculated. Four plants per genotype were inoculated, one served as control. Approximately 35 ml of colonized vermiculite was spread evenly on the soil surface of each pot (7 × 7 cm) containing one plant. The pots were placed in plastic boxes and also covered with boxes with moistened paper on the inner side to maintain high humidity. The plants were kept for 3 weeks in the dark at + 1 °C. Within this period all plants had been colonized by the pathogen, wheras the non-inoculated control plants showed no symptoms or damage at all. After 3 weeks, the plants were uncovered, the temperature raised to 10 °C and artificial light (12 hrs, day/night; 3000 lx) given. One week later, at the end of September plants were placed outdoors for regeneration. During this phase most of the plant damage took place. Snow mould resistance was scored on a 1–9 scale (0 = no damage, 9 = dead plant).

202

Table 1. Callus selection in populations

Induction		D0	D200
No. explants		1000	1000
Callus size*		3.06	1.94
Induction rate		79%	26%
No. calli selected		400	200
Subculture	D0	D400	D400
No. calli	200	200	200
Callus size*	5.38	4.96	2.74
Regeneration	26%	16%	8%
No. regenerants per reg. callus	4.62	4.86	8.42

*Scores, D = DON

Results

In vitro selection

Already during callus induction callus size and induction rate were reduced
to 60 and 30% in the D 200 compared to D 0. Regeneration was 26%, 16%
and 8% in D0/D0, D0/D400 and D200/D400, respectively. However, in the
latter variant almost twice as much regenerants per callus could be obtained
(see Table 1).

Snow mould test (Ro-plants)

Though most of the regenerated plants were tested for snow mould resistance,
statistical analysis was performed on a stratified sample. Each selection variant
was represented by 4 genotypes, each tracing back to an individual explant.
Plants originating from the same callus showed a similar pattern of resistance.
On average of both populations and within each one, seed control, D0/D0 and
D0/D400 were not significantly different, while D200/D400 was significantly
superior in its snow mould resistance. According to Table 2 the improvement
in the turf type population (WDØ2) was 1.3 score units. Already in the seed
control the forage type (WD51) with 5.75 in the seed control was 1 score
better than WD02. The improvement through in vitro selection by 1.8 units
was even more pronounced than in WD02. The very best genotype was scored
3.25 (WD51).

Table 2. Snow mould resistance after in vitro selection (Ro-plants) (0 = no damage, 9 = dead plants)

Variant	WD02	WD51
Seed control	6.75	5.75
DON 0–0	6.13	5.19
DON 0–400	6.25	5.25
DON 200–400	5.44	3.88
LSD 5	0.89	0.93

The non-inoculated control plants were transferred to the breeding nursery on the Suebian Alb (700 m altitude) last autumn. Unfortunately, because of a very mild winter with little snowcover, no scoring for snow mould resistance in the field was possible.

Toxin test (R1-plants)

From each population and selection variant 3 HS-families (40 explants each) were tested for DON-tolerance. On average of both populations (see Fig. 1) and for each of them, no significant differences in germination percentage and seedling growth between D0/D0 and D0/D400 could be found. Compared to D0/D0 a 55% higher germination rate and 72% faster seedling growth could be observed in D200/D400. The HS-families within each variant were significantly different from each other (data not given).

Snow mould test (R1-plants)

The same HS-families used in the toxin test were tested for their snow mould resistance (see Table 3). However, only D0/D0 and D200/D400 were compared. On average of the two populations no significant differences between the two groups could be found. The same was true for WD02. However, in WD51, a significant difference (0.6) could be recognized. On average of both selection variants, WD51 was still better (0.44) than WD02. There were no significant differences between the HS-families.

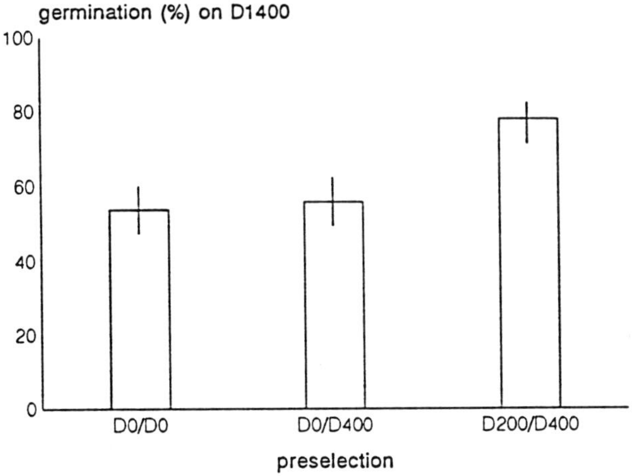

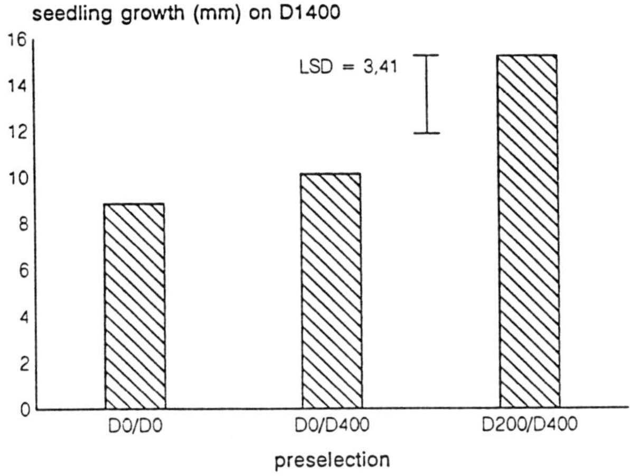

Fig. 1. DON-tolerance of sexual progenies from in vitro selection (av. of 2 populations).

Table 3. Snow mould resistance of sexual proge-
nies from in vitro selection

Variant	Av.	WD02	WD51
DON 0–0	5.60	5.63	5.57
DON 200/400	5.39	5.80	4.98
LSD5	0.26	0.40	0.33

Discussion

Schroeder & Christensen (1963) suggested that wheat plants have two basic types of resistance to *Fusarium* head blight:

1. resistance to the establishment of the initial infection and
2. resistance to hyphal invasion of the plant tissue.

The same holds true for resistance to *M. nivale*. However, according to our experience, no type 1 resistance could be detected, i.e. in all cases all inoculated plants were colonized by the pathogen. Miller et al. (1985) suggested a third level of resistance which is due to the toxin. According to their profound studies, DON-synthesis is either prevented or enzymatic degradation of DON is promoted or both. Until now it is not yet well documented whether the ability of toxin production of an isolate is a factor of agressiveness.

Our data clearly demonstrate that in vitro selection with DON as selective agent can improve pathogen resistance. According to our data, DON has to be applied already during callus induction. It is not clear whether the selection response is due to the variation within the populations or induced by mutation (somaclonal variation). The differences between the two populations suggest, that in WD51 a higer level of both toxin and pathogen resistance was available. This is probably due to previous selection for snow mould resistance with a toxigenic isolate. The high level of DON-resistance in the sexual progenies indicate, that there are heritable genetic factors for toxin resistance. It is assumed that the ability for toxin degradation was improved by in vitro selection. However, the results in the snow mould test were somewhat disappointing. Though in WD51 a significant higher snow mould tolerance in the D200/D400 compared to the D0/D0 variant could be observed. From these results several conclusions can be drawn: toxin and pathogen resistance are not closely correlated, and the association between these two objectives seem to be material dependant (a closer relationship in WD51).

The test for DON-tolerance seems to be a powerful tool for preselection before performing the laborious snow mould test. Such selection experiments are in progress. However, comparable field data are still lacking.

Previous investigations (Posselt, 1987) have shown, that within perennial ryegrass genetic variation for snow mould resistance exists. Though the correlation between artificial infection tests and field data is fairly weak (Nilsson & Weibull, 1981), breeders probably have no other choice than to apply such tests. Compared to the widespread application of colonized wheat kernels as inoculum, we believe, that the described inoculum production using vermiculite will improve the precision of the test remarkably.

From a breeders point of view cloning all plants to have true replicates is not practical. The use of some type of progeny (i.e. HS-families) is recommended with 10–15 plants per replication and at least four replications. In previous studies (unpublished results) it could be shown, that heritability on a single plant basis is very low and therefore mass selection is not very promising.

Acknowledgements

This project was supported by a grant of the Bundesministerium für Forschung und Technologie (BMFT No. PBE 0318897).

References

Altpeter, F. & U.K. Posselt, 1994. Production of high quantities of 3-Acetyldeoxynivalenol and Deoxynivalenol. Appl. Microbiol. & Biotechnol. 41: 384–387.

Arsvoll, K., 1977. Effects of hardening, plant age and development in *Phleum pratense* and *Festuca pratensis* on resistance to snow mold fungi. Meld. Norg. LandbrHögsk. 56: 1–14.

Jönsson, H.A. & C. Nilsson, 1985. Selection for resistance to snow mould Proc. XV Int. Grassl. Congr.: 291–293.

Marasas, W.F.O., P.E. Nelson & T.A. Toussoun, 1984. Toxigenic *Fusarium* Species: Indentity and Mycotoxicology, Pennsylvania State University Press. University Park, Pa., 350 p.

Miedaner, T., H. Höxter & H.H. Geiger, 1993. Development of a resistance test for winter rye to snow mold (*Microdochium nivale*) under controlled environment conditions in regard to field inoculations. Can. J. Bot. 71: 136–144.

Miller, J.D., J.C. Young & D.R. Sampson, 1985. Deoxynivalenol and *Fusarium* head blight resistance in spring cereals. Phytopath. Z. 113: 359–367.

Nilsson, C. & P. Weibull, 1981. Selection for improved resistance to *Fusarium nivale* (Fr) Ces. Proc. 4th Intern. Turfgrass Res. Conf., Guelph, pp. 21–26.

Nirenberg, H.I., 1981. A simplified method for identifying *Fusarium* spp. occurring on wheat. Can. J. Bot. 59: 1599–1609.

Posselt, U.K., 1987. Untersuchungen zur Resistenz gegenüber dem Schneeschimmel (*Fusarium nivale*). 29. Fachtung der DLG, Fulda, pp. 82–89.

Posselt, U.K., 1991. In vitro selection in forage crops. In: Fodder Crops Breeding: Achievement, Novel Strategies and Biotechnology. Proc. 16th EUCARPIA Fodder Crops Sect. Meeting, Wageningen, 18–22 Nov. 1990, pp. 117–121.

Schmidt, F. & U.K. Posselt, 1991. Reproducable regeneration of callus cultures derived from mature embryos in *Lolium perenne*. In: Fodder Crops Breeding: Achievement, Novel Strategies and Biotechnology. Proc. 16th EUCARPIA Fodder Crops Sect. Meeting, Wageningen, 18–22 Nov. 1990, pp. 205–206.

Schroeder, H.W. & J.J. Christensen, 1963. Factors affecting resistance of wheat to scab caused by *Gibberella zeae*. Phytopathology 53: 831–838.

Smiley, R.W., 1983. Compendium of Turfgrass Diseases. Amer. Phytopathol. Soc. St. Paul, USA.

O.A. Rognli et al. (eds.), Breeding Fodder Crops for Marginal Conditions, 207–214.
© 1994 Kluwer Academic Publishers. Printed in the Netherlands.

Development of procedures to identify red clover resistant to *Sclerotinia trifoliorum*

P. MARUM, R.R. SMITH & C.R. GRAU
Løken Research Station, Norway, and USDA-ARS and University of Wisconsin, USA

Summary. Sclerotinia crown and stem rot is a destructive disease on red clover. In this study we investigated appropriate procedures for producing and storing ascospores in the laboratory and compared the reaction of selected red clover germplasm, when inoculated with either ascospores or mycelium. The two methods produced fairly similar results, although there were exceptions. The procedures described to produce, store and inoculate with ascospores, will provide an opportunity to select germplasm resistant to *Sclerolinia trifoliorum* using ascospores, as inoculum.

Introduction

Sclerotinia crown and stem rot, caused by *Sclerotinia trifoliorum* Eriks., is one of the most destructive diseases on forage legumes in the eastern and north central areas of the U.S. and in Europe. On red clover (*Trifolium pratense* L.), Sclerotinia is especially destructive on seedling stands, those established in late summer or early fall. Under optimum conditions initial stands can be completely destroyed. On established stands, the disease kills individual plants, causing a gradual but hastened reduction of stand. This disease is one of the most important factors acting on yield and perenniality of red clover.

Sclerotia of *Sclerotinia trifoliorum* form on diseased plants during the winter and spring. The sclerotia remain dormant throughout the summer. Mycelia growth occur rarely in the soil and is apparently of no significance in the disease cycle. Cool, wet conditions in the fall induce carpogenic germination of sclerotia. Apothecia start to form when the daily soil temperature have declined to about 10 °C. Ascospores are forcibly ejected from asci and may be carried long distances by wind to new plants. Ascospores deposited on leaves germinate and penetrate directly. Dijkstra (1964) has described a lag phase of the pathogen, which occurs immediately after penetration, producing brown spots. Further progress into the tissue appears to be stimulated by frost or by continuous moisture on the plant surface. Colonisation of the tissue continues throughout the winter, with secondary infections occurring as mycelia grow from plant to plant. This secondary infection can be very destructive.

Control of the disease with fungicides has been met with limited success and is expensive. Therefore, the most ideal control would be to develop red clover cultivars resistant to the fungus. Selection of more resistant cultivars, based mainly on the observation of better perenniality, is generally made in the field, where the disease is endemic. Although many factors seem to influence the expression of resistance, artificial techniques in growth chambers are very useful to set up the primary screening for resistant plants.

Development of resistant germplasm was achieved with slow progress only, even though scientists have attempted to select for resistance for many years. Mycelium has been used as the source of inoculum. The question may be asked if the method of mycelia inoculation applied in the laboratory is in agreement with what happens in nature. The primary inoculum are ascospores and not the mycelium. This natural inoculum is produced by apothecia borne on sclerotia in the fall. When ascospores are important in the field it is perhaps explicable why mycelial infection alone does not afford a good possibility of selection for conditions prevailing in practice (Dijkstra, 1964). The use of this natural inoculum has been difficult because apothecia can be difficult to find, laborious to collect and can only be used for a short time (Raynal & Picard, 1985).

Until recently ascospores have not been used for selection tests because they are not easily produced in the laboratory. Raynal & Picard (1985) described one method for production of ascospores in the laboratory. A critical step is breaking the dormancy of the sclerotia to produce apothecia in the laboratory. Raynal & Picard (1985) broke dormancy of the sclerotia by keeping the sclerotia at 30 °C for 30 days. Several procedures are described in the literature to break dormancy and improve the formation of apothecia. McGimpsey & Malone (1979) obtained better results when the sclerotia, that were placed on 1% tap water agar, first were placed at − 18 °C for 48 h. The best results were obtained by simulating late autumn temperatures, i.e. alternating a 16 h period at 2 °C with 8 h at 8 °C. To induce apothecia production Jayachandran et al. (1987) air dried the sclerotia for 24–48 h after harvest before they were placed on 1% water agar. Kohn (1979) cold conditioned the sclerotia for 4 weeks at 0 °C. In a closely related species, *Sclerotinia sclerotiorum*, Radke & Grau (1986), first air dried the sclerotia for one week and then placed them on moist filter paper in a petri dish, and stored them at 5 °C for 30 days. According to these studies it looks like there are several ways to initiate the production of apothecia.

The objectives of this study were to investigate the appropriate procedures for producing and storing ascospores *in vitro* in the laboratory so that they are readily available for inoculation over time, and to compare the reaction of selected red clover germplasm when inoculated with either ascospores or mycelium.

Materials and methods

Initially we had difficulties producing ascospores in the laboratory. The method described by Raynal & Picard (1985) was not effective for us. In a preliminary study we were not able to get any formation of apothecia. To study this more closely we selected four strains of the fungus, Mar.1-B, S-26, Hank., and Racine, from different areas in Wisconsin and produced large quantities of sclerotia of each. To do this we used the following procedure.

Potatoes were sliced and put in a wide mouth 2 l Manson Jar with a 2.5 cm diameter hole in the lid. PDA solution (19.5g/l) were added to about 2 cm from the bottom. Absorbent cotton was placed in the hole and the jar was autoclaved for 20 minutes. After the jar had cooled, 15 mycelium plugs were added. The jars were placed in a dark room at room temperature (about 20 °C). After 4 weeks the sclerotia were harvested, rinsed in water and air dried at room temperature for one week. The sclerotia were stored in the refrigerator (4 °C) until use.

To break dormancy we tried different methods of preconditioning. About 50 sclerotia of each strain were placed in petridishes and exposed to the following temperatures: room temperature (about 20 °C), + 30 °C, + 5 °C, and − 17 °C. The sclerotia at 5 and − 17 °C were placed on wet filter paper.

After 5 weeks the sclerotia were planted in a soil mix in small glass jars with glass lids to maintain the moisture, and placed at 15 °C with 12 hr of 160 μmole of light. After 2 weeks there was no sign of growth from the apothecia.

To overcome this problem, the glass jars were maintained very moist at 25 °C for four weeks. (A condition not to different from the summer climate in Wisconsin.) After this treatment the temperature was reduced to 15 °C with the same light conditions as before. After this treatment stipes began to form after 10–14 days.

Even though we did not get any formation of apothecia after only the first pretreatment, they influenced the results. The two temperatures + 30 °C and + 5 °C produced the best results (Table 1). There were large differences between the strains. The strains Mar.1-B and S-26 gave a large number of apothecia, while the strain Hank. and Racine hardly produced any apothecia at all. For further studies we used the strain Mar 1-B.

In a later test we demonstrated that we could get good production of apothecia by only keeping the sclerotia in moist soil at 25 °C for four weeks. Each sclerotia of the Mar 1-B strain produced on the average about 1.5 apothecia. The maximum number of apothecia producing ascospores occurred 35 days after the sclerotia were placed at 15 °C after pretreatment. In this test we were able to collect ascospores for about 40 days.

In the last test we used the following procedure to produce, collect and store the ascospores in the laboratory.

Table 1. Number of apothecia produced per sclerotia planted
after 4 weeks in wet soil at 25 °C

Strain	Pretreatment				Mean
	Room temp.	+ 30 °C	+ 5 °C	− 17 °C	strain
Mar. 1-B	.46	1.13	1.16	.18	.73
S-26	.88	1.07	1.20	.04	.80
Hank.	.04	.10	.00	.00	.04
Racine	.00	. 00	. 00	.00	.00
Mean treat.	.42	.69	.72	.08	

[a] Approximately 20 °C

Procedure for in vivo production of ascospores

Sclerotia were seeded at a depth of 1–2 mm in 8 cm peat pots containing sterilised mix of soil, sand, and peat (1:1:1; v/v/v) and placed in a plastic flat containing 2 cm of water to keep the sclerotia and soil mix moist at all times. The sclerotia were maintained at 25 °C and 12 hr day-length for 28 days to break dormancy. After 28 days the peat pots, with sclerotia, were placed in small glass jars with glass tops in order to maintain the sclerotia at 100% relative humidity. The sclerotia were maintained at 15 °C with 12 hr of 160 μmole light. Stipes began to form after 10–14 days. The asci started to produce ascospores at 3–4 weeks after they were placed at 15 °C. Ascospores were released from the asci when the glass lid was removed, and were collected on 0.45 m cellulose nitrate membrane filter in a Millipore apparatus connected to a vacuum pump (Radke & Grau, 1986). The ascospores were stored on the filter paper at − 18 °C in parpafilm-sealed glass bottles containing silica gel to absorb the moisture. Ascospores have now been effectively stored for 12 month with good viability.

Ascospore inoculum

To prepare the inoculum for the ascospore test we cut a smaller piece of a filter containing ascospores that had been stored in the freezer, and placed it in a testube with 3ml of water. The testube were swirled for about 3 minutes to get as many spores into the water as possible. The final inoculum contained 10000 spores/ml, 10 g glucose/l, and 3 drops of Tween 80/100 ml.

Production of mycelium inoculum

For production of mycelium inoculum we adapted a procedure described by Rhodes (1991) for testing alfalfa with slight modifications. Three mycelium plugs, from the isolate Mar. 1-B., from active growing mycelium were placed in PDA broth and continuously rotated at 160 rpm. In one week the three plugs had developed into mycelium balls with a diameter of about 2–3 cm. The three mycelium balls were added to 250 ml of water and blended for about 5 seconds. The inoculum was filtered through a 50 m sieve. To the inoculum 3 drops of Tween 80/100 ml were added.

Plant material and methods

Four Scandinavian cultivars (Molstad, Bjursele, Nordi, and Kolpo-4X), two U.S. cultivars (Arlington and Pennscott), and one experimental strain (C369-Arlington selected for field tolerance to *Sclerotinia*) were inoculated and evaluated for their reaction to *Sclerotinia trifoliorum*. Two separate sets of tests were conducted: one using ascospores as the source of inoculum and the second set using mycelium as the source of inoculum. Because of the early problems with the procedure to produce ascospores, all 21 replicates using mycelium as the source of inoculum were completed before any inoculations were done with ascospores. Because of space limitations of the growth chambers normally 4 replicates were tested at a time. A total of 16 replicates were inoculated with ascospores.

Growing and inoculating red clover plants

In the original procedure described by Rhodes (1991), he seeded the plants directly and then thinned them to get an equal number of plants per variety. We had, however, problems to get equal establishment, because of variable seed viability. Therefore, we decided to transplant three-days-old seedlings into plastic trays containing a soil mix. In each replication we used 14 plants. The design was a randomised complete block design, where the replicates corresponded to flats.

The plastic trays were then inserted into a second non-draining plastic flat such that the trays could be watered from below with Hoaglands's solution. Two-week-old plants were spray-inoculated with ascospores or mycelium, depending upon desired test. After inoculation a plastic top was placed over the plastic tray to keep the plants at 100% relative humidity.

Plants were incubated at 15 °C at 100% relative humidity in 12 h day-length for 10–14 days for mycelial inoculations and for 14 days for ascospore inoculations. Plants were evaluated on a Disease Severity Index (DSI): 1 =

Table 2. Reaction to red clover cultivars and strains to *Sclerotinia trifoliorum* using either ascospores or mycelium as inoculum source

Cultivar	Source of Inoculum			
	Mycelium (21 reps)		Ascospores (2 reps)	
	DSI[a]	% Surv.[b]	DSI	% Surv.
Kolpo (4 ×)	3.57	54	3.04	68
Bjursele	3.61	44	3.75	35
C369	3.64	48	3.61	46
Molstad	3.67	45	3.54	46
Nordi	3.82	44	3.42	46
Arlington	3.91	39	3.64	35
Pennscott	3.92	39	3.14	59
Mean	3.73	45	3.45	48
LSD 5%	.20	10	1.00	21
C.V. %	8.4	35	12	17

[a]Disease Severity Index: 1 = healthy, 5 = dead

[b]Percent plants surviving 28 days after inoculation

healthy plant, 2 = slight necrosis, 3 = moderate necrosis, 4 severe necrosis, and 5 = dead plant. At 28 days after inoculation the number of surviving plants was determined.

Results and discussion

Twenty-one replicates of 14 plants per replicate for each cultivar/strain were inoculated with mycelium. There were differences both in DSI and % Survival depending on where the plants were grown in the flat. There was a trend for plants in the outside rows to survive better than the plants in the middle. The column values were adjusted to minimise this effect.

A separate 16 replicates were inoculated with ascospores. In several of these reps we tried different ways to inoculate the plants. In 14 of the replicates, we were unable to differentiate between the cultivars. In 8 reps most plants survived (80–100% survival), because of an error we had used too little glucose in the inoculum and in 6 reps most plants died (5–18% survival). In two reps we observed about 50% survival and detected a reasonable separation between the cultivars. The results from these two reps are given in Table 2 together with the results from the mycelium test.

With only two reps of the ascospore test it is difficult to make a conclusive comparison between the methods, but the ascospore method seems to give fairly similar results with the mycelium method.

The tetraploid Norwegian cultivar Kolpo was most resistant in both tests. The three cultivars/strains (Kolpo, C369 and Nordi) are all result of previous selection for resistance to the fungus. Also the strain C369 showed consistently good results in the two tests. In both tests C369 is more resistant than Arlington as expected since C329 is result of selection in Arlington for resistance against *Sclerotinia trifoliorum*. Arlington is among the least resistant cultivars in both tests.

Nordi is not more resistant than Molstad. That was a little surprising since Nordi is selected from Molstad after six generations of recurrent selection against *Sclerotinia trifoliorum*. There could be several possible explanations for this result. The selection in Norway was done on hardened 3 month old plants in comparison to the tests in this study that were done on non hardened 2 weeks old plants. This may cause different reactions in the plants. Different strains of Sclerotinia were used and Norwegian and American strains may give different results. There is also the possibility that the test was not good enough to separate the two cultivars, although we do not favor this conclusion.

The old U.S. cultivar Pennscott was one of the least resistant in the mycelium test and one of the most resistant in the ascospore test. If this difference is due to different mechanisms controlling resistance or if it happened just by chance is to early to determine.

Conclusions

In these artificially produced epiphytic tests, inoculation of red clover germplasm with either ascospore or mycelium produced fairly similar results, although there were exceptions. The results suggest that some red clover germplasm expresses a reasonable level of resistance to *Sclerotinia trifoliorum*. However, the mycelium-inoculated derived germplasm has not proven to express acceptable resistance under field conditions. The procedures described to produce, store, and inoculate with ascospores, will provide an opportunity to select germplasm resistant to *S. trifoliorum*, the natural method of field infection in USA.

References

Dijkstra, J., 1964. Inoculation with ascospores of *Sclerotinia trifoliorum* for detection of clover rot resistant red clover. Euphytica 13: 314–329.

Jayachandran, M., H.J. Willetts & S. Bullock, 1987. Light and scanning electron microscope observations on apothesial development of *Sclerotinia sclerotiorum*, *S. trifoliorum* and *S. minor*. Trans. Br. mycol. Soc. 89: 167–178.

Kohn, L.M., 1979. A monographic revision of the genus *Sclerotinia*. Mycotaxon. 9: 365–444.
McGimpsey, H.C. & J.P. Malone, 1979. Production of apothecia of *Sclerotinia trifoliorum* in the laboratory. Bull. British Mycological Society 13: 104.
Radke, V.L. & C.G. Grau, 1986. Effects of herbicides on carpogenic germination of *Sclerotinia sclerotiorum*. Plant Disease 70:19–23.
Raynal, G. & J. Picard, 1985. Laboratory production of the sexual stage of *Sclerotinia trifoliorum*, the winter crown-rot agent of red clover, consequences for improving control methods. Proc. XV Intern. Grassl Cong., Kyoto, Japan, Aug. 24–31 1985, pp. 782–783.
Rhodes, L.H., 1991. Sclerotinia crown and stem rot resistance. In: C.C. Fox, R. Berbert, F.A. Gray, C.R. Grau, D.L. Jessen & M.A. Peterson (Eds.), Standard Tests to Characterise Alfalfa Cultivars. North American Alfalfa Improvement Conference.

Cold hardening – a physiological mechanism for resisting biotic as well as abiotic stress factors

ANNE MARTE TRONSMO
Norwegian Plant Protection Institute, Fellesbygget, N-1432 ÅS, Norway

Summary. Plants adapted to a northern climate respond to autumn conditions with cold hardening. Cold hardened plants have higher resistance to freezing and other abiotic winter-stress factors than unhardened ones, but also increased resistance to snow mould fungi. This is regarded as a natural adaptation to a sub-arctic climate. Cold hardening also affects resistance to other fungal diseases, as rust, powdery mildew and leaf spot. The effect of hardening is similar to resistance induced by microorganisms. Biochemical studies have shown increased sucrose content as well as enhanced invertase activity after cold hardening of timothy and reed canary-grass. Mobilisation of sucrose in the plants may be of importance for both resisting fungal invasion and freezing injury. Cold hardened spring barley contained RNA-species and PR-proteins described from mildew-inoculated plants, amongst them a putative chitinase. Cold induced gene expression have several similarities to the gene expression in plants exhibiting microbial induced disease resistance.

Introduction

Perennial plants which are adapted to northern marginal conditions survive our winter conditions better than plants adapted to milder winter conditions. The reason for this can be either:

1. The plants have a constitutive ability to resist or tolerate the winter-stress factors due to physiological or morphological traits, or

2. The plants have an inducible ability for responding to autumn conditions with 'cold hardening', an acclimatization process which results in enhanced resistance to winter-stress factors.

A definition of 'hardening' is "An exposure to sublethal stress which results in resistance to an otherwise lethal stress factor" (Levitt, 1980). In agreement with the definition, cold hardened grasses have a higher resistance to freezing stress than unhardened and dehardened ones (Table 1) (Tronsmo, 1985).

A strong increase in resistance to snow mould fungi as well as other abiotic winter stress factors in cold hardened grass and forage species is also found (Tronsmo, 1984a). The phenomenon is regarded as a natural adaptation to a sub-arctic climate. Although grasses from a more temperate climate have the ability to cold harden, they do not obtain the same level of resistance to winter stress factors as the northern ones do (Larsen and Tronsmo, 1992).

216

Table 1. Resistance to freezing in the timothy varieties 'Grindstad' and 'Engmo' after hardening and dehardening treatments (From Tronsmo, 1985)

Treatment of plants	Resistance to freezing*	
	'Grinstad'	'Engmo'
Unhardened	0.7	0.8
Hardened 2 weeks	7.5	8.0
Hardened 2 weeks, dehardened 1 week	3.6	4.8
Hardened 2 weeks, dehardened 2 weeks	2.6	4.6
$LSD_{0.05}$	1.0	0.3

* Rating for resistance to freezing from 0 to 9, 0 = all plants killed, 9 = no visible injury.

Cold hardening

Accumulation of carbohydrates is regarded as an important part of the cold hardening process. It has long been known that the storage carbohydrates in grasses are fructans, and they accumulate in grasses during autumn (Smith, 1968; Pollock and Ruggles, 1976). However, in my opinion, better knowledge about the carbohydrate composition is necessary to understand the physiological mechanisms behind the cold hardening and its effects on resistance to winter-stress factors. Biochemical studies have shown that timothy and reed canary-grass have increased content of mono-and oligo-saccharides following cold hardening treatment at + 1° C for 2 weeks (Tronsmo et al., 1993a). In timothy we mainly found an enhanced sucrose content, in reed canary grass, both sucrose and the trisaccharide 1-F-fructosylsucrose were increased (Fig. 1). Dehardening in the greenhouse at 12–20° C led to a drop in the content of the mono- and oligo-saccharides (Fig. 1). The contents of total hot water soluble carbohydrates were approximately equal in hardened and dehardened plants. But dehardened plants contained more fructan than hardened ones. This indicates that at low temperature, a significant portion of the fructans is mobilised as sucrose.

The mobilisation of sugars in cold hardened plants is probably facilitated by changes in gycosidase activities. In cold hardened timothy and reed canary-grass we found an increased activity of invertase (Fig. 2), an enzyme which splits sucrose into fructose and glucose. This is necessary to get the sugar transported across the cell membrane. The role of mono- and oligo-saccharides in resisting freezing injury can simply be by lowering the

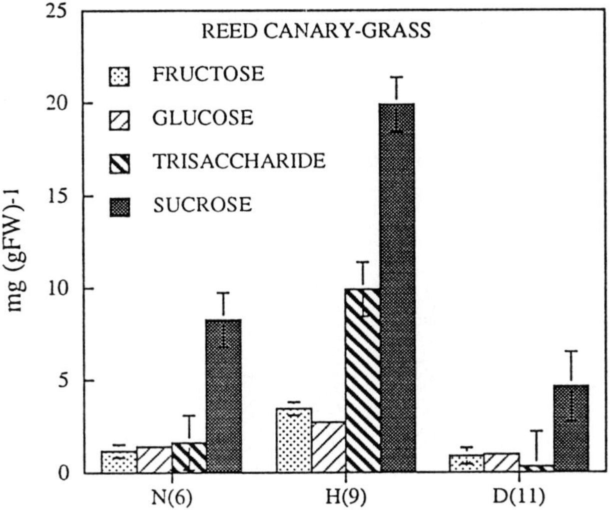

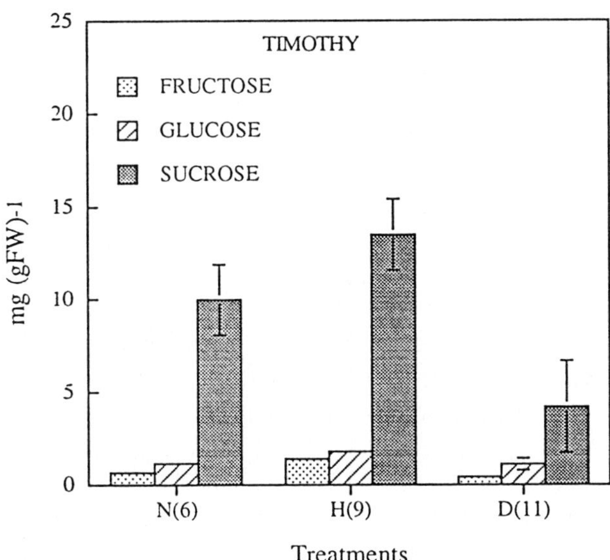

Fig. 1. Content of LMW-carbohydrates in timothy and reed canary-grass in untreated (N), hardened (H), and dehardened (D) plants. The data presented are least square means of 3 replicate experiments, each with 4 parallel determinations. The age of plants in weeks is given in brackets ( ). (From Tronsmo et al., 1993a.)

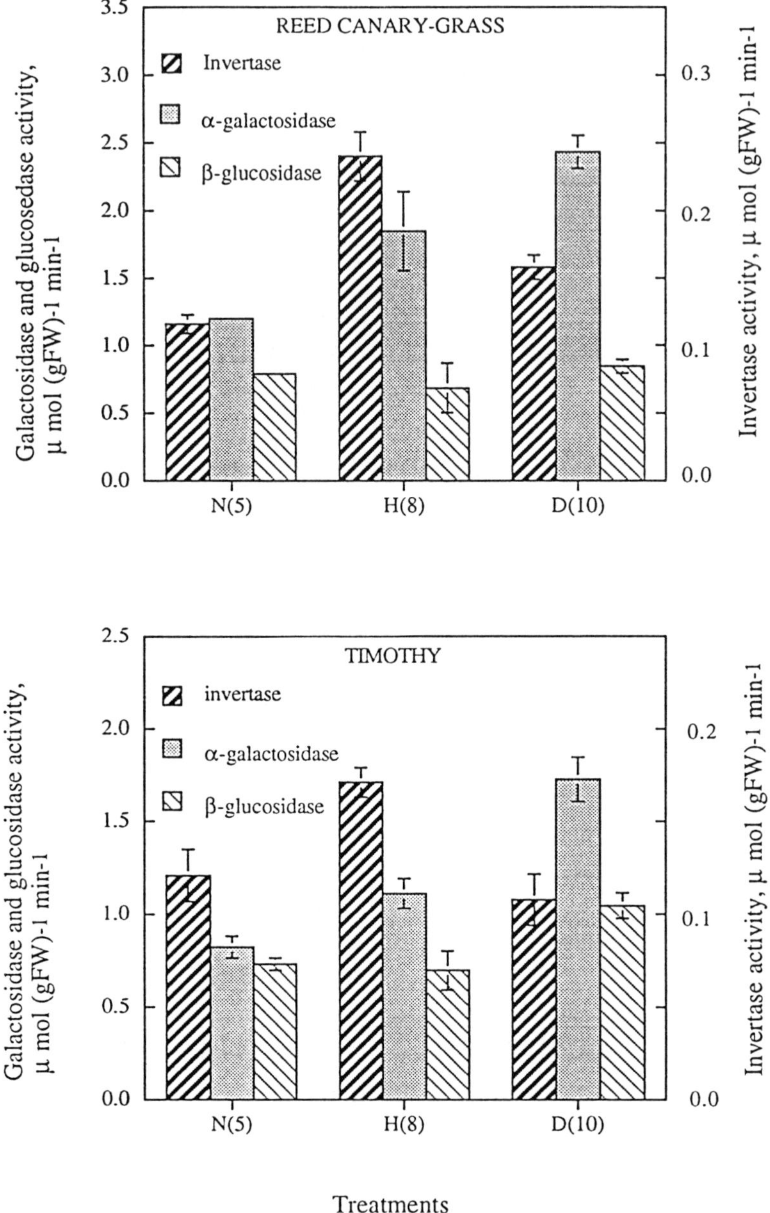

Fig. 2. Glycosidase activity (invertase, α-galactosidase, β-glucosidase) in leaves of timothy and reed canary-grass. Enzyme activities are presented as μmol $(gFW)^{-1}$ min^{-1}. The data are means of 3 replicate samples. Standard error of the means are shown as bars. Otherwise as in Fig. 1. (From Tronsmo et al., 1993a.)

freezing point of the cytoplasm, but it is also possible that they can act as cryoprotectants in cell membranes (Santarius, 1982; Tronsmo et al., 1993a). The soluble sugars are probably also important for the ability of the plant to resist fungal invasion. The low molecular weight (LMW) sugars are easily transported within the plant as a readily available energy source. This may be of significance for preventing as well as repairing injury caused by either abiotic or biotic stress factors.

Induced disease resistance by cold treatment

Another effect of cold hardening of grass species is increased resistance to several fungal diseases, as rust, powdery mildew and leaf spot (Tronsmo, 1984b and unpublished). In barley, resistance to powdery mildew can be induced by both virulent and avirulent strains of the pathogen and by saprophytes (Smedegaard-Petersen et al., 1992). In response to infection, plants activate new genes (de Wit, 1992; Keen, 1993) and enhance expression of others in response to cold hardening treatment (Lee and Chen, 1993; Thomashow et al., 1993). Our research is currently aiming at the question: Does cold treatment induce similar gene expression as found in plants exhibiting biotic induced resistance? So far we have approached the question by comparing physiological and biochemical changes induced by cold with resistance-responses induced by microorganisms. In a Nordic collaborative project, using spring barley as a model plant, proteins were analysed by gel electrophoresis and Western blots with antibodies to PR-proteins from barley (Bryngelsson and Collinge, 1991). We have found that cold hardened plants contain similar PR-proteins as mildew-inoculated plants, amongst them may be chitinase (Tronsmo et al., 1993b). The role of chitinases in defense is probably due to their ability to degrade the fungal cell-wall, in those fungi where chitin is a main cell-wall component (in asco- and basidiomycetes). Expression of genes induced by cold treatment in barley has to a limited extent been analysed by Northern blots, using probes from cDNA libraries prepared from m-RNA isolated from barley inoculated with powdery mildew (Smedegaard-Petersen et al., 1992; Thordal-Christensen et al., 1992). RNA from cold-hardened barley plants hybridized to a probe from a putative sucrose synthetase gene. We believe that induction of this gene is related to the sugar mobilisation in the plants, as also reported by Crespi et al. (1991).

Conclusion

Freezing resistance and snow mould resistance are supposed to be different traits. However, in grass species cold hardening induces several responses which are important for resisting a pathogen infection. Both proteins and nucleic acids originally described as induced by plant pathogen are also induced or enhanced by cold hardening. This indicate that resistance induced by cold stress involves the same defense mechanisms as resistance induced by biotic stress. Further studies might elucidate specific responses for resistance to pathogens, and which cannot be induced by cold. We are aiming at separating resistance due to specific genes for the disease resistance from the cold induced responses.

References

Bryngelsson T and Collinge DB 1991 Biochemical and molecular analyses of the response of barley to infection by powdery mildew. *In*: Barley: Genetics, Molecular Biology and Biotechnology. Ed. PR Shewry. pp. 459–480. C.A.B. International, Wallingford.

Crespi MD, Zabaleta EJ, Pontis HG and Salerno GL 1991 Sucrose synthase expression during cold acclimation in wheat. Plant Physiol. 96, 887–891.

de Wit PJGM 1992 Molecular characterization of gene-for-gene systems in plant-fungal interactions. Annu. Rev. Phytopathol. 30, 391–418.

Keen NT 1993 An overview of active disease defense in plants. *In*: Mechanisms of Plant Defense Responses. Eds. B Fritig and M Legrand. pp. 3–11. Kluwer Academic Publishers, Dordrecht.

Larsen A and Tronsmo AM 1992 Natural hardening in grasses. Poster at the 4th International Plant Cold Hardiness seminar, Uppsala, Sweden 1991. Poster abstracts, SLU Rapport 53, p. 26.

Lee SP and Chen THH 1993 Molecular biology of plant cold hardiness development. *In*: Advances in Plant Cold Hardiness. Eds. PH Li and L Christersson. pp. 1–29. CRC Press, Boca Raton, FL.

Levitt J 1980 Responses of plants to environmental stresses. Second Edition. Vol. 1. Academic Press. New York.

Pollock CJ and Ruggles PA 1976 Cold-induced fructosan synthesis in leaves of *Dactylis glomerata*. Phytochemistry 15, 1643–1646.

Santarius KA 1982 The mechanism of cryoprotection of biomembrane systems by carbohydrates. *In*: Plant Cold Hardiness and Freezing Stress, Vol. 2, Eds. PH Li and A Sakai. pp. 475–486. Academic Press, New York, NY.

Smedegaard-Petersen V, Collinge DB, Thordal-Christensen H, Brandt J, Gregersen PL, Cho BH, Walter-Larsen H, Kristensen HJ and Vad K 1992 Induction and molecular analyses of resistance to barley powdery mildew. *In*: Biological Control of Plant Diseases: Progress and Challenge for the Future. Eds. EC Tjamos, G Papavizas and RJ Cook. pp. 321–326. NATO-ASI Plenum Press, New York.

Smith D 1968 Carbohydrates in grasses. IV. Influence of temperature on the sugar and fructosan composition of timothy plant parts at anthesis. Crop Sci. 8, 331–334.

Thordal-Christensen H, Brandt J, Cho BH, Gregersen P, Rasmussen SK, Smedegaard-Petersen V and Collinge DB 1992 c-DNA cloning and characterization of two barley peroxidase transcripts induced differentially by the powdery mildew fungus. Physiol. Molec. Plant Pathol. 40, 395–409.

Thomashow MF, Gilmour SJ and Lin C 1993 Cold regulated genes of *Arabidopsis thaliana*. *In*: Advances in Plant Cold Hardiness. Eds. PH Li and L Christersson. pp. 31–44. CRC Press, Boca Raton, FL.

Tronsmo AM 1984a The effects of hardening, dehardening and freezing on resistance to snow mould fungi in timothy and meadow fescue. *In*: Proceedings of the 10th general meeting of the European grassland federation. Eds. H Riley and AO Skjelvåg. pp. 292–296.

Tronsmo AM 1984b Resistance to the rust fungus *Puccinia poae-nemoralis* in *Poa pratensis* induced by low-temperature hardening. Can. J. Bot. 62, 2891–2892.

Tronsmo AM 1985 Effects of dehardening on resistance to freezing and to infection by *Typhula ishikariensis* in *Phleum pratense*. Acta Agric. Scan. 35, 113–116.

Tronsmo AM, Kobro G, Morgenlie S and Flengsrud R 1993a Carbohydrate content and glycosidase activities following cold hardening in two grass species. Physiologia Plantarum 88, 689–695.

Tronsmo AM, Gregersen P, Hjeljord L, Sandal T, Bryngelsson T and Collinge DB 1993b Cold induced disease resistance. *In*: Mechanisms of Plant Defense Responses. Eds. B Fritig and M Legrand. p. 369. Kluwer Academic Publishers, Dordrecht.

O.A. Rognli et al. (eds.), Breeding Fodder Crops for Marginal Conditions, 223–232.
© 1994 Kluwer Academic Publishers. Printed in the Netherlands.

Morphological and biochemical variation in Sardinian populations of *Medicago polymorpha* L. suitable for rainfed mediterranean conditions *

S. BULLITTA[1], R. FLORIS[1], M.D. HAYWARD[2], A. LOI[1],
C. PORQUEDDU[1] and F. VERONESI[3]
[1]*Centro Pascoli-CNR, Via De Nicola, 07100 Sassari, Italy;* [2]*Iger, Welsh Plant breeding Station, plas Gogerddan, Aberystwyth, SY233EB, UK;* [3]*Dipartimento biotecnologie agrarie ed ambientali, Via Brecce Bianche, 60131 Ancona, Italy*

Summary. Forty five accessions of Sardinian germplasm of *Medicago polymorpha* L., derived from a wide range of climatic and edaphic conditions, were evaluated to identify useful genetic resources for the development of cultivars for rainfed Mediterranean conditions. The accessions were assessed for variation in morphological, agronomic and biochemical traits. Considerable variation was found between populations indicating the potential for selection.

Introduction

Burr medic, *Medicago polymorpha* L. syn. *Medicago hispida* Gaertn. (2n = 2x = 14), is an annual, autogamous and self reseeding species widely distributed in Mediterranean pastures. It is widespread in temperate Europe, the middle East, and both northern and southern Africa (Lesins & Lesins, 1979). According to Aitken (1981) and to Clarkson & Russel (1975) the wide diffusion and adaptability of the species can be explained by its low sensitivity to photoperiod and vernalization.

Heyn (1963) recognized three botanical varieties: *brevispina* Heyn, with spineless or tubercled pods; *polymorpha* spined and *vulgaris* Shin., spined but with pods smaller than *polymorpha*.

The species is interesting because of its adaptability to difficult soils and climates; its persistency related to summer survival as seed and self reseeding; its good winter growth; its ability to be grazed using high stocking rates; its possible use in rotation with cereals and in association with tree crops, and its low input requirements.

Burr medic, like other annual medics, is well adapted to alkaline soils and together with *Medicago murex* Willd., is most tolerant to acid soils (Gillespie, 1987). Its adaptability to soil pH lower than 5.5 has been reported by several authors (Cunningham & Munns, 1984; Munns & Keyser, 1981) but the persistency of the species is reduced by the lack of rhizobia resistant to low

* Work supported by the Italian Ministry of Agriculture and Forestry (MAF), Special Project 'Foraggicoltura Prativa', subproject 'Miglioramento Genetico'.

Table 1. Average and range of variation of the population means for each character evaluated

Characters		Avg	Min	Max	F (among populations)
Plant height	cm	23	15	34	***
Stem length	cm	53	42	63	***
Leaflet width	mm	13.6	9.9	16.9	***
Leaflet length	mm	17.8	12.8	23	*
Pod height	mm	4.6	3.3	7.3	***
Pod width	mm	5.8	5.1	6.8	**
Coils number	no.	2.5	1.5	4	***
Spine length	mm	1.4	0.5	2.2	***
Pods per plant	no.	331	40	599	***
Seeds per pod	no.	4.5	3	7	***
1000 seeds weight	g	2.4	1.3	4	***
Seed yield per plant	g	3.7	0.9	11.2	***

* P = 0.05; ** P = 0.01; *** P = 0.001

pH. Cold resistance is also well documented (Masson & Gintzburger, 1989; Cocks & Ehrman, 1987; Bullitta et al., 1991; Loi et al., 1992). In comparison to other medics, it is quite adaptable to poorly drained soils (Andrews & Hely, 1960; Francis & Poole, 1973).

In spite of the polymorphism and variation present in the species, the commercial varieties of *M.polymorpha* are very few. Only three Australian varieties, all belonging to subvariety *brevispina*, are present in the European seed market. Australian selected material is not well adapted to the different environmental conditions and stocking rates of Europe, Middle East and north Africa (Cocks, 1991; Olea et al., 1989). This has also been confirmed by comparisons with different ecotypes made in Sardinia (Porqueddu pers. com.) and in Tuscany (Talamucci & Pazzi, 1982).

Sardinian germplasm of *M.polymorpha* collected throughout the island has been evaluated for agronomic, biochemical and morphological traits to identify useful genetic resources for the development of cultivars for rainfed Mediterranean conditions.

Materials and methods

Burr medic accessions were from a Sardinian germplasm collection, the map of the collection sites is shown in Fig. 1. The environments of collection ranged from 0–1000 m (a.s.l.) and soil pH was between 5 and 8.5. Forty five

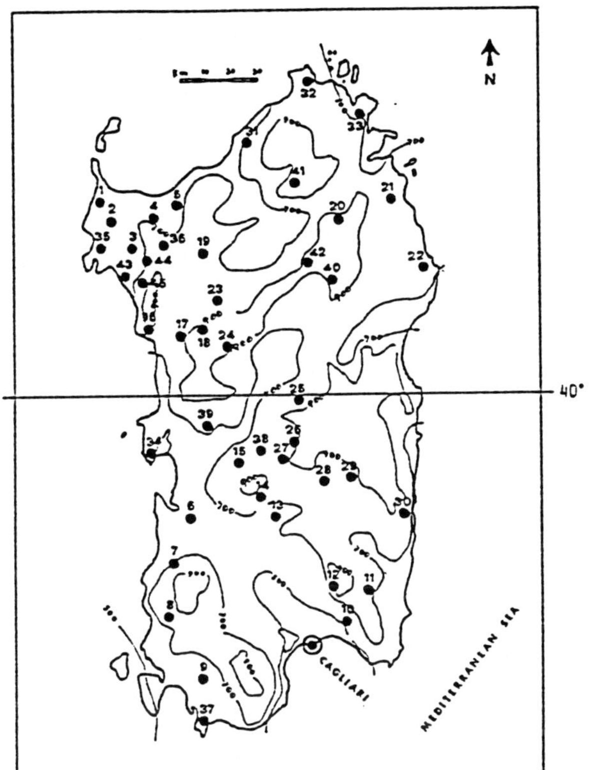

Fig. 1. Distribution of the collection sites of burr medic accessions in relation to the average annual rainfalls in Sardinia.

populations were assayed in N.W. Sardinia (Italy) at the Ottava experimental field of the Institute of Agronomy, 80 m a.s.l., pH = 7.5, average annual rainfall 547 mm. Seeds were inoculated with a commercial strain of *Rhizobium melilotii* and germinated in Petri dishes in autumn 1989. Seedlings were transferred into Jiffy pots and grown in a greenhouse. In February 1990, 18 plants per populations were transplanted in a spaced plant nursery (80 cm between rows, 25 cm on the row). N and P_2O_5 fertilizers were applied at a rate of 50 and 100 kg ha^{-1} respectively. The experimental design was a randomized complete block with three replications.

Data were collected on: plant and pod morphology and seed yield components. Plant height (cm), central leaflet width and length (mm) and stem length (cm) were measured at flowering on a single plant basis. Height and width of pods (mm), spine length (mm) and number of coils were measured on ten pods per plant at seed harvest. Total pod yield per plant was determined, samples of 200 pods per plant were threshed manually to determine

Table 2. Enzymes, loci, alleles and number of populations showing polymorphism

Enzyme	Locus abbreviation	Number of alleles	Number of populations showing allelic variation
Acid phosphatase	ACP1	3	6
Esterase	EST1	N.C.	12
Glutamate Oxaloacetate	GOT1	2	4
Transaminase	GOT2	3	24
Leucine Aminopeptidase	LAP1	1	0
	LAP2	2	5
Malate Dehydrogenase	MDH1	3	31
Malic Enzyme	ME1	1	0
	ME2	1	0
Peroxidase	PRX1	1	0
	PRX2	1	0
	PRX3	1	0
	PRX4	1	
6-Phosphogluconate	6PGD1	1	0
Dehydrogenase	6PGD2	1	0
Phospho-Gluco-Isomerase	PGI1	2	6
Phospho-Gluco-Mutase	PGM1	1	0
	PGM2	1	0
Shikimic Acid Dehydrogenase	SKD1	1	0
Superoxide Dismutase	SOD1	1	0
	SOD2	1	0
	SOD3	1	0

N.C. = not calculated

the number of seeds per pod, 1000 seed weight (g) and seed yield per plant (g).

In order to study the genetic variation present, the same collection was also utilized for electrophoretic analysis using the starch gel technique described by Hayward & McAdam (1977). The following enzymatic systems were assayed: phospho-gluco isomerase (PGI), leucine amino-peptidase (LAP), peroxidase (PRX), shikimate dehydrogenase (SKD), malic enzyme (ME), superoxidedismutase (SOD), phosphoglucomutase(PGM), malate dehydro-

Table 3. Linear correlation coefficients based on average values between agronomic and biochemical characters in 45 burr medic populations and some environmental characteristics of collection sites

Characters	1	2	3	4	5	6	7	8	9	10	11	12
1 Plant height	1.00	0.73***	0.37*	0.32*	n.s	0.30*	n.s	0.53***	n.s	n.s	n.s	n.s
2 Leaflet length	–	1.00	0.54***	0.52***	−0.41**	0.45**	n.s	0.53***	n.s	n.s	n.s	0.34*
3 Pod height	–	–	1.00	0.89***	−0.32*	0.75***	−0.30*	0.58***	n.s.	−0.51***	n.s.	n.s
4 Coils number	–	–	–	1.00	−0.37*	0.83***	−0.34*	0.68***	0.30*	−0.53***	n.s.	0.34*
5 Spine length	–	–	–	–	1.00	−0.38*	n.s.	−0.51***	−0.32*	n.s.	−0.38**	n.s.
6 Seeds per pod	–	–	–	–	–	1.00	n.s.	0.72***	0.45**	−0.49***	n.s.	n.s.
7 Pod per plant	–	–	–	–	–	–	1.00	n.s.	0.70***	n.s.	n.s.	n.s.
8 1000 seeds weight	–	–	–	–	–	–	–	1.00	0.48***	n.s.	0.34*	0.51***
9 Seed yield per plant	–	–	–	–	–	–	–	–	1.00	n.s.	0.36*	n.s.
10 Altitude	–	–	–	–	–	–	–	–	–	1.00	n.s.	n.s.
11 pH	–	–	–	–	–	–	–	–	–	–	1.00	n.s.
12 GOT-2	–	–	–	–	–	–	–	–	–	–	–	1.00

* = significant at 0.05 probability level

** = significant at 0.01 probability level

*** = significant at 0.001 probability level

228

Table 4. Matrix of principal components for 12 characters of the 45 burr medic populations

	P.C.1	P.C.2	P.C.3	P.C.4	P.C.5
Plant height	−0.284	−0.041	0.439	0.142	−0.145
Leaflet width	−0.275	−0.076	0.526	−0.109	−0.139
Leaflet length	−0.341	−0.041	0.414	−0.040	−0.091
Stem length	−0.151	0.283	0.124	0.747	0.397
Pod height	−0.355	−0.077	−0.233	0.189	0.125
Pod width	−0.315	−0.182	−0.240	−0.004	−0.455
Coils number	−0.364	−0.086	−0.290	0.067	0.147
Spine length	0.223	−0.170	−0.085	0.570	−0.658
Pods per plant	0.104	0.666	0.039	−0.066	−0.235
Seeds per pod	0.351	0.036	−0.330	−0.011	−0.021
1000 seed weight	−0.356	0.077	−0.128	−0.178	−0.076
Seed yield per plant	−0.180	0.619	−0.106	−0.065	−0.229
% var.	45.80	15.96	13.05	8.05	5.77
cumul.	45.80	61.76	74.81	82.86	88.63

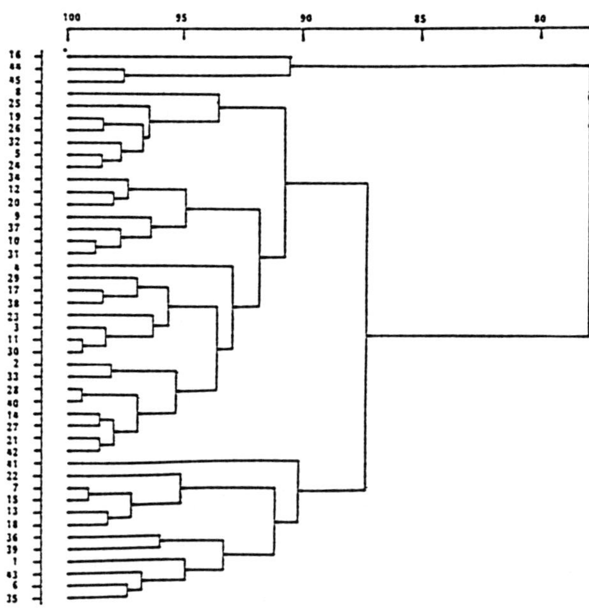

Fig. 2. Dendrogram of the 45 burr medic accessions clustered with average linkage method.

genase(MDH), 6 phospho-gluco dehydrogenase (6PGD), esterase (EST), acid phosphatase (ACP) and glutamate oxalacetate transaminase (GOT). When the products of more than one locus were observed, loci were numbered sequentially with 1 being the most anodally migrating isozyme. Different alleles at a locus were designated by letters with 'a' controlling the most anodal fast band, the next slower band being controlled by 'b'. Staining protocols followed Quiros (1981) for PRX and LAP, Soltis & Soltis (1989) for ACP, GOT, EST and the Genetics laboratory protocols of IGER-Aberystwyth for PGI, 6PGD, ME, SKD, SOD, MDH and PGM.

Linear correlation coefficients were determined using the morphological, agronomic and biochemical data together with altitude, precipitation and pH of collection sites.

A principal component analysis and cluster analysis were also performed with average linkage method.

Results

The averages and the range of the population means for the morphological and agronomic characters are shown in Table 1. Significant differences were found for all the characters measured. Population 19 seems to be the most promising regarding seed production characters (11.2 g per plant).

Table 2 shows results of the electrophoretic analysis of 12 enzymatic systems. Twenty one loci were scored, 7 showed polymorphism (ACP-1, EST, GOT-1, GOT-2, LAP-2, MDH-1, PGI-1) while all the others were monomorphic. The largest variability was found for the loci GOT-2 and MDH-1 with respectively 24 and 31 populations showing polymorphism. Almost all populations were homozygous except five that showed the presence of heterozygous individuals.

Table 3 shows the correlations at different level of significance for 12 of the characters showing the most interesting relationships. Considering the correlations between collection site environmental characters and morphological and agronomic characters, altitude is negatively correlated with pod height ($r = - 0.51^{***}$), number of coils ($r = - 0.53^{***}$), and seed per pod ($r = - 0.49^{***}$) while pH was negatively correlated with spine length ($r = - 0.38^{**}$) and positively correlated with 1000 seed weight ($r = 0.34^{*}$) and seed yield per plant ($r = 0.36^{*}$).

Of the correlations between biochemical and morphological and agronomic characters, only the frequency of alleles at the GOT-2 locus showed significant correlations. The frequency of 'b' allele was positively correlated with leaflet length ($r = 0.34^{*}$), number of coils in the legume ($r = 0.34^{*}$) and 1000 seed weight ($r = 0.51^{***}$).

230

Results of principal component analysis are reported in Table 4. The analysis showed that the first two factors accounted for 61% of the variation between populations. The major characters involved in this differentiation were pod morphological characteristics for the first component and number of pods per plant for the second.

Results of cluster analysis are shown in Fig. 2. Populations 16, 44 and 45 looked the most dissimilar from the others and had the following common characters: erect plants, pods of high dimensions and spineless, highest 1000 seed weight and highest self reseeding capacity. A second cluster grouped accessions with the following characters: small dimensions of pods, higher spine length, smaller plant height. A third cluster grouped accessions with lower pods per plant production and intermediate morphological characters of pods and plants.

Discussion

The present set of results shows that there is a considerable amount of useful variation among the Sardinian populations of *M. polymorpha*.

Among the morphological characters, populations differed in plant height which should allow the selection of prostrate types suitable for grazing and erect types for growing in mixtures with grasses. The variation for pod size indicates that several populations could be useful in a selection program to enhance self reseeding because small pod size helps self reseeding.

The large variation present for 1000 seed weight also could be useful in selecting populations with higher seedling viability as seed dimension is directly correlated with seedling vigour (Cocks, 1991), larger seeded populations having greater viability. This character is not necessarily important for the dry Mediterranean areas. In fact ecotypes producing small seeds give higher seed yield and have higher seed hardiness (Cocks, 1990). Both characters are important for self reseeding and the latter is essential to overcome drought periods. Some populations were spineless or tubercled, and therefore valuable to develop spineless varieties. This character is particularly useful for areas such as Australia where wool contamination is a problem. However, the presence of spines in the pod represents a mechanism of diffusion of the species and the absence of spines makes the pods more palatable to animals and thus limits seed resources. In the Mediterranean areas where wool is not valuable, the selection for more palatable spineless pods is more important to increase summer feed availability than to avoid wool contamination.

The isozyme analysis did not show a high level of variability at isozyme loci. Some allelic variation was present in some populations, individuals were almost all homozygous; the presence of a few heterozygotes would suggest possible outcrossing or gene duplication.

Allele 'b' of GOT-2 was correlated with 1000 seed weight, the presence of this allele might be useful to select higher seed yielding populations. The number of pods per plant seems to affect the seed yield more than the 1000 seed weight or seeds per pod. The plant morphological characters were highly correlated with 1000 seed weight so that selection for herbage production should not affect seed yield. Environmental characteristics showed to affect pod morphology, accessions with shorter spines and bigger legumes seem to be more widespread on coastal areas and lowlands, maybe in relation to the lower stocking rate of such areas in Sardinia.

Acknowledgements

The skillful technical assistance of Dr Antonello Franca, Istituto di Agronomia, Sassari (Italy), is gratefully acknowledged.

References

Aitken, Y., 1981. Temperate herbage grasses and legumes. In: Handbook of Flowering. Halevy, CRC, Boca Raton, Florida.

Andrews, W.D. & F.W. Hely, 1960. Frequency of annual species of *Medicago* on the major soil groups of the Macquaire region of N.S.W. Aust. J. Agric. Res. 11: 705–711.

Bullitta, S., M. Falcinelli, S. Lorenzetti, V. Negri, A. Pardini, S. Piemontese, C. Porqueddu, P.P. Roggero, P. Talamucci & F. Veronesi, 1991. Prime osservazioni su specie perenni ed annue autoriseminanti in vista della organizzazione di catene di foraggiamento in ambienti mediterranei. Riv. di Agron., XXV, 2: 220–228.

Clarkson, N.M. & J.S. Russel, 1975. Phasic development of *Medicago* species. Flowering responses to vernalisation and photoperiod in annual medics (*Medicago* spp.). Aust. J. Agric. Res. 26: 831–838.

Cocks, P. & T.A.M. Ehrman, 1987. The geographic origin of frost tolerance in Syrian pasture legumes. J. Appl. Ecol. 24: 678–683.

Cocks, P.S., 1990. Dynamics of flower and pod production in annual medics (*Medicago* spp.) I in spaced plants. Aust. J. Agric. Res. 41: 911–921.

Cocks, P.S., 1991. Ley farming, an integrated cereal/livestock system for small farms in West Asia and North Africa. In press.

Cunningham, S.D. & D.N. Munns, 1984. The correlation between extracellular polysaccharide production and acid tolerance in *Rhizobium*. Soil Sci. Soc. Am. J. 48: 1273–1276.

Francis, C.M. & M.L. Poole, 1973. Effect of waterlogging on annual medics. Aust. J. Agric. Anim. Husb. 13: 71–73.

Gillespie D.J., 1987. Murex medic, a new medic for acid soils. In: Temperate Pastures, Their Production, Use and Management. CSIRO. 172 p.

Hayward, M.D. & N.J. McAdam, 1977. Isozyme polymorphism as a measure of distinctiveness and stability in cultivars of *Lolium perenne*. Z. Pflanzenzuchtg. 79: 59–68.

Heyn, C.C., 1963. The Annual Species of *Medicago*. Scripta Hierosolymitana, vol. XII. At the Magnes Press, The Hebrew University, Jerusalem.

Lesins, K.A. & I. Lesins, 1979. Genus *Medicago* (Leguminosae). A Taxogenetic study. Dr. W. Junk Publishers, The Hague/Boston/London.

Loi, A., J.G. Howieson, P.S. Cocks & S. Caredda, 1992. The adaptation of *Medicago polymorpha* to a range of edaphic and environmental conditions: effect of temperature on growth, and acidity stress on nodulation and nod gene induction. Aust. J. Exp. Agric. 33: 25–30.

Masson, P. & G. Gintzburger, 1989. Role potentiel des legumineuses annuelles et ressemis en France. Proc. XVI Congrès Int. des Herbages, Nice, France, 4–11 Octobre 1989.

Munns, D.N. & H.H. Keyser, 1981. Response of *Rhizobium* strains to acid and aluminium stress. Soil. Biol. Biochem. 13: 15–25.

Olea, L., J. Paredes & P. Verdasco, 1989. Caracteristicas productivas de los pastos de la dehesa de S.O. de la peninsula Iberica. SEEP. XXIX Elvas (Portugal): 147–172.

Quiros, C.F., 1981. Starch gel electrophoresis technique used with alfalfa and other *Medicago* species. Can. J. Plant Sci. 61: 745–749.

Soltis, D.E. & P.S. Soltis, 1989. Isozymes in Plant Biology. Dioscorides Press, Portland, Oregon.

Talamucci, P. & G. Pazzi, 1982. Possibilità di inserimento di alcune leguminose autoriseminanti nei sistemi foraggeri asciutti della Maremma Toscana. Riv. Agron. 2: 223–230.

O.A. Rognli et al. (eds.), Breeding Fodder Crops for Marginal Conditions, 233,
© 1994 *Kluwer Academic Publishers. Printed in the Netherlands.*

The role of flowering intensity in adapting perennial ryegrass to different production systems

P.W. WILKINS
*Institute of Grassland and Environmental Research, Welsh Plant Breeding Station,
Aberystwyth, Dyfed SY23 3EB, UK*

Summary. Most current cultivars of perennial ryegrass vary markedly in productivity between harvests during the growing season. Such varieties produce high annual yields of dry matter when harvested infrequently and are suitable for animal production systems which rely heavily on grass silage. New varieties such as cv. Aberelan have been produced which are much better suited to grazing systems. They grow more evenly through the season and maintain dry matter production better when harvested frequently. One such variety (Ba11316) was compared with three commercial cultivars (Merlinda and two others) in a replicated field plot trial with six levels of fertiliser. Merlinda gave the highest total dry matter yields over two harvest years (5% more than Ba11316), but Ba11316 yielded significantly (16%) more leaf lamina than Merlinda. This substantial discrepancy in varietal ranking between total dry matter yield and total leaf yield was mainly because Ba11316 significantly outyielded Merlinda at several of the lower-yielding harvests, which all had high leaf contents, whereas Merlinda significantly outyielded Ba11316 only at harvests with a low leaf content. The mean percentage of flowering tillers over four sampling dates was significantly lower in Ba11316 than in the three cultivars. This, together with other circumstantial evidence already published, suggests that flowering intensity may be the primary factor controlling seasonal yield distibution of perennial ryegrass varieties and their suitability for different production systems.

O.A. Rognli et al. (Eds.) Breeding Fodder Crops for Marginal Conditions, 235–236.
© 1994 *Kluwer Academic Publishers. Printed in the Netherlands.*

CHARACTERIZATION OF DIFFERENT POTATO IDIOTYPES IN RESPONSE TO DROUGHT STRESS

CHR. BALKO, S. SEDDIG
Federal Centre for Breeding Research on Cultivated Plants
Institute for Stress Physiology and Quality of Raw Materials
Institutsplatz 2
18190 Groß Lüsewitz
Germany

Introduction

In order to select successfully for drought tolerance two preconditions should be given: (I) criteria for the assessment of drought tolerance in plants and (II) genetic variability regarding these criteria [1]. The potato (Solanum tuberosum L.) is known to react relatively sensitive to water deficit [2], influencing yield, therefore yield stability and also quality parameters of the harvested products. Consequently yield parameters as well as tuber constituents should be considered to characterize idiotypes in response to drought stress and to assess variability of this response.

Material and Methods

13 idiotypes including 8 cultivars, 1 retetraploid and 4 dihaploid forms were subjected to two different water regimes 40 and 70 % of the maximum water capacity of the soil respectively (stress and control variant) in a pot trial 1992 and repeated 1993.

Water relation parameters were compared to changes in morphological characteristics, yield and yield components as well as parameters of tuber quality. The following parameters were included:

- water consumption and water use efficiency referring to the tuber yield (WUE)
- morphological characteristics
  - soil covering of leafs
  - plant height
  - number of shoots
  - stomata frequency
- yield and -components
  - fresh and dry matter tuber yield /plant
  - number of tubers /plant
  - fresh and dry matter tuber weight
- tuber constituents
  - starch content
  - size of starch granules
  - total N, protein N content
  - P, K content
  - content of crude cell wall components

236

Results

Application of water deficiency stress resulted in differences in nearly all characteristics mentioned above.

As expected water deficit resulted in a reduced vegetative growth of potato plants and the number of shoots /plant was nearly constant. Although in stomata frequency dihaploids had on average the 1.5 fold compared with the tetraploid forms, stomata frequency and it's changes in response to water deficiency stress were unrelated to drought tolerance.

Interactions between idiotypes and waterregimes and therefore variability in the response of idiotypes to the stress factor were especially distinct in WUE and tuber yield. Regarding WUE all idiotypes were able for adaptation to water deficit, but the increase ranged from 0,4 to 3,3 g tuber fresh weight /l H_2O (3.8...19.6 %). More distinct was the loss of tuber yield - here differences between idiotypes varied from 47 to 204 g /plant (10.2...35.9 %) which is in correspondence with field trials [3], but no correlation between the increase in WUE and the yield loss could be found.

The starch content was first of all dependent on the genotype just as the distribution of the size of the starch granules. But analogous to the increase in the dry matter content, the starch content was also always higher in the tubers of the stressed plants, differences ranging from 1.3...3.7 %. The content of crude cell wall components showed the same tendency with differences from 0.1...7.2 % between stressed and nonstressed tubers.

Total N, protein N , P and K content of tubers showed differences between the two water regimes. Whereas total N content was generally higher in tubers of stressed plants, P content was up to 35 % lower. No correlations to WUE or yield could be found.

Conclusions

Results show, that in the potato there exists variability in the different characteristics in response to water deficit But changes in yield and yield components do not correlate with changes in analysed tuber constituents and therefore quality parameters showing that drought tolerance is a very complex characteristic. But the existence of idiotypes combining a high water use efficiency with little changes in both complexes of characteristics leads to the assumption, that a successful selection for drought tolerance is possible, provided that current field trials confirm these results.

References

[1] Parlevliet, J.E. (1987) 'Strategies for breeding for tolerance to abiotic stress factors that occur heterogenous in time and space such as drought', in L.M. Monti and E. Porceddu (eds), Drought Resistance in Plants, 1.-8. EUR 10 700, Luxembourg Office for Official Publications of the European Community, Luxembourg, pp. 277-285.

[2] Levy, D. (1992) 'Osmotic potential of potatoes subjected to a single cycle of water deficit', Potato Research 35, 17-24.

[3] Hoogendorn, J. and Groot, P.J. (1992) 'Drought tolerance and earliness', Potato Research 35, 65.

O.A. Rognli et al. (Eds.) Breeding Fodder Crops for Marginal Conditions, 237–238.
© 1994 *Kluwer Academic Publishers. Printed in the Netherlands.*

SELECTION FOR SNOW MOULD RESISTANCE OF *LOLIUM* AT A HIGH ALTITUDE SITE

B. BOLLER, S. GÜNTER ADELMANN, W. WINTER, and I. BÄNZIGER
Eidgenössische Forschungsanstalt für landwirtschaftlichen Pflanzenbau
FAP Reckenholz
CH-8046 Zürich
Switzerland

ABSTRACT. Snow mould resistance of advanced breeding material, as observed at 1000 m a.s.l., was compared to resistance to winter diseases found in lowland (400 to 500 m a.s.l.) trials. The correlation between the two altitudes was acceptable for varieties within *Lolium* species but poor for the ranking of the three species, *L. perenne* (normally having the highest level of resistance), *L. hybridum* and *L. italicum*. Analysis of the spectra of plant pathogenic fungi revealed that disease scores given at the end of winter at low altitude do not adequately predict snow mould resistance because *Microdochium (=Fusarium) nivale* does not predominate clearly among other pathogenic fungi.

Introduction

Damage caused by fungal diseases which develop under a snow cover ("snow mould", main causal agent *Microdochium nivale*) limits the use of ryegrasses (*Lolium spp.*) at higher altitudes of Central Europe. We use natural infection at an experimental field at 1000 m a.s.l. to evaluate our advanced breeding material. Here, we report on the relationship between snow mould resistance measured at this high altitude site and that predicted from disease scores given in lowland trials at the end of winter.

Materials and Methods

Between 1989 and 1991, candidate and standard varieties of *L. (multiflorum ssp.) italicum*, *L. hybridum* and *L. perenne* were sown in 3 m lines, replicated 4 times, in a field at Gibswil (1000 m a.s.l.) in the "Zürcher Oberland". Each year, the corresponding entries were used in plot trials at three lowland sites (400 to 500 m a.s.l.). Visual scores of disease severity were given at the end of each of two winters after each sowing date, and transformed fo relative disease resistance scores by subtracting them from the mean disease score of all varieties at a given date and place of observation. Spectra of plant pathogenic fungi were determined by plating pieces of 2-3 mm length of apparently diseased tissue (leaf blades or sheaths) on malt agar. Fungal colonies developing from the plant tissue pieces were identified visually after 5 to 7 days.

Results and Discussion

Over all 132 varieties of the three *Lolium* species tested, snow mould resistance, as measured at 1000 m a.s.l., was poorly correlated with resistance against winter diseases at the lowland sites (Table 1). However, within each *Lolium* species, the correlation was much better. Additionally, the correlation over all three *Lolium* species was greatly improved when we included only those lowland observations where *L. italicum*, normally the most susceptible of the three species, was given an average disease score of at least 4 on a 1 to 9 scale.

TABLE 1. Correlation between snow mould resistance observed at high altitude (1000 m a.s.l.) and resistance against winter diseases in lowland trials.

Calculation of r includes for lowland trials	Coefficient of correlation (r) between resistance against winter diseases at 1000 m a.s.l. and at 400 to 500 m a.s.l.			
	within *L. italicum*	within *L. hybridum*	within *L. perenne*	over all 3 species
- all observations	0.46 ***[1]	0.47 **	0.41 **	0.21 *
- only where score of *L. italicum* >4	0.48 ***	0.47 **	0.40 **	0.45 ***
Number of entries	55	37	40	132

[1] p (r≠0): * < 0.05, ** < 0.01, *** < 0.001

Analysis of the spectra of plant pathogenic fungi revealed that, at the end of winter, *Microdochium nivale* was present on 89 % of the apparently diseased plants collected at 1000 m a.s.l. where no other pathogenic fungi were found. In sharp contrast, *M. nivale* was identified on only 22 % of apparently diseased plants collected at the lowland sites (Figure 1). An additional 14 % was colonized with several other plant pathogenic fungi, among which *Drechslera siccans* was most prevalent. On more than half of the pieces of diseased plants, only secondary parasites such as *Epicoccum purpurascens* were found.

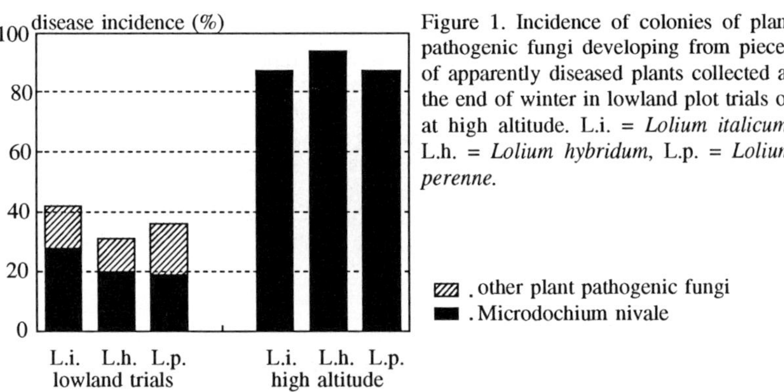

Figure 1. Incidence of colonies of plant pathogenic fungi developing from pieces of apparently diseased plants collected at the end of winter in lowland plot trials or at high altitude. L.i. = *Lolium italicum*, L.h. = *Lolium hybridum*, L.p. = *Lolium perenne*.

These results show that relatively small scale experiments at high altitude can contribute significantly to improve selection for snow mould resistance of *Lolium* varieties. As compared to lowland plot trials, the main reason for the more reliable assessment of resistance at high altitude appears to be the much more uniform spectrum of fungal diseases, with *Microdochium nivale* being the highly dominant species.

O.A. Rognli et al. (Eds.) Breeding Fodder Crops for Marginal Conditions, 239–240.
© 1994 *Kluwer Academic Publishers. Printed in the Netherlands.*

STRAW QUALITY OF BARLEY IN THE DRY AREAS OF NORTH SYRIA - FROM A BREEDER'S POINT OF VIEW

M. MAYER,[1] C.H.P. EINFELDT[2], S. CECCARELLI[1],
M. BLÜMMEL[2], A. GLAND[2] and H.H. GEIGER[2]
[1] *ICARDA, P.O. Box 5466, Aleppo, Syria*
[2] *University of Hohenheim 762, D-70599 Stuttgart, Germany*

1. Introduction

In Syria, barley is the most important crop in areas receiving less than 300 mm annual precipitation. Both grain and straw are used exclusively as livestock feed, mainly for sheep. They contribute about 53 percent to metabolizable energy (ME) needs (THOMSON, 1987).

In this study we investigated the potential of straw quality as an additional new breeding target.

Specific objectives were to
- examine the influence of environment and genotype on straw quality,
- estimate quantitative genetic parameters for straw quality,
- analyse the relationship between straw quality and other agronomic traits.

2. Materials and Methods

One hundred and thirty-six entries were derived from double crosses between drought adapted and high-yielding spring type cultivars. They were tested in Syria together with eight checks in three environments with severe drought stress. Furthermore trials were conducted with partly different genotypes from the same double crosses in one moderate and two non-stress environments in Syria and Germany. ME content was determined indirectly by near infrared spectroscopy. Agronomic traits recorded were total biological yield, grain yield, ME yield, harvest index, days to heading and number of fertile tillers.

3. Results

Grain yield and harvest index had significantly smaller means in stress environments than in moderate or non-stress environments. In contrast, ME content improved with increasing drought stress. As a consequence straw quality was better in stress environments than in favorable environments.

Golf, a non-adapted, European high yielding variety was low yielding under stress but had extremely high straw quality. Arabi Abiad, a Syrian landrace, Rihane, a six-rowed improved variety, and Harmal, a two-rowed improved variety, had similar grain yields but differed significantly with regard to straw quality. Due to a higher ME content, straw quality of Arabi Abiad was significantly higher than that of Rihane and similar to that of Harmal. However ME yield of Arabi Abiad was similar to Rihane and greater for Harmal.

The heritability estimate for ME content was high and comparable to those for grain yield and harvest index. The genetic coefficient of variation was low for ME content but rather high for grain yield, harvest index, and number of fertile tillers.

Genotypes which were well adapted to severe drought stress conditions (early genotypes with many fertile tillers and good yielding performance) had low straw quality as indicated by the coefficients of genotypic correlation. The relationship between total biological yield and straw quality was weak.

4. Discussion

The nutritive value of barley straw improved at increasing levels of stress. This can be explained by a higher number of non-fertile tillers and a reduced translocation of assimilates into the grain under stress. Both leads to higher contents of soluble carbohydrates and proteins in the straw and on the other hand to lower harvest indices.

A simultaneous improvement of grain yield and straw quality in drought-prone environments is difficult due to the strong negative correlation between both traits. Furthermore, selection for ME content seems to be limited because of a small genetic variation.

Landraces seem to have a higher straw quality than improved varieties, while producing at least similar grain and ME yields. Therefore, incorporation of landraces into breeding programs could be a simple way to maintain a certain level of straw quality.

Selection for total biological yield would combine the need for high grain and ME yield and additionally for a certain ME content.

For maximization of selection response development of a selection index is advisable. This would imply the determination of economic weights for the various agronomic and straw quality characters.

5. References

THOMSON, E.F. (1987) 'Feeding systems and sheep husbandry in the barley belt of syria', ICARDA-106 En, Aleppo, Syria.

O.A. Rognli et al. (Eds.) Breeding Fodder Crops for Marginal Conditions, 241–242.
© 1994 *Kluwer Academic Publishers. Printed in the Netherlands.*

MORPHOLOGICAL ADAPTATION TO DROUGHT OF DIFFERENT POPULATIONS OF <u>LOLIUM PERENNE</u> L.

V. NEGRI, M. FALCINELLI
Plant Breeding Institute,
Faculty of Agriculture,
Borgo XX Giugno, 74
06100 Perugia
Italy

Introduction

In breeding cultivars for a sustainable agriculture the identification of morphological traits conferring drought resistance may be an useful tool in screening germplasm. Traits conferring adaptation to drought need to be highly penetrant also in not limiting conditions such as those under which germplasm is generally evaluated. In this research morphological adaptations induced in seedling leaves by drought stress were investigated under controlled conditions.

Materials and Methods

Three populations of <u>L. perenne</u> from contrasting climatic and edaphic conditions were evaluated: cv Cropper from Northern Europe and two natural populations from Italy one collected in a dry meadow at 700 m a.s.l. on the Maritime Alps, Po valley, and one from an uncultivated area at sea level on the Adriatic coast, Cesenatico.
48 plants per populations were grown in pots in growth chamber (25 °C, 16/8hs day/night and 20,000lux); half of them were submitted to drougth stress maintainig the soil to 20% moisture content by weighed daily water addition (S), half full watered daily (W). The arrangment followed was a split plot with three replication, the whole plot represented the population and the subplot the treatment. Rate of extention (RLE) of 5th, 6th and 7th leaf was recorded. The 6th leaf of each plant was collected and examined for stomata width (SW) and number under unit area (SN) utilizing a striping technique. The median part of the 7th leaf of each plant was also collected, preserved in 70% ethanol, sectioned, stained and observed at the microscope for abaxial epidermal thickness (AbET), maximum and minimum leaf thickness (LT), ridge angle (RA), mesophyll cell number under unit area (MCN), vascular bundle diameter (VBD).

Results and Discussion

For each character recorded significative differences between treatments and populations were found with the exceptions of RA where treatments were not significant and VBD where populations were not significant (data not shown).
In Cesenatico RLE (not shown) was generally lowest in both watered and stressed conditions; in stressed conditions RLE was 82, 88 and 90% of the other two populations on the average for

each leaf evaluated, respectively. Cesenatico also showed the greatest percentage reduction of RLE in stressed conditions in respect to the other populations. Drought stress increased SN and MCN and decreased SW, AbET and LT (Tab. 1). Cesenatico, the population coming from the environment where drought stress is more likely to occur, shows these features to a greater extent than the other populations also in not limiting conditions. A high SN and MCN under unit area, small RLE, SW, AbET, and LT appear to be traits linked with drought resistance. Since differences for morphological traits are heritable in Lolium [1,2] these traits should be useful in detecting valuable germplasm in breeding for stress conditions. Some of them are reported to confer lower yielding ability [3], but in breeding varieties for a sustainable agriculture more importance has to be given to capability to withstand adverse conditions and to persist.

Table 1 - Morphological characters in watered and stressed populations of L. perenne.

	SN mm^{-2}			SW μm			AbET μm		
	Crop	Po	Ces	Crop	Po	Ces	Crop	Po	Ces
W $\bar{x}$ watered =	171	150	198 / 173A	24	24	20 / 23B	7.8	7.9	6.9 / 7.5B
S $\bar{x}$ stressed =	214	184	247 / 215B	18	21	18 / 19A	5.7	7.3	6.5 / 6.5A
$\bar{x}$ p.=	193b	167a	223c	21b	23c	19a	6.8a	7.6b	6.7a

	maxLT μm			minLT μm			MCN 5.5mm^{-2}10^{-4}		
	Crop	Po	Ces	Crop	Po	Ces	Crop	Po	Ces
W $\bar{x}$ watered =	557	516	476 / 516B	266	291	246 / 268B	5.0	5.0.	5.9 / 5.3A
S $\bar{x}$ stressed =	470	495	459 / 475A	223	285	236 / 248A	6.0	5.3	7.1 / 6.1B
$\bar{x}$ p.=	514b	506b	468a	245a	288b	241a	5.5a	5.2a	6.5b

means followed by the same letter are not different for P$\leq$0.05

[1] Wilson, D. (1972) 'Effect of selection for stomatal length and frequency on theoretical stomatal resistance to diffusion in Lolium perenne L.'. New Phytol. 71, 811-817.
[2] Wilson, D. and Cooper, J.P. (1969) 'Diallel analysis of photosynthetic rate and related leaf characters among contrasting genotypes of Lolium perenne'. Heredity 24, 633-649.
[3] Cohen, C.J., Chilcote, D.O. and Frakes, R.V. (1982) 'Leaf anathomy and stomatal characteristics of four tall fescue selections differing in forage yield'. Crop Sci. 22, 704-708.

O.A. Rognli et al. (Eds.) Breeding Fodder Crops for Marginal Conditions, 243–244.
© 1994 *Kluwer Academic Publishers. Printed in the Netherlands.*

COMPARISON OF AGRONOMIC AND QUALITY TRAITS OF NAKED AND HULLED OATS

P. Peltonen-Sainio
Department of Plant Production
Section of Crop Husbandry
Box 27, Viikki
FIN-00014 University of Helsinki, Finland

1 INTRODUCTION

Naked oat (*Avena sativa* var. *nuda* L.), the caryopsis of which threshes free from both lemma and palea, has excellent nutritional quality, but lower grain yields than conventional hulled oat. However, increasing grain yield of naked lines by up to 25% is probably easier than improving the quality of other cereals [1]. In Finland, breeding for high yielding naked oat began in the early 1970's and several breeding lines have been produced [2]. The aim of the present study was to compare the differences between naked and conventional oat lines in grain yield, groat yield, and morpho-physiological traits - i.e. to identify characteristics limiting grain yield of naked oat lines.

2 MATERIALS AND METHODS

The plant material included three naked spring oat cultivars (*Caesar*, *Terra*, and *Rhiannon*), seven naked breeding lines developed at Hankkija Plant Breeding Institute, and six Finnish conventional oat cultivars released in 1921-1985. Field experiments were carried out at the Viikki Experimental Farm of the University of Helsinki, Finland (60°13' N) in 1991 and 1992 in a randomized complete block design with three replications. Plot size was 10 m² and seeding rate was 500 viable seeds m^{-2}. The plots were fertilized with 80 kg N ha^{-1} as NH_4NO_3, and weeds were controlled with MCPA.

The following morpho-physiological traits were measured in each plot: grain yield (kg ha^{-1}), hull content (%), groat yield (kg ha^{-1}), number of sprouts m^{-2}, days to heading, days to yellow ripeness, length of grain-filling period, number of panicles m^{-2}, phytomass and vegetative phytomass (g plant^{-1}), panicle weight (g), number of spikelets and grains per panicle, number of grains per spikelet, spikelet and grain weight (mg), and HI (%). Significant differences between lines in morpho-physiological traits were tested with ANOVA.

3 RESULTS AND DISCUSSION

Hulled lines out-yielded naked ones by 30%. However, one quarter of the grain yield produced by the conventional lines was hull, and hence, they produced only 10% higher groat yields than the naked oats. Moreover, the highest yielding naked oat, *Rhiannon*, out-yielded the bred landrace. Naked lines had, however less panicles per m², which resulted from their lower sprouting ability and not from decreased tillering. Thus, improving management of naked oats - e.g. increasing seeding rate of naked lines by 10% - may already result in equal groat yields of naked and conventional lines. Further identification of factors limiting yield of naked oat and a successful attempt to overcome them by breeding would increase competitive ability of this high yielding cereal crop.

This study showed that naked lines produced higher above-ground vegetative biomass at the expense of panicle weight (Table 1). Allocation of assimilates into the caryopsis did not, however differ significantly between naked and dehulled conventional lines. Further improvement in partitioning assimilates into grain is needed to increase the competitive ability of naked lines. This study showed that naked lines produced significantly lower number of spikelets per panicle when compared with hulled ones, even though the number of grains per panicle was equal. Therefore, spikelets of naked lines often included the upper caryopsis. Increasing spikelet number by plant breeding may result in reduced number of grains per spikelet. Such changes in spikelet-grain interaction are likely to result in increased allocation of assimilates into grains. This is supported by Housley and Peterson [3], who showed that increases in the number of spikelets per panicle were associated with larger area of vascular tissue. The significant differences between naked lines in the number of spikelets per panicle, number of grains per spikelet, and filling rates of both of these components suggested that these traits can be manipulated in breeding programs. Moreover, naked lines mature early enough to be cultivated in northern growing conditions. These findings associated with relatively high groat yields of naked lines indicate that naked oat is a potentially useful grain crop for northern growing conditions.

Table 1. Significance of difference between hulled and naked lines in yield components.

Trait	Mean		Significance
	Hulled	Naked	
Grain yield (kg ha^{-1})	3270	2210	***
Hull content (%)	25.6	5.0	***
Groat yield (kg ha^{-1})	2460	2100	**
Sprouts m^{-2}	642	558	***
Panicles m^{-2}	591	523	***
Spikelets/panicle	16	13	***
Grains/spikelet	1.9	2.5	***
HI (%)	53	43	***

***, ** significant at $P \leq 0.001$ and $P \leq 0.01$, respectively

4 REFERENCES

[1] Doyle, C.J. & Valentine, J. 1988. Plant Varieties Seeds 1:99-108.
[2] Peltonen-Sainio, P. 1993. Agron. J., submitted.
[3] Housley, T.L. & Peterson, D.M. 1982. Crop Sci. 22: 259-263.

O.A. Rognli et al. (Eds.) Breeding Fodder Crops for Marginal Conditions, 245–246.
© 1994 *Kluwer Academic Publishers. Printed in the Netherlands.*

THE EFFECT OF WATER STRESS DURING FLOWERING ON SEED YIELD OF SUBTERRANEAN CLOVER: VARIATION AMONG STRAINS AND INFLUENCE OF FLOWERING PATTERN

E. PIANO and L. PECETTI
Plant Breeding Section,
Fodder Crops Research Institute,
viale Piacenza 29
20075 Lodi
Italy

Persistence of annuals such as subterranean clover (*Trifolium subterraneum* L.) depends primarily on seed yield. In marginal, Mediterranean environments the occurrence of sudden and anticipated closure of the rainy period, or intermittent moisture stress during the reproductive phase may adversely influence seed yield.

This experiment assessed the effect of different moisture regimes during the reproductive period on seed yield and components of subterranean clover strains differing in time of commencement of flowering and duration and rate of inflorescence production. On two early (Geraldton and Seaton Park) and two later (L39 and L42) strains four water treatments were imposed: withholding water at an early (T1), intermediate (T2) and late (T3) stage, and continuous water supply during flowering and beyond (T4) (Fig. 1). Plants were re-watered (T1 to T3) when further moisture stress would prejudice survival. This generally occurred at a soil water content of about 7% (w/w).

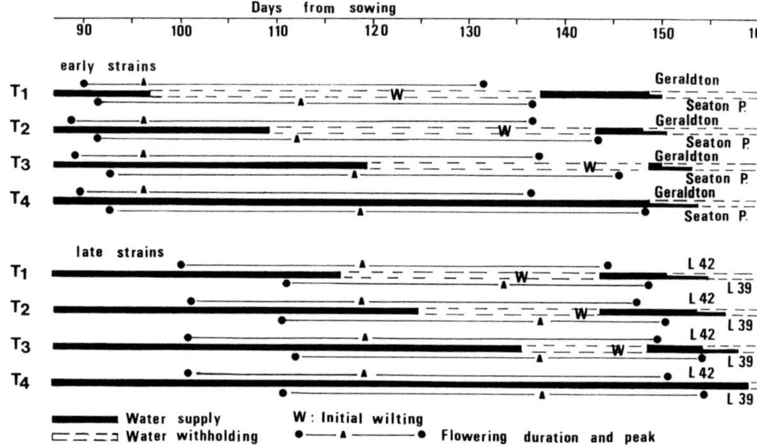

Figure 1. Scheme of water treatments and strain phenology.

In all strains the characters significantly influenced by the moisture treatments were seed yield and total number of seeds and burrs. Number of seeds per burr and individual seed weight were not affected. Hence, the reduction of total number of seeds was a simple consequence of the reduction of burr number, which appeared the critical seed yield component.

There was significant strain x treatment interaction. For the treatments involving water restriction, in the early lines a trend was evident towards a decrease from T3 to T1, i.e. on shortening of the growing season. Seaton Park was more affected than Geraldton in which T1 and T3 did not significantly differ (Table 1). The differential response appeared related to differences in pattern of flower production. Due to the rapid attainment of flowering peak, when the effective stress occurred Geraldton had already produced a great part of its inflorescences which had, therefore, a better chance than those formed later to develop into mature burrs. The two late flowering strains, particularly L39 which was the latest, yielded less seed than the early ones. The reduction caused by water restriction was much more severe in L39 than in L42 (Table 1). The remarkable advantage of L42 over L39 could be attributed to its earlier beginning of flowering and more intense initial inflorescence production, which allowed a greater part of seed to develop under more favourable conditions.

TABLE 1. Seed yield (g/plot) of the early and late strains in the four water treatments.

Treatment	early lines			late lines		
	Geraldton		Seaton Park	L39		L42
T1	9.7	*	5.8	0.6	@	3.4
T2	12.0	**	7.7	0.2	*	4.7
T3	12.5	*	9.4	0.1	*	4.1
T4	6.3	ns	4.3	1.8	*	5.1
LSD treat. $_{(0.05)}$		3.4			3.4	

ns, @, *, **: line means not different, different at $P \leq 0.1$, ≤ 0.05 and ≤ 0.01, respectively

Early and late lines showed opposite behaviour under continuos water supply. T4 had a negative effect on the former strains, whose seed was likely subject to an excess of moisture after the end of the growing cycle and, hence, to germination and losses by attack of soil-borne pathogens. In contrast, T4 provided a good fulfillment of the increased evapo-transpirative demands in the late lines, which, flowering later in the season, produced most of their seed under more severe environmental conditions.

High initial rate of inflorescence production seems to confer some advantage in short-season, marginal environments, where early moisture stress may occur during the reproductive phase.

Genetic and genomic aspects of adaptation to marginal conditions

O.A. Rognli et al. (eds.), Breeding Fodder Crops for Marginal Conditions, 249–259.
© 1994 *Kluwer Academic Publishers. Printed in the Netherlands.*

Genetic markers and the selection of quantitative traits in forage grasses

M.D. HAYWARD[1], N.J. MCADAM[1], J.G. JONES[1], C. EVANS[1],
G.M. EVANS[2], J.W. FORSTER[2], A. USTIN[1], K.G. HOSSAIN[1],
B. QUADER[1], M. STAMMERS[2] and J.K. WILL[2]
[1]*AFRC Institute of Grassland and Environmental Research, Aberystwyth, Wales, SY23 3EB,
UK;* [2]*School of Agricultural Sciences, University of Wales, Aberystwyth, Wales, UK*

Summary. Marker assisted selection is based upon the principle that if a gene (or block of
genes) is linked to an easily identifiable genetic marker it may be more efficient to select
in a breeding programme for the marker than for the trait itself. The recent developments
in molecular marker technology has allowed several approaches to be applied to the forage
grasses. The most effective methods involve the production of detailed genetic maps which can
be used for determination of the location of Quantitative Trait Loci (QTLs). Application of these
methods to *Lolium* has lead to the identification of 10 QTL's affecting mainly phenological
characteristics. Up to 80% of the variation in inflorescence production in the establishment
year may be accounted for by one region of the genome.

Introduction

The development of new cultivars of forage grasses is dependent upon two
main processes: firstly our ability to generate new variation and secondly
the efficiency of selection of improved genotypes which, when combined
together, will produce superior varieties. The creation of new and novel forms
of variation involves many processes such as the introduction of germplasm
from different eco-geographic regions to provide genotypes with enhanced
adaptation to environmental stress (Hayward, 1982); the use of interspecific
and intergeneric hybrids *per se*, often coupled with polyploidy, or for the
introgression of specific characteristics such as in the *Lolium/Festuca* complex
(Thomas, 1993). In the not too distant future we shall undoubtedly have
available germplasm genetically engineered for resistance to stress.

The selection of elite genotypes to form the parents of synthetic cultivars,
F1 hybrids or for the construction of recombinant inbred lines, is dependent
upon the ability to identify superior genotypes from their phenotype. The
majority of characters of interest in the production of new forage grasses are
quantitative in nature with heritability often being relatively low (Breese &
Hayward, 1972), in a breeding programme therefore considerable effort has to
be devoted to the conduct of progeny testing procedures to identify superior
mother plants. The recent rapid progress in the development of 'genetic
marker' technologies offers the prospect of more precisely identifying the
genotype and hence enhancing the selection of superior individuals. The
present paper considers a series of different approaches to the establishment

of associations between agronomic traits and genetic markers in *Lolium* sp. and the prospects for marker assisted selection in grass breeding programmes.

Principles of marker assisted selection (MAS)

Genetic markers

The utility of marker assisted selection (MAS) is based upon the establishment of a linkage relationship between an easily identifiable major gene marker and a character of agronomic importance. The classic work of Sax (1923), who showed that there was an association of seed coat colour in *Phaseolus vulgaris* with seed weight, established the principle that by selecting for the major gene difference a correlated response could be obtained in a quantitative trait. This response may have been due to a pleiotropic effect of the major gene and not linkage of the polygenes controlling seed weight. The work of Rasmusson (1935) on peas showed however that by selection of the appropriate parents and recombination, that the effects were due to genetic linkage and not to a pleiotropic effect of the gene itself. In order to apply this selection method the primary requirement is thus for polymorphic genetic markers and linkage of the genes controlling the agronomic trait to the marker(s).

The identification of a large number of highly polymorphic loci in plant species has come about with the advent of isozymes, restriction fragment length polymorphisms (RFLP's) and more recently RAPD's (Random Amplified Polymorphic DNA). They have been shown to provide a wealth of major gene markers applicable to most major crop species, (for a general review see Perez de la Vega, 1993). In *Lolium* sp. isozyme polymorphism is well known and has been utilized for variety discrimination (Hayward & McAdam, 1977), as markers for the identification of hybrids (Hayward et al., 1989) and in the characterization of genetic resources (Charmet et al., 1993). More recently RFLP and RAPD polymorphisms have been shown to be present in large numbers (Evans et al., 1991). Genetic analysis in pair cross families within both *Lolium perenne* and *L. multiflorum* have shown many of these polymorphisms to be controlled by single loci with multiple alleles present at each locus (for isozymes see Hayward & McAdam, 1975, 1977, RFLP's, Stammers, 1991; Will, 1991). For RAPD's, the methods used for their identification, involving use of random primers and the amplification of segments of the genome with the aid of the Polymerase Chain Reaction, mean that in a segregating family from a pair cross, at an individual locus only two 'allelic states' are observed, a presence or an absence. Unlike isozymes and RFLP's, RAPD's express dominance which can create difficulties in identification of the true genotype at a heterozygous RAPD locus. In all the forage grasses, including both temperate and tropical species, that we have examined, considerable levels of polymorphism have been found by using one or more of these procedures. The first requirement for marker assisted selection in the forage grasses has thus been met.

Linkage of the marker to the selected trait locus

The effectiveness of marker assisted selection is dependent on the strength of linkage of the marker to the locus controlling the character of interest ie. the degree of recombination, and the genetic control of the trait. The selected trait may be controlled by a single major gene such as in the case of disease resistance, or, under the control of many genes each of small effect (polygenes or quantitative trait loci, QTL's). For the former loci MAS can be a most effective means of enhancing the transfer of the desired gene by means of a backcross programme. This is well exemplified by the elegant work of Tanskley & Rick (1980) on tomato. In the forage grasses we have very few important traits controlled by single loci. In *Lolium* the incompatiblility system is under the control of two loci, *S* and *Z*, which are known to be linked to some isozyme marker loci (Cornish et al., 1980). To date there does not appear to be any reported cases of the direct use of MAS in forage grass breeding programmes for a single major gene trait. It has, however, been used very effectively in monitoring the introgression of blocks of genetic material into a *Lolium* background from *Festuca*, where a segment of the *Festuca* genome has been successfully transferred by selecting for a specific *Festuca* allele at the *Pgi/2* locus (Humphreys, 1989). In this case the segment of the *Festuca* genome around this locus behaves in the same manner as a single major gene.

The utility of MAS in the manipulation of quantitative traits is more complex in that by their very nature they are controlled by many genes each of small effect. Past selective forces will have lead to the establishment of groups of these genes linked together into co-adapted complexes (Mather, 1973; Hayward & Breese, 1993). Very often in the exploitation of forage grass genetic resources, particularly in breeding for adaptation to stress, it is these gene complexes that we seek to utilize (Breese & Hayward, 1972). The utility of MAS in these instances depends upon the ability to identify these blocks of genes (the effective factors of Mather, 1973) or as they are now generally known 'Quantitative Trait Loci' (QTL's). The development of the extensive range of polymorphic markers previous outlined provides a most powerful tool for locating QTLs by means of genetic mapping procedures (Soller & Beckmann, 1983; Stuber et al., 1987; Paterson et al., 1988; Lander & Botstein, 1989; Arus & Moreno-Gonzalez, 1993).

The various methods for the identification of QTL's have been comprehensively considered by Arus & Moreno-Gonzalez (1993). Basically they involve the establishment of a genetic model which will allow estimation of the contribution of the marker linked loci to the characteristic being assessed. The efficiency of these models depends upon the number of markers examined, their distance apart, the possible linkage of the QTL's themselves and the form of segregating generation being examined. For the outbreeding forage grasses 'F2' populations may be created by single pair crosses. In these instances difficulties may be encountered in the analysis due to inadequate information on the linkage phase in the parental plants. Whilst individual marker loci can be quite effective in the location of QTLs it is generally more efficient if markers can be obtained which flank the QTL on either side (Lander & Botstein, 1989, Arus & Moreno-Gonzalez, 1993). Ideally, makers should be located some 20 cM apart thus reducing the liklehood of double cross-overs occurring either side of the QTL. This clearly requires a well saturated linkage map of the species concerned.

Identification of QTLs in *lolium*

Association with single marker loci

Three different approaches, which differ in their relative efficiency and practical requirements, have been used to establish possible linkages of quantitative trait loci to marker loci. The first two are retrospective in that they examine the association of markers with the trait in populations which have already undergone selection, in order to determine possible relationships whilst the third, based upon segregating generations and the establishment of linkage maps, is prospective. The retrospective methods can of course be used to ascertain likely relationships which may be further exploited by selection in the population in question.

Correlated changes in marker gene frequency associated with selection for a quantitative trait

Selection for a quantitative trait may lead to a correlated change in gene frequency at marker loci if they are closely linked to the genes controlling the former. This principle was exploited by Stuber et al. (1980) in maize to assess the changes in isozyme gene frequency in populations selected for yield. Significant differences were established at seven loci. Later experiments showed that selection for these isozyme alleles was an effective means of increasing yield (Stuber, 1989). We have carried out a similar series of investigations in selected populations of perennial ryegrass.

Selections from within the cultivar S23 for yield and water soluble carbohydrate content were found to have been accompanied by correlated changes in isozyme gene frequency at the *Pgi/2* locus. Selection for high yield, which lead to the development of the cultivar 'Mascot', was associated with an increase in the frequency of the 'c' allele from 6% to 22%. The selections for WSC content were divergent and were associated with differing frequencies of the 'b' and 'c' alleles. These selection lines were multiplied through four generations to establish potential cultivars. Unfortunately, however, the selected character regressed towards the base population which it derived from (see Hayward & Abdullah, 1985). This change was closely accompanied by a change in frequency of the 'b' allele. Whilst this effect may be fortuitous it would suggest that the WSC% is closely related to whichever allele is present at the *Pgi/2* locus.

From these early experiments it was concluded that there may well be some linkages between isozyme markers and quantitative trait loci. In order to establish whether this is the case the second approach was adopted, namely selection for the specific isozyme marker.

Selection in L. perenne for isozyme markers

In order to establish whether any quantitative traits could be associated with one or more isozyme loci Hayward & McAdam (1988) created a number of populations which were homozygous for differing alleles at the loci *Pgi/2*, *Got/2*, *Got/3* and *Acp/1* by selecting within the cultivars 'Cropper', 'Aurora' and 'Gwennol'. Earlier studies had shown that these loci were effectively neutral in ryegrass for some agronomic traits (Hayward et al., 1978). A number of individuals were selected within each cultivar which were homozygous for the differing alleles found at each locus and across combinations of loci. Each genotype class was multiplied in isolation to create lines which were unique for the specific allele. These populations were evaluated for a number of agronomic traits in the spaced plant nursery.

The results for yield, measured as a conservation cut taken at 21 days post-inflorescence emergence showed that for the cv Cropper the *Pgi/2* 'cc line' out-yielded the other two classes by 57% whilst for cv Gwennol the 'aa' class was the highest performer yielding 76% more than the other homozygous classes. The results for Cropper are in agreement with those for Mascot referred to earlier. Clearly the *Pgi/2* locus is either having a direct effect on yield or there are QTL's associated with it. The former is unlikely as different alleles are associated with high yield in the two varieties. This may be accounted for by there being linked loci with the linkage phase being in opposite directions in the two cultivars. Of the total variation in yield only 34% is accounted for by the allelic phase associated with this locus in cv 'Cropper' and 16% in Gwennol. Further experiments of this nature to determine possible linkages with this marker locus have shown it to be associated with dark mature leaf respiration rate, regrowth potential and water soluble carbohydrate content (Hayward & Wakelin, unpublished). The first two are undoubtedly major factors influencing yield in perennial ryegrass (Wilson & Jones, 1981). It may thus be concluded for these populations of *Lolium perenne* there is at least one QTL influencing production which is located near to the *Pgi/2* locus. To exploit this as a selection tool will however require determination of the strength of the linkage and its phase in the population under selection.

Linkage of QTLs with single loci – information from segregating generations
As indicated in section 2.2 a more effective means of identifying QTL's is by determination of their linkage to markers through the analysis of segregating generations, which for the outbreeding forage grasses generally means either a pair cross family or a backcross. Comparisons of segregating marker class means for the trait of interest will reveal the presence of a possible linkage. We have applied this approach to two F2 families of perennial ryegrass and twenty different backcross progeny families involving either *L. perenne* or *L. perenne* × *L. multiflorum*, back-crossed to the outbred parental species or to a doubled haploid *L. perenne*. A range of seedling and adult plant characters were measured and the plants assayed for segregation at up to five isozyme loci.

For the seedling characters, number of days to appearance of fourth, fifth and sixth leaves, there were associations with the *Pgi/2* locus in one family and with the *Got/3* in a second (Ustun, 1992). Seedling leaf length, area and dry weight were shown to be linked to both the *Got/2* and *Sod* loci in half of the families (Quader, 1991). The absence of any valid test for the association of the quantitative traits with the markers in the remaining families for both this set of seedling characters may be due to a lack of variation amongst the parents involved. For two of the families a clonally replicated trial harvested over six cuts showed that there was genetic variation for productivity present with a broad sense heritability ranging from 8% to 48% for individual cuts. Significant association of yield with the *Pgi/2* locus was established in one of the families and with *Acp/2* in the second family. In two unreplicated experiments involving sixteen families further evidence of association with the former locus and with the *Got/3* locus was established (Ustun, 1992).

Multipoint mapping of quantitative trait loci

The rapid progress in the development of genetic maps using the various marker systems outlined in section 2.1 has created the potential for the precise identification of the location of genes controlling quantitative traits and their eventual manipulation. We described earlier our approach to the mapping of

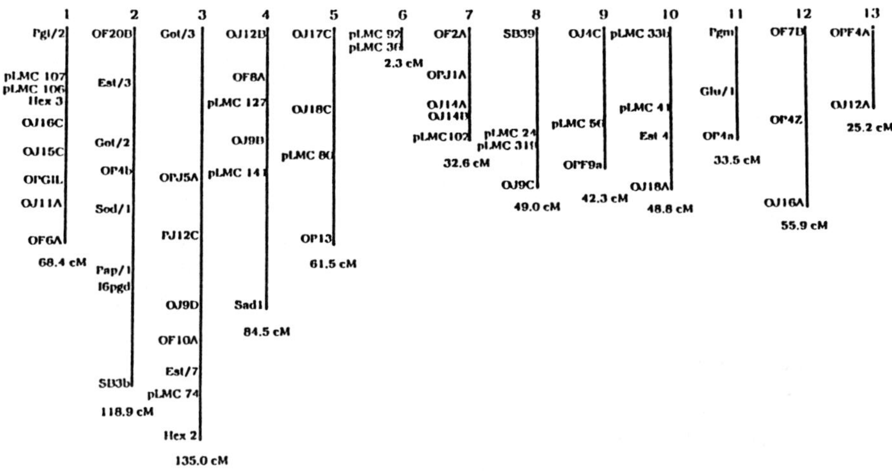

Fig. 1. Linkage groups in *Lolium*. Map lengths are in centimorgans.

the *Lolium* genome (Evans et al., 1991) so it will only be briefly considered here. We have analysed the segregation of 101 loci over 89 plants in our mapping family which is of the form (*L. perenne* × *L. multiflorum*) × *DH. L. perenne*. The markers employed were isozymes RFLP's and RAPD's. With the aid of the linkage analysis programme – 'MAPMAKER,' (Lander & Botstein, 1989) thirteen linkage groups, at a LOD score of 3 and a maximum recombination of 35%, have been identified with nineteen of the markers being unlinked (see Fig. 1). The preponderance of RAPD markers (65),is associated with map expansion leading to unrealistically long linkage groups; as such a further twenty-one have been omitted which showed particularly disturbed segregations or on the multipoint analysis gave rise to distances greater than 50 cMs. Under these conditions the total map length is of the order of 750 centimorgans. When related to the cytological data for *Lolium* (Rees & Ahmad, 1963), it is still rather long particularly when one has to consider that these groups will eventually be joined together. Nevertheless it does provide a basis for determining possible markers linked to loci controlling traits of agronomic importance.

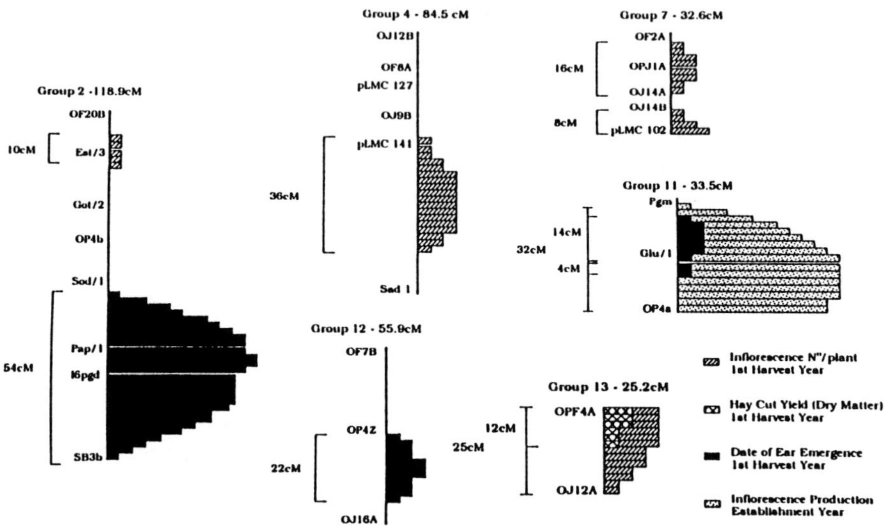

Fig. 2. Location of mapped QTLs in *Lolium*. Vertical scale of histograms represents a LOD score in units of 0.25 over the base of 2.

A clonally replicated field experiment has been conducted over two seasons and a range of agronomic traits measured. A one-way analysis of variance has revealed for all phenological and productivity characters that there is considerable variation present in this mapping family. With the use of the programme Mapmaker/QTL ten quantitative trait loci have been identified on six separate linkage groups (Fig. 2). Of these ten QTL's nine are concerned with differing aspects of the flowering processes. Three QTL's, on groups 2, 11 and 12, control date of inflorescence emergence. In the same region of group 11 we also have a factor controlling the degree of inflorescence production. For ear emergence the three QTLs control something of the order of 40% of the genetic variation with the major QTL located between the isozyme loci *Pap/1* and *6Pgd/1*. Under the assumption of a simple additive model for the genetic control of ear emergence, selection of the *perenne* alleles at these two loci will have the effect of bringing foreward timing of ear emergence by five days.

The region of group 11 around the two isozyme loci, *Pgm* and *Glu/1*, and RAPD marker, *OP4a* is of particular interest in its effects on the flowering processes. As well as having an influence upon the date of ear emergence it also has a major effect upon the number of inflorescences produced in the establishment year as it accounts for 80% of the genetic variation in that trait. As these physiological processes are controlled by photoperiodic and cold treatment factors there may well be a gene in this region equivalent to some of the 'day length' genes known in cereals. Here again, selection of the perennial ryegrass alleles will have the effect of eliminating inflorescence production in the establishment year. Clearly the ability to identify and manipulate such a gene or gene complex will have a considerable impact upon our breeding procedures to extend the adaptation of the forage grasses.

Conclusions

The results presented here provide evidence for the location of some of the genes in the *Lolium* genome controlling traits of importance in breeding for adaptation. They give an indication of the manner in which MAS may be used in breeding programmes. As our understanding of the organisation of the grass genome improves this tool will undoubtedly have a role to play in grass breeding technology. Before these methods can be widely applied however there is a requirement to make them cheaper and easier to apply. The recent developments in the chemi-luminescent procedures for RFLP analysis and their application to such crops as maize and rice means that the requirements for radioactive handling facilities has been removed. Their applicability will also be enhanced by the increasing numbers of universal probes which are now becoming freely available. The developments in comparative genome mapping between rice and wheat (Moore et al., 1993) show a high degree of collinearity between the genomes. Some studies which we are currently undertaking already show a common homology of ryegrass and wheat. This implies that in the future, when coupled with the transformation systems that have been developed at IGER for the grasses, that genes may be more readily transferred across the species thus offering the potential to increase the adaptation of the forage grasses.

References

Arus, P. & J. Moreno-Gonzalez, 1993. Marker-assisted selection. In: M.D. Hayward, N.O. Bosemark & I. Romagosa (Eds.), Plant Breeding: Principles and Prospects, pp. 314–331. Chapman and Hall, London.
Breese, E.L. & M.D. Hayward, 1972. The genetic basis of present breeding methods in forage crops. Euphytica 21: 326–336.

258

Charmet, G., F. Balfourier & C. Ravel, 1993. Isozyme polymorphism and geographic differentiation in a collection of French perennial ryegrass populations. Genetic Resources and Crop Evolution. In press.

Cornish, M.A., M.D. Hayward & M.J. Lawrence, 1980. Self-incompatibility in ryegrass iii. The joint segregation of S and PGI/2 in *Lolium perenne*. Heredity 44: 55–62.

Evans, G.M., M.D. Hayward, J.W. Forster, N.J. McAdam, M.J. Scanlon, M. Stammers & J.A.K. Will, 1991. Genome analysis and its manipulation in *Lolium*. In: A.P.M. den Nijs & A. Elgersma (Eds.), Fodder Crops Breeding: Achievements, Novel Strategies and Biotechnology. Proceedings of the 16th Meeting of the Fodder Crops Section of Eucarpia, Wageningen, Netherlands, 1990, pp. 141–146.

Hayward, M.D. (Ed.), 1982. The Utilization of Genetic Resources in Fodder Crop Breeding. Proceedings Eucarpia Fodder Crops Section Meeting, Aberystwyth, p. 345.

Hayward, M.D. & I.B. Abdullah, 1985. Selection and stability of synthetic varieties of *Lolium perenne* 1. The selected character and its expression over generations of multiplication. Theor. Appl. Genet. 70: 48–51.

Hayward M.D. & E.L. Breese, 1993. Population structure and variability. In: M.D. Hayward, N.O. Bosemark & I. Romagosa (Eds.), Plant Breeding: Principles and Prospects, pp. 16–29. Chapman and Hall, London.

Hayward, M.D., L.D. Gottleib & N.J. McAdam, 1978. Survival of allozyme variants in swards of *Lolium perenne* L. Z. Pflanzenzuchtg. 81: 228–234.

Hayward, M.D. & N.J. McAdam, 1975. Isozyme Polymorphism in *Lolium perenne*. Report of the Welsh Plant Breeding Station for 1975, pp. 12–13.

Hayward, M.D. & N.J. McAdam, 1977. Isozyme polymorphism as a measure of distinctiveness and stability in cultivars of *Lolium perenne*. Z. Pflanzenzuchtg. 79: 59–68.

Hayward, M.D. & N.J. McAdam, 1988. The effect of isozyme selection on yield and flowering time in *Lolium perenne*. Plant Breeding 101: 24–29.

Hayward, M.D., M.J. Kearsey, X. Xu & J. Chave, 1989. Outcrossing amongst inbred lines of *Lolium perenne*. Vortr. Pflanzenzuchtg.: 15–1, 10–10.

Humphreys, M.W., 1989. The controlled introgression of *Festuca arundinacea* genes into *Lolium multiflorum*. Euphytica: 42, 105–116.

Lander, E.S. & D. Botstein, 1989. Mapping mendelian factors underlying quantitative traits using RFLP linkage maps. Genetics 121: 185–199.

Mather, K., 1973. Genetical Structure of Populations. Chapman and Hall, London.

Moore G., M.D. Gale, N. Kurata & R.B. Flavell, 1993. Molecular analysis of small grain cereal genomes; current status and prospects. Biotechnology 11: 584–589.

Paterson, A.H., E.S. Lander, J.D. Hewitt, S. Paterson, S.E. Lincoln & S.D. Tanskley, 1988. Resolution of quantitative traits into mendelian factors by using a complete linkage map of restriction fragment length polymorphisms. Nature: 335, 721–726.

Perez de la Vega, M., 1993. Biochemical characterization of populations. In: M.D. Hayward, N.O. Bosemark & I. Romagosa (Eds.), Plant Breeding: Principles and Prospects, pp. 184–200. Chapman and Hall, London.

Quader, S.M.B., 1991. Genetic markers and QTL's in *Lolium*-marker assisted selection. MSc. thesis University of Wales.

Rasmusson, J.M., 1935. Studies on the inheritance of quantitative characters in *Pisum*: 1. Preliminary note on the genetics of flowering. Hereditas 20: 161–180.

Rees, H. & K. Ahmed, 1963. Chiasma frequencies in *Lolium* populations. Evolution 17: 575–579.

Sax, K., 1923. The association of size differences with seed coat pattern and pigmentation in *Phaseolus vulgaris*. Genetics 8: 552–560.

Soller, M. & J.S. Beckmann, 1983. Genetic polymorphism in varietal identification and genetic improvement. Theor. Appl. Genet. 67: 25–33.

Stammers, M., 1992. Molecular mapping and biosystematics of the *Festucae*. PhD Thesis, University of Wales.

Stuber, C.W., 1989. Marker based selection for quantitative traits. Vortr. Pflanzenzuchtg. 16: 31–49.

Stuber, C.W., R.H. Moll, M.M. Goodman, H.E. Schaffer & B.S. Weir, 1980. Allozyme frequency changes associated with selection for increased grain yield in maize (*Zea mays* L.). Genetics 95: 225–236.

Stuber, C.W., M.D. Edwards & J.F. Wendel, 1987. Molecular marker facilitated investigations of quantitative loci in maize. ii. Factors influencing yield and its component traits. Crop Sci. 27: 639–648.

Tanskley, S.D. & C.M. Rick, 1980. Isozymic gene linkage map of the tomato; applications in genetics and breeding. Theor. Appl. Genet. 57: 161–170.

Ustun, A., 1992. Identification of QTL's in *Lolium*. MSc. thesis, University of Wales.

Will, J., 1991. Genome analysis in *Lolium*. PhD. thesis, University of Wales.

Wilson, D. & J.G. Jones, 1981. Effects of selection for dark respiration rate of mature leaves on crop yields of *Lolium perenne* cv. S23. Ann. Bot. 49: 313–320.

O.A. Rognli et al. (eds.), Breeding Fodder Crops for Marginal Conditions, 261–271.
© 1994 Kluwer Academic Publishers. Printed in the Netherlands.

Genetic control of frost tolerance in wheat (*Triticum aestivum* L.)

J. SUTKA

*Agricultural Research Institute of the Hungarian Academy of Sciences, H–2462 Martonvásár,
Hungary*

Summary. The frost tolerance of winter wheat is one component of winter hardiness. If seedlings are frost resistant, it means that they can survive the frost effect without any considerable damage. To study the genetic control of frost tolerance, an artificial freezing test was used. Frost tolerance is controlled by an additive-dominance system. The results of diallel analyses indicate the importance of both additive and non-additive gene action in the inheritance of this character. The dominant genes act in the direction of lower frost tolerance and the recessive genes in the direction of a higher level of frost tolerance. The results of monosomic and substitution analyses show that at least 10 of the 21 pairs of chromosomes are involved in the control of frost tolerance and winter hardiness. Chromosomes 5A and 5D have been implicated most frequently. The gene *Fr1* (Frost 1) was located on the long arm of chromosome 5A. Crosses between cultivars, chromosome manipulation and the induction of somaclonal variation may be suitable methods for broadening the gene pool for frost tolerance.

Introduction

In Europe winter wheat is predominantly grown, giving yields 30 to 40% higher than spring wheat, provided frosts in snowless winters to early spring do not damage the crop. Under Hungarian conditions the wheat yield is influenced not only by the genetic yield potential and disease tolerance of the cultivars but also to a great extent by their winter hardiness. The winter exposes young wheat seedlings to many kinds of stresses: direct frost effect, cold winds, snow cover, intense freezing and glaciation of the soil, frost lifting in spring and various diseases which thrive in or can withstand the cold.

Frost tolerance is one component of winter hardiness. If seedlings are frost resistant, it means that they can survive the frost effect without any considerable damage.

Methods

Over the last 50 years many methods have been devised for studying frost tolerance. According to the method developed in the Martonvásár phytotron for the testing of genetic material, the growth and hardening of the plants are carried out in autumn-winter type plant growth units (Sutka, 1981). The growth period lasts for 5 weeks with decreasing temperature and illumination. During the 6th week hardening is carried out at a day temperature of $+2\,°C$ and a night temperature of $0\,°C$ with 20 h illumination. After hardening the boxes are transferred to the frost tolerance testing chamber, where the temperature is reduced by 1 °C/h to a value of − 4 °C. Hardening is continued in this chamber for another 2 days in the dark, after which the frost treatment is carried out at various temperatures depending on the genetic material. After 24 hours of freezing without illumination, the temperature is raised by 2 °C an hour to + 1 °C and the plants are kept at this temperature for 15 hours. The boxes are then transferred to a growth bench (GB) unit for recovery at a day temperature of 16 °C and a night temperature of 15 °C with a 14 hour day for 18 days.

To study the relationship between hardening period and the expression of frost tolerance plants were kept during two weeks of preliminary growth at day and night temperatures of 15 °C and 10 °C, respectively, with a 12 hour day. After this, the temperature was maintained at 2 °C continuously for 90 days, again with a 12 hour day. During the 90-day hardening period frost tests were carried out every 10 days in the freezing chamber. In this plant growth unit, plants were further hardened for 2 days at − 4 °C after which the temperature was lowered by 2 °C per hour to − 11 °C. The intensity of illumination during the growth and hardening of the plants is $Q = 260\ \mu Es^{-1}$ m^{-2} (15 klx), using Sylvania Gro-Lux/WS fluorescent tubes.

After freezing, the leaves are cut off with scissors a few centimetres above the soil. This is in order that regrowth can be more accurately evaluated, and to avoid the risk of infection by fungal diseases. Frost tolerance is assessed in terms of regrowth on a 0 (dead) to 5 (undamaged) scale and also as percentage survival.

Results

Genetic determination and gene interaction

The genetics of frost tolerance was studied in detail in winter wheat with a method using complete diallel crosses (Gullord, 1974; Puchkov & Zhirov, 1978; Parodi et al., 1983). Their data showed that frost tolerance is controlled by an additive-dominance system.

In our experiments two diallel crosses involving six and ten wheat varieties were tested for frost tolerance under controlled freezing conditions (Sutka, 1981, 1984). In the analysis of variance for combining ability, variance due to the general combining ability (GCA) and specific combining ability (SCA) was significant (Table 1).

This indicates the importance of both additive and non-additive gene action in the inheritance of frost tolerance. The high GCA:SCA ratio (14:6) revealed a preponderance of additive genetic variance. No significant average maternal differences or other reciprocal differences were found between the reciprocal crosses.

Table 1. Analysis of variance for combining ability and reciprocal differences of parents and F_1 hybrids for frost tolerance from a six-parental diallel

Source of variation	df	SS	MS	F
General combining ability (GCA)	5	37.4	7.473	202.76*
Specific combining ability (SCA)	15	7.6	0.5066	13.74*
General reciprocal effect (GRE)	5	0.4	0.08901	2.41
Specific reciprocal effect (SRE)	10	0.2	0.03686	
Error	35	1.3	0.03686	

*Significant at P = 0.001

Table 2. Effect of *Aegilops* cytoplasm on the frost tolerance (%) of *T. aestivum* L.

Cytoplasmic background	Nuclear background			
	Chinese Spring		Cappelle Desprez	
	−12 °C	−14 °C	−12 °C	−14 °C
Ae. mutica Boiss.	62.0	4.0	100.0	92.0[a]
Ae. squarrosa L.	66.0	12.0	92.0	82.0
Ae. umbellulata Zhuk.	32.0[b]	6.0	80.0	12.0[c]
Ae. variabilis Eig.	72.0	4.0	96.0	68.0
T. aestivum L.	72.0	8.0	84.0	68.0

[a], [b], [c] Significant at the 0.05, 0.01 and 0.001 probability levels, respectively, in comparison with the *T. aestivum* cytoplasmic background

The variance (V_r) and covariance (W_r) were calculated for the freezing test, averaged over the reciprocal crosses. The regression coefficient is significantly different from zero but not significantly different from unity. This indicates that non-additive genetic variation is present as dominance only. The dominant genes acted in the direction of lower frost tolerance and

Table 3. Frost tolerance of F₃ lines, homozygous for chromosome 5A of Chinese Spring (CS) or Rannyaya 12 (Ran.12) or Mironovskaya 808 (Mir.808), derived from the reciprocal crosses

Hybrid background	Source of chromosome 5A	−12 °C		−14°C	
		Average rating	Survival %	Average rating	Survival (%)
CSxMir.808	Mir. 808	2.32	92	1.47	78
Mir.808xCS	CS	0.46	32	0.07	7
Difference		1.86*	60*	1.40*	71*
CSxRan.12	Ran. 12	1.70	81	0.82	54
Ran.12xCS	CS	0.59	36	0.24	16
Difference		1.11*	45*	0.58*	38*

*$P = 0.001$

the recessive genes in the direction of a higher level of frost tolerance. In our experiments the values of narrow and broad heritability are 81.10% and 97.55%, respectively. From these data one can expect successful selection for frost tolerance.

In our experiments with one exception the cytoplasm has no significant effect on frost tolerance in varietal reciprocal F₁ hybrids. The survival of alien alloplasmic lines are presented in Table 2. In this experiment *Ae. umbellulata* cytoplasm combined with a nuclear background of Chinese Spring or Cappelle Desprez significantly reduced frost tolerance in comparison with *T. aestivum* cytoplasm. This could probably be explained by the *Ae. umbellulata* cytoplasm causing a decrease in plant vigour and in the case of the variety Cappelle Desprez interacting to produce winter variegation (Worland et al., 1987).

Location of genes on chromosomes

Several cytogenetic studies have been conducted in wheat using monosomic and substitution analyses which have allowed the chromosomal locations of the quantitative trait loci (QTL) to be established for frost tolerance (Goujon et al., 1968; Puchkov & Zhirov, 1978; Sutka & Rajki, 1979; Rigin & Barashkova, 1984). The results of monosomic analysis suggest that considerable variation exists between the effects of different chromosomes. This difficulty can be overcome by using reciprocal monosomic analysis (Sutka & Kovács, 1985). To demonstrate this idea the monosomic lines for chromosome 5A of the wheat varieties Chinese Spring, Mironovskaya 808 and Rannyaya

12 were used as parents. In the F_1 the 5A monosomics were selected and then self-pollinated. In the F_2 generation the disomics were selected and selfed. Seedlings of F_3 disomic lines were used for the freezing test. The average rating and percentage survival at freezing temperatures of $-$ 12 °C and $-$ 14 °C reveal a significant difference between 5A chromosomes from different varieties (Table 3). For the given hybrid backgrounds the 5A chromosomes of Mironovskaya 808 and Rannyaya 12 have a greater effect on frost tolerance than that of Chinese Spring.

Intervarietal chromosome substitutions provide one of the best means of studying the cytogenetic control of frost tolerance. The survival of Chinese Spring (Cheyenne) substitutions was tested under artificial conditions (Sutka, 1981). In each of the substitution lines one pair of chromosomes from Chinese Spring was replaced by the corresponding homologues from the frost resistant variety Cheyenne. Freezing tests in the Martonvásár phytotron confirmed earlier observations which indicated that the chromosomes of homoeologous group 5 of Cheyenne carry major factors controlling frost hardiness (Jenkins, 1971; Cahalan & Law, 1979). When comparing phytotron frost testing and nursery winter hardiness it can be seen that chromosomes of homoeologous group 5 and the 2B and 4B chromosomes play an important role in both environments, but considerable differences were also observed (Table 4).

A number of other studies have been conducted to determine which wheat chromosomes contain genes that affect frost tolerance (Roberts, 1986; Sutka, 1989). The results are consistent with the notion that frost tolerance is a complex character, at least 10 of the 21 pairs of chromosomes are involved in the control of frost tolerance and winter hardiness. Chromosome 5A and 5D have been implicated most frequently and they appear to carry major genes.

The location of the gene(s) responsible for frost tolerance on chromosome 5A was studied using chromosome recombinant lines from a cross between the substitution line Hobbit (*Triticum spelta* 5A) and Hobbit. In this sample of recombinant lines the locus for frost tolerance, designated *Fr1* (Frost 1) was completely linked to the locus *Vrn1* controlling the vernalisation requirement. The results can be explained by a pleiotropic action of the *Vrn1* locus or by close genetic linkage between *Vrn1* and *Fr1* (Sutka & Snape, 1989). The locus involved in the control of cold hardiness on chromosome 5A of wheat was also identified by Roberts (1990).

There was a substantial difference between Chinese Spring (CS) and Cheyenne (Ch) not only in the level of frost tolerance, but also in the dynamics of tolerance, making it possible to study the effects exerted by the individual chromosomes in the course of the hardening period. The substitution line 5A reached the maximum level of hardiness on the 40th day of hardening. Substitution line 7A did not increase frost tolerance during the initial stages

Table 4. Frost tolerance and winter hardiness of Chinese Spring/Cheyenne chromosome substitutions under phytotronic and nursery conditions

Chromosome substitution	Phytotron	Nursery
1A	59	17
2A	45	12
3A	39	25
4A	58	25
5A	94[c]	71[c]
6A	31[a]	56[c]
7A	75[c]	22
1B	63	19
2B	74[c]	31[a]
3B	62	19
4B	74[c]	40[c]
5B	73[b]	47[c]
6B	65[a]	30
7B	48	19
1D	61	21
2D	43	28
3D	36	23
4D	75[c]	17
5D	93[c]	41[c]
6D	59	31[a]
7D	37	22
Chinese Spring (recipient)	49	19
Cheyenne (donor)	100[c]	70[c]

Significance of differences compared to Chinese Spring. [a], [b], [c] P = 0.05–0.01, P = 0.01–0.001 and P = 0.001, respectively

of hardening, but caused a significantly higher rate of survival from the 50th to the 80th day than in the variety Chinese Spring (Fig. 1). This confirmed that the frost tolerance gene on chromosome 7A became activated during the second half of the hardening period, thus providing reliable protection against late frosts.

Table 5. Survival percentage of varietal chromosome substitution
5A into wheat variety Saratovskaya 29 (S 29)

Genotypes	Freezing temperatures		
	− 12°C	− 14°C	− 16°C
Recipient			
Saratovskaya 29	0	0	0
Donors			
Mironovskaya 808	100	100	95
Albidum 11	100	100	100
Ulyanovka	95	100	100
Lutescens 230	100	100	100
Substitutions			
S29/Mironovskaya 808 5A	81	7	0
S29/Albidum 11 5A	81	40	3
S29/Ulyanovka 5A	81	23	2
S29/Lutescens 230 5A	80	13	5

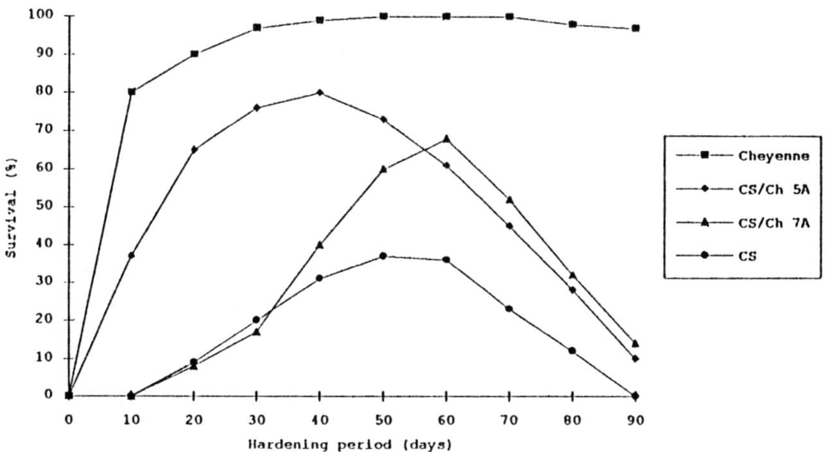

Fig. 1. Mean % plant survival of the parents and various Chinese Spring/Cheyenne chromo-
some substitution lines following increasing periods of hardening at 2°C and freezing treatment
at -11°C

Table 6. Survival percentage of wheat cultivars, species and alien chromosome addition lines

Genotypes	Chromosome number	Freezing temperature	
		$-16\,°C$	$-18\,°C$
Chinese Spring	42	0	0
Martonvásári 8	42	93	50
Martonvásári 14	42	23	10
Cheyenne	42	100	90
Aegilops cylindrica	28	90	87
Aegilops squarrosa	14	17	0
Agropyron glaucum	42	100	100
Agropyron elongatum	14	100	100
Amphidiploid of *T. aestivum/Ag. glaucum* (PPG 829)	84	100	100
Disomic additions of *T.aestivum/Ag.glaucum* (I–VII)	44	100	100

Increase in genetic variation

Several methods exist for the expansion of the gene pool. By means of interspecific crosses, transgressive segregants can be selected from progeny generations with frost tolerance exceeding that of the parents. A further possibility is to improve the frost tolerance of frost sensitive wheat varieties by substituting chromosomes from highly frost resistant varieties into the frost sensitive wheat. The frost tolerance of the very frost sensitive spring wheat variety Saratovskaya 29 can be improved to such an extent by substituting the 5A chromosome with that of the extremely frost resistant varieties Albidum 11, Ulyanovka or Lutescens 230, that it becomes capable of surviving freezing at $-14\,°C$ (Table 5).

Wild species related to cultivated wheat are extremely promising sources of increased genetic variation. *Aegilops cylindrica, Agropyron glaucum (intermedium)* and *Agropyron elongatum* have proved to be very resistant to frost. The addition of *Agropyron glaucum* chromosomes to the chromosome set of cultivated wheat led to a pronounced increase in frost tolerance; disomic additions are able to survive freezing to a temperature as low as $-18\,°C$ (Table 6).

Table 7. Survival percentages of 'GK Csongor' SC_4 somaclones at a freezing temperature of $-13\,°C$

SC_4 families	Survival (%)	Difference from control
1	86	12
2	76	2
3	46	-28^b
4	94	20^a
5	48	-26^b
6	44	-30^b
7	36	-38^c
8	60	-14
9	90	16
10	50	-24^a
11	66	-8
12	48	-26^b
13	66	-8
14	52	-22^a
15	74	0
16	58	-16
17	46	-28^b
18	26	-48^c
19	42	-32
20	86	12
21	60	-14
22	40	-34^c
23	56	-18
24	70	-4
25	44	-30^b
26	56	-18
27	54	-20^a
28	88	14
29	54	-20^a
30	92	18
31	40	-34^b
Control	74	

[a], [b], [c]Significant at the 0.05, 0.01 and 0.001 probability levels, respectively

270

Tissue culture techniques now make it possible to initiate callus cultures from immature embryos and to regenerate plants from the calli. Regenerants known as somaclones, produced from calli of various wheat varieties, including GK Csongor, were propagated for three generations. When the frost tolerance of the somaclonal plants was tested in the SC_4 generation it was weaker than that of the control, which consisted of GK Csongor wheat plants of non tissue culture origin (Table 7). The tolerance of 6 somaclones tended to be better than that of the control, but only somaclone No. 4 proved to be significantly better and thus of practical importance (Galiba & Sutka, 1989).

In summary it can be stated that interspecific crossing, chromosome manipulation and the induction of somaclonal variation may be suitable methods for increasing the genetic variation of frost tolerance.

Acknowledgements

The author is grateful to Mrs. B. Harasztos for revising the manuscript linguistically and to B. Kőszegi for his help in carrying out the preparation of the manuscript. This work was carried out under a research programme supported by the Hungarian National Scientific Research Fund.

References

Briggle, L.W., 1980. Origin and botany of wheat. In: E. Häflige (Ed.), Wheat, pp. 6–13. Documenta Ciba-Geigy, Basel, Switzerland.

Briggle, L.W. & B.C. Curtis, 1987. Wheat worldwide. In: E.G. Heyne (Ed.), Wheat and Wheat Improvement, pp. 1–32. American Society of Agronomy, Madison, Wisconsin, USA.

Cahalan, C. & C.N. Law, 1979. The genetical control of cold resistance and vernalisation requirement in wheat. Heredity 42: 125–132.

Galiba, G. & J. Sutka, 1989. Frost resistance of somaclones derived from *Triticum aestivum* L. winter wheat calli. Plant Breeding 102: 101–104.

Goujon, C., N. Maia & G. Dossinault, 1968. Frost resistance in wheat II., Reaction at the coleoptile stage studied artificial conditions. Ann. Amelior. Plant (Paris) 18: 49–57.

Gullard, M., 1974. Genetics of freezing hardiness in winter wheat (*Triticum aestivum*). PhD. dissertation, Michigan State University, East Lansing.

Jenkins, G., 1971. Breeding for Cold Resistance in Winter Cereals. Eucarpia Proc., Dijon, pp. 163–172.

Parodi, P.C., W.E. Nyquist, F.L. Patterson & H.F. Hodges, 1983. Traditional combining ability and Gardner-Eberhart analyses of a diallel for cold resistance in winter wheat. Crop Sci. 23: 314–318.

Puchkov, Y.M. & E.G. Zhirov, 1978. Breeding of common wheat varieties with a high frost resistance and genetic aspects of it. World Sci. News, India 15: 17–22.

Rigin, B.V. & E.A. Barashkova, 1984. Genetic analysis of resistance to frost in the variety Mironovskaya 808 with the use of Chinese Spring aneuploid. Sel. Genet. Charac. Sort. Pshen. 85: 23–29.

Roberts, D.W.A., 1986. Chromosomes in 'Cadet' and 'Rescue' wheats carrying loci for cold hardiness and vernalization response. Can. J. Genet. Cytol. 28: 991–997.

Roberts, D.W.A., 1990. Identification of loci on chromosome 5A of wheat involved in control of cold hardiness, vernalization, leaf length, rosette growth habit, and height of hardened plants. Genome 33: 247–259.

Sutka, J., 1981. Genetic studies of frost resistance in wheat. Theor. Appl. Genet. 59: 145–152.

Sutka, J., 1984. A ten-parental diallel analysis of frost resistance in winter wheat. Z. Pflanzenzuecht. 93: 147–157.

Sutka, J., 1989. Genetic control of frost resistance in wheat. Sveriges Utsädesförerings Tidskrift 99: 135–142.

Sutka, J. & G. Kovács, 1985. Reciprocal monosomic analysis of frost resistance on chromosome 5A in wheat. Euphytica 34: 367–370.

Sutka, J. & E. Rajki, 1979. Cytogenetic study of frost resistance in the winter wheat variety 'Rannyaya 12' by F_2 monosomic analysis. Cereal Res. Commun. 7: 281–283.

Sutka, J. & J.W. Snape, 1989. Location of a gene for frost resistance on chromosome 5A of wheat. Euphytica 42: 41–44.

Worland, A.J., M.D. Gale & C.N. Law, 1987. Cytoplasmic inheritance. In: F.G.H. Lupton (Ed.), Wheat Breeding, pp. 149–153. Chapman and Hall, London, New York.

O.A. Rognli et al. (eds.), Breeding Fodder Crops for Marginal Conditions, 273–283.
© 1994 *Kluwer Academic Publishers. Printed in the Netherlands.*

Assessing success in gene transfer between *Lolium multiflorum* and *Festuca arundinacea*

M.W. HUMPHREYS[1] & M. GHESQUIÈRE[2]
[1]*AFRC Institute of Grassland and Environmental Research, Plas Gogerddan, Aberystwyth, Dyfed, SY23 3EB, UK;* [2]*INRA Centre Poitou-Charentes, Station d'Amelioration des Plantes Fourrageres, 86600 Lusignan, France*

Summary. A *Festuca arundinacea* (2n = 6× = 42) plant with three PGI/2 homoeoalleles marking three homoeologous chromosomes was crossed with a *Lolium multiflorum* plant (2n = 4× = 28) with a different PGI/2 phenotype to give a pentaploid hybrid (2n = 5× = 35) with five chromosomes each marked by a different PGI/2 allele. This hybrid plant was backcrossed twice with diploid *L. multiflorum* (2n = 2× = 14) with a different PGI/2 phenotype. Numbers of interspecific recombinants involving chromosomes marked by PGI/2 were then determined in both backcross generations. In the BC1, recombinants involving only one PGI/2 allele were found but in the BC2, all three homoeologous *F. arundinacea* chromosomes carrying the PGI/2 locus recombined with *Lolium* with one in greater frequency and the others in equal but lower frequency. The evidence supports claims made for *F. pratensis* (2n = 2× = 14) and *F. arundinacea* var. *glaucescens* (2n = 4× = 28) being progenitors for *F. arundinacea.*

Introduction

The *Lolium/Festuca* complex comprises a range of characters (Thomas and Humphreys, 1991) which could if combined, offer good seasonal productivity and nutritional quality with persistence at low input management and tolerance to climatic stress. Between the two genera the combination of *Festuca arundinacea* and *Lolium multiflorum* has been claimed to offer the greatest complementation of characters (Breese *et al.*, 1981). *F. arundinacea* has a wider distribution than *L. multiflorum* and generally greater adaptation to climatic and edaphic conditions with superior persistency and ability to withstand extremes of temperature and water availability. However, compared to *Lolium* it has poor establishment, seedling vigour and lower nutritive value.

There are indications that in breeding for improved tolerance to environmental stress, there may be advantages of introgressing a limited number of genes from one species into another rather than combining complete genomes which may produce genetic imbalance and thus diminish the adaptive response (Humphreys *et al.*, 1993; Thomas and Evans, 1990). Humphreys and Thomas (1993) describe such a breeding programme between *L. multiflorum* and *F. arundinacea* which gave rise to *L. multiflorum*-like diploid plants (2n = 2× = 14) with drought resistance equivalent to that found in *F. arundinacea*, albeit at low frequency. Plants derived from this breeding programme are currently being agronomically assessed in drought conditions under rain

274

shelters at IGER, Aberystwyth, and in the field at INRA, Lusignan, in central France where a substantial water deficit is expected during the summer months.

Traits such as drought resistance are polygenically controlled, and genes which determine such a character may well be located on chromosomes in each of the three sub-sets of homoeologous chromosomes that make up the genome of *F. arundinacea*. Thomashow (1990) found that cold tolerance genes were located on every chromosome in each of the three homoeologous chromosome sets of wheat, although chromosome 5A and 5D were most implicated.

Lewis *et al.* (1980) demonstrated that a locus determining the isozyme marker phosphoglucoisomerase (PGI/2) was located on three different chromosomes in *F. arundinacea*, and they assumed that they would constitute one homoeologous group. They confirmed the close relationship between the three ancestral genomes reported by other researchers (Malik and Tripathi, 1970; Thomas *et al.*, 1983; Jauhar, 1975; Kleijer, 1984; Thomas and Thomas, 1993).

Thomas *et al.* (1983) demonstrated that the pentaploid hybrid between *L. multiflorum* and *F. arundinacea* left very few chromosomes unpaired and showed high levels of homoeologous chromosome pairing. Recombination between *L. multiflorum* and *F. arundinacea* at the PGI/2 locus was observed, in derivatives of such a pentaploid hybrid by Humphreys (1989) in a backcross breeding programme with diploid *L. multiflorum*. The data, however, only described recombination between one of the three PGI/2 homoeoalleles and *L. multiflorum* and gave no indication whether the levels of interspecific recombination observed would be similar between *Lolium* and the *Festuca* chromosomes carrying the PGI/2 locus in the other two homoeologous chromosome sets. To make an accurate assessment of the feasibility of recovering recombinants in a backcross breeding programme involving chromosome segments derived from all three homoeologous sets and to determine whether recombination frequency was the same in each, it is necessary to use genetic markers located in all three homoeologous chromosome sets.

This paper describes a hybrid of *L. multiflorum* × *F. arundinacea* ($2n = 5\times = 35$) which was labelled at the PGI/2 locus with five different homoeoalleles. The hybrid and its derivatives were backcrossed onto diploid *L. multiflorum* with a different PGI/2 genotype and the transmission of *Festuca* alleles and the frequency of interspecific recombinants in the BC1 and BC2 determined.

The data are compared with the frequency of interspecific recombination at the PGI/2 locus between *L. multiflorum* and the allotetraploid *F. arundinacea* var. *glaucescens* ($2n = 4\times = 28$), one of the two putative progenitors of *F.*

arundinacea (Malik and Tripathi, 1970; Chandrasekharan and Thomas, 1971; Sleper, 1990). The implications for plant breeding are briefly discussed.

Materials and methods

The backcrossing scheme for introgression of *F. arundinacea* PGI/2 alleles into diploid *L. multiflorum* and the isozyme procedures used were described by Humphreys (1989). Briefly a *L. multiflorum* cultivar Tetrone (2n = 4× = 28) with PGI/2 phenotype *"ab"* was hybridized with a *F. arundinacea* plant (2n = 6× = 42) from a natural Swiss population and a PGI/2 phenotype *"a$^+$ce"*. This resulted in a pentaploid hybrid (2n = 5× = 35) with a PGI/2 phenotype *"a$^+$abce"*, the *"a"* and the *"b"* PGI/2 alleles labelling the two homologous *Lolium* chromosomes, and the *"a$^+$"*, *"c"* and *"e"* alleles labelling three homoeologous *Festuca* chromosomes carrying the PGI/2 locus.

The hybrid as the male parent was backcrossed onto *L. multiflorum* cultivar RvP (2n = 2× = 14) homozygous *"d"* at the PGI/2 locus. The BC1 plants had 21 ± 2 chromosomes, containing the complete diploid complement of *Lolium* chromosomes and around seven *Festuca* chromosomes (Humphreys, 1989). The BC1 plants would, if no recombination had occurred, be expected to carry two *Lolium* PGI/2 alleles, a *"d"* allele from the *L. multiflorum* female parent and either an *"a"* or *"b"* from the hybrid. Any BC1 plant containing neither *"a"* nor *"b"* PGI/2 alleles from the hybrid but instead one or more of the three *Festuca* PGI/2 alleles together with the *"d"* allele of the *Lolium* parent indicates that recombination may have occurred between the relevant homoeologous *Lolium* and *Festuca* chromosomes. A test cross involving such a BC1 plant and a *L. multiflorum* plant with a different PGI/2 phenotype would verify whether or not the BC1 plant contained an interspecific recombinant. The *Lolium* and *Festuca* PGI/2 alleles should segregate at a 1:1 ratio. The transmission of the three *Festuca* PGI/2 homoeoalleles into the BC1 and the numbers of putative recombinants with *Lolium* was determined.

BC1 plants required one or two further backcrosses to return to the diploid (2n = 2× = 14) *Lolium* genotype of the recurrent parent. BC1 and BC2 plants with no interspecific PGI/2 recombinant and retaining a *Festuca* chromosome carrying the PGI/2 locus were backcrossed onto *L. multiflorum* cultivar Tribune (2n = 2× = 14) with a PGI/2 phenotype *"d"* one or two times to give diploid *Lolium*-like BC2 or BC3 plants respectively.

The frequency of recombination at the PGI/2 locus between the relevant three homoeologous *Festuca* chromosomes and that of *Lolium* was determined by scoring numbers of diploid (2n = 2× = 14) *"a$^+$d"*, *"cd"*, and *"de"* backcross derivatives. The transmission of the three *Festuca* PGI/2 alleles into the BC2 and BC3 populations was also calculated.

Table 1. BC1: *L. multiflorum* × (*L. multiflorum* × *F. arundinacea*)

	Lm (PGI/2 = dd) (2n = 2× = 14)			×	LmFa (PGI/2 = a^+abce) (2n = 5× = 35)				
				Number of *Festuca* PGI/2 alleles					
	0	1			2			3	Total
	–	a^+	c	e	a^+c	a^+e	ce	a^+ce	
Putative recombinant (with no Lm a or b)	–	–	7^x	–	–	–	4^{xx}	1^{xxx}	12 (10%)
Non-recombinant (with Lm a or b)	21	10	32	23	11	5	3	–	105 (90%)
Total BC1	21	10	39	23	11	5	7	1	117
With *Festuca* PGI/2 allele	–	72 (61%)			23 (20%)			1 (1%)	96 (82%)

$^x = cd$
$^{xx} = cde$
$^{xxx} = a^+cde$

Table 2. Transmission of *F. arundinacea* PGI/2 alleles into the BC1 and BC2

	Nos. of plants with *Festuca* PGI/2 allele / Total no. of plants			
	a^+	c	e	Total
BC1	27/117 (23%)	58/117 (50%)	36/117 (31%)	96/117 (82%)
BC2	57/374 (15%)	10/120 (8%)	36/488 (7%)	103/982 (10%)

Results

One hundred and seventeen BC1 plants were produced of which 96 (82%) carried one or more *Festuca* PGI/2 alleles (Table 1). Only 20% of the BC1 carried two *Festuca* alleles while 61% carried one *Festuca* allele, half of which were "c". The two *Lolium* PGI/2 alleles, "a" and "b" of the hybrid were recovered in 90% of the backcross derivatives and were at equal frequency but the numbers of the three *Festuca* alleles in the progeny differed (Table 2). The "c" allele was found in half of the BC1 plants and was as frequent as the two *Lolium* PGI/2 alleles. There was no significant difference in the recovery of the two other *Festuca* PGI/2 alleles, the "a^+" and "e", but they appeared at a frequency of 23 and 31% respectively. The frequency of the two

Table 3. BC2 (+ BC3): *L. multiflorum* × BC1 (or BC2)

Lm (PGI/2 = *dd*) (2n = 2× = 14)	×	BC1 (or BC2) (PGI/2 = *ad* or *bd* + "*a*⁺", "*c*" or "*e*") (2n = 2× + n = 15)	
		Possible recombinants and PGI/2 phenotype	Total no. BC2 / BC3
		"*a*⁺*d*" 17 (4.5%)	374
		"*cd*" 8 (7%)	120
		"*de*" 19 (4%)	488
Total		44 (4%)	982

Lolium PGI/2 alleles "*a*", and "*b*" should represent the number of plants with intact *Lolium* chromosomes and no recombinants involving the PGI/2 locus, recovered from the hybrid in the BC1 plants. The unequal transmission of the three *Festuca* PGI/2 alleles, with the "*c*" allele most commonly found in the BC1, would indicate that the *Festuca* chromosome carrying the "*c*" allele was more commonly transmitted into the BC1 than either of its homoeologous chromosome partners.

The only possible interspecific recombinants (with no *Lolium* "*a*" or "*b*" PGI/2 allele) all carried the *Festuca* "*c*" allele and were found in 10% of the BC1 (Table 1). Seven BC1 plants were "*cd*", one plant had an "*a*⁺*cde*" PGI/2 phenotype and four BC1 plants were "*cde*". The "*a*⁺*cde*" phenotype could be explained by recombination involving a *Lolium* chromosome and any one of the three homoeologous *Festuca* chromosomes and the "*cde*" by recombination with any one of two *Festuca* chromosomes. For any of the three putative recombinant PGI/2 phenotypes, an alternative explanation would be that neither *Lolium* chromosomes from the hybrid were transmitted through into the BC1 and that only intact *Festuca* chromosomes carrying the relevant PGI/2 alleles were recovered in those BC1 plants. A test-cross involving two randomly selected BC1 plants having a "*cd*" phenotype with *L. multiflorum* plants with a "*d*" gave a 1:1 segregation which was evidence that the "*c*" allele (at least in two of the BC1 progeny) had been successfully introgressed into *Lolium* during the first backcross (Table 4).

278

Table 4. Transmission of introgressed *F. arundinacea* PGI/2 alleles

BC2 × *L. multiflorum*	Plants with Fa PGI/2 allele	Plants without Fa PGI/2 allele	Total	X^2 (1:1)
$a^+ d \times dd$	40	64	104	5.54*
$cd \times dd$	2	6	8	+
	14#	21	35	1.40 NS
	24#	34	58	1.72 NS
	30	29	59	0.02 NS
	12	9	21	0.43 NS
Total	82	99	181	1.60 NS
$de \times dd$	3	12	15	+
	6	14	20	3.2 NS
Total	9	26	35	8.26**

\# = Derived from the BC1
* = P < 0.05
** = P < 0.01
+ = X^2 not calculated, less than 5 in one class

Backcross 1 plants retaining the *Lolium* "a" or "b" together with one *Festuca* PGI/2 allele from the hybrid in addition to the "d" allele from the *L. multiflorum* parent were in effect single chromosome addition lines. Such BC1 plants containing any one of the three *Festuca* PGI/2 alleles were backcrossed again onto the recurrent *Lolium* parent with a "d" PGI/2 phenotype to produce the BC2. In some cases, where the *Lolium* "a" or "b" PGI/2 alleles from the original hybrid were retained in the BC2 and the *Lolium* chromosomes expected to be intact, at least in regard to the locus determining PGI/2, the BC2 were backcrossed again with *L. multiflorum* to produce the BC3. The results are summarised in Tables 2 and 3. From a total of 982 BC2 and BC3 plants, 103 (10%) carried a *Festuca* PGI/2 allele and of these 44 (4%) neither contained an "a" nor a "b" *Lolium* allele and thus were putative interspecific recombinants.

When the BC2 and BC3 data are divided into populations according to whether the BC1 parent carried an "a^+", "c" or "e" *Festuca* PGI/2 allele in addition to two *Lolium* alleles (Table 2), the transmission of the three *Festuca* PGI/2 alleles in the backcross generations, could be calculated. As with the BC1, the transmission of the three *Festuca* PGI/2 alleles indicates both recovery of intact *Festuca* chromosomes and possible interspecific recombinant genotypes in the BC2 and BC3. The transmission of the three *Festuca* PGI/2 alleles was 72% lower in the BC2 and BC3 than in the BC1. If all *Festuca* chromosomes are lost at the same frequency as the *Festuca* chromosomes carrying the PGI/2 locus, then the low frequency of *Festuca* PGI/2 alleles would indicate that BC2 and BC3 plants are primarily *Lolium* in genotype.

There was no significant difference between the BC1 and BC2 ($X^2_{[1]}$ = 0.99 (Table 3)) in numbers of putative recombinants between the *Lolium* and *Festuca* chromosome carrying the "*c*" PGI/2 allele. However, in the BC2 some recombination involving *Lolium* and the two other homoeologous *Festuca* chromosomes was also found. The frequency of interspecific recombination involving both the chromosome carrying the "a^+" and the "*e*" *Festuca* allele with *Lolium* was nearly equal at 4% for the "*e*" and 4.5% for the "a^+" PGI/2 allele. The BC2 and BC3 plants were confirmed as recombinants by their chromosome number ($2n = 2\times = 14$). Eight arbitrarily selected BC1 and BC2 recombinant plants carrying an introgressed *Festuca* PGI/2 allele were test crossed with a *L. multiflorum* plant with a "*d*" PGI/2 phenotype to assess the transmission rate of the introgressed *Festuca* allele in *Lolium* germplasm (Table 4).

The 1:1 segregation "*cd*":"*dd*" from both BC1 and BC2 plants indicated no apparent selection against the introgressed "*c*" allele in any of five populations, nor when data from the five populations were combined.

Overall the introgression lines carrying both the *Festuca* "a^+" and "*e*" PGI/2 alleles showed some deviation from the expected 1:1 ratios with a deficiency of the *Festuca* PGI/2 allele in both cases (Table 4).

Discussion

Humphreys (1989) described the backcrossing programme between *L. multiflorum* ($2n = 2\times = 14$) and the pentaploid hybrid ($2n = 5\times = 35$) between *L. multiflorum* and *F. arundinacea*, and Morgan *et al.* (1988) did the equivalent in *L. multiflorum* and the closely related but structurally distinct *Festuca* species *F. gigantea* respectively. They described how using the hybrid and its derivatives as male parent, it was possible to return to the genotype of the recurrent parent in two generations and that over 80% of the BC2 were diploid ($2n = 2\times = 14$). The chromosome pairing in the BC1 reflected the origin of the chromosomes transmitted through the hybrid pollen where 80% of cells had up to seven bivalents or trivalents with the remainder unpaired. We would expect the bivalents to be predominantly between homologous *Lolium* chromosomes but the trivalents would include an additional *Festuca* chromosome illustrating the ability of the chromosomes of the two species to pair.

The retention here in the BC1 of one or other of the two *Lolium* PGI/2 alleles from the hybrid supported the meiosis data of Humphreys (1989) and Morgan *et al.* (1988) and showed that their respective chromosomes were transmitted at a 1:1 ratio in a regular Mendelian manner. Only one of the three *Festuca* PGI/2 alleles was transmitted into the BC1 at an equal frequency to those of *Lolium*, the "*c*" allele, while the other two were transmitted at a lower frequency. If the transmission rate of the three *Festuca* PGI/2 alleles reflects the transmission of chromosomes from the three ancestral diploid species which make up the genome of *F. arundinacea*, then chromosomes particularly from two of the *Festuca* genomes are lost in large numbers in the BC1. The BC1 contain circa 21 chromosomes (Humphreys, 1989) of which only seven will be *Festuca*, and these mainly from one of the three homoeologous sets. Clearly when genes which govern important agronomic characters such as drought and cold resistance are probably located on chromosomes in all three sub-sets of *F. arundinacea*, it is important to use as wide a selection of BC1 plants as possible to improve the chances of recombination involving the relevant *Festuca* chromosomes and *Lolium* in the BC2.

In addition to the greater transmission of the *Festuca* "*c*" PGI/2 allele, compared with the other two *Festuca* PGI/2 alleles, putative recombinants involving this allele and *Lolium* were also found in 10% of the BC1. Two randomly selected plants were confirmed as recombinants in a test cross with *Lolium* and segregated in accordance with Mendelian expectations. The combined PGI/2 recombination and transmission data would suggest that of the three ancestral progenitors of *F. arundinacea* that one, containing the chromosome marked by a "*c*" PGI/2 allele, was more closely related to *L. multiflorum* than were the other two. Kleijer (1984), who studied the relative chromosome affinity between the two species based on chromosome pairing in the tetraploid hybrid (2n = 4× = 28) also concluded that one of the ancestral *Festuca* genomes was closely related to *Lolium*. In the pentaploid hybrid three homoeologous *Festuca* chromosomes are each competing for pairing sites and the results demonstrate that the chromosome donated by one *F. arundinacea* genome (that carrying the "*c*" PGI/2 allele) had greatest success of forming a chiasmate association with its homoloeogous *L. multiflorum* counterpart.

If throughout the pentaploid hybrid, interspecific chromosome pairing was consistent with that between the PGI/2 labelled chromosomes, then only one of the putative diploid ancestors which gave rise to *F. arundinacea*, would pair and recombine with *Lolium*. However, in the BC2 all three *Festuca* PGI/2 homoeoalleles were found as recombinants in diploid *Lolium*-like (2n = 2× = 14) hybrid derivatives. Backcross 2 plants, with a recombinant involving the "*c*" allele were found in greatest frequency equal to that observed among the BC1 but backcross derived plants carrying a recombinant including the "a^+"

and the "*e*" *Festuca* PGI/2 alleles were also found in the BC2, both at equal frequency (4%), which was only half the value obtained for the "*c*" allele.

Backcross 2 progeny with recombinants including the "a^+" and the "*e*" *Festuca* PGI/2 allele were derived from BC1 plants with a single *Festuca* PGI/2 allele (in addition to two *Lolium* PGI/2 alleles). They were in effect chromosome addition lines. In the absence of any competition for pairing sites between homoeologous *Festuca* chromosomes, M1 associations between all three homoeologous *Festuca* chromosomes carrying the PGI/2 locus and *Lolium* were possible.

F. pratensis is widely believed to have donated one sub-set of chromosomes (Borrill *et al.*, 1977), and retains close genetic similarities with *F. arundinacea* (Lehvaslaiho *et al.*, 1987; Perez-Vicente *et al.*, 1992). The other two homoeologous chromosome sets may have been derived from the allotetraploid (2n = 4× = 28) species *F. arundinacea* var. *glaucescens* (Malik and Tripathi, 1970; Chandrasekharan and Thomas, 1971; Sleper and Nelson, 1990). The two homoeologous chromosome sets which make up the genome of *F. glaucescens* have been considered to be very closely related and some researchers have referred to *F. arundinacea* as an autoallopolyploid (for example Malik and Thomas, 1967). This view is generally not supported nowadays since chromosome pairing in *F. arundinacea* var. *glaucescens* (Ghesquière *et al.*, 1991a) and *F. arundinacea* (Jauhar, 1975) is known to be controlled by a gene (or genes) which is inactive in the hemizygous state and chromosome pairing is restricted to homologous partners conferring disomic inheritance (Lewis *et al.*, 1980). Such systems would not be expected to function in an autoallopolyploid.

Ghesquière *et al.* (1991b) measured recombination between *L. multiflorum* and *F. arundinacea* var. *glaucescens* using three isozyme loci including PGI/2. They used haploid anther culture derived plants from *L. multiflorum* × *F. glaucescens* (2n = 4× = 28) hybrids and backcross derivatives from fertile triploid hybrids between the two species. They achieved an overall recombination frequency of around 5% between *F. arundinacea* var. *glaucescens* and *L. multiflorum*. This recombination frequency was very similar to that observed in the BC2 between *L. multiflorum* and two of the three *F. arundinacea* homoeologous chromosome sets. The PGI/2 data from the BC2, although not providing any substantial evidence for the origin of the two diploid progenitors which together with *F. pratensis* gave rise to *F. arundinacea*, nevertheless clearly show that two *Festuca* homoeologues are both equally related to *L. multiflorum* since recombinants with the "a^+" and "*e*" *Festuca* PGI/2 alleles were found in equal numbers.

We propose that in the hybrid, the close structural similarities between *L. multiflorum* and *F. pratensis* allow some interspecific chromosome pairing and that the *F. arundinacea* chromosome carrying the *"c"* PGI/2 allele was derived from *F. pratensis*. Close structural similarities between the two *F. glaucescens* PGI/2 labelled homoeologues also encouraged their preferential chromosome pairing in the hybrid. Indeed Ghesquière *et al.* (1991a) demonstrated that homoeologous *F. arundinacea* var. *glaucescens* chromosomes can exhibit complete bivalent pairing in the absence of their homologous chromosome partner. This together with the closer chromosome affinity found between *L. multiflorum* and *F. pratensis*, prevents any interspecific recombination at the PGI/2 locus between *F. glaucescens* and *L. multiflorum* in the BC1. In the BC1 plants used for the BC2, only one or other of the *F. glaucescens* chromosomes marked by the *"a^+"*, and *"e"* PGI/2 alleles were present and in the absence of another *Festuca* homoeologue each was able to pair with *Lolium*.

The use of fluorescence *in situ* hybridization (FISH) techniques currently being employed at IGER, Aberystwyth, and INRA, Lusignan, for identifying *Lolium* and *Festuca* chromosomes should finally remove doubts as to the phylogeny of *F. arundinacea*. The technique will greatly aid selection procedures for introgressed genes through marker assisted selection and will also indicate the location of genes controlling important agronomic traits on specific chromosomes in ryegrass.

References

Borrill, M., M. Kirby & W.G. Morgan, 1977. Studies in *Festuca*. II. Interrelationships of some putative diploid ancestors of the polyploid broad-leaved fescues. New Phytol. 78: 661–674.

Breese, E.L., E.J. Lewis & G.M. Evans, 1981. Interspecific hybrids and polyploidy. Philosophical Transactions of the Royal Society of London B 292: 487–497.

Chandrasekharan, P. & H. Thomas, 1971. Studies in *Festuca*. 5. Cytogenetic relationships between species of *bovinae* and *scariosae*. Z. Pflanzenzüchtg 65: 345–354.

Ghesquière, M., Z. Zwierzykowski, C. Poisson & J. Jadas-Hecart, 1991a. Amphitetraploid *Festulolium*: chromosome stability and female fertility over intercrossing generations. Proc. of the Eucarpia Fodder Crops Section Meeting Alghero, Italy.

Ghesquière, M., F. Durand, P. Le Quilliec & F. Gaullier, 1991b. Use of Electrophoretic markers in chromosome manipulating of *Festuca* × *Lolium* hybrids. Proc. of the Eucarpia Fodder Crops Section Meeting Alghero, Italy.

Humphreys, M.W., 1989. The controlled introgression of *Festuca arundinacea* genes into *Lolium multiflorum*. Euphytica 42: 105–116.

Humphreys, M.W. & H. Thomas, 1993. Improved drought resistance in introgression lines derived from *Lolium multiflorum* × *Festuca arundinacea* hybrids. Plant breeding 111, 155–161.

Humphreys, M.O., M.W. Humphreys & H. Thomas, 1993. Breeding grasses for adaptation to environmental problems. Proc. of the International Grassland Congress, New Zealand.

Jauhar, P., 1975. Genetic control of diploid-like meiosis in hexaploid tall fescue. Nature (London) 254: 595–597.

Kleijer, G., 1984. Cytogenetic studies of crosses between *Lolium multiflorum* Lam. and *Festuca arundinacea* Schreb. Z. Pflanzenzüchtg 93: 1–22.

Lehvaslaiho, H., A. Saura & J. Lokki, 1987. Chloroplast DNA variation in the grass tribe *Festuceae*. Theor. Appl. Genet. 74: 298–302.

Lewis, E.J., M.W. Humphreys & M.P. Caton, 1980. Disomic inheritance in *Festuca arundinacea* Schreb. Z. Pflanzenzüchtg 84: 335–341.

Malik, C.P. & P.T. Thomas, 1967. Cytological relationships and genome structure of some *Festuca* species. Caryologia 20: 1–39.

Malik, C.P. & R.C. Tripathi, 1970. Mode of chromosome pairing in the polyhaploid tall fescue (*Festuca arundinacea* Schreb. 2n = 42). Z. Biol. (Munich) 116: 332–339.

Morgan, W.G., H., Thomas & E.J. Lewis, 1988. Cytogenetic studies of hybrids between *Festuca gigantea* Vill. and *Lolium multiflorum* Lam. Plant Breeding 101: 335–343.

Perez-Vicente, R., L. Petris, M. Osusky, I. Potrykis & G. Spangenberg, 1992. Molecular and cytogenetic characterization of repetitive DNA sequence from *Lolium* and *Festuca*: applications in the analysis of *Festulolium* hybrids. Theor. Appl. Genet. 84: 145–154.

Sleper, D.A. & C.J. Nelson, 1990. Breeding and genetics: potential use of haploids and doubled haploids. In: Biotechnology in Tall Fescue Improvement. Ed. by M.J. Kasperbauer. CRC Press Inc.

Thomas, H., W.G. Morgan, M. Borrill & M. Evans, 1983. Meiotic behaviour in polyploid species of *Festuca*. Proc. of the Kew Chromosome Conference II. George Allen and Unwin: 133–138.

Thomas, H. & C. Evans, 1990. Influence of drought and flowering on growth and water relations of perennial ryegrass populations. Anns Appl. Biol. 116: 371–382.

Thomas, H. & M.O. Humphreys, 1991. Progress and potential of interspecific hybrids of *Lolium* and *Festuca*. J. Agri. Sci. Cambridge 117: 1–8.

Thomas, H.M. & B.J. Thomas, 1993. Synaptonemal complex formation in two allohexaploid *Festuca* species and a pentaploid hybrid. Heredity 71, 305–311.

Thomashow, M.F., 1990. Molecular genetics of cold acclimation in higher plants. Adv. Genet. 28: 99–131.

DETECTION OF RAPD MARKERS LINKED TO CROWN RUST TOLERANCE IN LOLIUM MULTIFLORUM L.

M. De Loose, A. Ghesquiere, D. Reheul and E. Van Bockstaele
Governement Plant Breeding Station (R.v.P. - C.L.O.-Gent)
Burg. Van Gansberghelaan 109, 9820 Merelbeke, Belgium

Introduction

Crown rust (*Puccinia coronata* Corda) is a cosmopolitan pathogen that infects annual (*Lolium multiforum* L.) and perennial (*L. perenne* L.) ryegrasses, which are both cross-pollinating species. The fungus parasitizes the host plants by depleting their carbohydrate reserves. Crown rust infected ryegrass is less palatable and the nutritional value is lower. Severe infections have a negative effect on growth, recuperative potential and resistance to cold winter conditions.

Chemical control of crown rust is expensive. Therefore a lot of effort is put in breeding for genetic resistance. Generally cloning of plant disease resistance genes has been hindered by a lack of information on the patterns of expression and on the products of these genes. Recently, marker-facilitated selection has received attention as a viable method in breeding for disease resistance in crop plants. Especially restriction fragment length polymorphism (RFLP) has been used extensively to tag useful genes in tomato, rice, soybean, maize, etc. (for a general overview see Melchinger 1990).

A modification of the polymerase chain reaction (PCR) has resulted in the availability of a relatively new form of molecular marker : the random amplified polymorphic DNA (RAPD) marker (Williams *et al.* 1990). RAPD markers are polymorphic DNA sequences separated by gel electrophoresis after PCR amplification using random oligonucleotide primers of 10 - 12 nucleotides. Polymorphisms are caused by base changes in the primer binding sites or by chromosome rearrangements within the amplified sequences. RAPD markers are usually scored as dominant alleles.

The identification of RFLPs or RAPDs linked to important resistance genes is dependent on the availability of pairs of backcross derived near-isogenic lines (NILs) for the identification of genomic regions linked to the gene of interest (Young *et al.* 1988). The development of these NILs is time consuming. An alternative strategy is to use "bulked segregant analysis" (Michelmore *et al.* 1991), which allow the rapid development of populations useful for the identification of RFLP or RAPD markers linked to important plant genes.

Since marker based selection would greatly facilitate the transfer of rust resistance genes in susceptible *Lolium* germplasm, a study was initiated to identify molecular RAPD markers linked to crown rust tolerance gene(s). While constructing experimental populations for "bulked segregant analysis", we started already to screen three independently obtained populations of annual ryegrasses (1 → 3) for the presence of RAPD markers. The objective was to identify two groups of individual genotypes with high (S) or low sensitivity (T) to crown rust.

Material and methods

Under controlled conditions 2000 plants belonging to different *L. multiforum* populations were inoculated with spores of *P. coronata* Corda in the spring of 1993. After a hydratation of 5 hours, the spores were dissolved in water and sprayed over the plants. The relative humidity was kept at 100% for about 20 hours after the inoculation. During this period the temperature fluctuated between 17°C and 29°C.

We scored each plant two weeks after the inoculation in a scale from 1 to 9 ; 1 = no symptoms, 9 = > 2/3 of the leafs are covered with pustules. In each population the least infected plants (scores 1 and 2 ; T) as well as the most infected ones (scores 5 to 9 ; S) were selected and retained for subsequent DNA isolation.

The DNA was prepared by a standard phenol extraction method starting from a mixed sample of either tolerant or sensitive recuperated healthy grass plants grown in the field. For each population we made two DNA preparations containing between 10 and 15 plants per group. The DNA concentration was determined by both fluorometric measurement and a comparison of staining intensity in agarose gels.

The RAPD screening is done by using 60 different 10-mer primers purchased from Operon Inc. The PCR reactions were carried out as described by Williams *et al.* 1990. Approximately 25 ng of genomic DNA template and 0.35 μM of decamer primer was used in a 20 μl reaction that contained 0,8 units of Taq DNA polymerase (Boehringer Mannheim) ; the buffer, containing each dNTP (Pharmacia Inc.) was as recommended by the company. This mixture was overlaid with 20 μl mineral oil.Amplification was carried out in a Hybaid Omnigene programmed for 35 cycles of 5 sec 94°C, 30 sec 35°C and 1 min 72°C. Before starting the program a denaturation of 1 min at 94°C was carried out. The final elongation step was prolonged for 10 min. Approximately 20 μl of the completed reactions were run in 2 % NUSIEVE (FMC Inc.) agarose and the DNA was visualised by UV fluorescence after staining the gel with ethidium bromide. Subsequently the DNA profiles or fingerprints were fixed on a photographic record and the RAPD patterns were compared manually.

Results

By using 60 different primers we could evaluate about 250 different loci for their heterozygosity and for their potential linkage with the sensitivity for crown rust. Only one primer with the sequence GACCGCTTGT revealed a polymorphism between sensitive and tolerant plants , which could be observed in the three populations. With this primer a $\pm$ 1,1 kb fragment is obtained in the PCR reaction with DNA isolated from the sensitive plants as template.

Conclusion

Three populations were divided in sensitive and tolerant genotypes in order to screen for RAPD markers that are typical for either the tolerant or the sensitive genotypes and are present in all three populations. The three populations were therefore artificially infected with *P. coronata* Corda under controlled conditions. By using RAPD analysis we were able to identify a polymorphism that is possibly linked with crown rust tolerance. To locate, confirm and map this marker other segregating populations have to be constructed and analyzed. Furthermore other primers will be used in PCR reactions to detect new polymorphisms.

References

MILCHELMORE, R.W. , PARAN, I. and KESSELL, R.V. 1991. Identification of markers linked to disease resistance genes by bulked segregant analysis : a rapid method tot detect markers in specific genomic regions using segregating populations. Proc. Natl. Acad. Sci. USA, 88, 9828-9832.

MELCHINGER, A.E. 1990. Use of molecular markers in breeding for oligogenic disease resistance. Plant Breed., 104, 1-19.

WILLIAMS, J.G.K. ; KUBELIK, A.R., LIVAK, K.J., RAFALKSI, J.A. and TINGEY, SV 1990. DNA polymorfisms amplified by arbitrary primers useful as genetic markers. Nucleic Acids Res., 18, 6531-6535.

YOUNG, N.D. ; ZAMIR, D., GANAL, M.W. and TANKSLEY, S.D. 1988. Us of isogenic lines and simultaneous probing to identify DNA markers tightly linked to the Tm-2a gene in tomato. Genetics, 20, 579-585.

O.A. Rognli et al. (Eds.) Breeding Fodder Crops for Marginal Conditions, 287–288.
© 1994 *Kluwer Academic Publishers. Printed in the Netherlands.*

HYBRID BREEDING BY MEANS OF INCOMPATIBILITY IN *LOLIUM MULTIFLORUM*

FRED EICKMEYER and GÜNTER WRICKE
Institute of Applied Genetics
University of Hannover
Herrenhäuser Str. 2
30419 Hannover, Germany

Introduction: F_1-hybrid varieties in forage grasses can exploit a higher degree of heterozygosity than the currently available synthetics. This requires a genetical mechanism that allows multiplication of inbred lines as well as it ensures a sufficient outcrossing between the lines. ENGLAND (1974) proposed a breeding scheme based on the use of the gametophytic 2-loci self-incompatibility system (SI) that is widely distributed in the outcrossing grasses.
Pseudocompatibility under normal environmental conditions is very low in *L. multiflorum*. If a selfed plant is heterozygous at both SI-loci (het-het) it is possible to multiply the I-line. After 2 generations of random mating an equilibrium is reached. In this case 50% hethet and 50% homhet genotypes are produced. Crossing of 2 lines results theoretically in 83% hybrids. The remainder being sibs which are derived from pollination within the I-lines.
Aim of this work was to improve pseudocompatible seed-set under special environmental conditions, to determine outcrossing between inbred-lines and to check if heterosis is high enough to justify F_1-hybrid-breeding.

Materials and Methods: Non inbred single plants were cloned and selfed by bagging with parchment bags. One clone-part was kept at 14°/18°C and the other at 30°C permanent temperature during anthesis (WRICKE, 1978; WILKINS AND THOROGOOD, 1992). Multiplication of the derived $I_{0,1}$-lines was carried out in the greenhouse in order to avoid foreign pollination. After one generation of multiplication 7 $I_{0,2}$ lines were planted as a complete diallel in rye isolations with 10 m distance between the isolation plots. Outcrossing , sibs portion and pollution through foreign pollen was determined by means of isozymes. Yield trials of the hybrids were carried out in 6.6 m^2 plots at two locations with two replications each. Inbred-lines were tested at one location with 2 replications. The standard varieties were 'Lema', 'Lemtal' and 'Lipo'.

Results: Under 14°/18°C condition most of the plants set no or just a few self-seeds whereas under 30°C permanent temperature in most cases seed set is sufficient to propagate the lines. Outcrossing of the line-combinations and relative dry-matter (DM) yield of the hybrids after the second cut compared to the standards is given in table 1. Relativ DM-yield of the parent lines and heterosis of the hybrids compared to the parents are given in table 2.

Table 1: Outcrossing percentages (above diagonal) and relative DM yield of hybrids (below d.) after 2nd cut in *L. multiflorum*

Parent Lines	WW 1	WW 4	WW 6	WW 9	WW16	WW20	WW21
WW 1		63	49	62	25	62	74
WW 4	109		76	80	59	57	73
WW 6	99	103		40	39	36	69
WW 9	100	115	109		48	53	68
WW16	91	105	101	101		29	54
WW20	99	109	101	97	90		68
WW21	96	107	106	94	90	93	

Table 2: Relative DM-yield of parent mean (above diagonal), parents (d.) and heterosis of hybrids (below d.) after 2nd cut in *L. multiflorum*

Parent Lines	WW 1	WW 4	WW 6	WW 9	WW16	WW20	WW21
WW 1	70	75	62	67	63	72	67
WW 4	146	80	67	71	67	77	72
WW 6	160	155	54	59	54	64	59
WW 9	150	161	186	63	59	68	64
WW16	146	156	185	171	55	64	59
WW20	138	142	158	142	140	74	69
WW21	144	149	180	148	151	135	64

Discussion: The low seed-set under 14°/18°C conditions demonstrates the high-efficient SI-system. The theoretically expected outcrossing rate of 83% was only reached once (WW4xWW9). Lower outcrossing results are probably due to non adapted flowering times of the lines or to different pollen pressures.   POSSELT (1992) found heterosis up to 115% and high performance inbred-lines in *L. perenne*. In our experiment heterosis related to the parents with an inbreeding coefficient of 0,5 is between 138 and 186% and the DM-yield of the inbred-lines was only 54 to 80% of standard varieties. The different results in this trial are presumably due to the multiplication of inbred lines in greenhouse isolation cabins instead of field isolations, where the danger of pollution through foreign pollen is great. Impurities of the inbred lines in this experiment can be excluded since every generation was checked by means of isozymes for foreign alleles.

Conclusions: The above results show that the SI-system in *L. multiflorum* is highly effective. There is a high amount of heterosis which could be used to breed better varieties in *L. multiflorum*. It depends however on the pure propagation and additionally on a good adaptation of the flowering time of the parent lines.

References:
ENGLAND F.W.J., 1974: Heredity <u>32</u>, 183 - 188.
POSSELT U.K., 1992: XIIIth EUCARPIA Congress, July 06-11th Angers, France, Book of Poster-Abstracts 263 - 264.
WILKINS P.W. AND D. THOROGOOD, 1992: XIIIth EUCARPIA Congress, July 06-11th Angers, France, Book of Poster-Abstracts 279 - 280.
WRICKE G., 1978: Z. Pflanzenzücht. <u>81</u>, 140 - 148.

O.A. Rognli et al. (Eds.) Breeding Fodder Crops for Marginal Conditions, 289–290.
© 1994 *Kluwer Academic Publishers. Printed in the Netherlands.*

LINKAGE RELATIONSHIPS OF ISOZYME MARKERS AND INCOMPATIBILITY GENES IN *LOLIUM*

FRED EICKMEYER and GÜNTER WRICKE
Institute of Applied Genetics
University of Hannover
Herrenhäuser Str. 2
30419 Hannover, Germany

Introduction: Molecular and biochemical markers offer a unique tool for e.g. description of variability and studying interesting traits in the course of a breeding program. They can help to understand inheritance and behaviour of physiological characteristics under different environments if the degree of linkage is strong enough. For the calculation of linkage an unequivocal genetic analysis of banding patterns is necessary. After selfing heterozygous plants a 1:2:1 or 3:1 segregation for codominant or dominant inheritance is expected. Deviations from these relations are hints for selection mechanisms like e.g. chlorophyll-deficiency or self-incompatibility (SI) genes.

Materials and Methods: 18 inbred-lines of *L. perenne* and *L. multiflorum* were produced by selfing cloned plants at 14°/18°C and at 30°C permanent temperature during anthesis. Only 3 of the *L. perenne* clones set a certain amount of seed under both conditions whereas all other clones only set sufficient seed for genetical analysis under 30°C conditions.
3 electrophoresis techniques were applied to study the inheritance of 20 isozyme systems with 42 loci. In addition one DNA locus (SPLAT 107) was studied using a primer-pair in the PCR that was derived from the end sequences of the *L. multiflorum* c-DNA probe pLMC 107 (STAMMERS, 1992).
Single locus segregations and recombination values were calculated using the program LINKAGE-1 (SUITER ET AL. 1983). In case of codominant single locus segregation and a significant x^2-value orthogonal comparisons for both degrees of freedom were performed: $x^2_2=(\mathrm{hom1+hom2-het})^2/n$ points to zygotic and $x^2_3=2*(\mathrm{hom1-hom2})^2/n$ points to gamete selection.
Recombination values for one gene-pair in different progenies were combined using the tables of ALLARD (1956). In order to find the most probable order of markers in one linkage group, linkage data of different families were combined with the program JOINMAP. If for an isozyme-locus in more than one family distorted segregations were found and the x^2 values gave hints for gamete selection, the data were combined and a recombination value between the marker locus and the hidden selection locus was calculated.

Results: Most of the single locus segregations followed the expected

distributions. In case of segregation distortion at least one locus shows codominant inheritance. Therefore all deviating families could be used, too, for linkage analysis (WAGNER ET AL. 1992).
3 linkage-groups that were derived from the data of the 18 families are given in figure 1. Markers were found around the S- and Z-loci of the SI-system. Group 1 covers 79 cM, group 2 covers 48 cM and group 3 is 7 cM long.

Figure 1: Linkage relationships between 32 isozyme-loci, one DNA-locus and incompatibility genes in *Lolium*.

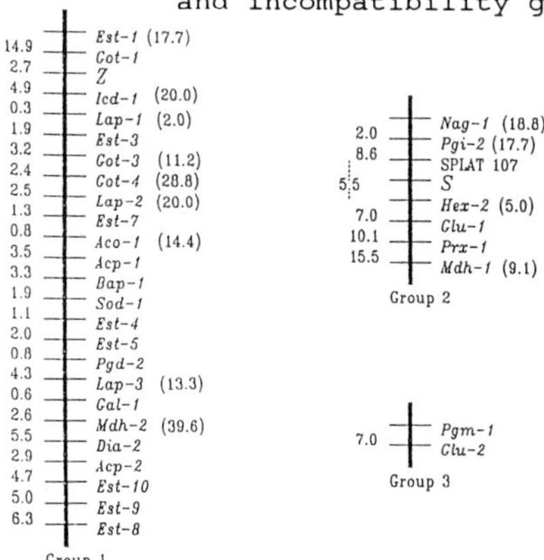

Map distances are given in centimorgans. Distances between marker-loci and incompatibility genes (in brakkets) were calculated using distorted segregations of different families.

Discussion: The linkage groups are in a good agreement with results obtained by STAMMERS (loc. cit) and HAYWARD (unpublished results). HAYWARD found more than 3 linkage groups showing markers in different groups which are allocated in this work to group 1. Differences between the two maps are perhaps due to the use of one mapping family on the one side and by combining data of many different families on the other side. In deriving an order of loci from combined data of different families there are often found contradictions to data from single families, because the recombination values can vary in a certain range from family to family. These variations are not found if only one mapping family is used. But then generalizations could be difficult because the results may be only correct for the observed family. An allocation of the linked markers to the corresponding chromosomes would therefore be a very useful help to compare different linkage maps.

References: ALLARD R.W., 1956: Hilgardia <u>24</u>, 235 - 278
STAMMERS M., 1992: Ph.D. Thesis, University College of Wales
SUITER K.A., J.F. WENDEL and J.S. CASE, 1983: The Journal of Heredity <u>74</u>, 203 - 204
WAGNER H., W.E. WEBER AND G. WRICKE, 1992: Plant Breeding <u>108</u>, 89 - 96

Acknowledgement: We thank Dr. O.A. Rognli and Dr. M.D. Hayward for provision of the primers for SPLAT 107 and Dr. P. Stam for provision of the program JOINMAP.

O.A. Rognli et al. (Eds.) Breeding Fodder Crops for Marginal Conditions, 291–292.
© 1994 *Kluwer Academic Publishers. Printed in the Netherlands.*

SEEDLING VIGOUR, AGRONOMIC TRAITS, AND ISOZYME MARKERS IN BACKCROSSES *LOLIUM PERENNE X FESTUCA* spp.

A. GARCIA, W.G. MORGAN, M.D. HAYWARD and H. THOMAS.
Plant genetics & Breeding/Cell Biology. AFRC-IGER.
Aberystwyth. Dyfed SY23 3EB. UK.

The introgression of useful *Festuca* characters such as cold tolerance, drought resistance, and persistence into *Lolium* is an approach to breeding for adverse conditions. Triploid (Thomas et al., 1991) and pentaploid hybrids (Humphreys, 1989) have been succesfully used to accelerate the recovery of the parental type.

Two experiments involving backcross 1 families, one derived from a cross between 4x *Lolium perenne* L. and 2x *Festuca pratensis* Huds. (experiment 1), and the other (experiment 2) between 4x *Lolium perenne* and 6x *Festuca arundinacea* Schreb. were set up. The seeds were sown in a completely randomized design in trays in an unheated greenhouse, and plants were subsequently transplanted to the field after measuring seedling traits.

Experiment 1

There were significant differences among backcross families for all seedling traits considered. There were also reciprocal differences between the crosses, which could either be due to maternal effects or to different chromosome numbers of the progeny, imposed by the gametic selective filter in the pollen of the triploid hybrid, in favour of haploidy. This could also explain the higher vigour of the plants whose male parent was the hybrid. Among seedling traits, tiller number was not significantly correlated with tiller fresh weight, presumably due to the small size of the seedlings, preventing any serious intertiller competition. Seedling dry matter content was negatively correlated with seedling fresh weight, possibly because early seedling weight (heterotrophic stage) is mainly achieved by water uptake. Third leaf lamina length and width were positively correlated.

There were also differences among field characters excepting conservation yield, showing that most of the variability for yield at this stage is found within groups, confirming the necessity of individual selection. The reciprocal differences observed in seedling vigour were maintained in field survival and regrowth. Seedling fresh and dry weight were strongly and positively correlated with field survival, spring growth scores, conservation yield (dry weight) and regrowth, and negatively with heading date, which correlated positively with days to seedling emergence. Seedling tiller fresh weight and third leaf length were also significantly correlated with conservation yield. All this indicates that seedling vigour influences the adult plant performance. Spring growth was also positively correlated with third leaf length, seedling tiller number and tiller fresh weight, but not so highly as with conservation yield and regrowth, stressing the advantage of visual scores for spaced plant assessment. Heading date correlated negatively with spring growth and conservation yield, suggesting, along with the above, that early types develop faster and produce more. The heads produced by the hybrid and the backcross 1 plants were all "loloid", without branching. The hybrid also presented narrow, "loloid" leaves, but an erect, festucoid habit. The predominance

292

of "loloid" traits reflects the effect of the double dose of that genome.
    Segregation ratios for some isozyme markers and their association with
seedling traits was determined for 77 plants from the backcross family
P172/184, the results of which are as follows:

<pre>
        Bc parent   F1   Fescue allele X^2, 2:1

        Ba11254(5) x P168/234(1)   abs. pres.

PGI/2   bc   ab<u>d</u>#   63   14   9.1**
SOD/1   bb   a<u>bb</u>   71   6   24.2***
ACP/2   ab   ab<u>f</u>   66   11   13.9***
</pre>

underlined letters indicate fescue alleles

The X^2 test for minimal presence revealed a significant deficiency of the
F. pratensis alleles, which could be due to haploid pollen selection: as
the *F. pratensis* chromosome is not completely homologous to the *L.
perenne*'s, only recombined alleles would be included. Some of the backcross
plants which contain the fescue allele can be interspecific recombinants.
    The only significant associations of isozyme loci with the
quantitative traits evaluated were: 1) between SOD/1 and third leaf length,
with longer leaf associated with the presence of the fescue allele (a),
accounting for 10% of the variation. 2) between ACP/2 and heading date,
with early heading associated with the fescue allele (f), accounting for
just 3% of the total variation.

Experiment 2

As in experiment 1, there was no significant correlation between seedling
tiller number and tiller fresh weight. Here there is also a negative
correlation of seedling fresh weight with dry matter content, but the same
holds with seedling dry weight. The absence of a correlation between third
leaf lamina length and width in this experiment is due to a higher
variation in leaf shape. Due to field mortality, only seven plants survived
in the field. Their chromosome numbers were either 2n=20 or 21. All of them
had vegetative aerial tillering in some of the tillers. Two, with 2n=21,
remained vegetative. This trait was already seen in monosomic addition
lines (Morgan, 1991), and was selected succesfully in *L. perenne* in this
Institute, associated with a reduction in flowering potential. It could be
seen as a reversion to an ancestral type. All plants were transferred to
the glasshouse and the five that produced inflorescences were crossed with
the paternal *Lolium* variety to obtain the backcross 2 generation.

<u>References</u>

Humphreys, M.W. (1989) The controlled introgression of *Festuca arundinacea*
genes into *Lolium multiflorum*. **Euphytica** 42:105-116.

Thomas, H., W.G. Morgan and M.W. Humphreys (1991) Strategies for gene
transfer in the *Lolium/Festuca* complex. In: **Ploidy and chromosome
manipulation in forage breeding**, 53-59. Eucarpia.

Morgan, W.G. (1991) The morphology and cytology of monosomic addition lines
combining single *Festuca drymeja* chromosomes and *Lolium multiflorum*.
Euphytica 55:57-63.

O.A. Rognli et al. (Eds.) Breeding Fodder Crops for Marginal Conditions, 293–294.
© 1994 *Kluwer Academic Publishers. Printed in the Netherlands.*

LEAF GROWTH GENETIC VARIABILITY AMONG VARIOUS POLYPLOID RYEGRASS X FESCUE HYBRIDS INVOLVING FESTUCA ARUNDINACEA VAR. GLAUCESCENS

M. GHESQUIERE, F. MI*, L. HAZARD and C. POISSON
Institut National de la Recherche Agronomique
Station d'Amelioration des Plantes Fourrageres
86600 Lusignan (France)
* College of Agriculture and Animal Husbandry
010018 Houhehot (China)

Breeding for marginal conditions emphasizes the interest of ryegrass x fescue hybrids combining productive and adaptative traits as well. Within the *Festuca* complex, utilization of wild species related to hexaploid tall fescue ($2n = 6x = 42$) is of major importance for the development of interspecific hybrids adapted to even more extreme environmental conditions. In this respect, *F. arundinacea* var. *glaucescens* which is found in the Alps is specially well adapted to cold and dry growing conditions and poorly fertile soils. Also, as a tetraploid species ($2n = 4x = 28$), *F. glaucescens* can be used either directly for developing synthetic amphiploid hybrids or as a bridge species for tranferring genes of Lolium species into tall fescue. As potential productivity allowed by *F. glaucescens* might be limiting to some extent, the objective of this communication is to assess genetic variability and heredity of leaf growth components among various polyploid hybrids involving *F.glaucescens*.

Populations of *L. multiflorum* and *F. glaucescens*, both at natural ploidy level (diploid and tetraploid resp.) and after polyploidization induced by colchicine ($2n = 4x = 28$ and $2n = 8x = 56$ resp.) were compared together with five hybrid populations. Two hybrid populations were tetraploid and resulted from crosses between tetraploid *L. multiflorum* ($2n = 4x = 28$) and tetraploid *F. glaucescens* ($2n = 4x = 28$). The two populations consisted of direct hybrids and one first intercrossing generation (G0 versus G1 generation). A third tetraploid hybrid population was recovered by back-crossing the previous G0 hybrids into tetraploid *L. multiflorum* (BC1). A triploid hybrid population ($2n = 3x = 21$) was obtained from direct crosses between diploid *L. multiflorum* and tetraploid *F. glaucescens* and can be considered to some extent as the symetrical back-cross of the previous BC1 population. As chromosome doubling of triploid hybrids was impossible to achieve, hexaploid hybrid population ($2n = 6x = 42$) was finally derived by doubling first the chromosome number of the parental species and crossing therefore tetraploid *L. multiflorum* ($2n = 4x = 28$)

with octoploid *F. glaucescens* (2n = 8x = 56). All first generation
hybrids were recovered after *in-vitro* culture of immature embryos.
Growth of 3 succesive leaves and heading date were recorded in spring
on 3 tillers of 10 plants (parental populations) and 20 plants (hybrid
populations). Six leaf growth components were observed or estimated :
Adult Leaf Length, Phyllochron, Leaf Elongation Rate, Leaf Elongation
Duration, Number of Growing Leaves per tiller, Leaf Life. As leaf
growth was overlapping among plants and tillers, estimates were
weighted by temperature expressed in degree x day. Main Component
Analysis was performed on single genotype means as well as Hierarchical
Multivariate Analysis of Variance within parental and hybrid
populations.

Results confirmed that leaf morphogenesis is quite contrasted between
F. glaucescens and *L. multiflorum*. *F. glaucescens* appeared as a typical
species growing in moutainous areas and characterized by late heading
date and slow growing rate. In overall, leaf growth components were
inherited in an additive way by hybrid populations which ranged
therefore gradually between parental populations. As expected,
tetraploid BC1 and triploid hybrid populations appeared closer to
either ryegrass or fescue populations (resp.). However, the hexaploid
population was found in average more similar to the tetraploid G0 and
G1 amphiploid populations than to the triploid hybrid population
despite the relative genome contribution of parental species was the
same. Although the effect of chromosome doubling was not observed
between parental populations within both species, this effect might be
more obvious in the hexaploid hybrids by restoring the balance between
each homeologous genomes. Within hybrid populations, Leaf Elongation
Rate was highly correlated to Adult Leaf Length and had the largest
genetic variability when compared with the other growth traits
surveyed. For no trait, within hybrid genetic variability was found
higher than within parental populations. Also, no obvious increase of
variability was recorded within tetraploid G1 and BC1 populations when
compared to tetraploid G0 population as it might be expected if
homeologous recombination had occurred significantly.

Although the potential growth rate of *F. glaucescens* is low, large
genetic variability of leaf growth including *Lolium*-like genotypes is
recovered among hybrids. Selection within either amphiploid populations
should be therefore possible and maybe within BC1 population if stable
introgression can be achieved in next generations. Using leaf length as
a predictor of leaf elongation rate should be also very helpful in this
respect. Further studies are now required to determine physiological
and genetic relationships between growth rate and adaptative traits as
persistency for selecting genotypes retaining optimum combinations of
traits.

THE VALUE OF INTERSPECIFIC HYBRIDISATION IN BREEDING FOR IMPROVED TOLERANCE OF CLIMATIC STRESS

M.O.HUMPHREYS
AFRC Institute of Grassland and Environmental Research, Welsh Plant Breeding Station, Plas Gogerddan, Aberystwyth, Dyfed SY23 3EB, UK

Interspecific hybridisation and polyploidisation have played a large part in extending the distribution of grasses in Europe. Allopolyploids generally have a higher genetic diversity and are distributed over a wider range of habitats than related diploid species. Thus despite considerable adaptive radiation among diploid species of *Dactylis* in the Mediterranean Basin and central southern Europe, only tetraploid species (particularly *D. glomerata* L.) are commonly found further to the north, west and east of Europe and hexaploid species are found in N. Africa. In the *Lolium/Festuca* complex, hexaploid *F. rubra* extends well beyond the northern limit of diploid *F. pratensis* in Scandinavia. In the south of Europe, tall fescue extends beyond the range of diploid ryegrasses and fescues through the Mediterranean Basin to N. Africa where higher polyploid forms are also found.

Increased DNA content in polyploids may have adaptive significance associated with increases in cell size and minimum cell doubling time. However it seems likely that improved climatic adaptation in many polyploid species is due to increased heterozygosity and the novel gene combinations produced by hybridisation. Grass breeders can exploit this potential by creating novel polyploid hybrids for new agronomic niches.

Successful tetraploid hybrids have been produced between *Lolium multiflorum* and *L. perenne* which show a very flexible response to cutting or grazing and tend to switch from an Italian to a perennial growth form in mid-season (Jones & Humphreys 1993). Regrowth during late summer and autumn is more leafy and based on a greater number of tillers in hybrids compared to Italian ryegrass. This benefits high quality forage production particularly during dry summers. Tetraploid hybrids between meadow fescue (*F. pratensis*) and perennial ryegrass also show improved summer growth based on good root development and crown rust resistance derived from meadow fescue. These features can be retained in backcrosses to ryegrass. Similarly enhanced drought tolerance in Italian ryegrass has been obtained by gene transfer from tall fescue (Humphreys et al 1993). Thus there are good prospects to improve the climatic stress tolerance of ryegrass through the introgression of genes from fescues. For areas were stresses are extreme, the direction of introgression may be reversed to transfer genes for improved nutritive value from ryegrass into a fescue background.

In *Dactylis*, water use efficiency differs between *D. glomerata* and *D. marina*. Low leaf conductance in *D. marina* is associated with the presence of large epidermal papilla cells (Wilson et al 1980). This trait was found to be heritable in hybrids between *D. glomerata* and *D. marina* and it should be possible to improve the water use efficiency of *D. glomerata* by incorporating large papilla cells from *D. marina*.

Winterhardiness is a complex trait involving resistance to frost and ice/water cover, dessication and resistance to low-temperature fungi. The distribution of assimilates between shoots and roots also affects persistency of grasses during winter. This varies in relation to differences in patterns of seasonal growth found among populations within species (such as *D. glomerata* and ryegrass from Scandinavia and the Mediterranean Basin) but also between different species. Fescues generally have good winterhardiness compared to ryegrasses and improved winter survival compared to the ryegrass parent has been observed in hybrids between meadow fescue and perennial ryegrass and between tall fescue and Italian ryegrass.

Amphiploid hybrids, which combine complete genomes from ryegrass and fescue parents, unfortunately express both advantageous and disadvantageous parent traits. Introgressive breeding can be more selective in combining only advantageous characteristics and may offer greater long term potential particularly with the development of genetic labelling techniques including use of DNA markers (RFLP's and RAPD's) and "in situ" chromosome hybridisation.

References

Jones M.LL. and Humphreys M.O. (1993) Progress in breeding interspecific hybrid ryegrasses. Grass and Forage Science 48, 18-25.

Humphreys M.O., Humphreys M.W. and Thomas H. (1993) Breeding grasses for adaptation to environmental problems. In: *Proceedings of XVII International Grassland Congress*, New Zealand and Australia (In Press).

Wilson D., Abdullah I.B. and Trickey S.A. (1980) Variation in transpiration rate in *Dactylis*. In: *Proceedings of XII International Grassland Congress* (Eds E. Wojahn & H. Thons), Leipzig, pp. 207-210.

O.A. Rognli et al. (Eds.) Breeding Fodder Crops for Marginal Conditions, 297–298.
© *1994 Kluwer Academic Publishers. Printed in the Netherlands.*

POSSIBLE GENE MODELS EXPLAINING ANDROGENETIC RESPONSE IN PERENNIAL RYEGRASS (*Lolium perenne* L.)

H-G. OPSAHL-FERSTAD and O. A. ROGNLI
Dept. of Biotechnological Sciences, Agric. Univ. of Norway,
P.O. Box 5040, N-1432 Ås, Norway

1. Introduction

Androgenetic response is determined by three genetic processes: 1) induction of embryo-like-structures (ELS), 2) ability to regenerate plants, and 3) frequency of green plants produced (Henry and de Buyser 1985), where the last factor is particularily important in grass species. A number of studies in several species of *Poaceae* have shown nuclear genetic control of anther culture response, with mainly additive, but also some dominance and epistatic effects (Agache et al. 1989; Tuvesson et al. 1989). In order to assess the natural variability for androgenesis in perennial ryegrass, nine Norwegian populations (90 genotypes), were screened for androgenetic response. Based on the results of the screening experiment three genotypes (7-5, 9-5, and 245) were selected because they exhibited differences in all androgenetic response processes. A detailed genetic analysis was performed on the 63 F_1 plants from all crosses between these genotypes.

2. Results

2.1 EXPERIMENT 1 - THE SCREENING

Of the 90 genotypes screened, 74 (82%) produced ELS, albino plants were regenerated from 64 (71%) genotypes, and green plants from 15 (17%) genotypes. The total production was 8 451 ELS, 2 971 albino and 90 green plants from 34 290 anthers plated, an average of 24.6 ELS, 8.7 albino and 0.3 green plants per 100 anthers. Heritabilities around 0.80 and high or complete positive genotypic correlations, were found for most characters of androgenetic response.

2.2 EXPERIMENT 2 - THE CROSSES

From 24 264 anthers plated in a crossing experiment, 20 021 ELS, 2 894 albino plants and 1 391 (32%) green plants were generated, an average of 82.5 ELS, 11.9 albino and 5.7 green plants per 100 anthers. The best producer of green plants (F_1 donor plant no. 25) produced 118 GRP/100 ANT. The crosses were not significantly different for embryogenic ability (62 of the 63 F_1 donor plants produced ELS), but were different for total regeneration (PL/100 ELS), albino and green plant production. The correlations from the cross experiment (63 F_1 plants) ranged from r=-0.99*** to 0.81***.

3. Discussion

The considerable differences in correlations are most likely a result of changed allelic frequencies caused by the strong selection of parents in the crosses, and a relatively simple genetic control.

Three possible gene models explaining the processes of androgenetic response in perennial ryegrass have been constructed. The existing but variable embryogenic ability is most likely controlled by several additive genes (loci) (E_1/e_1, E_2/e_2,..., E_n/e_n). Total regeneration may be explained by two additive genes (R_1/r_1, R_2/r_2) and green plant production by four duplicate genes (A/a, B/b, C/c, D/d). These gene models are further based on pleiotropy or linkage between the genes controlling embryogenic ability, total regeneration of plants, and green plant production (Table 1). All models were tested by a goodness-of-fit test which all gave nicely low Chi-squares. The hypotheses are consistent with the high heritabilities and correlations found in the study of the initial 90 genotypes and the changes found after selection of parental plants and segregation in the 63 F_1 plants for androgenetic response.

Genotype	Regeneration	GRP	Linkage		
7-5	$R_1r_1R_2R_2$	aabbCcDd	E	R_2	a
9-5	$R_1r_1r_2r_2$	AABBCCDD	e	r_2	A
245	$R_1r_1R_2r_2$	AaBbccDd			

Fig 1. Postulated gene models explaining the segregation for androgenetic response in the 63 F_1 plants from the crosses between 7-5, 9-5 and 245, selected from the screening experiment.(GRP; Green plants production)

4. References

Agache S, Bachelier B, de Buyser J, Henry Y, Snape J (1989) Genetic analysis of anther culture response in wheat using aneuploid, chromosome substitution and translocation lines. Theor Appl Genet 77:7-11

Henry Y, de Buyser J (1985) Effect of the 1B/1R translocation on anther culture ability in wheat (*Triticum avestium*). Plant Cell Reports 4:307-310

Tuvesson IKD, Pedersen S, Andersen SB (1989) Nuclear genes affecting albinism in wheat (*Triticum aestivum* L.) anther culture. Theor Appl Genet 78(6), 879-883

O.A. Rognli et al. (Eds.) Breeding Fodder Crops for Marginal Conditions, 299–300.
© 1994 *Kluwer Academic Publishers. Printed in the Netherlands.*

POTENTIAL OF TETRAPLOID ×*FESTULOLIUM* (*FESTUCA PRATENSIS* × *LOLIUM MULTIFLORUM*)

Z. ZWIERZYKOWSKI [1], W. JOKŚ [2] and B. NAGANOWSKA [1]
[1] *Institute of Plant Genetics, Polish Academy of Sciences,
Strzeszyńska 34, 60-479 Poznań, Poland*
[2] *Szelejewo Plant Breeding Station, 63-813 Szelejewo, Poland*

Introduction

For over 30 years a number of efforts have been made to utilize interspecific and intergeneric hybrids of the *Lolium–Festuca* complex in grass forage breeding. These hybrids, which combine complementary characters of the parental species, often offer excellent potential for producing new valuable grasses. In the *Lolium–Festuca* complex it is attempted to combine the high yield and nutritive value of ryegrasses with the persistency, winter hardiness and drought tolerance of fescues. Within this complex a special breeders' interest is directed to *Festuca pratensis* (4x) × *Lolium multiflorum* (4x) hybrids, from which several cultivars have already been obtained (e.g. 'Elmet' – in Great Britain, 'Paulita' – in Germany and 'Perun' – in Czechoslovakia). In Poland, the *F. pratensis* (4x) × *L. multiflorum* (4x) hybrids were obtained for the first time in 1981 at the Institute of Plant Genetics in Poznań (Zwierzykowski 1987; Zwierzykowski et al. 1993) and now an extensive breeding program based on them is in progress.

The objectives of this investigation were: 1) to examine the cytotype stability and fertility in F_2-F_6 generations, 2) to evaluate of some agronomic characters in the best strains selected from the F_5 and F_6 generations.

Materials and methods

As a result of controlled crossing between colchitetraploid forms of meadow fescue (*F. pratensis*, 2n=4x=28; female parent) and Italian ryegrass (L. multiflorum, 2n=4x=28) partly fertile F_1 hybrids (2n=28) were produced. In the F_2-F_6 generations, morphological characters and fertility were studied under field conditions on single plants, spaced 50×50 cm apart. Somatic chromosome number was analysed in root tips of plants in the F_2, F_3, F_5 and F_6 generation. Great variation in fertility and other characters was observed in the F_2 generation. It was found that plants of ryegrass type (with spike-shaped inflorescences) had a higher female fertility than plants of fescue type (with panicle-shaped or intermediate inflorescences). In the successive generations (F_3-F_6) selection for the female fertility was performed as follows: in the F_3 generation only the progeny of the F_2 plants showing fertility higher than the average for the F_2 generation was included; the F_4-F_6 generations were produced on the same way. Five

Festulolium strains (all in ryegrass type) characterized by the relatively high fertility as well as by a great vigour and persistency were selected from the F_5 and F_6 generations. These strains were examined in 3-year field trials (10 m^2 plots with four randomized replicates). Some agronomic traits, e.g. fresh and dry matter yield, seed yield, crude protein content, in vitro dry matter digestibility, persistency and winter hardiness, were evaluated. Five tetraploid cultivars were used as controls: *Festulolium* 'Paulita' and 'Perun', *F. pratensis* 'Koa-186', *L. perenne* 'Solen' and *L. multiflorum* 'Kroto'.

Results and discussion

The tetraploid forms (2n=28) decidedly prevailed amongst the studied plants of all generations. The frequency of aneuploids (from 2n=25 to 2n=31) in the analysed progenies was low and slightly differed between the generations (4.5-11.7%).

Male fertility (pollen grain stainability) was high (mean about 80%) and differed a little between the analysed generations . As a result of selection for the female fertility it was found that seed set in the F_2-F_4 generations increased from generation to generation (from 28.4% to 61.0%, respectively) and stabilized on the level over 50% in two successive generations. It seems that *Festulolium* forms with that degree of fertility can be successfully used in breeding.

Regarding the green and dry matter yield, protein content and digestibility the studied strains were equal to the control cultivars 'Paulita', 'Perun' and 'Kroto' and sometimes exceeded them. All our strains had significantly higher green and dry matter yield than the cultivars 'Solen' and 'Koa-186'. The studied strains were characterized by a similar persistency and winter hardiness as the cultivars 'Paulita' and 'Solen' but were evidently better compared to the cultivar 'Perun'. The seed yield of the strains in a wide-spaced plant trial reached values from 7.8 to 9.6 q/ha.

Conclusions

1. The studied strains of *Festulolium* are satisfactorily stable and fertile and they maintain hybridity through the generations of seed multiplication.
2. The best strains have high potential (high yield and quality forage, good persistency and winterhardiness) for development into valuable cultivars – the first Polish *Festulolium* cultivars.

References

Zwierzykowski, Z. (1987) 'Interspecific and intergeneric hybridization in the *Lolium-Festuca* complex', Proc. Intern. Conf., Hladké Životice, Czechoslovakia, May 1987, pp. 29-38.

Zwierzykowski, Z., Jokś, W. and Naganowska, B. (1993) 'Amphitetraploid hybrids *Festuca pratensis* Huds. × *Lolium multiflorum* Lam. [=*Festulolium braunii* (K. Richter) A. Camus]: obtaining and characterization of F_1 hybrids, cytotype stability and fertility in successive generations', Biuletyn IHAR (in press).

O.A. Rognli et al. (Eds.) Breeding Fodder Crops for Marginal Conditions, 301–302.

IN VITRO APROACH TO PRODUCTION OF *LOLIUM - FESTUCA* AMPHIPLOIDS

I. Pasakinskiene
Lithuanian Institute of Agriculture
Department of Genetics and Physiology
5051 Dotnuva - Akademija, Kedainiai
Lithuania

1. Introduction

The importance of hexaploid fescues, *F. arundinacea* and *F. gigantea*, as donors providing a trait of persistency under extreme conditions in *Lolium - Festuca* hybridization programmes, has been emphasized by Thomas and Humphreys (1991). Chromosome doubling is necessary in order to restore fertility in these hybrids. Recently, a new and original technique for *L. perenne* polyploid induction was developed (Pasakinskiene 1992). The efficiency of this method, which is based on application of colchicine to embryos in *in vitro-*culture, has already been demonstrated in *Lolium* spp. x *F. pratensis* hybrids (Pasakinskiene and Petniuniene 1992). The specific objective of this work was to restore fertility of *Lolium* spp. x *F. arundinacea* hybrids by using original *in vitro* technique for induction of polyploids.

2. Materials and Methods

L. perenne, *L. multiflorum* and *L. multiflorum* var. *westerwoldicum* were used as female parents in crosses with *F. arundinacea*. Hybrid embryos were isolated 16 days after pollination and placed for germination on solid MS medium (2/3 of salts) with 0,4 mg/l of IAA and 0,25 mg/l of kinetin. Concentration of sucrose varied as 30, 50, 70 or 90 g/l. The seedlings were treated with 0.3% colchicine for 4 hours. Afterwards the seedlings were maintained on the medium for rooting and establishment. Dehiscence of anthers and pollen fertility was evaluated in the field next season.

3. Results and Discussion

352 (37%) out of 955 treated hybrid embryos survived. The highest survival rate was 48% when 90 g/l of sucrose had been used in the germination medium, and the lowest was 16% in case of 30 g/l. Three initial populations of hybrids were characterized by non-dehiscent anthers, and sterile pollen. Concerning Co material, 20% of hybrids had got dehiscent anthers and pollen fertility increased up to 21% on average. Although from the viewpoint of fertility restoration, *L. multiflorum* var. *westerwoldicum* x *F. arundinacea* hybrids were most feasible, the use of *L. perenne* and *L. multiflorum* was more valuable as regards agronomic characters, such as vigour, tillering and leafiness.

4. Conclusions

1.   Treatment of embryos with colchicine *in vitro* is suitable for *Lolium* spp x *F. arundinacea* amphiploid production, if initial initiation of hybrid embryos is sufficiently high.

2.   There is specific response of hybrids to procedure of fertility restoration as regards parental material.

5. References

Pasakinskiene, I. (1992). Method of production of mitotic polyploids of perennial ryegrass. USSR Gospatent, SU 1774843 A3.

Pasakinskiene, I. and Petniuniene, D. (1992). Application of *in vitro* methods for polyploids induction in *Lolium x Festuca* hybrids. Eksperimentine biologija 3-4: 82-83.

Thomas, H. and Humphreys, M.O. (1991). Progress and potential of interspecific hybrids of *Lolium* and *Festuca*. J. Agri. Sci., Cambridge 117: 1-8.

Miscellaneous topics

O.A. Rognli et al. (Eds.) Breeding Fodder Crops for Marginal Conditions, 305.
© 1994 *Kluwer Academic Publishers. Printed in the Netherlands.*

CHARACTERIZATION OF COCKSFOOT MOTTLE VIRUS (CFMV)

K. MÄKINEN[1], T. TAMM[2], V. NÆSS[3], E. TRUVE [2], L. JÄRVEKÜLG[2], T. MUNTHE[3], D.-R. BLYSTAD[3], Ü. PUURAND[1&2] & M. SAARMA[1&2].
1, Institute of Biotechnology, Karvaamokuja 3A, P.O.box.45, FIN-00014 University of Helsinki, Finland.
2, Insttitute of Chemical Physics and Biophysics, Estonian Academy of Sciences, Akadeemia tee 23, EE0026 Tallinn, Estonia..
3, Norwegian Plant Protection Institute, Fellesbygget, N-1432 Ås, Norway.

Cocksfoot is an important herbage grass species in Norway. Rapid spread of CfMV in the cultivated areas has resulted in substantial yield losses, and in certain areas CfMV is becoming a threat to continued cocksfoot cultivation.

We have isolated the virus from naturally infected cocksfoot plants and purified it from mechanically infected oat plants. We have produced poly- and monoclonal antibodies (pabs & mabs) which recognize the virus particles and the coat protein (CP) in various immunological assays. All the 8 mabs were of IgM type. The detection limit for purified CfMV with indirect double antibody sandwich-ELISA was $\geq 0.3\ \mu g/ml$ plant sap.

We have subjected purified CP to fragmentation with trypsin, V8 protease and CNBr and identified the fragments containing the antigenic determinants using time-resolved fluoroimmunoassay (TRFIA). We have sequenced 18 amino acids from the N-terminal end of the CP, and we are planning further sequencing of the antigenic proteolytic fragments. We also intend to do a further mapping of the epitopes using recombinant CfMV CP and its deletion fragments and to do the precise mapping using the pepto-scan method.

We have cloned and sequenced >90% of the genome ($\approx$4000 nucleotides). Sequence comparisons verified that CfMV belongs to the sobemovirus group. We have identified the putative open reading frames (ORFs) coding for the CfMV VPg, protease, replicase and CP. The CP gene was verified by comparison with the direct amino acid sequencing data. The 5'end of the CfMV genomic RNA has a secondary structure similar to that of many (+)-strand RNA viruses. A conserved motif similar to the subgenomic RNA initiation region of some picornaviruses was found $\approx$ 40 bp upstreams to the CP gene.

We have done *in vitro* translation studies using natural viral RNA purified both from virus particles and from infected plants and RNA generated from cDNA, in order to establish the genome organization. In wheat germ extract the CfMV RNA direct the synthesis of at least four proteins with molecular weights of 95, 65-67, 32-35 and 12-14 K.

We plan to make fusion proteins of the ORF coded proteins, and to raise pabs against them. These pabs are to be used for immunoelectron microscopical studies of the infection process. We are also looking for transcriptional or translational enhancers in the viral genome. The gene coding for the CP is in the prosess of being cloned. It will later be cloned in suitable vectors for transformation of possible transformable Norwegian varieties of cocksfoot. The expression of the CfMV CP in plants will be verified with mabs. The virus resistance of these plants will be studied. Virus resistant, transgenic plants may then form the basis for a conventional breeding program in cocksfoot.

O.A. Rognli et al. (Eds.) Breeding Fodder Crops for Marginal Conditions, 306–307.

IN VITRO EMBRYO SPECIFICALLY EXPRESSED TRANSCRIPTS IN *POACEAE* ISOLATED FROM BARLEY

H-G. OPSAHL-FERSTAD, R.B. AALEN, C. LINNESTAD and O-A. OLSEN
Dept. of Biotechnological Sciences, Agric. Univ. of Norway,
P.O. Box 5040, N-1432 Ås, Norway

1. Introduction

Embryo specific markers are of interest to increase efficiency in *in vitro* techniques e.g. suspension cultures. They make it possible to identify embryogenic cultures at an early stage, and make it possible to study the molecular aspects of *in vitro* embryogenesis. This may lead to improvements of the techniques and eventually increase their use in plant breeding. Hopefully they will also elucidate the molecular basis of zygotic embryo development and reveal differences between somatic and zygotic embryogenesis. Such markers will automatically be self selectable *in vitro*, when used in e.g. transformation.

Results from RFLP studies give strong indications of gene conservation over genomes in many species of the Poaceae, which may defend the use of barley as a model species in the grass family. The *Bar*ley *al*eurone and *em*bryo expressed clones *Balem*1, *Balem*2, *Balem*3 and B22E (from an aleurone cDNA library from seeds 20 days post anthesis (dpa)) have been studied, characterized and related to somatic embryogenesis in several species in the family *Poaceae*.

2. Results & Discussion

Most cDNA clones expressed in the aleurone layer in barley seeds are also expressed in the embryos, which support the hypothesis that the endosperm has evolved from a secondary embryo (Friedman 1992).

By Northern hybridization *Balem*1 and *Balem*2 were found to be specifically expressed in anther derived embryos of barley and perennial ryegrass (*Lolium perenne* L.) and in embryogenic suspension cultures of barley and wheat (*Triticum aestivum* L.), but not in fresh or cold pretreated anthers nor in nonembryogenic suspension cultures (Aalen et al. in press, Stirn pers. comm.). The *Balem*1 transcript is homologous to a 18 kDa oleosin from maize (Qu & Huang 1990) and the *Balem*2 transcript is homologous to a dormancy related transcript pBS128 in *Bromus secalinus* L. (Goldmark et al. 1992). B22E (Klemsdal et al. 1991) also called pZE40 (Smith et al. 1992) and *Balem*3 are expressed in anthers, in nonembryogenic suspension cells, and in soft callus as well as in embryogenic cells, which makes them unsuitable as embryogenic markers.

While *Balem*1 and *Balem*2 transcripts appear in zygotic embryos at 15-18 dpa and persist until seed maturity, these transcripts seem to appear at earlier stages during somatic embryogenesis.

We will further characterize the development of embryo-like-structures from barley microspore cultures by means of novel molecular markers of embryogenesis from zygotic embryos, i.e. by existing markers and by identifying new markers.

3. References

Aalen RB, Opsahl-Ferstad H-G, Linnestad C, Olsen O-A (in press) Transcripts encoding an oleosin and a dormancy related protein are present both in the aleurone layer and in the embryo of developing barley (*Hordeum vulgare* L.) seeds. The Plant Journal

Friedman WE (1992) Evidence of a pre-angiosperm origin of endosperm: implications for the evolution of flowering plants. Science 255:336-339

Goldmark PJ, Curry J, Morris CF & Walker-Simmons MK (1992) Cloning and expression of an embryo-specific mRNA up-regulated in hydrated dormant seeds. Plant Mol Biol 19:433-441

Klemsdal SS, Hughes W, Lønneborg A, Aalen RB, Olsen O-A (1991) Primary structure of a novel barley gene differentially expressed in mature aleurone layers. Molecular and General Genetics 228:9-16

Laurie DA, Snape JW, Gale MD (1991) DNA marker techniques for genetic analysis in barley. In: Barley genetics, biochemistry, molecular biology and biotechnology, Ed (PR Shewry) Biotechnology in agriculture No 5:115-132

Smith LM, Handley J, Li Y, Donovan L, Bowles D (1992) Temporal and spatial regulation of a novel gene in barley embryos Plant Molecular Biology 20: 255-266

Vance VB, Huang AHC (1987) The major protein from lipid bodies of maize. J Biol Chem 262:11275-11279

Qu R, Huang AHC (1990) Oleosin KD 18 on the surface of oil bodies in maize. J Biol Chem 265:2238-2243

O.A. Rognli et al. (Eds.) Breeding Fodder Crops for Marginal Conditions, 308–310.
© 1994 *Kluwer Academic Publishers. Printed in the Netherlands.*

GENETIC VARIATION IN RESISTANCE TO COCKSFOOT MOTTLE VIRUS IN COCKSFOOT (*DACTYLIS GLOMERATA* L.).

O.A. ROGNLI, K. AASTVEIT, AND T. MUNTHE[1].
*Department of Biotechnological Sciences, Agric. Univ. of Norway,
P.O.Box 5040, 1432 Ås, Norway.*
[1] *Norwegian Plant Protection Institute, 1432 Ås*

1. Introduction

Cocksfoot mottle virus (CfMV) can be found in many countries in Western Europe and has been reported to cause severe damage. CfMV infection causes clear chlorotic symptoms on leaves of cocksfoot plants, associated with necrotic leaf tips and plant death when infection is heavy. CfMV is mostly transmitted mechanically from one plant to another, and it is assumed that the most important way of virus transmission in Norway is by the fodder harvester. Seed transmission has not been detected. Differences between cultivars in resistance or tolerance towards CfMV infection have been reported by Engsbro (1978), Catherall (1985), and Munthe (1988).

In an experiment with clones of cocksfoot selected among surviving plants in nine-year old swards, a severe attack of cocksfoot mottle virus (CfMV) was observed. We have used this to study the genetic variation in rate of injury within and among Norwegian varieties and experimental selections of cocksfoot, and the relationships between CfMV-injury and some agronomic characters. Artificial field inoculation has also been used to study variation in tolerance among populations.

2. Materials and methods

Experimental populations were produced by open pollination after phenotypic selection of clones with high and low raw-matter (RM) yield within three Norwegian cultivars (Table 1). A long-term yield trial (4 replications, 12 m^2 plot size) was established in 1975 with the populations listed in Table 1, and harvested for 9 years with 3 cuts/year. More detailed information on the populations 'Leikund', 'Hattfjelldal' and 'Holt' have been presented by Aastveit *et al.* (1991).

TABLE 1. Experimental selections and cultivars used in the long-term yield trial.

Name	Origin
Leikund	Commercial cultivar from South Norway
Leikund Low	Leikund selected for low RM-yield
Leikund High	Leikund selected for high RM-yield
Hattfjelldal	Commercial cultivar from Mid-Norway
Hattfjelldal High	Hattfjelldal selected for high RM-yield
Holt	Local population from North-Norway
Holt High	Holt selected for high RM-yield

In order to study differences between genotypes, 20 plants from each of the 7 populations were selected at random among surviving plants in the swards of the long-term yield trial. In 1985 a total number of 190 clones were laid out in a randomized block experiment with 4 replicates (5 clonal ramets/plot). Already in the planting year, but especially in the two following years, a wide and continous range of variation in CfMV-symptoms between clones occurred. The rate of injury based on the symptoms was visually estimated on a plot basis by use of a scale ranging from 0 (no symptoms) to 100 (all leaves chlorotic and dying).

In 1989 a special experiment, comprising the same populations and with plants raised from the same seed lots as the long-term yield trial, was laid out designed to measure effects of artificial CfMV infection. Each plot consisted of 210 plants in a simulated sward design (spaced 15cm x 15 cm), and divided in two halves. All leaves on 20 plants on one half-plot was infected with CfMV-inoculum, the other half-plot serving as a control.

3. Results

The variation in CfMV injury was highly significant and continous in nature. Although not significant, there was a tendency that phenotypic selection for high RM-yield led to a decrease in tolerance to CfMV. Broad sense heritabilites for CfMV injury ranged from 0.52 to 0.91 within populations, and genotypic correlations between CfMV injury and total DM-yield ranged form -0.46 to -0.80. The relationship between CfMV injury and DM-yield could be described by a smooth curve of second degree (Fig. 1.). CfMV injury was positively correlated with crude protein content and digestibility (IVDDM-%), and negatively with crude fiber content. Artificial infection with CfMV did not reveal any significant differences between populations in resistance to CfMV infection. Infection caused a 54.5 % increase in the number of dead plants, estimated in the third harvest year, but only to a 4.5 % reduction in dry matter yield, averaged over two years.

It is concluded that the type of resistance against CfMV found in these cocksfoot materials is a sort of tolerance. The results indicate that the tolerance can be improved by selection to such a level that the harmful effects become negligible in practical cultivation of cocksfoot.

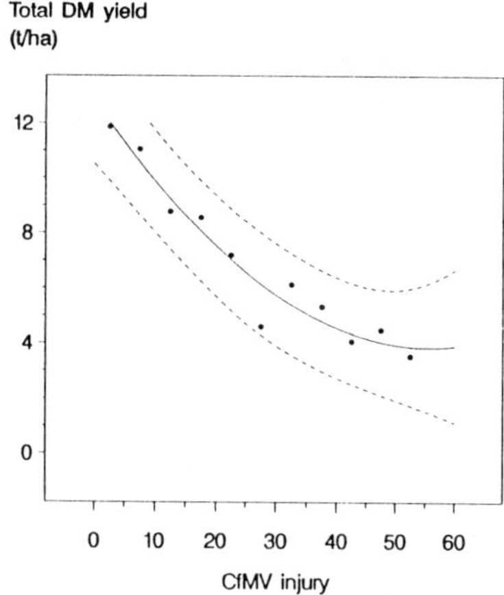

Figure 1. The relationship between CfMV injury and total DM-yield (calculated on a tonnes/ha basis). Fitted equation: DM = 12.8 - 0.32 CfMV + 0.003 CfMV^2.

4. References

Aastveit, K., Aastveit, A.H. and Marum, P. 1991. Polycross progenies in cocksfoot (*Dactylis glomerata* L.) grown under variable environmental conditions. Norwegian. J. Agric. Sci. 1:23-38.

Catherall, P.L. 1985. Resistance to cocksfoot mottle virus (CfMV) in cv. Cambria cocksfoot. Welsh Plant Breeding Station, Annual Rep. 1985.

Engsbro, B. 1978. Investigations on virus diseases of grasses in Denmark. Nordisk Jordbruksforskning, **61**:51-52.

Munthe, T. 1988. Norske undersøkelser vedrørende hundegrasmosaikkvirus. Nordisk Växtskyddskonferens, Malmø, Sverige, 25.-27. okt. 1988.

310

In order to study differences between genotypes, 20 plants from each of the 7 populations were selected at random among surviving plants in the swards of the long-term yield trial. In 1985 a total number of 190 clones were laid out in a randomized block experiment with 4 replicates (5 clonal ramets/plot). Already in the planting year, but especially in the two following years, a wide and continous range of variation in CfMV-symptoms between clones occurred. The rate of injury based on the symptoms was visually estimated on a plot basis by use of a scale ranging from 0 (no symptoms) to 100 (all leaves chlorotic and dying).

In 1989 a special experiment, comprising the same populations and with plants raised from the same seed lots as the long-term yield trial, was laid out designed to measure effects of artificial CfMV infection. Each plot consisted of 210 plants in a simulated sward design (spaced 15cm x 15 cm), and divided in two halves. All leaves on 20 plants on one half-plot was infected with CfMV-inoculum, the other half-plot serving as a control.

3. Results

The variation in CfMV injury was highly significant and continous in nature. Although not significant, there was a tendency that phenotypic selection for high RM-yield led to a decrease in tolerance to CfMV. Broad sense heritabilites for CfMV injury ranged from 0.52 to 0.91 within populations, and genotypic correlations between CfMV injury and total DM-yield ranged form -0.46 to -0.80. The relationship between CfMV injury and DM-yield could be described by a smooth curve of second degree (Fig. 1.). CfMV injury was positively correlated with crude protein content and digestibility (IVDDM-%), and negatively with crude fiber content. Artificial infection with CfMV did not reveal any significant differences between populations in resistance to CfMV infection. Infection caused a 54.5 % increase in the number of dead plants, estimated in the third harvest year, but only to a 4.5 % reduction in dry matter yield, averaged over two years.

It is concluded that the type of resistance against CfMV found in these cocksfoot materials is a sort of tolerance. The results indicate that the tolerance can be improved by selection to such a level that the harmful effects become negligible in practical cultivation of cocksfoot.

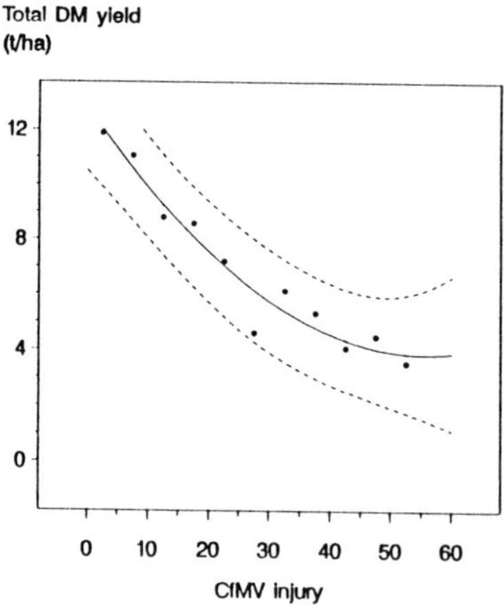

Figure 1. The relationship between CfMV injury and total DM-yield (calculated on a tonnes/ha basis). Fitted equation: $DM = 12.8 - 0.32\ CfMV + 0.003\ CfMV^2$.

4. References

Aastveit, K., Aastveit, A.H. and Marum, P. 1991. Polycross progenies in cocksfoot (*Dactylis glomerata* L.) grown under variable environmental conditions. Norwegian. J. Agric. Sci. 1:23-38.

Catherall, P.L. 1985. Resistance to cocksfoot mottle virus (CfMV) in cv. Cambria cocksfoot. Welsh Plant Breeding Station, Annual Rep. 1985.

Engsbro, B. 1978. Investigations on virus diseases of grasses in Denmark. Nordisk Jordbruksforskning, 61:51-52.

Munthe, T. 1988. Norske undersøkelser vedrørende hundegrasmosaikkvirus. Nordisk Växtskyddskonferens, Malmø, Sverige, 25.-27. okt. 1988.

O.A. Rognli et al. (Eds.) Breeding Fodder Crops for Marginal Conditions, 311–312.
© 1994 *Kluwer Academic Publishers. Printed in the Netherlands.*

IN VITRO MINIBEET INDUCTION SYSTEM IN SUGARBEET AND REDBEET (*BETA VULGARIS L.*)

O. TOLDI[1] É. PREININGER[2] É. VÁRALLYAY[1] AND M.FÁRI[1]
1.*Agricultural Biotechnology Center,*
   H-2101 Gödöllő, PO.Box 170, Hungary
2.*Eötvös Loránd University, Department of Anatomy,*
   H-1088 Budapest, Puskin u.11-13, Hungary

ABSTRACT. How can we explain that sugarbeet produces a storage organ in one hundred days under field conditions but it never occures *in vitro*? The genetic determinisme of the storage organ's differentation is also present in *in vitro* seedlings but changes in gene expression and/or gene activity somehow must be induced. As a result of a pretreatment with gibberellic acid and using an induction medium containing abscisic acid we could succesfully induce *in vitro* minibeet and multi-minibeet formations in 45% and 5%, respectively of the seedlings. We proved the structural and functional beet origin of minibeets by using comparative histological analysis and by measuring saccharose accumulation.

1.   Introduction

In vitro induction of tuberisation in potato provided the opportunities for plant breeders to produce a virus free propagation material [1] and to analyse environmental factors affecting tuber formation [2]. Molecular genetic studies in tuberisation afforded a possibility for the isolation of tuber specific genes and for the analysis of gene regulation [3]. Sooner or later the manipulation of tuber induction will be feasible on a molecular level and it could be modelled *in vitro*. We hope that our *in vitro* minibeet induction system will be the first step to obtain similar results in sugarbeet as in potato.

2.   Materials and Methods

2.1.   Plant material, seed surface sterilization and hormone induced germination

The following sugarbeet genotypes were used in our experiments : DM.8803, SZM.2, TMI.8049, TM.8714 (Sugarbeet Research Institute, Sopronhorpács Hungary); K.1002, K.1047 (Maribo Seed, Holeby Denmark). Redbeet plants were originated from commercial seeds.
Seeds were shaked in 70% ethanol for 1 min., then in 0.05% $Hg(II)Cl_2$ for 10 min., washed 10-15 times in sterile distilled water contained Tween 20 for 5 hours. After soaking the seeds overnight they were incubated on IG medium for 15 days. IG medium contained half concentration of MS macro, micro elements, 10 mgl^{-1} thiamine and 0.1 mgl^{-1} GA_3.

2.2.   Minibeet induction

After preincubation of the seedlings the lower part of their rooting system, namely the absorption and branching zones were removed.

312

After this preparation the explants were placed on modified MSB5 medium contained BAP and ABA in 0.2 mgl^{-1} concentration, respectively.

2.3. Comparative histological and sugar content analysis

Shoot, beet and root cross-sections, originated from minibeets and normal sugarbeets grown in greenhouse, both in the same developmental stages, were fixed in Carnoy solution, dehydrated in different alcohol concentrations, embedded in paraffin and observed in light microscope.
D-glucose and saccharose concentrations were measured by the method of Bergmeyer and Bernt (1974)[4] in shoot and beet samples of minibeets and normal sugarbeets compared to noninduced controls.

3. Results

We worked out a modified surface strilization method and a new hormone induced germination system which resulted an 80% germination rate of the seeds. Using our medium we could succesfully induce minibeets for the first time. After about 100 days of induction, genotype dependent minibeet and multi-minibeet formation were observed in 45% and in 5% of the explants, respectively. 70% of the minibeets developed into complete plants in the greenhouse. Histological analysis proved that the polycambial vascular system is a typical character not only in normal sugarbeet but also in minibeet. By measuring saccharose concentrations we determined the same amount of saccharose accumulation in minibeet as in normal beet.

4. Discussion

In vitro minibeet induction is a combined tissue culture method including a hormone induced germination on a special medium and the minibeet induction itself. As a result of a two years long synchronised optimisation, we can state that both steps influence quantitatively and qualitatively the results of the procedure.

5. Acknowledgements

We would like to thank Dr. Judit Mitykó and Michael Krackhardt for critical reading of the manuscript.

6. References

1. Wang, P.J. and Hu, C.Y.(1982) In vitro mass tuberisation and virus-free seed potato production in Taiwan. Am.Potato J. 59,33-37
2. Koda, Y. Okasawa, Y.(1983) Influences of environmental, hormonal and nutritional factors in potato tuberisation in vitro. Jpn.J.Crop.Sci. 52(4),582-591
3. Taylor, M.A. Kumar, A. George, L.A.and Davies, H.V.(1992) Isolation and molecular characterisation of a tuberisation-related cDNA clone from potato (Solanum tuberosum L.). Plant Cell Rep. 11,623-626
4. Bergmeyer, H.U.and Bernt, E.(1974) in Bergmeyer, H.U.(ed) Methods of Enzymatic Analysis, Academic Press, New York and London, 2nd ed.Vol.3 pp.1176-1179

Workshop reports

O.A. Rognli et al. (eds.), Breeding Fodder Crops for Marginal Conditions, 315–318.
© 1994 *Kluwer Academic Publishers. Printed in the Netherlands.*

Why should we breed for marginal conditions:

Report of workshop I

The importance of marginal conditions

Marginal conditions may occur throughout Europe in space and/or time although their effects on agricultural output can vary considerably in different regions. Climate and soil factors have a primary role in creating marginal conditions, but land management is also important. Thus the influence of political policies (economic and social) on, for example, grazing pressures, fertiliser inputs, irrigation use and industrial pollution can be critical in determining the agricultural value of marginal areas. Agriculture is also often supported in less favoured regions in order to maintain inhabitation and community structure. Set-aside schemes may remove marginal land from agricultural production while reduced inputs and lack of proper land management may expand areas of marginal status. Decisions on whether to initiate breeding programmes for marginal conditions are also determined by seed marketing prospects. Therefore economic considerations are more often likely to influence decisions on breeding for marginal conditions than biological limitations. Unfortunately, economic policies often have a shorter time span than breeding programmes which may create difficulties in meeting political aims. If marginal conditions occur rarely then the costs of incorporating specific adaptations into breeding material is probably not justified and occasional sward damage may be rectified by reseeding. At the other extreme, if marginal conditions are a permanent feature of an area (as in Northern Scandinavia or the Mediterranean Basin) varieties possessing specific adaptations are essential. Between these extremes are areas where marginal conditions are not uncommon but occur in a fairly unpredictable and random manner. Broadly adapted varieties are often used in these areas and the extent to which these possess adaptations necessary to survive specific environmental stresses is often dictated by the assessment policies and techniques of variety testing systems. Extreme adaptation to an environmental stress often involves a cost in terms of dry matter yield. The extent to which Recommended List Authorities rate adaptative traits as opposed to dry matter yield under optimum conditions, is often a critical factor in the weighting of objectives in commercial breeding programmes.

316

Prospects for alleviating marginal conditions by breeding

Climatic factors

Temperature and/or moisture stress are the primary climatic limitations which are present in many marginal areas. Survival of severe northern winters and dry southern summers both depend on plants possessing appropriate growth rhythms with optimum photosynthetic and respiration rates and correct assimilate distribution. Carbohydrate reserves are important in the survival of plants during periods of intense stress (cold or drought) and must be built up during more favourable growth conditions. Balanced root/shoot growth and adapted leaf morphology are important in drought tolerance and hardening/dehardening responses are vital features of winter survival. It appears that relevant research in field physiology has been neglected through diversion of funding to exciting developments in molecular techniques for work on basic biochemistry. A good balance should be maintained between research at various biological levels to obtain maximum benefit for agriculture. Plant breeding is an important focus for technology transfer and has a proven record of success in improving characteristics such as winter hardiness and drought tolerance. New traits must be identified which breeders can use as selection criteria so that progress can be maintained.

Management factors

Products of plant breeding can help to alleviate a range of management problems in marginal areas. Economic and environmental considerations in these areas often permit only limited use of fertilisers. Breeding can improve the uptake and utilisation efficiency of nitrogen and phosphate and enhance compatibility with nitrogen fixing legumes. Other mineral stress problems such as high salinity, possibly caused by poor irrigation practices, may also be overcome with the help of specifically bred varieties. Breeding can also help the environment by reducing the need for pesticides and herbicides. Disease resistance continues to be a successful objective in plant breeding and new genetic technologies offer new pathways for progress. Forage quality is an increasingly important feature of efficient animal production and has maximum significance in marginal conditions. Many plant traits affect quality including the chemical composition of leaves (digestible carbohydrate and protein content) and patterns of seasonal growth. The timing of forage harvests for maximum yield, quality and persistence do not necessarily coincide and this has particular significance in the short growing seasons often found in marginal areas. Amenity grassland offers a different range of management stresses associated with both frequent close mowing and infrequent cutting together with a range of trampling pressures. Varieties specifically bred for amenity purposes are of increasing value in helping to satisfy the expanding demand for leisure activities which often have particular importance in marginal areas.

Genetic resources for marginal conditions

The basic genetic resources for marginal areas are in the native natural pastures which contain species of variable use. Appropriate management can encourage those species of greatest value and 'wild' harvested seed may be sown. Selection of particular genotypes from 'wild' material leads to the development of land races and local varieties (e.g. timothy in Scandinavia). Such varieties are very important for marginal areas and it is vital that seed certification regulations do not promote the eradication of these valuable genetic resources. Previously unexploited local species may also be found to have valuable attributes (e.g. *Medicago polymorpha* in Italy). Thus protection of a wide range of genetic resources in marginal areas is a vital part of breeding for marginal conditions. Finally, exotic introductions can be significant in improving the attributes of marginal grasslands. However, considerable breeding effort is often required either to select within exotic material for adaptations to local conditions or to transfer traits from exotic into native material. Commonly this gene transfer has been restricted to plants within the same species, however, new genetic technologies now open up wider possibilities.

Conclusions

1. There is considerable potential to breed forage varieties with specific adaptations for marginal conditions.
2. Genetic resources in marginal areas must be protected to preserve useful adaptations. Loss of land races due to restrictive seed regulations must be avoided.
3. There is still a need for physiological research to identify useful selection criteria for marginal conditions. Balanced research funding is required to allow transfer of technology from basic work to practical use.
4. Seed trade economics promote widespread sale of broadly adapted varieties. More attention should be paid to the use of more specifically adapted varieties in niche markets.
5. National Variety Testing Authorities must question whether their variety assessment policies and techniques serve agriculture in the best way possible, especially with regard to marginal areas. Too much emphasis

on total dry matter yield, as opposed to specific adaptive traits affecting persistency and nutritive value, should be avoided.

Dr. M.O. Humphreys
Chairman of the Workshop

Dr. A. Helgadóttir
Secretary of the Workshop

O.A. Rognli et al. (eds.), Breeding Fodder Crops for Marginal Conditions, 319–320.
© 1994 Kluwer Academic Publishers. Printed in the Netherlands.

Specific versus general adaptation – What should be the breeding strategies for marginal conditions?

Report of Workshop II

The chairman gave an introduction and, assuming the question for Workshop I was given a positive answer, proposed the following topics for discussion:
- Definition of marginal – conditions
- environments
- areas
- How to deal with genotype-environment interactions?
- Role of locally adapted germplasm
- Selection in marginal areas: how?
- Adaptation (specific vs. wide) in relation to:
- genetic diversity
- crop vulnerability
- seed production

Participants of the workshop wanted to include a discussion of predictable vs. unpredictable environmental factors and responses under the first topic, and the cost of breeding for general vs. specific adaptation under the last topic. During the discussion a number of aspects of the various topics were touched upon, but only the main conclusions are mentioned below. To have a common concept of general or wide adaptation vs. specific adaptation, the workshop found it necessary first to establish a definition of those traits, and predictable vs. unpredictable environmental factors was brought into it. Also much of the discussion was based on a Finlay and Wilkinson type of graph, and for marginal conditions it was principally concentrated upon the lower left corner of such a graph. The common concepts and definitions that came out of the discussion may be summarized as follows:
- General or wide adaptation: The ability to perform under a wide range of unpredictable environmental conditions;
- Specific adaptation: The ability to perform under a restricted range of predictable environmental conditions.

Marginal conditions were considered in biological sense, and taken to be equivalent to stress. Marginal environments and –areas then, are where stress conditions prevail, i.e. where abiotic factors are limiting the production/yield to a consistently low level compared to the usual or optimal level of the crop/culture. (Stress from biotic factors then were left out in this discussion.) It was suggested that general adaptation might be found among forms/varieties of amenity grasses and sugar beets, but mainly one should breed for specific adaptation to marginal conditions. This does not mean adaptation to small areas, as the same abiotic factor(s) may consistently be limiting the production of a crop over a geographically wide area. Concerning selection, this lead to the conclusion that one should select under the marginal conditions for which one breeds. If varieties bred with specific adaptation should ever reach the market as recommended varieties, it was argued that variety testing must be conducted over a wider range of environments than present official testing. (Official variety testing at present only under non marginal conditions.) It was also argued and recommended that experimental design and conduction under marginal conditions should be given special attention, because experimental error is usually large here. Diversity (genetic within variety and species diversity in mixtures?) is good in an unpredictable situation (general/wide adaptation?). The workshop could not be concluded with any consensus of a comprehensive breeding strategy for marginal conditions, but some elements have been given above.

Dr. S. Ceccarelli
Chairman of the Workshop

Dr. B.I. Honne
Secretary of the Workshop

Can *high quality* and *adaptation to stress* environments be *combined*?

Report of Workshop III

There are 3 central issues in this topic:
1. High quality: we defined high quality as all genetically based characteristics of fodder grasses improving animal health and performances;
2. Adaptation to stress: the issue of the meeting;
3. Combined: regards simultaneous breeding both for stress and quality.

General opinion of the group

1. If you've to do with marginal conditions adaptation to stress is far more *important than quality*. If your crop doesn't survive the winter it is of no use to have a good quality: *quality comes second*.
2. It was the audience's opinion that it *is not impossible to combine* breeding for stress situations and quality at the same time; someone thought quality reacts neutral in these situation. Examples:
   1. Drought resistance breeding in the Festuloliums did not seem to effect quality in a negative sense in the UK. In comparison to the basic population, drought resistant Festulolium reacts very differently in many physiological parameters.
   2. In Poland breeding for a higher seed yield in lucerne did not decline protein.
   3. In Italy the variability in protein and fibre content of comparable lucerne (both morphological and physiological (age-maturity)) is that quality characters are not likely to be improved. Producing more protein/ha has to be done by increasing the yield or changing the stem/leaf ratio, and as said under 1, this seems not to effect quality. Saponines, an anti nutritional factor, offers enough variability for breeding potential.
   4. In maize temperature influences the lignification of the stems. It is not known whether or how this temperature dependency is under genetic control.
   5. Breeding takes time and different approaches according to the species under control. Combining complete different genomes as e.g. crossing very winterhardy with very wintersusceptible plants to improve the winterhardiness in the susceptible strain – may have no direct effect due to genomic unbalanced situations. One needs back crosses and

hence time. The same is true for the introgression in Fescue of Lolium genes and vice versa.
6. Frequent cutting to improve quality might weaken persistency in marginal areas in grasses.

Conclusion

If one talks about marginal situations, quality comes second; improving the quality in adapted material seems not be impossible but anyway hard to achieve and this is no big news.

Dr. P. Marum
Chairman of the Workshop

Dr. D. Reheul
Secretary of the Workshop

List of participants

Andersson, Bengt
Svalöf Wibull AB, S-26881 Svalöv, Sweden

Balfourier, Francois
Plant Breeding Station, 63039 Clermont-Ferrand, France

Beerepoot, Laurens
Barenbrug Holding BV, P.O. Box 4, 4900 AA Oosterhout, The Netherlands

Berner, Phillipp
Saatzucht Steinach GmbH, Straubinger Strasse 17, 8441 Steinach, Germany

Bócsa, Ivan
GATE Agricultural Research Institute, H-3350 Kompolt, Hungary

Bockstaele van, Erik
*Rijksstation voor Plantenveredeling, Burg. Van Gansberghelaan 109, B-9820 Merel-
beke, Belgium*

Boller, Beat
*Eidg. Forschungsanstalt f. ldw. Pflanzenbau, Reckenholz, CH-8046 Zürich, Switzer-
land*

Bulinska-Radomska, Zofia
Plant Breeding and Acclimatization Institute, P.O. Box 1019, 05-870, Poland

Bullitta, Simonetto
Centro Pascoli-CNR, Via E. De Nicola, 07100 Sassari, Italy

Buraas, Trond
*Felleskjøpets Agricultural Experimental and Seed growing Station Bjørke 2344
Ilseng, Norway*

Caradus, John
Agresearch Grasslands, Private Bag 11008, Palmerston North, New Zealand

Caredda, Salvatore
Instituto Agronomia Wa de Nicola, 07100 Sassari, Italy

Ceccarelli, Salvatore
International Center for Agricultural Research in the Dry Areas, P.O. Box 5466, Aleppo, Syria

Dragiyska, Roumiana
Institute of Genetic Engineering, 2232 Konstinbrod-2, Bulgaria

Dyba, Stanislawa
Academy of Agriculture, Department of Genetics and Plant Breeding, 60-625 Poznan, ul. Wojska Poskiego 71c, Poland

Eickmeyer, Fred
University of Hannover, Institute of Applied Genetic, Herrenhauser Str. 2, 3000 Hannover 21, Germany

Entrup, Ernst Lütke
Deutsche Saatveredelung, Lippstadt-Bremen GmbH, Wiessenburger Str. 5, 4780 Lippstadt, Germany

Falcinelli, Mario
Istituto di Miglioramento Genetico Vegetale, Universita de Perugia, Borgo xx Giugno 72, 06100 Perugia, Italy

Floris, Rosanna
Centro Miglioramento Pascoli (CNR), Via Enrico Denicola, 07100 Sassari, Italy

Fritsen, Hugo
Dansk planteforædling A/S, DK-4660 Store Heddinge, Denmark

Garcia, Alvaro
AFRC Institute of Grassland and Environmental Research, Welsh Plant Breeding Station, Plas Gogerddan, Aberystwyth, Dyfed SY23 3EB, U.K.

Ghesquiere, Marc
Station d'Amèlioration des Plants, Fourragères – I.N.R.A., 86600 Lusignan, France

Hayward, Michael Dennis
AFRC Institute of Grassland and Environmental Research, Welsh Plant Breeding Station, Plas Gogerddan, Aberystwyth, Dyfed, SY23 3EB, U.K.

Helgadottir, Áslaug
The Agricultural Research Institute, Keldnaholt, 112 Reykjavik, Iceland

Hillestad, Ragnar
Hellerud Research Station and Seed Multiplication Farm, P.O. Box 115, 2013 Skjet-ten, Norway

Hintzen, Jacques J.
Mommersteeg International B.V., P.O. Box 1, 5250 AA Vlymen, The Netherlands

Honne, Bjørn Ivar
Kvithamar Agricultural Research Station, 7500 Stjørdal, Norway

Humphreys, Merryn Owen
AFRC Institute of Grassland and Environmental Research, Welsh Plant Breeding Station, Plas Gogerddan, Aberystwyth, Dyfed, SY23 2EB, U.K.

Humphreys, Michael W.
AFRC Institute of Grassland and Environmental Research, Welsh Plant Breeding Station, Plas Gogerddan, Aberystwyth, Dyfed, SY23 2EB, U.K.

Kleinhout, Arend
Dansk Planteforædling A/S, DK-4660 Store Heddinge, Denmark

Larsen, Arild
Vågønes Agricultural Research Station, 8010 Bodø, Norway

Lellbach, Hans
Federal Centre for Breeding Research on Cultivated Plants, Institutsplatz 2, D-2551 Gr.-Lüsewitz, Germany

Lindvall, Eva
Svalöf Weibull AB, P.O. Box 4097, S-904 03 Umeå, Sweden

Mariani, Anna
Istituto Miglioramento Genetico Piante, Forraggere del C.N.R., Via Madonna 130, 06100-Perugia, Italy

Marum, Petter
Løken Agricultural Research Station, Volbu, 2940 Heggenes, Norway

McNeilly, Thomas
D.E.E.B. Nicholson Building, University of Liverpool, P.O. Box 147, L69 3BX Liverpool, U.K.

Miettinen, Eero Juhani
Agricultural Research Centre, Kainuu Research Station, SF-88600 Sotkamo, Finland

Mlyniec, Waleria
Polish Academy of Sciences, Institute of Plant Genetics, 60-479 Poznan, ul. Strzeszyn-sku 34, Poland

Myhre, Astrid
Department of Biotechnological Sciences, P.O. Box 5040, 1432 Ås, Norway

Nemeskéri, Ezter
University of Agricultural Sciences-Debrecen, Department of Crop Production, Böszörmenyi ut 138, H-4032, Hungary

Nielsen, Niels Chr.
Prodana Seeds A/S, Fåborgvej 248, DK-5250 Odense SV, Denmark

Nurminiemi, Minna
Department of Biotechnological Sciences, P.O. Box 5040, 1432 Ås, Norway

Østrem, Liv
Fureneset Agricultural Research Station, 6994 Fure, Norway

Pärssinen, Pertti
Agricultural Research Centre of Finland, Institute of Plant Breeding, SF-31600 Jokioinen, Finland

Peltonen-Sainio, Pirjo
University of Helsinki, Department of Plant production, SF-00710 Helsinki, Finland

Piano, Efisio
Istituto Sperimentale per le Colture Foraggere, Viale Piacenza 29, 20075 Lodi (MI), Italy

Pietraszek, Wieslaw,
Society R.A.G.T., 18. rue de Sèguret Saincric, 12033 Rodez Cedex 9, France

Pinter, Lajos
Crop Science Department, Georgicon Faculty, Pannon University, Keszthely, P.O. Box 71, H-8361 Hungary

Posselt, Ulrich
University of Hohenheim, Plant Breeding Station, P.O. Box 700562, D-7000 Stuttgart 70, Germany

Praijsks
Institute of Genetic Engineering, 2232 Konstinbrod-2, Bulgaria

Pronczuk, Slawomir
Plant Breeding and Acclimatization Institute, Radzikow, 05-870 Blonie, Poland

Pulli, Seppo
Agricultural Research Centre of Finland, Institute of Plant Breeding, SF-31600 Jokioinen, Finland

Rapp, Kåre
Holt Agricultural Research Station, P.O. Box 2502, 9002 Tromsø, Norway

Reheul, Dirk
Rijksstation voor Plantenveredeling, Burg. Van Gansberghelaan 109, B-9820 Merelbeke, Belgium

Reijden, Anton van der
Limagrain Genetics B.V., P.O. Box 2, 9679 EG Scheemda, The Netherlands

Rhodes, Ian
ARRC Institute of Grassland and Environmental Research, Welsh Plant Breeding Station, Plas Gogerddan, Aberystwyth, Dyfed SY23 3EB, U.K.

Rogalska, Stanislawa
Academy of Agriculture, Department of Genetics and Plant Breeding, 60-625 Poznan, ul. Wojska Polskiego 71c, Poland

Rognli, Odd Arne
Department of Biotechnological Sciences, P.O. Box 5040, 1432 Ås, Norway

Rotili, Pietro
Istituto Sperimentale per le Colture Foraggere, Viale Piacenza no 29, 20075 Lodi, Italy

Scheller, Helmut
Bayerische Landesanstalt für Bodenkultur und Pflanzenbau, Vöttinger Str. 38, D-8050 Freising, Germany

Schjelderup, Ivar
Holt Agricultural Research Station, P.O. Box 2502, 9002 Tromsø, Norway

Simon, Uwe,
Technische Universität München, Lehrstuhl für Grünland und Futterbau, Hohenbechernstrasse 2a, D-8050 Freisung-Weihenstephan, Germany

Simonsen, Øystein
The Norwegian Agricultural Research Stations, P.O. Box 100, 1430 Ås, Norway

Sjödin, Jan
Svalöf Weibull AB, S-26881 Svalö, Sweden

Solberg, Eli
Løken Agricultural Research Station, Volbu 2940 Heggenes, Norway

Staszewski, Zygmunt
Plant Breeding and Acclimatization Institute (IHAR), Radzikow, 05-870 Poland

Stubsjøen, Magne
The Royal Ministry of Agriculture, P.O. Box 8007 Dep. 0030 Oslo, Norway

Sutka, Jozef
Agricultural Research Inst. of the Hungarian Academy of Sciences, Martonvasar, H-2462 Hungary

Szyrmer, Jerzy
Plant Breeding and Acclimatization Institute, P.O. Box 1019, Radzikow, 00-950 Warszawa, Poland

Tigerstedt, Peter
Department of Plant Biology, Plant and Tree Breeding, P.O. Box 27 (Viikki D), SF-00014 University of Helsinki, Finland

Toldi, Otto
Agricultural Biotechnology Center, Institute for Plant Sciences, P.O. Box 170, H-2101 Gödöllö, Hungary

Tronsmo, Anne Marte
The Norwegian Plant Protection Institute, P.O. Box 70, 1432 Ås, Norway

Užik, Martin
Research Institute of Plant Production, Bratislava cesta 122, 921 68 Piestany, Slovakia

Veronesi, Fabio
Dipartimento di Biotecnologie Agrarie e Ambientali, Universita Di Ancona V. Monte d'ago, Breece Bianche 60100 Ancona, Italy

Vestad, Reidar
Department of Biotechnological Sciences, Samfunnsveien 3, 1430 Ås, Norway

Wilkins, Peter William
AFRC Institute of Grassland and Environmental Research, Welsh Plant Breeding Station, Plas Gogerddan, Aberystwyth, Dyfed 2Y23 2EB, U.K.

Willner, Evelin
Institut für Pflanzengenetik und Kulturpflanzen Forschung Gatersleben, Aussenstelle Malchow, O-2401 Malchow/Poel, Germany

Wolters, Lukas
Zelder B.V., P.O. Box 26, 6590 AA Gennep, The Netherlands

Zwierzykowski, Zbigniew
Institute of Plant Genetics, Polish Academy of Sciences, Strzeszynska 34, 60-479 Poznan, Poland

Developments in Plant Breeding

1. H. Schmidt and M. Kellerhals (eds.): *Progress in Temperate Fruit Breeding.* 1994   ISBN 0-7923-2947-3
2. O.A. Rognli, E. Solberg and I. Schjelderup (eds.): *Breeding Fodder Crops for Marginal Conditions.* Proceedings of the 18th Eucarpia Fodder Crops Section Meeting, Loen, Norway (August 1993). 1994   ISBN 0-7923-2948-1

KLUWER ACADEMIC PUBLISHERS – DORDRECHT / BOSTON / LONDON